What Do Lions Know About Stress?

What Do Lions Know About Stress?

Majid Ali, M.D.

Associate Professor of Pathology (Adj)
College of Physicians and Surgeons
of Columbia University, New York
Visiting Professor
Liu Hua Qiao General Hospital, Guanzhou, China
Chief of Staff, Institute of Preventive Medicine,
Denville, New Jersey and New York City
Fellow, Royal College of Surgeons of England
Diplomate, American Board of Anatomic Pathology
Diplomate, American Board of Clinical Pathology
Diplomate, American Board of Environmental Medicine
Diplomate, American Board of Chelation Therapy
President, American Academy of Preventive Medicine
President, Capital University of Integrative Medicine,
Washington, D.C.

Library of Congress Cataloging Data Available
ISBN 1-879131-10-2

Ali, Majid

What Do Lions Know About Stress? Majid Ali.--1st ed.

Includes bibliographical references and index
1. Stress
2. Spirituality
3. Healing
4. Autoregulation
5. Language of Silence
6. The Fourth-of-July Chemistry
6. Adrenergic Molecular Hypervigilance
7. Environment and Human Biology
8. Oxidative Molecular Injury

10 9 8 7 6 5 4 3 2 1

Published in the USA by
LIFE SPAN PRESS
95 East Main Street, Denville, New Jersey 07834
(201) 586-9191

To Sarah

A Different View Of Stress

A physician does his most worthy work when he participates in his patient's suffering. In participating in their suffering, my patients with severe, chronic stress have given me two insights:

*First,
the common notion of stress being fight-or-flight response to a demand for change is so inadequate as to be clinically irrelevant.*

*Second,
spirituality makes psychology irrelevant.*

In this volume, I include many true-to-life stories of my patients and describe the energetic-molecular basis of their suffering. I relate how long hours of listening to them led me to conclude that the popular notion of mind-over-body healing is a cruel joke, and, in essence, pours salt on their wounds. I also recognized that the prevailing practice of searching for relief of the agony of the present through 'working out the problems of the past' is little more than a cortical trap-the mind endlessly recycles past pain or precycles feared, future misery. Psychology, by and large, keeps us incarcerated in obsolete models of disease and sufferings. Spirituality sets us free.

Acknowledgments

I am most grateful to my patients whose true-to-life suffering and healing gave me insights into the nature of the stress and recovery phenomena. They were—and will always remain—my most worthy teachers.

I am indebted to the medical, nursing and administrative staffs of the Institute of Preventive Medicine for creating and sustaining an environment in which I can freely pursue my clinical work. I'm also thankful for the many contributions to my work made by colleagues in the American Academy of Preventive Medicine.

I thank Jerrold Finnie, M.D., Dolores Finnie, R.N., Maria Lissandrello, Lisa Rosen, Cathy Johnson and Amy Lang for their review of some segments of the manuscript; Barry Weiner for his sketches of the title pages for book chapters; and the staff at Life Span Press for their unfailing support.

I am grateful to Sarah, our daughter, who invited us to see the "real" Kenya with her in the spring of 1995. In Masai Mara I saw "her" lion with a limp. This book begins with the story of that arthritic lion. Of course, I had no idea on that sunny, breezy morning in Mara where Sarah's lion would lead me.

Talat, my wife, is forever my best resource.

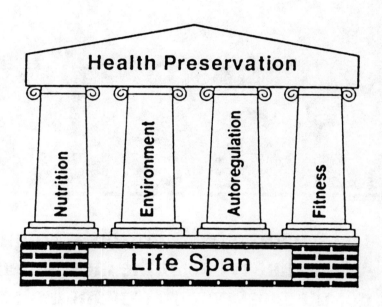

Prayer is the best antioxidant

The scientific basis for this is simple:
Adrenaline is one of the most potent,
if not the most potent, oxidant molecule
in the human body.
Prayer and meditation is the best way to
down-regulate adrenaline production.

A Prayer

Lord, Today may I simply be in your presence for a few moments.

Today I protest nothing.

Today I demand nothing.

Today may I simply be in your presence for a few moments.

From *The Canary and Chronic Fatigue*

AN ESSENTIAL NOTE

I do not recommend that any reader consider the therapies that I include in this volume
as recipes for treating any specific health disorder without the clinical supervision of a qualified
professional.

What Do Lions Know About Stress?

Majid Ali, M.D.

One of America's foremost spokespersons for preventive medicine and author of the Life Span Library of the Scientific Basis of Health.

* The Canary and Chronic Fatigue
* The Cortical Monkey and Healing
* The Ghoraa and Limbic Exercise
* RDA: Rats, Drugs and Assumptions
* The Butterfly and Life Span Nutrition
* The Dog, Directed Pulses and Energy Healing
* Battered Bowel Ecosystem
—Waving Away A Wandering Wolf
* The Principles and Practice of Nutritional Medicine
Part I: Intramuscular and Intravenous Therapies

TABLE OF CONTENTS

TABLE OF CONTENTS

PREFACE

When life begins, it begins to end. In essence, life consists of injury and healing, only to be followed by yet more injury. The injury-healing-injury continuum of life is the true nature of stress.

The prevailing notion of stress holds that it is an organism's fight-or-flight response to a threat to his survival, and that it is followed by an adaptation response by which the organism adjusts to its altered condition. Furthermore, the stress response is considered to be mediated by the adrenal gland. In my view, these notions are mere artifact created by animal mutilation experimenters, and are so inadequate as to be clinically irrelevant.

The adrenal gland, the putative seat of the fight-or-flight response, is not a hermit organ. It senses and responds to its internal and external environments like every other body organ. Similarly, adrenal hormones influence—and, in turn, are influenced by—all other hormones and messenger molecules in the body. The idea that stress can exist as a discrete adrenal malfunction is neither tenable on theoretical grounds nor consistent with my clinical observations.

Life is an ever-changing kaleidoscope of energetic-molecular events. In biology, when one thing changes in one way, everything changes in some way. We can neither understand nor effectively address issues of stress in clinical medicine by applying narrow-focused, reductionistic and artificial notions of the stress response. What is required for this purpose is a deep, holistic understanding of the energetic-molecular relationships in human biology.

This is an exciting time. Nearly each month I see scientific studies that validate at least one of the ancient healing arts or philosophies. *Science catches up with empirical medicine.* As far as stress in clinical medicine is concerned, this means an end to the era in which animals are burned, drugged, drowned, electrocuted, or decapitated by experimenters so they can develop "scientific" theories of what stress is and isn't. Science is not only self-correcting, it is also liberating.

CHILDREN ON METABOLIC ROLLER COASTERS

I see little children living troubled lives on metabolic roller coasters. They suffer wide mood swings—behaving as loving little angels one moment, then kicking their mothers' shins the next. Punishment is frequent at home, and they face daily indignities at school. They are tormented by sugar roller coasters that are recognized neither by their parents nor by school psychologists. Their food sensitivities remain undiagnosed, and their mold allergies remain unrecognized and untreated. School psychologists are quick to label them with learning disabilities, hyperactivity and attention deficit disorder—and their pediatricians are quick to offer Ritalin prescriptions. How does the suffering of these children coincide with the prevailing notions of fight-or-flight stress response?

ANTIDEPRESSANTS FOR HUMAN CANARIES

I see young women and men who not too long ago were athletic teenagers. Their common colds were aggressively treated with massive doses of antibiotics that battered their bowel ecosystems. Their sinus headaches were treated with painkillers, and the symptoms of caffeine addiction and anxiety were suppressed with Ativan and Valium. Their undue tiredness was chalked up to shirkers' syndrome, Yuppie syndrome, all-in-the-head and other insolent diagnostic labels. For indigestion and bloating they were prescribed antacids and ulcer drugs. Their physicians never bothered to look for nutritional and environmental causes of their suffering. Finally, when their symptoms became disabling, they were labeled with chronic fatigue syndrome and were awarded prescriptions for antidepressants. How does their anguish fit into the fight-or-flight stress response?

HOLLOW TIN DOLLS

I hear gynecologists praise synthetic estrogens and progesterones, speaking as if those hormones were little marbles rattling noisily in hollow tin dolls. I never hear a word about how female hormones are affected by sugar-insulin-adrenaline roller coasters. Nor do I hear gynecologists acknowledge roller   coasters. Nor do I hear gynecologists acknowledge interactions between female hormones and other hormones produced in the thyroid, pancreas, pituitary and pineal glands. They are always silent about the roles of yet other hormones produced in the bowel, lung or heart. They excitedly talk about their patients as if the female bodies were hollow vessels—as if estrogens and progesterones turn, twist and bump into each other in empty cells.

But my female patients are not hollow tin dolls. They are living, breathing beings. The tissues under their skin teem with a thousand ever-changing molecular kaleidoscopes. When they suffer wide mood swings, the jitters and headaches associated with PMS, it's not just estrogens that trick their bodies. When they are shocked with hot flushes one minute and cold waves the next, mere estrogenic pranks are not at fault. During the night, when they awaken drenched in sweat, it can't simply be chalked up to a frenzy of sex hormones.

How do sugar-insulin-adrenaline roller coasters feed—and how are they fed by—estrogen roller coasters? What does a confused thyroid gland have to do with hot flushes? What does a bowel in revolt against yeast overgrowth have to do with a patient's nocturnal misery? Allergic triggers light up oxidative fires in their blood streams. What do such fires in blood have to do with their brain fog and muscle symptoms? How do chemical triggers fan those oxidative fires? Gynecologists do not ever concern themselves with such questions —at least not the ones I know. How does all that fit in with the fight-or-flight stress response?

SLEEPING WITH MACHINES STUCK UP THE NOSE

Recently, *The New England Journal of Medicine* discovered that young people are sleepy during the day if they do not sleep soundly at night. (How desperately do we need such insight?) The *Journal* further reported that in a sleep study, one-fourth of the young male volunteers revealed evidence of sleep-disordered breathing (328:1230; 1993). Then the study concluded that those young men would benefit from sleeping with a sleeping machine stuck up their noses. Amazingly, the *Journal* does not bother to ask how the young sufferers' sleep patterns became deranged in the first place.

When we sleep, we are not dead. That is self-evident. What happened to those young men during the day to interfere with their sleep at night? After a sleepless night, people tend to drink large amounts of coffee to stay awake at work. The caffeine keeps their neurotransmitters revved all day and prevents deep restful sleep during the night. The next day begins just as the previous one. How does sleep-disordered breathing coincide with the fight-or-flight stress response?

THE UNSTOPPABLE HAS NO MOTIVATION NOW

Last evening, a 29-year-old man consulted me for chronic

fatigue, migraine headaches, recurrent sinusitis, irritability and heart palpitations. He had single-handedly built a small and highly successful commodity brokerage firm.

"I was athletic. I suffered sinusitis and migraine headache attacks, but I did okay with them. I was a very high-energy person. I always performed four or five tasks at a time. I was unstoppable, Dr. Ali." He spoke with pride, then added ruefully, "But now I'm drained all the time. I drink a lot of coffee, but still simple tasks seem impossible. I have no motivation left in me."

How does chronic fatigue and lack of motivation coincide with a fight-or-flight stress response?

WHEN HOSPITALS AREN'T HEALING PLACES

A patient kindly sent me a video of a Nova program. It showed sad stories of nurses who contracted a mysterious malady. They developed incapacitating weakness, confusion, headache, skin rashes, joint pains and breathing difficulties. Many of them cried as they described how they were finally disabled by the malady. After prolonged consultations with world-famous medical specialists and extensive batteries of diagnostic laboratory tests and scans, the illness remained undiagnosed.

What went wrong? The nurses made a grave error: They breathed the air in the operating rooms of Harvard's Brigham and Women's Hospital in Boston. The mystery was finally solved by some medical sleuths who identified the elusive offender molecule: glutaraldehyde, which is used to sterilize surgical instruments in operating rooms. The scene then changed and the video showed some high-powered environmental specialists talking about multi-million dollar renovations to eliminate the problem. I have doubts about their success. The diminished antioxidant and immune defenses of the hospital staff are as much a part of the problem as is the virulence of the offending molecule. All the millions spent on structurally renovating the hospital building will not restore the damaged antioxidant, enzyme and immune defenses of the hospital staff.

I know that to be true because I have seen too many people crippled by such stealth tormentors. How does Hans Selye's fight-or-flight stress response coincide with the unmitigated misery of those nurses?

NITRIC ACID: A GUARDIAN ANGEL OR KILLER?

I hear internists talk about the role of nitric oxide in high blood pressure and heart disease. That's their scientific rationale for prescribing their favorite drugs. Somehow the nitric oxide story is accepted as scientific validity for the long-term use of drugs that block one or more cellular receptors, enzymes, membrane channels and messenger molecules. Invariably, such blockade medicines create long-term chemical toxicities.

What my internist-friends do not see is that nitric oxide

is a molecular Dr. Jekyll and Mr. Hyde. Nitric oxide protects the healthy heart in some ways and attacks a damaged one in other ways. How does an internist know when nitric acid will be a guardian angel and when it will be a remorseless destroyer? Internists rarely ask such questions.

Iron is also a molecular Dr. Jekyll and Mr. Hyde. A part of hemoglobin, it is essential for transporting oxygen to the tissues. Yet excess free iron is also toxic, causing oxidant injury to the liver, adrenal glands and heart damage. Adrenaline also
plays dual roles—essential for survival in life-threatening emergencies as well as a dangerous oxidizing molecule. How do such molecular vagaries coincide with the adrenal fight-or-flight stress response?

How well does a psychologist understand stress if he is unfamiliar with the havoc wrought on his client by sugar-insulin-adrenaline roller coasters? How effective is a psychiatrist in depression caused chemical sensitivity if he vehemently denies that chemical sensitivity can cause depression? How competent can a cardiologist be in helping a young woman with mitral valve prolapse caused by stress of rampant yeast overgrowth? (Indeed, most cardiologists will probably scoff at the very idea.) How successful will a gastroenterologist be in soothing a rebellious bowel if he insists that food sensitivities cannot cause colitis? Surgeons enthusiastically perform sympathectomy —an operation that cuts sympathetic nerves out—for patients with arterial spasms. What is the true value of such an operation when arteries are tightened by unrelenting stress of oxidatively damaged blood cell membranes? Or, when the blood proteins are literally cooked by simmering oxidative coals kept lighted by viral activation syndromes?

Psychoneuroimmunology experts are a creative folks. They are busy propounding complex theories of how the psyche punishes the nervous and immune systems. In the past decades, we spent hundreds of millions of dollars on research establishing psyche, brain and the immune system as discrete segments of the human condition. How ironic that we are now wasting larger amounts of public funds trying to link them back again! Long live the gurus of our fight-or-flight stress industry!

Everyday in my clinical practice, I see the folly of fight-or-flight thinking through the true-to-life suffering of my patients. And everyday I wonder why our fight-or-flight experts cannot see something so obvious: Life is an injury-healing-injury continuum —and that is the *true* nature of stress.

SPONTANEITY OF INJURY, SPONTANEITY OF HEALING

The beginning of life as well as its ending are spontaneous phenomena. This is not a romanticist's view, nor is there anything metaphysical about it. These two aspects of life are observable phenomena and constitute the two sides of life's essential energetic-molecular equation.

Oxidation is the loss of electrons. It is a process by which high-energy molecules are turned into low-energy molecules. Common examples of oxidation are the wilting of fresh flowers, spoiling of fruit, decomposition of meat and rusting of iron. Spontaneity of oxidation in nature determines that the process of electron loss—breakdown of high-energy molecules —requires no external triggers. It is triggered solely by internal cues. It has nothing to do with demand for change. (I devote a large part of the companion volume *RDA: Rats, Drugs and Assumption* to this subject.)

Healing is also a spontaneous phenomenon —it occurs in response to inner cues. Some folks are enchanted by notions of spontaneous healing. I am at a loss as to the source of their excitement. For nearly three decades, as a hospital pathologist I studied the healing phenomenon in injured tissues with a microscope. I do not know of any *un*spontaneous healing. We pathologists have limited ideas about some observable aspects of the healing response. However, the truth is that we have no inkling about the internal energetic-molecular signals that molecules, cells and tissues heed during the course of healing. (I devote a large part of the companion volumes *The Cortical Monkey and Healing* and *The Dog, Directed Pulses and Energy Healing* to this side of life's equation.)

SPONTANEITY OF LIVING

In this volume, I include some personal observations and reflections on the third element of what I call the trio of spontaneities: the spontaneity of living.

Living was once spontaneous. For one thing, no one knew how to be *unspontaneous*. For another, everyone entered this world spontaneously —without any prior planning. People did what needed to be done—when it needed to be done. The ancients recognized that death was also a spontaneous process.

So where did things go wrong?

Doubt grows with knowledge, the German philosopher Johann Wolfgang Goethe wrote. The novelist Virginia Wolf lamented that literature is strewn with the wreckage of men who have minded beyond reason the opinions of others. At least, we have some understanding of what happened along the way—how we were reduced to living unspontaneously —and miserably.

Now here, you see, it takes all the running you can do to keep in the same place. If you want to get somewhere else, you must run at least as fast as that.

Charles Lutwidge Dogdson

How could the English mathematician, Dogdson (alias Lewis Carroll) see the future so clearly? How did he know that *all* we would do would be to keep running to keep in the same place? Did he know that would happen within a mere hundred years after his death? A perceptive rogue, that Mr. Dogdson!

Andy Warhol, our modern-day prophet, thought people forgot what emotions were supposed to be during the 1960s. "And I don't think they've ever remembered," he concluded. Mr. Warhol, it seems to me—mistook the 1960s for the beginning of the human era. The phenomenon of forgetting what human emotions are is much older.

How does one live spontaneously? Once lost, how does

one recapture one's lost innocence? When we know something, we cannot unknow it, my friend, Choua, often says. How do we say no to Goethe's knowledge that creates doubt? How do we *un*know? How do we detect —and sidestep —the wreckage of other men's ideas that Virginia Wolf warned us against?

Socrates pronounced that an unexamined life wasn't worth living. Now *all* we *ever* do is examine our lives. Could Socrates have ever imagined that? Then we re-examine and "re-re-examine" until the process of examining life totally excludes all possibility of *living*.

The past lives in the present, psychiatrists and psychologists teach us. Then they go on to promulgate their theories about solving the problems of the present through analysis of past suffering. We learn our lessons well. Under their able tutelage, we learn to recycle past misery—and when that doesn't suffice, we precycle feared, future misery.

My patients teach me something different. They have found that the endless recycling of past misery only causes endless misery—it does not free them from the misery of the moment. They have learned that they cannot clever-think their way out of all their problems. Neither stress nor healing are intellectual phenomena.

One clinical observation in my work has influenced my thinking more than anything else: *Tissues do not lie.* The thinking mind is the only part of the human condition that deceives. Where do the distortions in spontaneous healing come from? I asked. The Mind. That was the obvious answer. If the mind was the only part of the human condition that lies, why should I heed it in matters of healing? This simplistic notion was reassuring.

THERE AREN'T ENOUGH TIBETAN CAVES

The early African who walked out of the Rift Valley and looked up understood something about his linkage with the larger *presence* that surrounded him at all times. He understood something about injury-healing-injury cycles and about the real source of healing. The early African bequeathed those insights to the ancient Indians. The notion of the reverence for all life—and the ancient Jain concept of *Ahsima,* on which it is based, is rooted deep in human history.

In the West today, Eastern thought is reaching hundreds of millions of people through the popular New Age medium. That is good. Many people now look to the East for enlightenment —trekking all the way to Tibet. Others yearn for the opportunity and hope that someday they might complete the pilgrimage. But Tibet, the sacred land of enlightenment, has its problems.

Tibetan villages and towns are now strewn with as many Coke cans, beer bottles and candy wrappers as large cities in other parts of the world. Even if Tibet were as pristine and pure today as in its heyday, and even if higher states of consciousness were as achievable in Tibetan caves today as they were in the past, we would still face a problem: Tibet simply does not have caves to accommodate all of us.

Enlightenment and spirituality must now be sought on

Main Street, U.S.A. We must learn to live meditatively on our garbage-strewn city streets or abandon all pursuit of higher states of consciousness. The truth is, we do not need the high altitudes of the Himalaya to enter spiritual domains —our littered Main Streets will do. But, first we must divest ourselves of frivolous notions of fight-or-flight response and mind-over-body healing. This book is devoted to that idea.

Majid Ali, M.D.
New York, July 22, 1996

Chapter 1

The Arthritic Lion

"There! There is a big one!" Michael shouted as he turned his vehicle abruptly and pointed to something in the distance. "He has to have his pride with him."

Michael, our safari guide, had a sharp eye for the African savannah and—it seemed to me—an even sharper sense for the life in it.

"What big one?" I asked, peering into the tall grass in that direction. "What is it?"

"There!" This time Michael pointed straight into the grass. "Do you see him now? There, lying low in the grass is the huge, black-maned head of a patriarch lion," Michael beamed, obviously gratified.

"Where?" This time it was Sarah, our daughter, who asked as she looked excitedly in the direction of Michael's hand.

We had driven for more than two hours in the grasslands that morning before we lost sight of all the safari vans that were looking for lions. I stood up to look through the roof hatch. It was a clear day. The morning sun was warm, and I felt a mild rush of breeze on my face.

The day before, Michael had taken us on a safari in the Masai Mara Game Reserve —the northernmost part of the great Serengeti Plain. Mara is a place like no other. You don't need to look for wild animals—they come looking for you by the zillion. The savannah teemed with wildebeests, zebras, giraffes, warthogs, baboons, topies, bushbucks, impalas and tommies —gazelles named after Joseph Thomson, a Scottish geologist who walked across much of Kenya during 1879 and early 1880s. In 1884, he shot an antelope that proved to be a new species and was named *Gazella thomsoni*. The tommy is by far the most prolific gazelle, and in large herds sometimes dots the east African plains horizon to horizon.

Michael told us earlier that we might run into some rhinos if we were lucky. We were. We saw several up close. The rhinos reminded me of New York City's tollbooth attendants. Brooding and alone, the rhinos stood impervious to approach, disdainful when distracted.

Elephant herds were simply too large to miss even at great distances. The Serengeti elephants seemed as placid and limbic as the Asian elephants in Pakistan. I remembered reading that more than any other animal, elephants possess traits of sensitivity and tenderness. At one time during the safari, an elephant herd slowly ambled alongside our van, until it decided to cross the road ahead of us, passing us within several feet. One huge bull raised a foot, swayed toward the van as if to step on us, then changed his mind and moved on. An elephant calf walked along, nudging his mother and rubbing her underbelly with his small head. Mother-daughter bonding among elephants is legendary. I searched the eyes of the mom for some visible maternal tenderness and imagined I saw some.

THE LIMBIC LIONS

But the lions were different. Finding them wasn't difficult. All Michael had to do was drive toward any group of white safari vans gathered in a semicircle. Invariably, we would find the big cats in the grass or small thickets of trees, sunning themselves in the Serengeti sun or snoozing in the shade. They evidently had no chores and seemed to know that. They simply *were,* the essence of being limbic.

In one place a lioness was in heat, so the male entertained her—and us—with his mating performance. His taut and hunched torso bore down on her; his thigh muscles bulged and quivered; his black mane flared up; his lips curled and his bare teeth dug into her neck in such a way that only a lioness could call it a love bite. Then came a quick, eerie yowl. The king of beasts was through in less than a minute. I recalled reading that lions mate every 20 to 25 minutes when the female is in heat. This male obviously hadn't read that book. He was ready for a repeat performance in fewer than 10 minutes. This exhibitionist monarch was not intimidated by six vans full of voyeurs.

We stayed around the lions for some time. Yet it all seemed pure Disneyland: well-staged, superbly choreographed, utterly contrived. The cast of characters never really came alive. The only genuine items, I thought, were the irreverent American, German and Japanese tourists.

Sometime during that safari run, Sarah announced that the next day we would strike deep into the Serengeti savannah by ourselves. She said Michael had to find some real lions that we could call "all our own." When Sarah invited us to visit her in Nairobi, she promised to show us the "real" Kenya. Sarah had gone to Kenya on a scholarship after receiving her master's degree from the Harvard School of Public Health. She had traveled much throughout the country before we visited her, and she was determined to avoid the many tourist traps there. We admired her resolve and expressed our profuse gratitude for her detailed planning of our trip. She was evidently dissatisfied with merely looking for lions surrounded by safari vans. So she pushed Michael to do better. He promised to do his best. There we were the next morning, deep in the savannah, away from the nuisance of safari vans brimming with tourists.

"I don't see it, Michael," Talat spoke from the back seat, craning her neck for a better view between Michael and Sarah who were sitting in the front seat.

"We'll be there in a few moments," Michael laughed reassuringly. "And he isn't going anyplace. Lions never seem to be in a hurry."

I looked hard. There was nothing to be seen except endless fields of tall, gold-brown grass waving in the savannah breeze under an azure blue sky. Weaving his way through tall grass, Michael drove through the bumpy savannah as if the Mara grasslands grew on an unending paved airfield. I held fast to the roof hatch, trying hard to save my ribs from being bruised by rough jolts as Michael approached his object.

Then I saw the beast stand up and stretch his enormous torso as he shook large head and glistening black mane. He walked slowly toward a thicket of low trees without seeming to take notice of the approaching van. Then he disappeared into the thickets. I felt cheated by the lion and looked first at Sarah, then at Talat, who seemed to be equally dismayed. Moments later, the lion re-emerged from the thicket, swiveled and stared at us directly for a brief moment. Then, with the gruff indifference of a patriarch, he moved away. Looking from the rear, I thought I saw a limp. Yes, the lion favored his left leg.

Michael swung the van to the other side of the tree thicket, bringing into full view a stunning sight: a pride of five lionesses—sleek, sinewy and supreme. They walked with their heads up. Their powerful legs carried lithesome, long torsos. Their long tails described perfect sigmoid curves that ended in black-tasseled tail tufts. Their gold-brown pelts glistened as if illuminated by some radiant energy from within. The lionesses eyed us with regal nonchalance, then ambled away with easy and measured grace. Two of them moved side to side a few paces ahead of the remaining three, who followed Indian-file. I understood then why a grouping of lions is called a *pride.*

Mesmerized, my eyes remained glued to the lionesses as Michael slowly inched his way toward them. Some paces away, Michael veered his van so the lionesses and the van were parallel. The patriarch lion followed many steps behind. Thus we shared the savannah with the lions for about two or three miles. After the initial eye contact, the lionesses never acknowledged our presence. I was too absorbed in that unearthly scene to have any real sense of time.

"What do lions know about stress?" Choua's voice brought me back.
"Stress?" I asked, surprised.
"Yes, stress! What do lions know about stress?" he repeated.

I looked at Choua and wondered what might have raised such a question in his mind. "Hey, lion, what do you know about stress?" I shouted at the lions in jest, then looked at Choua and shrugged.
"What do lions know about stress?" he repeated, ignoring my stab at humor.
"Hey, lions, do you hear me?" I shouted at the lions again. "What do you know about stress? My friend here, Choua,

has an inquiring mind. He wants to know."

"What do lions know about stress?" Choua asked again, unimpressed by the questions I tossed at the lions.

"Hey, lions, what do you know about Hans Selye's fight-or-flight response?" I decided to continue the gag.

I looked at Choua after a few moments, then again at the lions. Choua kept quiet for some minutes, then tilted his head and raised his eyebrows in inquiry.

"What can I tell you, Choua?" I shrugged again. "You saw it. None of them cares to answer me. Why don't you try?"

"What do these cats know about..." Choua stopped in mid-sentence.

"Okay, you tell me," I replied, pretending to be serious that time. "What would lions know about stress anyway? They don't have to worry about anyone cutting them off in traffic. Right?"

"Right."

"They have this prodigious capacity for rest and seem to relax all the time."

"Yes, that they do."

"Even flies sitting on their muzzles don't seem to irk them."

"Right again," he added solemnly.

"They don't have a natural predator, do they?"

"Go on," he prodded.

"And I don't think any of them has ever read about Selye's stress reaction or about Bensen's relaxation response."

"Probably not."

"All I see them do is sun themselves in the grass. They seem to think they own the sun, don't they?"

"True, but..."

"And when they don't laze around in the sun, they snooze in the shade."

"That too."

"I read someplace that males generally don't hunt."

"Yes, most hunting is done by females."

"About the only time males seem to get excited is when some female is in heat."

"Don't beat about the bush," Choua spoke tersely. "I'm talking about the stress in lions' lives."

"How can I know what lions know about stress?" I replied, suppressing my irritation. "You saw them. They don't talk to me. They don't even look at us. How can I know what lions might or might not know about stress? As far as I can tell, the males excel at doing nothing. What they cherish most is their regal slumber. Even when they march, like the ones we see now, they walk indifferently. If there is anything dramatic about them, it is their inactivity. I don't think lions have much use for your notions of stress. I don't see how they can really know anything about stress."

Choua looked away, and I wondered if he heard the last few sentences I spoke.

A thicket of trees separated our paths, hiding the pride of lions from view. I turned back to look at the patriarch. He followed, somewhat strained, a few hundred feet behind, his head held low, his eyes downcast. Still, it seemed to me, he knew everything without having to scan the scene around him. He was clearly in no hurry to catch up with his harem. I looked ahead and to the side to see if the lionesses would reemerge from behind the thicket. They did some moments later and we resumed, sojourners in silence. The sun was blazing now, and I felt its heat on my head and neck when the breeze died every now and then.

OFFENSE BEGINS THE PLAY

In the distance I spotted a large herd of tommies, who seemed to be posing for a perfect still portrait. Two strong males stood at the periphery of the herd, closer to the approaching pride of lions—straight-legged necks stretched, ears perked, gazes fixed on the lions.

"They smelled the cats earlier and now they've seen them," Michael explained.

"Hamburgers for the lions," Sarah spoke excitedly.

"Frozen in fear, not in freezers," Talat added.

"Nah!" Michael replied in a matter-of-fact way. "Cats don't attack the prey that have spotted them."

"Why not?" I couldn't resist asking the obvious.

"Cats need a surprise advantage when they hunt," Michael explained. "Besides..."

"But what about the fawns?" Sarah interrupted. "Surely the little ones can't outrun the lions."

"Lions know a tiny fawn is not enough for a meal, except when a pregnant lioness needs extra calcium. Then it will target a fawn and eat it, bones and all. Right now the cats are going for zebras," Michael pointed. I strained to look but saw nothing. Pretty annoying, this habit of Michael's, spotting animals in tall grass before we can, I murmured to myself.

"But why don't the gazelles run away while they can?" Sarah asked.

"That would be dangerous," Michael replied. "Gazelles

know their best chance of survival is in letting the offense begin the play."

"Explain that," Sarah demanded, surprised by Michael's answer.

"Lions sometimes hunt in groups," Michael began. "Some of them use the strategy of hiding in the grass and crouching quietly on one side of the prey, while other lions approach their target visibly from the other side. When the lions charge, they know the gazelles will panic and hope some of them will run straight toward the lions in waiting. Gazelles also know their survival depends on denying the lions a surprise advantage."

"So they hold out. Frightened to their marrows and frozen in time, they wait for the lions to charge," I added.

"Yes," he agreed. "It's different with cheetahs. When a cheetah breaks into a hunting sprint, he becomes a ball of energy, moving like lightning. A cheetah *reads* the zigzagging flight of his prey and succeeds only if he correctly predicts the abrupt turns and twists of his victim—he cuts corners, so to speak. It's different with lions. They can't think once their ballistic charge begins. For a leaping lion, it's a straight line to the intended target or nothing at all. That's one reason why lion hunts are often unsuccessful."

"Are the lions moving upwind or downwind?" I asked, then added hurriedly, flustered at my own folly, "Don't answer, Michael. I can feel the wind on my back."

"Yeah, lions do that," Michael laughed. "They ignore the first rule of successful hunting."

"What's that?" Talat asked.

"They often approach the prey downwind. Cheetahs never approach their targets downwind. Leopards never do that. But lions do," Michael explained.

"But why?" I asked.

"Who knows?" Michael bared his white teeth.

"Maybe these kings of the jungle don't need the advantage," I offered an explanation.

"Oh yes, they do!" Michael said emphatically, then continued, "One out of four nighttime lion hunts ends with a lion biting the dust. During the day, the situation is worse."

"I see the zebras now, Michael," I said, recognizing black-and-white stripes moving among the distant trees. "But it looks like there's a river between the lions and the zebras."

"Yes, there is. That's the Mara River. But there's also a bridge. And cats know about that too."

The Thomson gazelles didn't budge. They stood still, like a field of statues planted in the grass. As the lionesses and our van slowly passed them by, I noticed their eyes still transfixed on us. So they did move their head, I thought to myself, only they did so imperceptibly. Abrupt movement adds to the stress of the prey. Then I noticed one large male gazelle at the far end. His head was cocked. His unwavering stare was fixed on the patriarch lion, who moved at a slower pace several hundred feet behind the lionesses. I watched the lion limp along and wondered how his right leg might have been injured.

I looked at the field of gazelle statues and wondered why Choua had asked me about stress in lions and not in gazelles. As far as I could tell, lions had no reason to be stressed. The gazelles had spotted the lions first so the cats lost their surprise advantage, but that didn't seem to trouble them. They simply moved to where the zebras grazed.

Why did Choua bring up the subject of stress on a ride through an African game reserve? Why on a bright sunny day in the open savannah, surrounded by tall, golden grass waving in the gentle breeze? Why, when we were in the surrealistic presence of five glorious lionesses and their powerful, full-maned patriarch, albeit with an arthritic leg? Why, when passing within yards of a stunning field of gazelle statues? Why bring up the subject of stress? If Choua was interested in stress, he should have asked me about the fear of gazelles—their utter terror of death. Choua often speaks cryptically, sometimes with a schizophrenic dissociation of ideas. I looked at him. He stared impassively at the lionesses. I decided not to disturb him.

ELEPHANTS AND MOTHS

Michael told us that elephants have no natural predators. They live free lives. A storybook image from my boyhood memories rose before me: the sight of an Indian maharajah's hapless elephant lying on his side, weeping as his trainer whipped him. Large tears rolled down from the elephant's sad eyes. Why don't these big animals fight back? I wondered then. Elephants are huge and their trainers are small men. Why don't the animals see something that simple? The trainers are in no position to control the huge beasts if the elephants were to challenge them. Indeed, I had heard stories of kept elephants suddenly losing their tempers and thrashing their mounts around them before trampling them to death and disappearing into the jungle.

At the time, I didn't know how wild animals are tamed. I didn't know how professional trainers get animals to march or dance to their drums. How do small men control huge elephants and fierce lions?

I learned something about the dynamics of animal training when I found out how young German boys were trained in eighteenth-century trading posts in Norway. During a visit to Bergen on the western coast of Norway, Talat and I visited Hanseatisk Museum at Finnegarden. It's a place worth visiting if one is interested in studying the effects of stress on young boys and how they cope with it as they grow up. The Hanseatisk were affluent German merchants who monopolized the dried fish trade in Norway and many other European countries.

The museum reveals in lucid and harrowing detail the lives of apprentices in the Hanseatisk trading posts. These apprentices were young 12- to 14-year-old boys. Considered difficult by their parents in Germany, the boys were shipped to far-flung trading offices for discipline, proper upbringing and trade skills. The boys worked 16 to 18 hours in small, unheated wooden cabins. During long, lightless Norwegian winter months, they were not permitted to use candles for light, let alone for heat, because of the risk of igniting fires. Fresh food was almost nonexistent. At night, the boys were locked into small wooden berths, two or three to a berth barely 30 inches wide. What any of them did when suffering from bladder infections or diarrhea is anyone's guess. The berths were constructed so that the boys could only sleep sitting up. This was done so that the boys could be awakened quickly and also because sleep in that posture was thought to prevent respiratory disorders. Talat and I looked at those narrow berths for several minutes trying to figure out how three boys could possibly sleep there. Claustrophobia evidently wasn't considered a designated mental disorder then. To keep a close watch on the boys, the merchant in charge of the trading post slept in a wooden cabin on one side of the boys' cabin while the merchant's assistant slept in a cabin on the other side. The thin, wooden walls partitioning their quarters wouldn't even muffle the sounds of breathing.

The rules of conduct for the boys were very strict, and the boys were frequently and ruthlessly beaten to enforce discipline and order. One corner of the wooden cabin displayed a whip with nail marks at its one end. (The nails evidently had fallen off with time.) The whip was used freely by trainers to bring the miscreants in line.

For years the boys never heard from their families—nor their families from them. Escape from the trading posts was impossible. The open sea in front and the steep rocks of Norwegian fjords in back thwarted all escape attempts. The apprentices, we were told by the museum curator, learned their lessons well. When they grew up and were promoted, they relished their new assignments and inflicted equal cruelty on the newcomers. And so the art of *training* was preserved and advanced.

The lessons we learned about stress and human endurance at the Hanseatisk Museum were long lasting. I suppose animals learn similar lessons in their training.

(Talat and I made another discovery in our travel through the Norway countryside from Oslo to Bergen: The Chinese immigrants in Norwegian hamlets do not make good pizza.)

My thoughts drifted from memories of the Norwegian coast to elephants. I remembered the picture of a gray elephant's eye I'd seen in *Nature* magazine. It showed an eye shaped like a teardrop —with tears rolling down from the point of the teardrop on the animal's head to a distance of about an inch. There, surrounding the tiny pool of tears in a large skin crevice, hovered a cluster of the Asian moths, *Hypochrosis baenzigeri*. The moths had gathered around the pool of tears to quench their thirst. Below the picture, a caption explained that moths sting the elephants' eyes, make them teary, then drink the lachrymal fluid as it spills from the teary eyes. Nature has its own sense of order, its own game plan to provide for the hydration of some moth species. Who could have imagined it would assign to tiny moths the role of predators for monstrous elephants?

Elephants don't shed crocodile tears, I mused. Crocodiles in African lakes with high water alkalinity purportedly shed tears to rid themselves of excess body alkalinity, not to weep. However, I'm not sure the naturalist who proposed this viewpoint ever asked a crocodile about it.

Elephant stories sometimes remind me of an account of an elephant baby emerging from a woman's womb by the Roman naturalist, Pliny the Elder, in the first century A.D. As Lance Morrow observed, a Pliny pattern persists—Elvis-sighters of rock music continue to thrive as do Einsteins of science.

Are any living beings ever truly free? I wondered. I began to see what Choua was leading to.

In 1963, Fosbrooke described a pestilence among Serengeti lions. Between April and June 1962 an outbreak of biting flies *(Stomoxus calcitrans)* occurred in Ngorongoro Crater in the Serengeti Plain. The blood-sucking flies bit the lions with such intensity and relentlessness as to leave behind large, confluent bare patches on the lions' skin. Many cats crawled into hyena burrows to escape the merciless flies—something they would never do under any other circumstances. Others climbed trees. But the flies didn't let up. Some lions deserted their home turf. Most lions became emaciated. Before the flies were finished with the lions, their number had dropped from 70 to 15. The kings of the jungle were hapless before mere flies.

Cape buffaloes in Africa are ill-tempered and, as Michael would say, are always having a "bad" day. Buffaloes in my boyhood in Pakistan were different. I rarely saw an ill-mannered buffalo in Kirto, my ancestral village. Do Cape buffaloes have an extra "anger gene"? I wondered. Or could it be that the Asian buffaloes who inherited the anger gene were selected over the millennia and eliminated for noncooperation? Or perhaps the ill-tempered buffaloes in the Indian subcontinent were taught to behave a long time ago by their trainers, just as the Hanseatisk merchants had trained the "difficult" German boys in Bergen.

I wondered how I might apply their experience to our established notions of stress. What happens when people or animals refuse to be "trained"? What happens when living beings are unable to follow someone else's script?

WHAT IS STRESS?

"What is stress?" Choua repeated the question and brought me back from my thoughts.
"That's not an easy question to answer," I replied. "Everyone knows how it feels to be stressed out, but putting that into words isn't easy."

"Take a stab at it," he coaxed.

"Most people probably can relate to the absence of stress rather than with its presence. Maybe I can answer your question by paraphrasing Leo Tolstoy: All absence of stress is the same, yet each stress is different in its own way."

"Not bad," he shook his head approvingly. "Tell me how would you say that in medical language?"

"Hans Selye defined stress as a fight-or-flight response," I replied.

"Selye didn't do that," he countered. "Walter N. Cannon described the fight-or-flight aspect of the stress response long before Selye did. Indeed, the expression fight-or-flight was Cannon's."

"Who was Cannon?" I asked, then remembered his work vaguely. "Was he the guy who experimented with decerebrate cats?"

"Yes. Cannon removed parts of cat's brains and then brought them to a maximal physical arousal state by creating sham rage conditions."

"Why did he do that?"

"He wanted to know if animals have some capacity for coping with life-threatening stressors at nonthinking, noncortical levels, so he took out parts of cats' brains to see how brainless cats cope with stress."

"Okay, but didn't Selye popularize the concept of fight-or-flight stress response?"

"Yes, that he did. Selye was a natural philosopher, a brilliant man. In 1925, as a second-year medical student, he recognized that many patients afflicted by what were considered separate diseases actually suffered from many common symptoms such as weakness, loss of appetite and anxiety. He labeled that state as the *syndrome of just being sick*. That was brilliant!"

"I didn't know that. I don't think too many people..."

"Brilliant, but too simple for Selye's teachers at the medical school and unimpressive for doctors outside the school. Nobody would have taken that sort of name for a syndrome seriously, and nobody did."

"Why?"

"Not enough medical authenticity in the name of the syndrome. What patient would have been impressed by that?"

"Oh, that!"

"And no editor of a medical journal worth his salt would have taken that kind of simplicity in medical jargon seriously either."

"Well, let's face it, the syndrome of just being sick is not exactly scientific terminology," I said, then asked, "So what did he do?"

"When he realized that the gods of medicine frowned upon the name of his syndrome, he changed it to *stress reaction,* and then he coined another term, *general adaptation response.* Now, that term sounded sufficiently technical and prestigious."

"So is that where the term general adaptation response comes from? I didn't know that."

"Selye was a clever man, and that was a brilliant solution to an awkward problem," Choua chimed.

"Why? Because the term general adaptation response was scientific and syndrome of just being sick wasn't. Is that it?"

"No, it wasn't that at all," he smiled impishly. "It had nothing to do with medicine at all."

"What was it then?"

"Don't you see, it was a marketing coup! I told you Selye was a smart man. He understood marketing."

"That's a cynical viewpoint, but go on."

"The name change made it easy for him to sell his ideas to doctors and editors of medical journals. They loved the new names because they could easily sell it to their patients. The patients, of course, understood nothing by the new terms, but that's the whole point of medical terminology, isn't it?"

"You're a rascal," I reprimanded.

"Don't you see the obvious?" Choua spoke churlishly. "The name syndrome of just being sick was not elegant, but it was true to life. It made a clear statement —that the patient was simply sick. It carried no pretense of pseudoknowledge, while the term general adaptation response was elegant but not true to life. It sounded so very scientific, but what did it actually say? Anything?"

"I don't understand that," I admitted.

"What's there to understand? If you tell someone who is sick that he is just being sick, he is likely to be offended and tell you, 'Of course, I'm sick. I know that! That's why I came to you. Don't simply tell me I'm just sick. Tell me what is making me sick.' Now that's an awkward question to answer, isn't it?" he smirked.

"I don't know where this is leading us, but go on."

"Well, if you tell a sick person that he has general adaptation response, he is likely to be impressed by the clinical sound of the diagnostic term. He is unlikely to ask questions about its cause."

"You are a cynic," I berated him. "You can't help but be yourself, can you?"

"Don't you see the simple truth there?" he groused.

"What truth?"

"No one adapts to serious injury! People either heal their injuries or continue to suffer from them. Adaptation is an illusion."

Selye's adaptation is an illusion? I was stunned. Choua has a way of dropping bombshells. But this hit me totally unprepared. I stared at him blankly for several minutes. Choua seemed to relish my surprise as well as my confusion. Then he looked away. I sensed he did that to hide his amusement at my reaction to his words. I looked ahead where the lions had spotted a zebra herd. There was only tall, golden grass and thickets of low trees. No zebras could be seen. I couldn't keep my mind off what Choua said so nonchalantly.

Selye's stress response is, of course, considered solid science. I've never heard anyone take issue with Selye's notions about stress. Indeed, many years after his death, he still reigns as the super guru of the stress community. What made Choua make a stunning statement like that? I wondered. We rode in silence for some distance. Every now and then, I looked at his turned face. He seemed lost in deep thought. Finally I broke the silence.

"You don't buy Selye's fight-or-flight response, is that it?"
"What is stress?" he asked, ignoring my question.
"Didn't we cover that before?" I asked, irritated. "Stress is a physiologic response that occurs when a person faces a threat and has to flee to save his life or dig his heels in and fight it out with the threatening being."
"What happens in stress? I mean physically," he pressed.
"Selye called it a nonspecific response to a demand for change. That demand brings about a host of changes in various body organ functions."
"For example?"
"Well, the heart rate quickens. The breathing becomes deeper and its rate increases. Muscles tighten, pupils widen, and the blood flow increases to the body organs that actively participate in the fight-or-flight response. The blood supply to other body organs decreases. Activity in the digestive-absorptive

organs ebbs and kidneys slow down."

"How are such changes brought about?"

"That's what Selye's work is all about, isn't it?" I returned to Selye's work. "There are bursts of adrenaline and other catecholamines —cousin molecules of adrenaline —from the adrenal gland. These stress hormones fire up a range of neurotransmitters and energize the whole body for a maximal survival response. Right?"

"Right!" He nodded, then asked, "What is eustress, and what is distress?"

"Selye divided stress into two types: eustress and distress. Eustress is produced by the demand for adaptation that the body can comfortably cope with—an optimal level of stress, so to speak. He further believed eustress promotes health. Selye described distress as demands on the body to adapt that exceed its capacity for adaptation. This excessive demand results in damage —and, in time, disease."

"Ah, a neat classification!" he murmured, then asked, "How do you separate the two? How does a person know whether the adaptation he's being asked to make is health-promoting and he should welcome it, or whether it's disease-causing and he should protest it?"

"That's..."

"Not easy," he completed my sentence. "Tell me, does an antelope know when the presence of lions in his vicinity is causing eustress and when it is causing distress?"

"Don't be ridiculous," I chastised him. "How can you question adaptation? That's amazing. I know you are a contrarian, but don't you think this is going too far? Wasn't adaptation the centerpiece of Darwin's theory of natural selection?"

"Darwin was partially right," he replied impassively.

"But Selye wasn't?" I shook my head in disbelief.

"Don't confuse the two," he replied curtly. "Genes don't adapt to demands for change in seconds. That's not what Darwin's core theory was about. It was about natural selection."

"But he wrote about adaptation, didn't he?"

"Yes, genes can change in seconds. But that has nothing to do with the demands put upon them for change. Genes are randomly—and oxidatively, as you say—mutating all the time. If the product of that gene mutation strengthens the animal—favors its long-term survival, so to speak—it increases the chances of that gene being passed on to that animal's offspring. If the gene mutation weakens the animal, the opposite happens."

"Now, isn't that adaptation?" I persisted.

"Then there is the matter of an intelligent design needing an intelligent designer," Choua went on, ignoring my question.

"Are you an evolutionist or a creationist?" I asked, baffled by his sudden deviation from the subject of natural selection.

"Neither," he grinned broadly, then continued. "It's a gene selection, and not an adaptation process. When injured, living beings either heal or continue to hurt. They don't adapt. Have you ever seen a mother adapt to the loss of her child?

"They do recover after a period of bereavement, don't they?" I countered.

"I don't believe that," he scowled. "Is that how much you truly understand about human suffering?"

"You don't have to insult me," I squirmed.

"No mother ever adapts to the death of her baby," he continued, his eyes softening.

"How about other less painful stressors?" I refused to yield.

"Living beings either heal their wounds or suffer from them. There is no adaptation." He spoke with finality.

We rode in silence. I could hear Sarah and Michael talking incessantly in the front seat, but I was too distracted by Choua's troubling assertions to make sense of what they were saying. Talat stared into the distance.

STRESS AND BEHAVIOR EXPERIMENTS

"How do you study the effects of stress on behavior?" It was Choua who broke the silence this time.

"Behavior," I repeated after him absent-mindedly.

"Yes, how is stress-behavior research conducted?"

"By controlled animal and human studies, just like research is conducted in other areas. Why do you ask?"

"How are stressful conditions created?"

"There are many established standard techniques."

"Like dunking rats in ice-cold water?" he pouted.

"That's one of the common practices." I ignored his sarcasm.

"Rats are dunked into freezing water so that researchers can see which ones can swim and live and which ones die. Isn't that the idea?"

"That's absurd," I replied curtly. "That isn't the purpose of those experiments. The objective is to measure physiologic responses evoked by the stress of exposure to cold water."

"And by the struggle to avoid drowning."

"Yes, that too," I agreed. "But the objectives of those experiments are to measure changes in animal heart rates, breathing cycles and neurotransmitter levels."

"What do you observe when you incarcerate animals in small cages, starve them, then make them fight among themselves for tiny morsels of food?"

"Changes in their..."

"Behavior?" he interrupted me.

"Yes, yes," I replied testily. "If you want to study the effect of stress on an animal's behavior, there's no other way except to create stressful conditions for the animals, then carefully record the changes in their behavior."

"Tell me, what do you learn from those experiments?" he pressed.

"Different things. Many different things. Why do you ask?" I inquired impatiently.

"So you learn that when an animal's life is in jeopardy, his behavior changes, is that it?"

"Yes, but what's the point of this inquisition?" I asked, exasperated.

"Sometimes the animals become incontinent and urinate and defecate," he continued evenly.

"Yes! That too!"

"Don't you think the ancients knew all that?" he persisted. "Don't you think they observed the behavior of animals when they were seriously injured or when they faced death?"

"Yes, but..."

"Don't you think the ancients ever witnessed an animal drowning in cold water?" He didn't let me complete my sentence. "Don't you think they ever watched how an animal recovers from the near-fatal experience of sinking in a lake? Do you think no humans ever experienced near-drowning episodes and lived to tell others about it?"

"Yes, but none of those were controlled, scientific observations," I replied.

"Scientific!" he erupted, then calmed down momentarily and asked, "Do you think no human ever felt a sudden thumping of his heart when faced with a pride of lions emerging out of the bush?"

I decided not to pursue the subject any further. Of course, I knew the purpose of those animal experiments was not merely to learn about their quickened heart rates and labored breathing. But Choua can be so unrelenting and, at times, utterly recalcitrant. His arguments were wearing me out. Silence seemed to be a sorely needed respite from his tirades. I looked to the side, away from him and pretended to search for animals in the bush. We rode in silence. The hypnotic effects of the savannah sun and grasslands soon restored my sense of the Serengeti. I saw some more impala herds, a family of ostriches and some crown cranes prancing in the grass. They seemed to be flapping their wings in celebration of life.

"Tell me about stress behavior in rats and drug research," Choua gently nudged me.

"Rats and drug experiments?" I couldn't suppress a smile. "Rats are subjected to stress before and after injections of drugs to study how their behavior under stressful conditions is altered by drugs."

"Tell me about forced-swim and tail-suspension tests used in drug research."

"The tests are what their names say they are. In forced swim tests, rats are forced to swim to avoid drowning. In tail-suspension tests, they are suspended by their tails and dunked into water intermittently."

"Why?"

"For obvious reasons. To see how drugs affect their ability to maintain a survival effort."

"That *effort*, of course, is the rat's last-ditch attempt to survive death by drowning."

"Yes, but..."

"Then the researchers found that animals valiantly struggle to escape their tormentors," he interrupted me, "until the experimenters win and the rats drown. Right?"

"Drug researchers didn't design experiments to torment rats," I protested. "You're distorting things again. It was all part of drug research so that..."

"Drug data can be procured to satisfy the drug lords at the FDA for drug approval."

"You're so irrational today," I reprimanded. "How else do you conduct drug research? There is no limit to your scorn, and..."

"Tell me about the ingenious 'learned-helplessness-model' experiments," he cut me off.

"In those experiments, rats and mice are exposed to stress with electrodes to see how electric shocks impair their ability to escape additional shocks," I replied with resignation.

"You first electrocute the hapless rodents, then study how they can survive additional electric shocks. Is that it?" he grimaced.

"I don't electrocute any rodents," I protested vehemently. "Drug researchers do. Though I see why they have to perform those experiments. The purpose of this research is to create such a fear of uncontrollable future shocks that the animals 'learn' to become helpless."

"What happens next?"

"The animals are injected with drugs to see how the use of drugs affects learned helplessness in animals, and..."

"And, by implication, humans. Right!"

"Right," I answered, exasperated. "How else do you establish the safety of drugs for human use?"

"Drug safety?" He suddenly stiffened and stared at me with cold eyes.

I immediately knew the folly of my statement. Of course, establishing the safety of any drug has nothing to do with drowning rats in ice-cold water. I bit my lips but said nothing. Choua seemed to sense my uneasiness and mercifully didn't follow through.

"Tell me about experiments in which rats are given electric shocks to see how they recover from electrocution."

"What's there to tell? I guess it is a tough thing for anyone to do, I mean, shocking laboratory animals. But I guess that's better than shocking people."

"Why?" he scowled. "Because animals can't talk back."

"Well, that..."

"I take that back," he interrupted me sarcastically. "How silly of me! I should know better. That's not quite right because we know you drug researchers also do evil things to people when they are in no position to know what you do to them, or when you know your research subjects can't fight back!"

"What are you ranting about?" I asked angrily.

"Between 1944 and 1974, more than four-thousand experiments were conducted with radioactive materials in which human subjects were told neither the truth about the nature of the experiments nor about the risks involved."

"Progress in science has its cost. Besides..."

"Ah, the things you do to innocent people in the name of scientific progress," he bluntly cut me off. "Like injecting highly radioactive plutonium into very ill patients without their knowledge."

"I don't believe that. Nobody in his right mind would do a thing like that. Don't make things up," I scolded him.

"You know me. I don't make things up. That's exactly what *Nature Medicine* reported in its November 1995 issue.

"Really! Tell me, what did *Nature Medicine* report?"

"The journal also reported something else," he laughed out loud.

"What?"

"It said some experimenters confessed that they injected radioactive materials into people to conduct experiments that offered 'no prospect of direct medical benefit.'"

"Why would anyone ever inject radioactive material into humans, knowing there is no prospect of direct medical benefit?"

"Who knows? But President Clinton did publicly apologize to the victims of those experiments. Of course, for most of the victims, the apology came a little too late. They had died years earlier."

"How did we get on that tangent? What does that have to do with stress?"

"I don't know," he grinned broadly.

I looked down the roof hatch. Talat seemed oblivious to everything. Utterly abandoned, her eyes were fixed on distant hills. Sarah chatted away with Michael. I looked around. There were a couple of topis near a cluster of acacia trees. I straightened up and looked out, avoiding Choua's eyes.

"How do drug researchers study depression in rats?"

"They create depression by using repetitive stressors," I replied hesitatingly, without turning to look at him.

"The way they're described in psychiatry and psychology books?" He grimaced.

"Yeah," I replied indifferently. "Do we have to talk about depression and anxiety here in Masai Mara?" I complained.

We were silent for a while. I knew what Choua was driving at. I had read several harrowing accounts about cruelty to animals. Often, I, myself, had wondered about the need for such cruelty. Below, I include an excerpt from the *Handbook of Depression and Anxiety* published by Marcel Dekker publishers to give the reader some sense of how such experiments are conducted:

> ***...3 weeks of exposure to electric shocks, immersion in cold water, immobilization, reversal of the light-dark cycle, and a variety of other stressors, caused a decrease in the activating effect of acute stress in an open-field test. However, the activating effect of acute stress was maintained in animals receiving daily antidepressant treatments during the chronic stress period.***

"How do the drug researchers treat poor rats in order to create what they call a 'defeat mentality'?" Choua gored in.

"You make it sound so awful," I protested. "I told you scientific animal experimentation has its downside."

"Downside?" Choua groused. "First they put the strong male rats through electric shocks and drowning, then they provoke them to molest the weaker ones. Do you call that the downside of science?"

"It's difficult to design experiments for measuring the effects of stress, depression and defeat on dominant and nondominant animals."

"Tell me, what was the purpose of doing those tests?" he pressed.

"The purpose of the tests was to see how drugs affect animals under high stress," I explained.

"Just give me the scientific test results, will you?" he asked testily.

"The defeated animals showed a gradual increase in passive behavior. Furthermore, those animals were then subjected to forced-swim and tail-suspension tests to show they had developed higher immobility times. In the end, the drug did help the stressed animals, didn't it?"

"How very nice!" Choua's voice brimmed with bitter sarcasm.

"In other versions of those tests, mice were kept in social contact, but were physically separated, except for single daily encounters of a few minutes," I continued, ignoring his comment. "Repeatedly, defeated animals in such experiments showed trouble with spontaneous movements —what the drug researchers called 'increased immobility times.' Next, the drug researchers concluded that the drugs protected the animals—the effects of extreme stress on rats could be eased with drugs."

"What did the rats do when they lost their ability to move?" he asked.

"That's the ugly underbelly of drug research. I agree with you," I confessed.

"Ugly and unnecessary," he added.

"I don't know if I agree with the part about necessity," I countered.

"Do stress researchers ever publish results that don't suit their purpose?"

"What do you mean?"

"The data of studies that do not support the use of drugs never see daylight. But that's not their concern, is it?"

"I really don't want to talk about electrocution of rats any more," I said, irritated. "Anyway, tell me, how do lions fit into all this? What do lions know about stress?"

STRESS RESEARCH AND ANIMAL MUTILATION

"Lions know as much about stress as lambs," he replied evenly.

"Pray, tell me what do lambs know about stress?" I asked sarcastically.

"Lambs know as much about mutilation as rats do in drug research laboratories."

"What did anyone do to you to make you so angry?" I teased.

"I'm thinking about gruesome animal experiments in which animals are mutilated," he replied.

"That's ludicrous. Didn't we cover it enough?" I protested. "You have a one-track mind. Once you're obsessed with something, no one can pull you out of it."

"I'm trying to make some sense of the experiments in which researchers burn, poison or mutilate parts of animals," he continued, seemingly unaffected by my upbraiding.

"That's a very unfair characterization, and..."

"All in the name of science," he bluntly cut me off.

"How else do you conduct research?" I screamed at him in indignation.

Choua stiffened at my outburst, looked puzzled for a moment, then smiled and looked away. It took several moments for my angst to subside. Then I suddenly recalled a boyhood image. I remembered the slaughter of a lamb on *Bhurri Eid*—the Muslim sacrifice festival after the month of Ramadan. Then followed many similar images of animal sacrifices, which I witnessed every year on *Eid* days. After the animal's throat was slit with the lightning-quick sleight of a butcher's hand, the animals fell to the ground, gasping for breath, their bodies convulsing, their nostrils fuming, their mouths frothing. Frequently they urinated and defecated. Their eyes would open wide before they glazed over. Sometimes I could see their hearts fluttering as the butcher pulled them out of their chests and threw them on a pile of other eviscerated organs. I don't remember if I ever thought about the stress response then. How could I? At that time, I didn't even know Selye existed.

"How do animals respond to the demand for change when they are slaughtered?" Choua asked, surprising me out of my reflection.

"How did you know I was thinking about lamb sacrifices on *Bhurri Eid* day?" I asked, perplexed.

"I didn't," he replied, surprised. "Tell me about the physiology of an animal having his throat slit open."

"What's there to tell? You've seen animals being slaughtered, haven't you?"

"Yes, I have. So if all you want to do is study and document the physiology of the dying process, why don't you study that in the slaughterhouses?"

"You're not serious, are you?" I was flabbergasted.

"Yes, I am. Why don't you study the dynamics of the physical mutilation of living beings by observing what happens in nature —such as when lions tear into impalas for a meal?"

"You can't set up scientific experiments in the wilderness."

"Why not?" he persisted.

"Serious research must be conducted in properly equipped laboratories, with a controlled environment."

"What was the purpose of the experiments in which cats were mutilated?"

"What experiments?"

"Those in which cats' brains were destroyed and the decerebrate cats were lifted several feet from the ground, then dropped."

"To observe how their bodies landed on the ground, on their paws or heads," I explained.

"Huh!" his eyes narrowed.

"You make those scientific experiments sound gory. What else could a physiologist do? Practice such experiments on humans? Those experiments are essential for learning the anatomy and physiology of the brain."

"Why do you have to mutilate cats to learn things about the human brain? Couldn't you do the same by watching how injured cats fall in real life?"

"That's absurd," I nearly screamed. "Where would any researcher go to find such animals?"

"How do you use such animal experiment data in treating people?"

"That's a real problem," I confessed.

"Why?"

"Because there are species differences. You can't blindly apply data from animals to people. Besides..."

"I was hoping you would say that," he interrupted me and grinned broadly.

"What's the point of all this?" I asked, flustered.

"Tell me, why do you perform autopsies on people who've suffered strokes?"

"That's obvious. At an autopsy examination, we try to correlate the location and type of brain injury to the type of functional problem the person had during life."

"So if you can gain the knowledge of human anatomy

and physiology in the autopsy room, why mutilate cats?"

"That's not practical at all," I posited. "You'll have to wait for years before you find the dead body of a stroke victim that is satisfactory for study."

"The feline researchers realized that cats have sharp instincts that can prevent head injury even when some parts of their brains have been destroyed," he sidestepped my comment. "Then there were other experiments in which the smell apparatus of rats were ablated. What do you call that, some sort of bulbectomy?"

"Yes," I replied. "It's called olfactory bulbectomy."

"Since the sense of smell is essential to the rats' survival, olfactory bulbectomy caused severe behavioral changes in the rats. Wasn't that predictable?"

"Yes. No!" I flustered. "But Choua, you're missing something important. In science, you cannot assume anything unless you actually observe it. Science is not mere speculation."

"What happened to the bulbectomized rats?" he asked, again ignoring my objections.

"The bulbectomized rats were stressed out. They became very hyperactive, irritable..."

"Just as children do when thrown into sugar-insulin-adrenaline roller coasters," he interrupted me.

"No, that's different," I replied, annoyed by his flight of ideas. "The rats showed elevated blood levels of steroids."

"Different?" Choua scowled, then stared at me in silence.

"Hyperactivity in children is a different problem altogether," I broke the silence after some moments.

"Tell me about those dog experiments in which their stomachs were amputated to see how stomachless dogs coped with the state of 'stomachlessness.'"

"That was it. The experiments were done to study the role of the stomach in digestion."

"And about dogs whose bowels were bypassed to see how they dealt with the stresses of indigestion and malabsorption?"

"What's the point of all this?" I asked, increasingly irritated by the tone of his questions.

"I am just asking simple questions about how you define what stress is and how you study its effects," he replied calmly. "Very few of those animal experiments are necessary," Choua resumed.

"I know it's rough on animals, but how else do you conduct stress research and develop drugs for stress and anxiety?"

"Rough on animals!" he exploded. "You don't understand, do you?"

"Calm down, Choua," I admonished him. "If drug researchers don't conduct research on animals, should they use a human subject? Would you be happier with that?" I held my ground.

"You can test the safety of new drugs on animals, but for that you don't have to electrocute or decapitate them. I'm not opposed to animal research as long as it can be done humanely."

"Animal rights advocates have been saying that for decades, but they don't understand the complexities of animal research."

"Tell me, what is it that you learn from electrocuting rats? What do you learn by decapitating cats?" he frowned.

"Be reasonable, Choua. How else do you observe the effects of severe stress in animals without putting them through such stress?"

"Observation, Mr. Pathologist! Observation!" he jeered.

"How do you observe the effects of stress on animals without doing experiments?" I asked, irritated.

"You could start here in the Serengeti," he dropped his

voice.

"Practice drug research in the Serengeti with wild animals?" I asked, incredulous.

"There is enough suffering among wild animals for observation, if that's what you want to observe."

"That's a new one for me," I said sarcastically.

"Things you see here in the Serengeti are real. The struggles you observe here are true to life. Stresses that animals sustain here in the dust are authentic. If you really want to study stress in animals, simply observe them. Simple observation is the purest of all sciences."

"That's fantasy! In medicine, we need..."

"The torture you put animals through in laboratory cages is not true to life," he interrupted me bluntly. "There is no purer science than the science of observation. Molesting cats in laboratories is not true science. Drowning rats in cages is not true science. Do we really need to electrocute rats and decapitate cats to study stress?" Choua heaved visibly as he finished, then looked away.

Suddenly the pride of lions reappeared from behind a thicket of trees. Lions don't make noise when they move around, I recalled reading somewhere. It was certainly true of that pride. They walked past us, not once acknowledging our presence.

"Amazing!" Choua murmured to himself. "How can these lions be so limbic yet so focused? There's a lesson in that about what being limbic means."

"I suppose they've learned to obliterate white tourist safari vans from their collective consciousness," I responded. "Our vans seem to cause no stress in them. But, then, why would anything else?"

"That may not be all there is to it."

"What do you mean?"

"Lions don't like to be stared at, just like people. Human eyes fixed on them make them uneasy. In particular, male lions don't like to be stared at. They take it as a challenge, just like most bosses do in American companies."

"So do you think they avoid eye contact with us because it stresses them?"

"When stared at with unblinking eyes, a lion's eyes glaze over within moments. He seems to look through you rather than at you, so wrote Chris McBride in *The White Lions of Timbavati,*" he explained.

"Fascinating. Something that simple unnerves the king of beasts and elicits a stress response. Amazing, isn't it?"

"Yeah, the stress response again." He winked mischievously.

In physiology class, I was taught much about animal experiments. No one ever raised any questions about the ethics of animal experimentation, torture and mutilation. Animals were, of course, simply dismissed as *animals,* to be used and sacrificed. There were never any awkward questions about animal sensibilities. No one recognized their suffering.

Is stress really as simple as Selye made it? The fight-or-flight response? I wondered. For many of my patients, stress was not a response. They *lived* stress. My thoughts wandered and settled on the case histories of my patients who lived difficult lives and suffered for months in spite of my best efforts.

DOES ANYONE EVER TRULY ADAPT
TO SUFFERING?

"No one adapts to electric shocks," Choua resumed.
"Does anyone really ever adapt to losing a part of his brain?"
"Didn't we cover that? Why..."I asked.
"Does anyone adapt to becoming decerebrate, as you
were taught in physiology class?" he cut me off. "Do rats really
adapt to ice-cold water? To hunger-starvation cycles? To
periods of darkness ended abruptly by flashing bright lights? To
poking and to repeated electrocution? Are those experiments
really valid?"

Choua's volley of questions jarred me. Doubt surged
through my mind. How would any rat adapt to an olfactory
bulbectomy —to losing his sense of smell? How does a gazelle
adapt to the sight of hunting lions?

"A lioness delivers her litter and usually cares for her
cubs all by herself," he resumed. "When she's forced to leave
the vulnerable cubs in her den to hunt, predators come looking
for the cubs and kill them—more to spite the mother, it seems,
than to feast on the tiny morsels of meat that the furry cubs
offer. How does a lioness adapt to finding bits and pieces of her
cubs left behind by predators?"
"I don't know. And I don't know if I like your
descriptions either."
"A cheetah mother ferociously attacks anyone who
approaches her cubs, no matter how peaceful their intentions,"

he continued. "Cheetahs are not known to kill their cubs. Yet when one of her cubs dies, a cheetah mom is known to eat the dead body to prevent the decomposed body from attracting more predators and threatening her remaining litter. How does a cheetah mother adapt to that?"

"Beats me," I replied with resignation.

"Nomad lions invade established territories of lion prides for hunting and for sexual favors from lionesses in heat. Whenever they can, they kill the patriarch lions to take over the pride. On such occasions, they are known to kill and devour small cubs right in the presence of their mothers."

"That's awful!"

"Awful, yes. Tell me, how does a lioness adapt to watching her cubs being eaten alive right before her eyes? Do you know what the naturalist, George Schaller, wrote about that?"

"What?"

"Schaller observed such events. On one such occasion, the lionesses who saw their cubs eaten alive by nomads remained restless, irritable and sullen while the new patriarch lions forced themselves on them. Some semblance of order returned to the pride only after two years, when the bereaved lionesses had new litters. But does a semblance of order really indicate that the lionesses had adapted to the memory of their cubs being eaten by their new lovers? Of course, George Schaller is too astute an observer of nature to imply that the semblance of order means the memory of their cubs' death is obliterated. How can any human fully understand animal suffering of that magnitude?"

"Sometimes women also lose their children equally violently," I replied.

"Does a woman ever adapt to watching her husband gamble his paycheck away while her children starve?" he continued. "Does anyone ever adapt to random mugging? To a terrorist's senseless murder?"

"What's the point of all of this?" I asked, irritated.

"Does a young girl ever adapt to paternal molesting?" he went on, without acknowledging my comment. "Does a woman ever adapt to rape? Does a child ever adapt to seeing his parents shot dead by random acts of violence? Susan Smith drowned her two little boys. Will she ever adapt to that evil memory? Can she ever adapt to the vision of her car rolling into a lake with two little boys strapped to their car seats? To the car slowly sinking in the water? How does Selye's adaptation apply to those situations?"

"What's eating you today?" I asked, exasperated.

"Of course, if Susan Smith also had fifteen million dollars, she would have hired a dream team of defense lawyers, and been acquitted. Don't you think she had a perfectly legal defense for temporary insanity? Who can claim insanity more than Susan Smith? And for what better reason?"

I listened to Choua's volley of questions in silence. I'd never thought about such things until that day in the Serengeti Plain. What is the true nature of stress? I wondered. My eyes followed the five sleek lionesses glistening in the bright Masai Mara sun, and Choua's question returned. What do lions know about stress? Yes, what do they know? I looked at Choua. His face seemed frozen.

> ## THE SUFFERING OF THE PAST
> ## CAN'T BE SOLVED.
> ## IT CAN'T BE RESOLVED.
> ## IT CAN ONLY BE DISSOLVED.

Suffering ennobles. I have been told that many times. But does it?

How much can one know about life if he lives without suffering? Can anyone truly know happiness except through sadness?

"I don't understand what happiness is, Choua once said. "I think I know what gratitude is," he went on. "How does one know gratitude except through suffering?

A core belief of many psychologists and psychiatrists is that the past is always alive in the present. They hold that the suffering of the present can be mitigated only through analyzing the past. Is that really true? Does recycling past suffering truly keep it from casting its long dark shadow on the present, or on the future?

A young English woman came to see me for chronic fatigue, ulcerative colitis, and difficulties of memory and concentration. Weeks passed, but she saw no relief with my management plan. One day she spoke to Talat about her childhood sadness and wondered if that was holding her recovery back. Talat listened to her patiently, then replied, "You cannot get better by continually returning to your past. Past suffering can't be solved; it can't be resolved; it can only be dissolved." (Talat is not a therapist and she recognizes that. She doesn't give therapy. However, she has a special gift of listening, and many chronically ill patients who do not obtain relief within several weeks at our Institute tend to gravitate to her for counsel.)

Years earlier, when I began my work with autoregulation, I had experimented with some breathing methods to control my own migraine headaches. After suffering with migraines for about thirty years and injecting myself with Demerol (a narcotic drug with a high addictive risk), I finally learned to dissolve my headaches with limbic breathing. I became intoxicated with the possibilities offered by autoregulation. Then one day a young woman who suffered from severe PMS came to see me. After listening to her describe her headaches, I enthusiastically told her I would teach her how to dissolve her PMS headaches, as I had learned to dissolve my own headaches. She listened to me with blank eyes and sank deeper into the chair. I later learned that she refused the blood tests I had recommended to diagnose food sensitivities and left the Institute distraught. I never saw her again. That experience taught me when to talk about dissolving suffering with breathing and when to keep my mouth shut. I also wondered how she might have misconstrued my comment about dissolving headaches. Did she think I meant some exotic Eastern ritual whereby some parts of the brain are physically dissolved?

Conversely, the young English woman seemed to have understood Talat quite well when she spoke about the futility of solving past problems. She seemed to understand what was meant by simply dissolving present suffering. She eventually recovered from chronic fatigue, and her ulcerative colitis healed to a degree that surprised her gastroenterologist during a colonoscopy performed some weeks later.

FEAR IS THE PRIMARY GOVERNING INFLUENCE IN LIFE

Four days earlier, we had stayed at the Ark, a mountain lodge built at the edge of a water hole, high on the Aberdares Mountain Range, near Nyeri, the self-styled capital of Kikuyuland. (Nyeri was the last home of Robert Baden-Powell, founder of the world-wide scouting movement.) The Ark is built like a large boat, with three observation decks where guests can lounge and observe wild game at their leisure. Staff at the lodge spray salt on a mud patch by the water every day to attract animals who oblige, rather regularly, all day and all night long. There we saw elephants, buffalos, antelopes, topis and gazelles wander in and out for water—clearly following some unwritten but orderly schedule in respecting the need for the privacy of other species.

Bushbucks, impalas, topis and tommies were an embodiment of fear at the water hole, forever making false starts for the water's edge, only to retreat for more scrutinizing looks. Past experience must have warned them of the dangers of big cats crouched behind the bush and ready to spring. It's different with us. We sipped our afternoon tea and nibbled at sandwiches some time earlier, absorbed in our individual reading materials. No false starts or nervous retreats for us.

"Life at an African water hole is a life of the unexpected, a chemistry of fear," Choua spoke. "One careless drink can provoke a murderous attack. One unguarded moment of lingering can mean death. The animals obviously know that. They must have watched too many near-death situations —or have been the target of some themselves."

I nodded. As a boy, I loved to watch sparrows approach bread crumbs on the ground. They, too, moved with countless false starts and nervous retreats, forever cocking their heads and twisting their necks, always on the lookout for trouble. If I stood still like a statue, the sparrows became bold and often approached within my reach. Suddenly I realized that's what lions and leopards do when they crouch low in the grass beside the water hole. They patiently wait for the prey to become acclimated and comfortable. Then they pounce.

"Life is difficult because the essential chemistry of life is that of fear," Choua continued. "Fear is the governing influence of life. The adrenal glands are ever so ready to disgorge their adrenergic load. Adrenaline blasts don't occur only when there is clear and present danger. The adrenals are trigger-happy. That's the chemical truth of life. The glands fire—and, more frequently, misfire—not only in response to a present threat, but just as readily to recycled past threats, and precycled feared, future threats. The sparrows suffer from their adrenals just as my patients with debilitating chronic disorders do."

"That's true," I agreed. "The lab staff at the hospital often talk about their enlarged adrenal glands. What they mean by that, of course, is the effect of chronic stress."

"The basic chemistry of fear is of oxidative fireworks, isn't it?" he asked.

"Yeah."

"Oxidation is the loss of electrons —those tiniest packets of energy in atoms and molecules. It's a process of decay and death."

"Yeah. Spontaneity of oxidation in nature is the root cause of aging and all diseases. At least that's what I think," I replied.

"High-energy molecules spontaneously decay and are turned into low-energy molecules," he continued. "That is the essential chemistry of aging in humans and other living beings."

"I can't disagree with that, can I? I mean, I wrote that stuff in *Rats.*"

"I know," he grinned, then continued. "Adrenaline —the well-known stress hormone —is a powerful aging-oxidant molecule. Along with its cousin catecholamine molecules, it oxidizes, breaks down, and mutilates life-sustaining enzymes and neurotransmitters. These adrenergic molecules first fan, then extinguish, the flames of life. How do they do both?"

"How?" I asked, without really meaning to.

"Initially, adrenaline and related adrenergic molecules energize nerve-muscle junctions to prepare them for coping with the increased demands of various stressors," he replied. "They fire up neurotransmitter molecules as well as many other messenger molecules in the body. Adrenergic overdrive initially is counterbalanced by another family of molecules called cholinergic transmitters."

"Are you saying stress is caused by too much adrenaline?"

"The problem begins when there is too much adrenergic activity—that is, there is adrenergic molecular hypervigilance. When not held in abeyance, it literally creates a state of molecular burnout. Let's consider an analogy of how a car engine works. A combustible mixture of gasoline and air is pumped into the combustion chamber of the engine, where it is ignited to release energy for the car's motion. The entry of the gasoline mixture, however, is regulated by a carburetor. We all know what happens when a car runs out of gas. It cannot move. We rarely consider what would happen if there was no carburetor to regulate the flow of gasoline mixture in an orderly fashion. An uncontrolled entry of gasoline would create a blast, and the car might blow up. Do you agree?"

"Yes."

"Under normal conditions, adrenergic sparks are quickly put out by life-span enzymes. In conditions of adrenergic overdrive, unregulated adrenergic sparks quickly turn into oxidative blasts that sear blood cells, cook plasma proteins, short-circuit nerve-muscle conduction sites, and damage life-span enzymes. Adrenergic molecules fly everywhere, lighting up a million oxidative flames in the blood, liver, heart and brain. The blood proteins get cooked. The blood cells are deformed, crumpled, and thrown into clumps that choke the tiny capillaries, bringing the flow of blood to a halt. The heart flutters under adrenaline blasts. The liver struggles. The brain seethes. Don't you see that every day in your patients?"

"Yes, I do," I replied.

"In men and women who live in sugar-insulin-adrenaline roller coasters? In people with viral activation and yeast overgrowth syndromes? In patients with battered bowel ecosystems?"

"Yes."

"The adrenergic molecular hypervigilance drives sparrows as mercilessly as it drives people in the throes of cancer, multiple sclerosis, lupus and disabling Lyme disease. And sparrows exhaust their adrenal glands just as chronically ill patients do. That's the essential chemistry of fear. That's the essential chemistry of life." Choua stopped and rubbed his face.

"Go on," I prodded.

"Your friends in psychiatry don't seem to recognize that clever thinking cannot turn off adrenergic hypervigilance —unrelenting thinking relentlessly stokes adrenergic fires."

"I know."

"Talat is right. Adrenergic crises cannot be solved, nor can they be resolved. They can only be dissolved."

I KNOW WHAT DID IT: A CALL FROM MY DOCTOR

Tom, a successful senior engineer, looked strong and spoke confidently when I first saw him. His wife consulted me for disabling chronic fatigue associated with sky-high levels of antibodies against the Epstein-Barr virus. She had received up to 200 grams of vitamin C intravenously twice weekly from another physician in the hope of eradicating the Epstein-Barr virus from her body. Even though Tom was very concerned about the safety of that therapy, he fully supported his wife. I cautioned them against such massive doses of intravenously administered vitamin C, but to no avail.

A few months later Tom consulted me for his own health problems. He looked distraught and depressed. His lips trembled slightly as he described the events that had taken place during the preceding two weeks. He suffered acute anxiety, developed tightness in his chest, lost his appetite, couldn't sleep, and began to "lose his ability to think" while making presentations at work. "I'm deathly afraid," he blurted out, painfully aware of his helpless condition.

Next, Tom told me how his mother came down with lupus, how she deteriorated progressively until she was finally crippled by the disease. He described how painful his mother's slow death had been for him. His wife was then a strong woman, who supported him all through his mother's illness. Some time later, his wife came down with progressive and disabling chronic fatigue. Her condition deteriorated in spite of all therapies. Tom helped his wife, even as she regressed from a vigorous young woman to a disabled person. He began to feel run down himself and developed minor joint symptoms. His doctor ordered some tests. Then it all began to happen. "I know what did it. It was that call from my doctor. He said my test for lupus came back positive." Tom ended the description of his present illness sadly.

I knew lupus, like all other autoimmune disorders, tends to run in families. I needed to find out what stresses might be injuring his immune defenses. So I tried to explore the possibility of adverse food effects, mold and pollen allergies, chronic viral activation syndromes, excessive use of coffee, an overactive thyroid gland, and some other issues that I thought might be contributing to his problems. He seemed to evade my inquiry, then blurted out:

"Doc, you write about listening to your patients. Why don't you listen to me?"
"You're right. I should practice what I write, shouldn't I?" I tried in vain to humor him.
"I know where the problem started."
"Where?" I asked.
"It started when my doctor called to tell me I had a positive test for lupus. That started it all," Tom spoke emphatically. "That brought back memories of my mom's illness.

She died in seven years—and those were seven years of hell."

How does a well-educated, well-heeled, successful engineer get thrown off the loop by a telephone call like that? How can he destabilize like that? I wondered. The thinking mind loves to recycle past misery. And when that isn't enough, it thrives on precycling feared, future misery endlessly and without interruptions. Intellectually, it is all so easy to understand. In my meditation and autoregulation training sessions, I often hear myself ask out loud, "Do I know if I will get home safely today? How do I know that some truck won't veer me off the road and kill me? How do I know an infected drop of blood will not abruptly end all my plans for an orderly life?" It all seems so clear. Yet none of this ever seems to help anyone in the throes of chronic suffering. Adrenergic hypervigilance continues to punish them relentlessly.

How do tommies do it in African savannah? How can they always be on the lookout for the big cats and not break down completely, as Tom did? They face fatal threats every moment of their life. How can they look so vivacious, edgy, nervous, suspicious and afraid, all at the same time? Why don't they get sick thinking of their miserable lives? Why doesn't the fear of death paralyze tommies in the Serengeti plains the way it did Tom, my patient, in New York? I began to see why Choua asked me about stress in Masai Mara Game Reserve.

PSYCHOSOMATIC AND SOMATOPSYCHIC MODELS OF DISEASE

Many teachers of stress management hold that 70%-80% of all diseases are psychosomatic in origin. They coined the term psychosomatic to indicate that problems of the mind (psyche) in these disorders lead to problems of the body (soma). To differentiate such diseases from those that are believed to be primarily caused by physical factors, the term somatopsychic is used.

It is a common practice for physicians to order a battery of tests to make a diagnosis. When the blood tests, x-rays, and scans come back negative, but the patient continues to suffer, they invoke the psychosomatic theory and refer the patient to their colleagues in psychiatry or psychology. The implication, of course, is that what a physician cannot diagnose really doesn't exist, and that psychiatrists and psychologists are good at managing imagined health disorders. I never questioned this practice during the 25 years I was engaged in mainstream medicine. Indeed, the psychosomatic model was a godsend to me when I worked as a surgeon. Patients who continued to complain after I had performed the indicated operation were a nuisance. Referring them to psychiatrists and psychologists was a convenient thing to do.

There is a profound irony here. Standard blood tests and scans are designed to detect diseases that have advanced to a state where one or more body organs have been badly damaged. Only a rare physician is knowledgeable about the direct microscopic methods of detecting the early stages of disease —the molecular phases of "dis-ease" states —caused by oxidative injury to which I alluded in the preceding paragraphs. Again, I describe these methods at length in *RDA: Rats, Drugs and Assumptions*. Hardly a week goes by that I do not hear some colleagues invoke the doctrine of psychosomatic medicine to dismiss a patient who doesn't fit into this thinking mold. Negative blood tests and scans are usually managed by psychiatric referrals. The old all-in-the-head dogma continues to thrive.

The internist draws the line between his diseases and those of the psychiatrist sharply and decisively. But how does he know that his inability to diagnose a problem is not an indication of his own inadequacy or of his own incompetence? How does he know if what he considers nonexistent really doesn't exist? How many textbook medical disorders are there that were once considered psychosomatic and are now considered organic?

And how does an internist know that the psychiatrist will succeed in making a diagnosis where he has failed? I have seen a very large number of patients enjoy vigorous health until they came down with disabling bowel and breathing problems or debilitating chronic fatigue. When multiple diagnostic tests and drug therapies failed, some of my most troubled patients were glibly told to see a psychiatrist. When one of my patients was told by the fifth gastroenterologist she consulted to see a psychiatrist, she was outraged. She said:

It was the most demeaning thing I had to endure in my life. What do they think psychiatrists know about severely bloated bowels anyway? About adhesions between the loops of the bowel? Do they understand the normal bowel flora and how yeast overgrows? Do they understand anything about the problems of digestion and absorption? Anything about parasites in the gut? Why didn't my bowel hurt me all those years I was well? Where were my unresolved childhood conflicts then? The truth is, I had a wonderful childhood. My dad loved me dearly and so did my mom. Tell me, what great insight into the turbulence in my bowel is any psychiatrist going to give me?

I think we need a new generation of psychologists who have the courage to say to their patients, "I'm sorry, but it's all in your bodies." The New Age gurus talk about mind-body-spirit connections. But before we can think of connections, we have to know what it is that we're trying to connect. How does one know where the body ends and the mind begins? How does one draw lines between the mind and spirit? And then, how does the spirit boomerang to find its seat in the body, if indeed that is what it does? Stress researchers exult about what they discover in their animal experiments. They thrive on their numbers. But how does that relate to my patients who continue to suffer after they are told their problems are in their heads?

WHAT COMES BETWEEN FIGHTING
AND FLEEING?

Without any apparent reason, all five lionesses assumed a low crouching position. I looked around but saw nothing. Minutes passed and the lionesses resumed their leisurely walk. My mind wandered to the scenes at Ark lodge. Late in the evening, a leopard appeared at the edge of the clearing around the water hole and lay there for several hours. Later he moved closer to the water hole—and to us. Then we saw a bushbuck fawn amble along within fifty feet of the cat. It eyed the leopard every now and then but continued to graze. Once, when the leopard moved a little, apparently to stretch, all of us froze in anticipation of the leopard's leap at the fawn within yards of us. But nothing happened. The leopard lay down again, and the fawn continued to graze.

"Cannon and Selye maintained stress was a fight-or-flight response," Choua resumed speaking. "But what comes between the two?"

"What do you mean?" I asked back.

"What do animals do when there is no fighting or fleeing to do?"

"I guess they rest and graze."

"How does the prey know when the predator is hungry and when he is not? How do warthogs know the safe distance between themselves and lions?"

"I don't know. They probably have some system of limbic

intelligence. They just know about those things."

"In what state are the wild animals when they neither flee for their lives nor stick around to dare their predators? What do stress experts think happens to living beings at other times? Do the stress gurus think there is nothing else there?"

"Whatever there is between the fight-or-flight periods, it must be restorative."

"Many of your patients are schoolteachers. They always tell you how stressful it is to teach these days. What are they running from? What are they fighting?"

"I don't think they are running from anything."

"Hospital laboratories are pressure cookers. What states are the laboratory technicians in? There is no room for error in their work, and they know that."

"Yes, I agree. Laboratory work is very stressful. They work with all kinds of chemicals."

"How does a pathologist go through his day? Diagnosing cancer is a risky business. What if the pathologist makes a mistake? Who pays for it?"

"The patient, of course. But eventually the pathologist as well. No pathologist can afford to make a mistake. He'll get sued. No one considers it justifiable for a pathologist to make one mistake in a year and be responsible for a woman's loss of her breast for the wrong reason."

"Or one mistake in five years?" he added. "What is a pathologist fighting when he diagnoses cancer all day long? If not fighting, what is he fleeing from?"

"Fear of jeopardizing his professional reputation. Fear of lawsuits. Fear of being fired."

"What does a homemaker do when the breadwinner is at work and the children are at school?"

"Household chores," I replied.

"What does she do when all chores are done?"

"Go shopping."

"And when that is done?"

"Listen to the radio. Watch TV. Do other things. I don't know."

"Boredom?" Choua's forehead wrinkled.

"Yeah, that too."

"When she is bored, what does she flee from? Or fight?"

"Fights boredom, of course."

"How?"

"Eats," I offered an option in jest.

"Eats?" Choua pouted, then broke out in a laugh and continued, "Someone thought that two more Fs should be added to the fight-or-flight thing—an F for feeding and another for making babies." Choua winked.

"Some people are quite good at those things," I prodded.

"I know, but for how long?"

"Okay, I give up. You enlighten me," I mocked.

"What happens when a person simply *is?* When he is not fighting, fleeing, feeding or making babies? What state is he in? Do gurus of the stress industry ever reflect on such questions?"

"I don't know, but are these questions leading us anywhere?" I asked, exasperated.

"Nowhere," he laughed out loud and looked toward the lionesses.

AREN'T YOU AFRAID THEY'LL PADLOCK YOUR OFFICE?

Last year Raymond Paul Russomano, M.D., of East Hanover, New Jersey, attended my postgraduate workshop for

holistic physicians conducted at the Institute of Preventive
Medicine in Denville, New Jersey. He joined me for lunch.
Some minutes later, he spoke.

"You have a very nice facility."
"Yes, it is nice," I thanked him.
"You have a good staff," he continued.
"Yes, we are blessed with wonderful nurses and
administrative staff."
"You have good laboratory equipment."
"That too."

Ray fell silent for a few moments. I could tell he had
something else on his mind. I waited.

"Aren't you afraid they'll padlock your office?" he asked
after some moments.
"Who?"
"The state board of medical examiners."
"Why would they do that?" I asked, feigning puzzlement.
"They don't endorse holistic medicine."
"Oh, that," I smiled and went back to eating.

A few minutes passed. Then Ray spoke again, "Aren't
you afraid they'll padlock your office?"
"Why would they do that?" I asked back. "All I do is try
to find nondrug solutions for patients who cannot tolerate
drugs."
"That's not the point," he frowned.
"Then what is the point?" I asked.
"Your practice violates the norms of medical practice in
the area. It's not—as they say in organized-crime movies—good
for business."

"I must confess I'm guilty of that offense."

Ray fell quiet for some moments. The conversation at the table shifted to other subjects. Several minutes later, Ray brought up the subject of the state licensing board padlocking my office again. I smiled and repeated my answer. A few minutes later, Ray returned to the same subject.

"Ray, the folks at the licensing board are not here, you are," I replied as gently as I could. "Right now the board is not putting my lunch in jeopardy, but you will if you persist with your warnings." We both laughed and moved to another subject.

WALL STREET HAS DISCOVERED THERE IS MONEY IN MEDICINE

One day, in the hospital dining room, a surgeon-friend complained bitterly that he couldn't practice medicine the way he was trained. "There are hordes of people at every step I take. There are these committee rulings thrown at me wherever I go. Someone is always telling me what to do. Twenty years ago, we had one hospital administrator, one assistant administrator and one administrative intern. Now there are fourteen vice-presidents. Then we had one director of nursing. Now we have a director of nursing at each nursing station. There are federal rules and state rules. There are lawyers everywhere. There is Medicare and Medicaid. FDA is busy rewriting its rules and so is OSHA. Patients want treatment. The insurance companies don't want to pay. There are HMOs and PPOs. Now Wall Street has found out there is money in medicine. Every day there is a new threat of one cap or the other on my fee schedule. I run like a chicken without a head. I feel run down. Where is it all going to end?" he moaned.

I listened sympathetically. Some other physicians walked in, and the range of complaints widened to include problems with nurses and patients. I finished my lunch and left the dining room.

"Is this what Hans Selye had in mind when he talked about his fight-or-flight response?" Choua asked.

"I don't know. They don't seem to be running, and they aren't fighting," I replied.

"So what do you call that?"

"Anger."

"And?"

"Frustration."

"And?"

"Fatigue! You heard him. He says he feels run down."

"And?"

"And stress."

"So you think stress can exist when there is no fighting or flighting to be done, do you?"

"Yes! Yes!" I answered emphatically.

"Right! Right!" Choua became animated.

"What excites you in all this?" I asked, surprised.

Choua looked at me, then grinned broadly.

I wondered what the fight-or-flight response has to do with my colleagues' anger over the changing patterns and practice of medicine. What I see above all is profound resentment. My colleagues are bitter and disillusioned. Medicine can be a gratifying and energizing profession. I know that. It can also be unnerving and draining. I have seen both. What did Choua have on his mind? I wondered.

THE HUNTER BECOMES THE HUNTED

As we approached the Mara River, our path came closer to that of the lionesses, who were moving to the left of us. We saw two bridges, one several feet below the other. Michael headed for the larger, higher bridge while the lionesses took the lower one. The lionesses were barely 10 feet from us at this point. I wondered whether the lionesses knew of their vulnerability. We were secure in the safety of our van. The lionesses were an easy target out in the open. A child with a gun could shoot them dead. How could anyone miss at such a distance? I recalled a description of a Masai lion hunt written by Anthony Cullen, a game warden in Samburu, Kenya, in *Downey's Africa:*

Not all encounters, of course, are between lions and other animals. Sometimes there is a two-legged foe...I was invited to witness at close quarters the spearing of a lion by Masai...My own personal feeling is that this is the most disgusting and brutal cruelty that I have ever seen...A good maned lion was singled out, then surrounded by about 25

*Masai, apart from the vehicles in which we
and the film-party were driven to the scene.
The wretched animal was so terrified and
bewildered by the number of its enemies that
he seemed unable to attempt to save himself.
It showed no fight whatever, and was simply
hacked to death.*

So here was the sad truth behind the myth of young
Masai warriors who claim manhood by hunting a lion!

*The time will come when men will look on
the murder of animals as they now look on
the murder of men.*

Leonardo da Vinci

Da Vinci was right. We now *do* seem to look on the
murder of animals as we look on the murder of men—neither
seems to perturb us much. But, was that what da Vinci really
foresaw?

TROPHY HUNTING

My thoughts drifted to trophy hunting that, incredible as
it seems, still continues on the Serengeti plains today. Every

year lions become trophies of those who travel long distances to hunt in East Africa.

What sort of sport is lion hunting? Natives who serve as guides transport the hunters-sportsmen in enclosed safari vans to within feet of lions snoozing in the sun or shade. Lions see the hunters coming and assume they are tourists. But the hunters pull their guns out and shoot the lions point-blank, as the placid eyes of the hunted turn into horror and glaze over. A lion dies. A hunter carries his trophy home. (The scene is reminiscent of a cartoon I had seen many years earlier. The cartoon showed a drunken European shooting at a lion while an African guide steadies his gun. The caption below the picture said something about a 'great white hunter'.)

Why do the natives encourage such trophy "hunting" by foreigners? They do so because hunters pay the poverty-stricken natives several thousand dollars for each lion killed.

So, this is the ugly reality of great European hunters bagging lions in East Africa!

Are any living beings truly free from predators? I wondered. How does one describe the anguish—and stress—of a lion who faces merciless death at the hands of hackers? What do lions know about stress? Choua's question returned to me. I turned to face him, but he seemed lost in the river water as it pummeled over rocky outcrops in the shallow riverbed. I decided not to distract him.

Looking backward I noticed the lionesses crouched in single file on the narrow bridge. I didn't think they needed to do that to avoid being seen by the zebras. The bridge level was low and the riverbank far too high for the zebras to spot the lionesses. I looked to our right on the other side of the riverbank and saw a large troop of baboons in trees. The baboons sat still, their eyes transfixed on the lions, just as the gazelles had done. Midway on the bridge, Michael stopped. I looked back and saw the patriarch standing on a high spot several hundred feet behind us. His head was raised, and his eyes were fixed in the direction of the zebras. Still favoring his left leg, he moved, turned and limped to the shade of an acacia tree. I watched the patriarch lion for several minutes and wondered if his leg injury had resulted in an arthritic hip.

THE DYING LION

Lions have fascinated man for eons. And killing lions has been a favorite royal sport since ancient times.

Ashurbanipal was a powerful Assyrian king who lived in Nineveh (present-day Iraq) during the sixth century B.C. In Assyrian ruins first unearthed by Sir Austen Henry Layard, a stunning wall sculpture of a hunting scene (c. 645-640 B.C.) was found. I saw the sculpture in an Assyrian exhibition at the Metropolitan Museum of Art. The sculpture depicts a king who fells a full-maned lion with an arrow shot from his hunting chariot. The following caption, written by J.E. Curtis, appears below the sculpture:

The lion itself is squatting on its haunches, facing right. It has been mortally wounded by an arrow that has penetrated deep into its chest...Blood is gushing out of the mouth of the beast, and it is straining every muscle and sinew in a last futile attempt to sit upright. The veins on the head are standing out. Its eyes are beginning to glaze over, and it is desperately gripping the ground with its claws.

A full-grown lion hunted down with an arrow shot by a mighty king! How did the king do that? I wondered.

Several feet from this exhibit, another wall hunting scene in three frames revealed the answer. In the first frame, the lion was shown leaping out of a cage and charging at the king. The king held a drawn bow, ready to shoot. A soldier stood beside the king, protecting him with a large shield. In the second frame, the lion appeared in a full and ferocious attack —a midair leap within yards of the king. The king's guard tensed with fear. Finally, in the third frame, the lion reached the king, face-to-face, before the king shot him dead.

How long was the lion incarcerated in the cage? How well had he been cared for in his small prison? Was the beast in good health, or was he sick? How debilitated had he become? The sculptor provides no answer to such questions.

What dangers did the king really face in his hunt? Again, there is no answer—except that a soldier stood ready to throw himself between the king and the lion, if the king's arrow were to miss the lion.

So is that how the mighty kings of Assyria hunted lions to demonstrate their prowess and establish their supernatural abilities to their subjects?

SHOWERS FOR LIONS

Suddenly some baboons screamed, and I turned to see what might have provoked them. The lead lioness now stood on the other bank of the river. She was evidently irked by the noise of the baboons and suddenly rushed toward them. The troop burst into frenzied activity, climbing out of the trees. Some fled as they screamed. Others plodded up a steep stone ledge behind the trees. There they stood defiantly, as if daring the lioness to pursue them farther. Naughty little rascals, I mused.

"What was that about?" Sarah asked Michael.

"Baboons making alarm calls to warn the zebras of approaching lions," he replied.

"What type of altruism is that? Aren't baboons fearful of the big cats?" Sarah asked.

"They have several babies with them. Isn't that dangerous for the babies?" Talat joined in.

"Yes, it is dangerous," Michael agreed, then explained, "Sometimes the baboons do it because they can't stop themselves. I guess being so frightened, they bring trouble upon themselves. Sometimes, when lions stand below the trees they are perched on, the baboons tremble with fear and rain showers of urine on the lions," he laughed.

"That must disgust the lions," Talat interjected.

"Not really!" Michael looked back and grinned. "Lions don't seem to mind—at least not in ways we can tell. In fact, sometimes it seems to egg them on. The lions then attempt to climb the trees to chase the baboons."

"I don't think animals care much about the notions of altruism that fascinate your biology professors," Choua spoke absently.

"Tell me, why do you think the baboons screamed if that wasn't an alarm signal?" I asked, ignoring his impertinent reference to the academics.

"I didn't say that wasn't an alarm signal, did I?" Choua asked back.

"If it wasn't an alarm call for the zebras, who was it for?" I asked, puzzled.

"Who knows?" he shrugged. "All alarm calls are not as altruistic as they might seem. Some of them are shamelessly selfish."

"What do you mean?" I asked, irritated.

"When hungry lions lay siege around their trees and bare their teeth, bigger baboons have been known to throw down smaller baboons from their perches to appease the lions. So much for the romantic ideas of altruism," he snickered.

"That's not difficult to understand," I countered. "If the sacrifice of one baboon saves the rest of the troop, it's a pretty good example of altruism."

"Sometimes the alarm call is intended to draw the attention of the approaching predator to a fleeing member of the group—a sort of a diversionary technique that saves the caller at the expense of someone else—perhaps to eliminate

some male from competition for female favors."
"That does strain credibility, doesn't it?" I taunted Choua.

Their cover blown, the remaining lionesses moved along on the last yards of the bridge nonchalantly. Then they crouched very low and disappeared in the tall grass. I looked back. The patriarch still stood on a high spot in the shade, scanning the savannah where we had seen the zebras earlier. What is he doing there? I wondered. In what possible way can he assist the lionesses in the hunt? What sort of walkie-talkie radio contact does he have with his lionesses moving so far ahead of him? And, if the hunt is successful, how does he plan to fly across the river to claim his lion's share of the kill? I learned that male lions have a different concept of a lion's share than humans. It is even different from that of the lionesses. To a patriarch lion, a lion's share is not the biggest portion—it is everything.

"Lions have an interesting sense of the distribution of labor," Choua chimed. "Lionesses hunt; male lions eat the kill."
"That's not fair," I protested.
"Feline feminism! Yes, that's what is in order here," Choua winked.
"So, is that what you were talking about earlier?" I asked. "Stress in a lion's life, or to be precise, stress in a lioness's life?"
"Stress is not merely an aspect of the fight for survival," he went on.
"What else is it?" I asked.
"Nor is stress merely an aspect of the flight to escape a threatening circumstance."
"Then what is it?"
"Stress is not a response." He didn't answer my question.
"No?"
"And it is not an adaptation!"

"So what is it?" I asked impatiently. "Don't keep saying what it isn't. I want to know what it is."

"Stress *is* life! Stress *is* living. It is an integral a part of the life-injury-repair equation," he replied.

"If it's that simple, why don't the stress researchers see that?"

"You see what you look for. And you look for what you know. Isn't that what Nietzsche wrote?" A gentle smile spread on Choua's face.

"But still,"I protested. "Some of them should have seen that."

"Of course, and some did!" Choua grinned. "Indeed, Selye himself saw that clearly when he wrote about his *syndrome of just being sick*. Then things changed for him. From a natural philosopher, he became a laboratory experimenter. Natural philosophers search for the truth in the "wholeness" of life experiences. Laboratory experimenters, I'm afraid, suffer from reductionism. They can't cope with the wholeness of life, so they limit themselves to looking at thin slices of life by dunking rats in ice-cold water and drowning some of them, or in taking the brains out of cats and thrashing them around. But it doesn't have to be like that," Choua lowered his voice to a whisper and looked away. "All that knowledge could have been gained by diligently observing life in nature."

We were both silent for some time. I searched for the patriarch lion with a limp. He was nowhere to be found.

OLD GREEKS AND YOUNG TURKS

"A lion's life is not a day by the beach, is it?" I asked.

"No, it isn't," Choua replied.

"I have heard lions keep out of the way of ill-tempered elephants. But, really, how much stress is that?"

"Not much," he agreed.

"Hyenas are known to gang up on lone nomad lions, but I don't know if they mean to just annoy them or if they really want to hurt them."

"Probably both."

"Lionesses must have to be under stress when their cubs are little. Even jackals like to kill their cubs. The poor mother lioness has to fend for her cubs as well as go out and hunt to feed them."

"Yes. Lions have fairly tight social structures in their prides. But when it comes to delivering cubs and baby-sitting, they are sometimes callous to each other."

"Mealtime is a notoriously violent time for lions," I continued. "They regularly maul each other at a kill, don't they?"

"Yes, they do. Then they make up and lick each other's wounds," he replied.

"Human bites often cause dangerous infections. Why don't lion bites cause similar problems?"

"They often do. That's how lions get those festering wounds. And they probably do have powerful lysosomal enzymes in their saliva that kill the bugs. Tell me about stress?" Choua brought back the subject.

"Hunger may be a problem for lions on some occasions," I replied. "But there again, it's the lionesses who might feel deprived. The big guys often bully the huntresses and push them away from their kill. Then they take the lion's share. I guess that must stress the females a little."

"Some."

"Hunting must be stressful in other ways as well. I have heard zebras can break a lion's jaw with a well-placed kick."

"But that obviously doesn't happen often. You don't see too many lions with splinted jaws."

"It's so cute to see lionesses play around with their cubs and grab them by their delicate furry necks. I guess that's how the little ones learn to go for the neck of the prey at killing times. I have heard lions sometimes kill giraffes. How do lions reach giraffes' necks?"

"It's hard to imagine, isn't it?" he grinned, then continued. "But that is exactly what they manage to do when that is the only possibility of a dinner for the pack. First the lions bite off the giraffes' legs, then climb on their fallen bodies and go for their jugulars."

"So what do lions know about stress?" This time I asked the question.

Choua smiled mysteriously, but said nothing. I waited for several moments for him to resume, but he didn't. Then I looked back and searched for the limping patriarch. He wasn't around.

"There is no peace for the old Greek, is there?" Choua broke the silence finally. "Some young Turk is always lurking behind."

"Who is the old Greek?" I asked, perplexed. "Do you mean the old limping patriarch?"

"Yes."

"And the young Turk?"

"Two- to three-year-old sub-adult lions who get chewed out by the patriarch lions when they are not strong enough to fight back. Then they are kicked out of the pride."

"Where do the sub-adult males go?"

"The patriarch doesn't care."

"Don't the mama lions protest?"

"Nah. But it wouldn't matter even if they did. When it comes to sex, the patriarchs don't much care for female opinions. Besides, lionesses have been through enough fights of their own. They know better than to interfere with the sexual conflicts of their males."

"Do they return to pester the old man when they grow older and more powerful?"

"Urgencies of the groin can be maddening," he winked.

"And the patriarch lions don't want them messing around with their harems?"

"Right. They don't want their genetic pools diluted."

"But some of the sub-adults must become very strong with time. How do old patriarchs keep them under control?" I asked.

"The young Turks have brute power, but the old Greeks have craft and experience. Of course, they often keep another male as an escort. The lionesses in a pride also fight back when their help is needed."

"Don't the young ones ever win?" I asked finally.

"In the end, they always do," he replied.

"Always?" I asked, puzzled.

"All strong beings become weak one day. Why should it be any different with patriarch lions?"

"Oh, that. How does the end come?"

"Not very pleasant for the patriarch lions. They get

pushed, shoved, beaten up and banished —that is, if the old guys are wise enough to see the handwriting on the bush."

"Otherwise?"

"Otherwise the old Greeks get killed by the young Turks."

"So the lions do have natural predators after all, don't they? Their own sons!"

"Yes, they do," he smiled. "Lions are their own natural predators."

"Is that why most adult lions wear scars on their haunches and rumps?"

"It's hard for patriarchs to keep horny sub-adults away from their lionesses peacefully."

"The possibility of mutilation and death is real for lions," I added.

"Yeah."

"And it is always there."

"Yes, real and ever present, just as real as the possibility of an FDA raid or inquisition by the state licensing board is for physicians practicing holistic medicine in the United States." He grinned broadly.

I felt a slight chill, but said nothing.

THE ARTHRITIC LION

Three days later, we stayed at Seranora Lodge. At the gift shop of the lodge, I picked up a picture book of East African animals. I opened the book randomly at about the middle. The two opposing pages showed a large, black-maned patriarch lion lying in a sprawl of bright blood. The lion evidently died moments before the picture had been taken, because the picture showed some blood still dripping from his body. Furthermore, there was no sign of any scavengers. The picture showed a second, huge, dark-maned lion walking away from the dead body, his rear to the camera, his shoulders drooping, his head low, his muzzle nearly touching the ground—the embodiment of regret. A third lion stood some feet away, staring at the dead body, as if in disbelief. The still picture evoked powerful images of the battle of life and death that preceded the events seen in the photograph. I thought I saw (or maybe imagined) a limp in the left hind leg of the lion who walked away. The limp seemed similar to the one that affected the patriarch lion we had seen three days earlier by the Mara River.

So is that how lions' legs get chewed up? I wondered. How they end up limping? And when the injuries do not heal, does arthritis set in?

"So, tell, me what is stress?" I asked as we left the gift shop at Seranora Lodge.

"Life *is* stress—and stress *is* life," Choua replied.

"Can life exist without stress?"

"What is life?"

"Life is life. What else?" I replied, annoyed.

Choua stared at me for a few moments, then spoke, "When life begins, it begins to end, isn't that what you wrote in *Rats, Drugs and Assumptions?*"

"Yes, I did."

"So the process of living is also the process of ending—of dying. Right?"

"Right."

"The range of experience in living and dying is broad, and so is the range of stress. Stress is not simply the fight-or-flight response. It's not just a small slice of life's mosaic. Stress is activity at the boundaries of life—where a single cell faces another, one body organ meets another, a living being interfaces with its environment."

"A change at a boundary of life or just the presence of that boundary?" I asked.

"It's not a change at the boundary of life. It is the boundary of life itself."

"But didn't Selye say stress is a response to change?" I pressed.

"I know what he said." Choua showed signs of irritation. "Don't you see that the boundaries of life cannot be static? Can biology be without change? Can a cell exist unless it is some dynamic equilibrium with its micro-environment? Can an environment ever be unchanging? And if biology and the environment cannot be unchanging, how can the boundary between the two be unchanging?"

"You have a point, but..."

"Is there a living being who is unchanging? Is there anything in the wild that is ever truly free of change? Is there a lion that is ever free of stress? The patriarch lion ambles along as if he doesn't have a care in the world. If that is so, why does he forever mark the boundaries of his pride's territory with the scent of his glandular secretions? Why does he roam about all night long roaring? Why doesn't he like to be looked in the eye? Is there a pet cat that is free of stress? Does a domestic cat ever sleep? Even when she is in bed with her mistress, a bed that she has shared for several years?"

"I guess marks of evolution don't fade that easily."

STRESS AND LIFE ARE THE SAME

"Stress is life—as life is stress," Choua went on. "It has as much to do with a woman incarcerated in a traffic jam while her child waits for her at the school door as it does with a bushbuck at the water hole, or with the baboons who saw the lions but couldn't help shrieking to warn the zebras, even though they must have known that would irk the lions. That's the way life is. Stress simply *is*."

"What does that have to do with the homemaker who is late for her child?" I asked.

"Everything!" he snapped.

"That's absurd," I protested, irritated.

"In *Rats, Drugs and Assumptions*, you wrote that when you change something in biology one way, you change everything in some way. Injury and healing are inextricably intertwined." Choua ignored the irritation in my voice. "What did you mean by that?"

"I meant what I said. Life is but a cycle of injury-healing-injury. That's the basic equation of life."

"Quite right! Quite right!" Choua shook his head condescendingly. "It's the same with stress and life. Stress isn't something that arrives with a demand for change—with a need to fight or a desire to flee. It's there all the time. *It simply is*."

"So, none of us can ever be free of stress, is that it?"

"Stress is a constant. It is the state of simply being. That's the way with both the predator and the prey—with lions and with bushbucks. There is no mystery about it. Each of us is a victim. There is a canary in each of us. Only the cages look different. *Stress and life are one and the same thing.* It's artificial to set them apart. Besides, that simply can't be done. Animals know that. People also knew that until, of course, your stress gurus burst on the scene with their elegant, but meaningless, jargon."

"So, do you think Selye was off the mark?" I asked.

"You don't understand, do you?" he groused, then stared at me with intense eyes.

RANDOMNESS OF LIFE AND THE ORGANIZING INFLUENCE

"To cope with stress," Choua spoke after a while, "you need to understand the essential randomness of life and know something about..."

"Essential randomness in life? What's that?" I interrupted, baffled.

"Misfiring of electrons, as some physicist might put it."

"Do you really believe stress is all about misfired electrons?" I asked.

"Or misdirected energy pulses," he added.

"So it's all physical, is it?" I expressed doubt.

"It matters little whether electrons misfiring are triggered by sad thoughts of a mother with a hungry child or the futile charge of a lioness with hungry cubs. Then there is the second element."

"What?" I asked, my confusion growing.

"The *organizing influence* in life," he replied cryptically.

"What organizing influence?" I asked.

"The larger *presence* that gives purpose and meaning to

existence—for a flower, a lion cub or a child."

"What is that presence?" I asked.

"The organizing influence that turns nonliving atoms of oxygen, hydrogen, carbon and nitrogen into living energy of enzymes."

"Now, you have lost me."

"The energy of the *presence* that surrounds each living being." He winked.

"Oh, that! You mean God, don't you?" I asked tentatively.

"Yes, if that's the name you choose for that *organizing influence*." Choua smiled mystically.

"God and science don't mix, do they?" I teased.

"That's your problem, not mine," he replied churlishly and looked away.

The spiritual is the unknown without any uncertainty. Fear cannot exist without a sense of loss, and there can be no sense of loss in the spiritual where there is no awareness. In the spiritual we do not plead for freedom from fear of suffering, but for the heart to reach a stillness that is beyond *any concept of freedom from fear.*

The Canary and Chronic Fatigue

Someday after mastering the winds, waves, the tides and gravity, we shall harness for God the energies of love. And then for the second time in the history of the world man would have discovered fire.

Teilhard de Chardin

It seems improbable that man will ever fully understand the healing energy of love, or, to be more precise, the healing energy of God. Medical technology, itself an expression of God's energy, is beginning to allow us to measure some things about love, and then reproduce them. Measurement and reproducibility make up the language of science. One day, it seems, the men of medicine and the men of spirits will meet at some summit of union. The energy of love will have brought them together.

The Cortical Monkey and Healing

Chapter 2

THE DERELICT MOTHERS

"Are those lionesses sisters?" Sarah asked Michael, referring to the pride of five lionesses and the one patriarch lion.

"Well, that's usually the way it is. A pride of lionesses are generally moms and sisters. But these lionesses probably are not," he replied.

"Why not?" she asked, puzzled by his unexpected response.

"Lion cubs have a high mortality rate. I wouldn't expect five female cubs of a single litter to survive."

"Why not?"

"They are often left unprotected."

"Unprotected? I thought lionesses were fiercely protective of their offspring. Isn't that true?"

"Yes."

"But you seem to imply that the high mortality of cubs is due to maternal negligence. Don't mom lions take good care of their cubs?"

"Not always. Sometimes their motherhood practices leave a lot to be desired."

"What practices?" Talat interjected, obviously puzzled by Michael's comment.

"Lionesses are often derelict mothers. They sometimes leave their cubs unattended when they go hunting."

"But I read somewhere that pregnant lions become secretive close to birthing time and select secluded places to make their dens."

"The African savannah has no secluded places," Michael answered emphatically, grinning. He then peered hard into the bush on the other side of the Mara River.

Michael's comments about derelict lionesses intrigued me. Animals are fiercely protective of their offspring. Nursing mothers in the animal kingdom sometimes continue to suckle long after they become severely malnourished. Cheetahs are agile cats with lithe bodies, almost totally bereft of body fat. Cheetah mothers are known to go hungry when their daily kill is not enough to satisfy their cubs. I wondered what Michael meant by derelict lionesses. I know lionesses are not magnanimous at their kills. They don't have good table manners. They push, shove and snarl viciously at whatever comes in their way at feeding times. In fact, they will bite the heads off their cubs if they try to sidle up to the carcass of the prey. I have seen pictures of large lion prides gnawing at each other, sometimes inflicting serious wounds while fighting for their share of the kill. Indeed, that is why many of their muzzles, heads and necks are scarred. But I know all that derelict behavior doesn't apply to lionesses and their tiny, furry newborns.

Still, I didn't want to contest Michael. He was an excellent safari guide. His information had been good to that point.

"Why are lionesses derelict mothers?" I asked Choua after some time.

"Derelict?" he frowned.

"Didn't you hear Michael tell us that lion moms leave their tiny cubs unattended, and that's the reason why cubs are wasted so often?"

"Motherhood is unique—sometimes irrational, often unyielding, but always utterly and unfalteringly devoted. It is never derelict in nature."

"Never? That's not always true," I challenged him.

"Give me an example."

"Snakes often swallow their newborns, don't they?"

"That's because they are snakes," Choua chuckled.

"But, seriously, what do you make of Michael's notion that lionesses are derelict moms, Choua?" I asked.

"He's off the mark," Choua replied flatly.

"How so?"

"Lionesses protect their cubs as fiercely as elephant moms and hippo moms," he replied emphatically, then seemed to have a second thought. "Well, at least they do most of the time."

"What do you mean? Do you mean sometimes they don't?"

"Sometimes they can't."

Mother and daughter elephants are known to keep their bonds for life. At Baringo Lake Lodge, where we stayed before leaving for Masai Mara, the hotel staff issued severe warnings not to go close to baby hippos should we happen to see them grazing by the lodge grounds at night. Hippo mothers are extremely dangerous to people, who may inadvertently come too close to their baby hippos. There are other species that guard their babies vigilantly. Beluga whales carry their stillborn calves balanced delicately on their snouts until the calves' bodies decompose and disintegrate.

"So, tell me, why are mother lions different from elephant moms and hippo moms?" I asked, returning from my thoughts.

"They are not," Choua snapped. "Lionesses don't have daycare services for cubs available to them."

"What do you mean?"

"The cubs have to be fed sometimes, don't they?"

"Yes."

"The elephant moms can graze and keep a close watch

on their babies. Lionesses can't do that, can they?"

"Why not?"

"Because they don't have babysitters when they leave the den for hunting."

"How about dad lions?"

"They're good for nothing when it comes to raising cubs. Patriarch lions only want to snooze or walk around, infatuated with their strong bodies and big, dark manes."

"Don't they protect their prides from invading nomad lions?"

"They're more proficient at protecting their turf than their prides. In any case, they desert their ladies at birthing time. They show no interest in newborn cubs. If the mom lion doesn't go out hunting, the cubs will starve to death. And when she does..."

"The cubs have to be left alone," I completed his sentence.

"Yes, she can't carry her litter on her back and hunt at the same time, can she? The big guys have no patience for babysitting," Choua winked.

"I get it now," I said, flustered.

"The savannah doesn't share Michael's sense of maternal responsibilities," Choua said. "It offers no protection to the cubs just because mom has to go hunt a warthog to bring home the bacon."

We were quiet for a while. Nature may not have malice, but it certainly has no remorse. Choua's words returned to me. The African savannah doesn't share Michael's notion of maternal obligations. Nature has its own sense of order and disorder. Life *is* stress. Stress is not merely an aspect of fight chemistry—nor the chemistry of flight.

"Cub retrieval can be a full-time job for the lioness," Choua resumed. "Lion cubs are like toddlers, forever poking their muzzles where they do not belong. There is but one mom lion and a whole litter of inquisitive little beasts."

"Housekeeping with a den full of cubs must be hard on the lionesses," I agreed.

I recalled that Amir, our younger son, was enamored with electric outlets. No toys could distract him from those electric sockets. He had an irresistible urge to stuff all sorts of things into them. I remember warning Talat not to inadvertently drop her hairpins on the floor where Amir's eyes—close to the floor as they were most of the time—could easily spot the shining metallic objects. And, of course, he would want to put the hairpins into the electric outlets. She was obviously aware of the danger. But preventing a two-year-old from such attractions can be a mission impossible even for a full-time mother.

I understood what Choua meant. Michael was right about the African savannah. It hides nothing. No secretive lion den is truly secret from the other beings that populate the wilderness. But Michael was wrong about labeling lion moms derelict. Michael can be forgiven this once, I told myself. He had told us about his own seven children, whom he left with his wife in Nairobi during his long absences on safari. Does he really know what it takes to keep seven children fed, clothed and satisfied? What would he have known about how the infant-retrieval game is played? How would he know what a lioness has to go through to protect her cubs and hunt for them at the same time?

MANTLE OF MARTYRDOM

A flotilla of anvil clouds hung in the sky. As I watched them move slowly, my thoughts drifted to Sally.

Sally, a woman in her early fifties, consulted me about the deterioration of her general health and persistent, progressive disabling fatigue. I asked if she knew what might have triggered the problem. She told me that it simply happened, that she didn't have a clue to the why or how of her health problems.

Extensive clinical experience with disabling chronic fatigue has convinced me that such fatigue does not simply happen. Fatigue sufferers often trace the onset of their illness to a single event, such as serious Epstein-Barr infections or extensive use of antibiotics for pneumonia. But this is not what really happens. The human body has an enormous capacity to sustain insults and recover. Persistent chronic fatigue sets in only when human antioxidants, enzymes and immune defenses have been slowly eroded. In clinical practice, I can almost always uncover energetic-molecular events that precede persistent chronic fatigue. The most common mistakes are made when underlying stressors such as mold allergy, food incompatibility, chemical sensitivity and severe stress are ignored. The patient's defenses are then further compromised by thoughtless and continuing antibiotic therapy. Chronic fatigue states, in essence, are states caused by doing the wrong things and by not doing the right things.

During the initial interview I explored such possibilities at length but could uncover no significant factors. Sally was a happily married woman who loved her children, husband and horses. She enjoyed her work most of the time. As much as I tried to find some predisposing factors, I drew a blank. Finally, I assured her that I expected her to recover fully. I prescribed some nutrient and herbal therapies and recommended training in autoregulation. Before she left, I said there was something in her case that puzzled me. I hoped that, at some point, she would provide a clue to the origin of her disabling fatigue.

Sally responded very well to the treatment. On her first follow-up visit about ten weeks later, she jubilantly announced that her health was back, and she had returned to work. I rarely see such dramatic responses during the initial weeks of therapy. I felt gratified and talked about the possibility of symptom relapse with common infections. We discussed how we would address such an event, and she smiled approvingly.

As she was leaving my office, she stopped at the door, turned back and said, "Oh, by the way, I think I know what triggered the whole problem. Remember, you said I was a puzzle for you because I gave no clues as to the origin of my fatigue?"

"Yes, I remember," I replied with interest. "So, what was it?"

"My dog."

"What happened to your dog?"

"He died. My baby died in my arms after he was run over by a car."

"I'm sorry to hear that."

"When you asked me all those questions about any unusual circumstances at home or work, I forgot about my baby dying in my arms."

"That's sad," I sympathized.

"It was awfully hard on me."

"I understand."

"I think that's what brought on the depression and fatigue."

"I once saw that in one teenager, but he was recovering from a severe case of mono when he lost his pet and relapsed."

"I felt guilty for weeks."

"But you didn't push the dog in the way of a speeding car. Why the guilt?" I asked.

"Why the guilt?" she stiffened.

"Yes, why the guilt?" I persisted.

"You know how it is being a mother, don't you?" she asked, then added with a smile, "The mantle of martyrdom. We mothers wear it around our necks at all times, don't we?"

JACKALS ARE FAIR GAME FOR LIONS, AS LION CUBS ARE FOR JACKALS

"Where did the other cubs go?" I asked Choua at the lodge gift shop, as I showed him the photograph of an emaciated lion cub lumbering along after his mom.

"Must have perished," he replied.

"Died of bacterial infections?" I asked.

"Not often."

"Viral diseases?"

"That happens, but not frequently."

"What about parasites? Don't lions often get infested with parasites?"

"Yes, they do. George Schaller reported finding *Trypanosoma* parasites in the blood smears of two-thirds of the lions whose blood was examined with a microscope."

"Why don't lions get sick with the blood parasites?"

"They know something that you apparently don't."

"What?" I asked, annoyed a bit.

"That there is such a thing as parasite-host balance in nature. Lions have antioxidant, enzyme and immune defenses against *Trypanosoma* parasites and so are able to fight them off."

"Are you saying lions are born with stronger immune defenses than those of people?"

"Not born with stronger defenses."

"But their immune defenses must be down sometimes."

"Then the infested lions get sick and sometimes die."

"Let's get back to lion cubs. The cubs cannot have very strong immune systems at birth. How do they fight off viral infections and parasitic infestation? What is different between humans and newborn lions?"

"Viral infections and parasites, by and large, are caused by overcrowding; poor sanitation and hygiene; and by damaged bowels, blood, liver and brain ecosystems. The antioxidant defenses of lions are not violated by pesticides and fungicides every day. The delicate bowel ecosystems of cubs are not decimated the way they are in human babies who are fed regular doses of antibiotics. Cubs on the Serengeti Plain don't breathe the polluted air that babies in New York City breathe, do they?"

"Okay, tell me, why is the mortality rate so high among lion cubs? How do the cubs get killed?" I asked.

"Jackals eat them when the mom lion is out hunting."

"Jackals, of all creatures? I thought jackals were cowardly, never wanting to face a danger squarely. Why would they mess with lions?"

"They face no danger when the mom lion is out hunting and the dad lion is snoozing in the sun at a distance. Cubs are tiny morsels of tender meat for them."

"The savannah's sense of justice, isn't it?" I felt pity for the cubs and the lionesses.

"Jackals are fair game for lions, and lion cubs are fair game for jackals," he grinned, then added with a laugh, "It isn't much different for lions than it is for people."

"What did you say?" I was jolted by Choua's comment.

"The predator-prey relationships in lions aren't much different from those in people." He smiled again.

"What do you mean?"

"The hunter-hunted drama is the same—whether it is played in the Los Angeles courtroom or in the Serengeti savannah," he mused and looked to the distant hills where Michael told us the Tanzanian Serengeti border was located.

"Too much of a swing for me, Choua," I protested. "I don't get it. What do the goings-on in an American courtroom have to do with a lioness losing her cubs on the Serengeti Plain?"

THE PREDATOR BECOMES THE PREY

"In a Los Angeles courtroom, Marcia Clark is the predator and O.J. Simpson, the prey."

"That's some flight of imagination," I chided Choua.

"In the courtroom, as the *National Enquirer* told its readers, Marcia is a tigress, ferociously battling O.J.'s dream team of defense lawyers. Conversely, according to the tabloid,

Marcia is a pussycat at home. In one court, she is prosecuting the trial of the century; in the other, she is a working mom fighting her former husband to keep her children. In court documents her former husband argued that Marcia saw her five-year-old and three-year-old boys no more than an hour a day, and was therefore unfit to be a real mother. So while Marcia attacks one person in court, someone else invades her den." Choua stopped and looked toward the pride of lionesses.

"Go on," I prodded.

"A lioness has to go out and hunt to bring food for her cubs just as Marcia has to. When the lioness is away, the jackals have their way. When Marcia is away in a courtroom, her children are free game for the former husband. Isn't the drama essentially the same? The theater is different. The cast of characters is different. But the chemistry of stress and anguish is the same. Do you think the lioness suffers any less than Marcia Clark when her cubs are snatched away?" Choua frowned.

"I never looked at it that way," I replied. "But is it true that jackals can eat lion cubs? I mean the cubs look stronger than jackals."

"Twelve inches in length! That's all there is to a cub at birth, and that includes its furry tail. Merely 12 ounces in weight. A jackal shouldn't have much problem with that, especially those who have narrowly escaped the lioness's fast, flat, galloping charges."

"So there is malice in nature. You don't think jackals hunt without malice or remorse, as they tell you in the nature movies, do you?"

"I don't think those movie makers ask jackals, hyenas and buffaloes such questions. Even if they did, I don't think the animals would care to answer. Hyenas detest lions as lions detest hyenas. Jackals remember who kills them, and so do buffaloes. They don't have many chances to get even, but when they do, they cherish the moment."

"Do buffaloes also kill lion cubs?" I asked, surprised.

Choua looked at me, then turned his face away. "So that's that," I told myself and walked out of the gift shop.

****

Another time two park rangers saw a herd of buffalo chase a lioness with three cubs. The mother and two cubs escaped into a tree but the third cub was trampled and killed by the buffalo. When we arrived on the scene, the buffalo were moving around the tree, paying no attention to the mangled cub.

Makacha and Schaller
E. Africa Wildlife J 7:99, 1969

KILLING BABIES TO SPITE THE PARENTS

"Most, but not all, lions are social beings," Choua said when he joined me later. "Some males are loners. They are called nomad lions. They brood alone, wandering about in their ranges. Sometimes you see them in pairs or even in groups. They are ill-tempered and always angry about something or other."

"They don't like female company, is that it?" I asked.

"Oh, they do. But sex can be very expensive for them," he said.

"Why? Do the lionesses fight back? They don't like the male's ill temper?"

"No, it's not that. Actually, given the opportunity, lionesses don't mind sneaking out of the pride for a quick rendezvous with the nomads. You know what biologists call it, don't you? A yearning for enlarging the gene pool for healthier, vigorous offspring. Sex is expensive for nomad lions because the patriarch lions of prides don't like to see them around their harems. If nomads persist in pursuing the females, the patriarchs grow irate and ugly battles ensue."

"Understandable! What happens?"

"It's sex at the risk of mutilation and death," Choua explained. "Sometimes that's exactly what happens."

"I thought the nomad lions would be hardier in their fight for sex. I thought they would prevail over the patriarch, who must become exhausted from those twenty-minute matings."

"That's probably true. I told you nomads are often ill-tempered and testy. So you might think the angry lions would fight more viciously. But the patriarch lions have an edge—their lionesses often join in and fight off the invaders. Also, the patriarch lions often keep a big male as their assistant. So it isn't that tempting for the nomad lion to mess around with the pride."

"That's tough! Do they ever succeed in mating?"

"Yeah, sometimes they do. I suppose the biologic need to pass the genes is stronger than the threat of torn limbs and brutal death. Horny lions are known to do crazy things."

"Give me an example."

"Example?" Choua rubbed his temple for a few moments, then continued. "Nomad lions are always on the lookout for aging and weakened patriarch lions, whom they can dislodge from the pride and take over. If they win, they will sometimes eat the cubs in the pride just to spite the displaced patriarch and his harem."

"Kill babies to spite their mom?" I asked, incredulous.

"It happens," he shrugged. "Since nomad lions don't eat the cubs they kill, one can assume they do so only to spite the moms."

I had read that very hungry carnivores will sometimes devour their own babies. Michael told us earlier that baboons —herbivores under ordinary circumstances —sometimes eat their babies for reasons naturalists are at a loss to explain. But to kill babies to spite their parents? That seems too brutal and senseless even for aroused and angry lions.

"Why do you think frustrated and angry nomad lions take it out on the cubs?" Choua asked.

"I don't know. Why?" I asked back.

"Nomad lions are no different from people," he replied indifferently.

"People don't kill babies," I retorted.

As I challenged Choua, I recalled a report I had read about Susan Smith's trial. It described a "fresh-faced killer mom" who cunningly conned the world into believing that her two children were killed by a carjacker. In reality, she had driven her two little boys, strapped to their car seats, to their deaths in a lake. Nine days later, she confessed her heinous crime. "Why?" an outraged world asked. Her attorney's explanation was insanity caused by the unrelenting cruelty of those around her and the grim demands of her boyfriend to rid herself of her kids.

"No? People don't kill babies?" Choua asked, as if he had read my thoughts. "How is baby killing by an angry bomber in Oklahoma different from cub killing by an angry nomad lion?"

"We really don't know why the bomber did what he did, do we?"

"For the same reason nomad lions kill lion cubs."

"Horrible! A horrible thought!" I groaned.

"Nomad lions are in the same quandary. The accused bomber was a hero one day, decorated in the Gulf War and considered for an elite force in the army. Then the war hero becomes an outcast —alone and consumed by anger. He doesn't understand where the anger springs from or how to dissipate it. It's the same with angry nomad lions. Nature doesn't seem to care much for a naturalist's notions of altruism, malice or remorse. Does it?"

"Still, there is some consistency in nature that lends meanings to life," I said in reply.

"Ah yes, the *meanings of life*!" Choua chuckled. "Isn't that the *in* thing now? The new buzzword foisted on the gullible by the wise of the New Age?"

"Well, you can't observe what is all around you and not try to draw a conclusion sometime, can you?"

"Conclusion!" Choua muttered. "Meanings of life and conclusions! Tell me, what conclusions do you draw from a Harvard premed student killing her roommate?"

"Awful! That was awful!" I recalled the news story. "They found forty-five stab wounds on the body of that poor Vietnamese girl. And for what?"

"Yes, for what?" Choua repeated after me solemnly. "Poor Trang Ho, she was knifed to death because she wished to room with someone else. Then the murderess, Sinedu Tadesse, hanged herself in a shower stall. She was from Ethiopia —a 'glittering jewel of the family' as her father would say. Both the murderess and the murdered won scholarships at Harvard and prepared for careers in medicine. So tell me, what conclusions do you draw from such observations?" Choua heaved as he finished the sentence.

"It's impossible to understand that kind of violence. Maybe criminologists can. Or perhaps some psychiatrists."

"Criminologists! Psychiatrists, eh?" he frowned. "They *do* know how to spin yarn, don't they? After every bombing, they concoct new theories. After every murder, they change their stories, don't they?"

"Someone has to try to make sense of such heinous crimes," I countered.

"You're always thinking about making sense, aren't you?" he mocked, then continued, "The basic scheme of things hasn't changed much as humankind moved away from the savannah, has it? Isolation, stress and anger remain the same, whether it be the open African plain or the Dunster House on the Harvard campus."

"Or the killing fields in the Persian Gulf and the Middle East?" I added.

"It's the same thing. The essential bestiality of human beings persists. Muslim women are raped by Christians in Bosnia and it takes President Clinton three years to define a moral imperative for interceding. When that doesn't sell, he claims that the United States has vital interests in Bosnia. What vital interests?"

"Christians rape Muslim women now because they know Muslims did the same. What's the difference?" I asked.

"West Pakistani Muslim soldiers raped Bengali Muslim women when Bangladesh separated from Pakistan."

"That's Muslims raping Muslims!" I said with disgust, then asked with resignation, "What's the answer?"

"The answer," he drawled, "The answer is..."

He stopped in midsentence, peered into my eyes for several moments, then looked away at the distant hills where Michael had told us the Kenyan Serengeti rolled into the Tanzanian Serengeti.

What is the chemistry of mindless violence? I wondered. What are the energetic-molecular basis of rage? A photograph of Shoko Asahara published in *Time* magazine flashed through my mind. Asahara is the Japanese guru who was accused of masterminding the gassing with sarin of commuters in a Tokyo underground station. Several people died. I wondered what populates the minds of disciples when they cook with or drink water in which their guru bathed. In Asahara's case the used bathwater, called "Miracle Pond," was sold to believers for about $300 an ounce according to *People* magazine. (These disciples also drew much "spiritual enlightenment" by sipping tea made with Asahara's hair.)

FELINE FEMINISM

*Male lions only form groups because they
have to secure and defend groups of females;
female coalitions are largely formed by
groups of mothers that have reared their
young in a creche. The fundamental reason
why lions live in groups lies with females.*

Craig Packer
Into Africa

"The social order of the Serengeti lions and the people
of Kirto, your ancestral village, have a lot in common," Choua
resumed.

"What?" I asked, amused by his flight of ideas.

"Males in both places carry a pretense of power and
control. They are quick to erupt when challenged, but the basic
social order is essentially female-oriented."

"I agree with the first part of your statement."

"Serengeti lionesses, like Kirto women, don't like to be
denied."

"I agree that Kirto women don't like to be denied. But
there's a difference between not wanting to be denied and
actually being denied."

"Lionesses and Kirto women know what they want. Both
groups have their sense of things in life. They understand that

males need to be tolerated for rather limited periods of time for their temporary procreation roles."

"Go on," I smiled.

"Kirto women and lionesses know their males are chauvinistic—consumed by their petty narcissistic self-indulgences," Choua chuckled. "They know males can't be depended upon for serious things in life."

"Such as?" I asked.

"Such as rearing cubs and children. So they tolerate them and let them impregnate them. Then they turn away. The opposite gender, they know well, must simply be ignored. Let them wallow in their frivolous notions of superiority and dominance."

****

I recalled a *National Geographic* video that showed a large pride of about 30 lions, all adult females and cubs, on a nightly prowl for food. Hunting targets are scarce. The pride ambles along for miles without food. The cubs wander away for short distances at times, then catch up with the pride as their moms turn around and wait. Suddenly through the darkness of the night come the sounds of nomad male lions roaring and yowling. The pride stops in its tracks, then moves noiselessly away from the direction of the nomads. Why bother with the rascals? All they ever want is sex. Next to that, what they love most is to mess around, squirting their glandular secretions on bushes and trees to mark them with their scent. They seldom bother to work, but at the kills, they devour most of the meat. Why not stay out of the way of vagabonds?

For every one of them, God is in her child.
Mothers of great men must have this feeling
particularly, but then, at the beginning, all
women are mothers of great men—it isn't
their fault if life disappoints them later.

Boris Pasternak
Doctor Zhivago

As I wandered wrapped up in thought, my eyes were struck with the hospital for the reception of deserted infants, which I surveyed with pleasure, till, by a natural train of sentiment, I began to reflect on the fate of the mothers. For to what shelter can they fly?

Samuel Johnson

Chapter 3

Of Ladies and Lionesses

Living alone is a tragic fate for a female lion. Solitary females almost never succeed in raising any offspring and often become nervous and furtive. However, they are not aberrant misfits, but perfectly healthy animals that have ended up alone through forces beyond their control...solitaryfemales almost never team up with females from other prides.

Craig Packer
Into Africa

How does isolation affect the basic equation of life? How does loneliness influence the essential injury-healing-injury cycles in biology? How do lions deal with loneliness? How do humans cope with isolation? How different are the problems of women from those of lionesses?

I care for a large number of patients with unrelenting chronic illnesses. I see patients so devastated by unmitigated suffering that they are irked by the mere mention of hope. Their suffering is unrelenting, their despair, profound. Yet I am amazed by the regenerative capacity of chronically injured tissues. When such patients are guided properly, following the appropriate procedures and avoiding the wrong ones, most of them eventually heal.

I recall a patient who suffered from multiple sclerosis

and couldn't walk fifty yards without falling. His MRI brain scans showed multiple white lesions characteristic of that disease. A year later, he was completely free of symptoms and a repeat MRI scan was completely normal. I don't often see such complete recoveries with our nondrug therapies, but the essential lesson this patient taught me was that complete recovery from a severe case of multiple sclerosis *is* possible.

I have also seen many cases of indolent ulcerative colitis and rheumatoid arthritis heal. I have witnessed many of my patients who suffered from Graves' disease (overactive thyroid gland) heal—without thyroid-burning radioactive iodine, without thyroid-removing surgery and without thyroid-destroying drugs. Indeed, such a clinical outcome has been a rule rather than an exception in my experience. And, of course, I have seen patients totally disabled with chronic fatigue syndrome regularly—albeit slowly—regain their energy patterns and return to work.

As I write this, I recall a patient who developed colon cancer. The operating surgeon told the patient he removed *all* the cancer. When the surgeon referred him to an oncologist, the patient asked why the referral was necessary if the tumor had been removed completely. The surgeon hemmed and hawed, then said something about chemotherapy being an insurance policy against the cancer recurring. Predictably, chemotherapy made him sick and weak. Two years after chemotherapy, the cancer returned to the patient's lungs. He suffered progressive difficulty in breathing and required hospitalization.

After the second surgery, he was again told that *all* the tumor had been removed. More chemotherapy was advised—again as an extra safety measure. That time chemotherapy made him sicker and for a longer period of time.

Nonetheless, after about two years, the tumor returned to his groin and lower abdomen. The scans outlined the extent of the tumor. Not surprisingly, additional surgery and yet more chemotherapy was advised.

By this time the patient had done some research into natural healing methods, some anticancer salves and herbs. He refused surgery as well as chemotherapy, and went on to apply a combination of yellow and black salves on the skin overlying the known tumor masses. He also put himself on a nutrient program. When I saw him about two years later, the lumps in the groin and abdomen had melted away. His wife—a wonderful, remarkably supportive woman—told Talat and me that he felt better than he had in years. He had more energy for his business and lived a full life. I know of other cancer patients who have also succeeded with holistic therapies after multiple surgeries and chemotherapy courses failed. While many patients hadn't successfully controlled their tumors, *many had*.

I recall a woman who had a highly malignant ovarian cancer removed in 1974. The tumor had broken through the surface—a sign of poor prognosis. In 1994 she was still alive and well when a needle aspiration biopsy of a pelvic mass showed cancer cells identical to those seen in the ovarian cancer twenty years earlier. I have also seen many other patients who lived for years after they had been pronounced terminal.

I also recognize some patterns of failure to heal. Most notably, even when sound integrated holistic therapies are used for sufficiently long periods, a dismal clinical pattern emerges in terribly lonely and hurt individuals, among people incarcerated in personal silos of isolation.

OF LONELINESS AND ISOLATION

Kim, a woman in her early forties, consulted me for recurrent viral infections, persistent vaginal yeast infections and chronic fatigue. Six years before I saw her, she had undergone a mastectomy for cancer and received chemotherapy. Not surprisingly, her general health deteriorated after chemotherapy. She had been an efficient worker before chemotherapy but was unable to cope due to failing health. Some months before I saw her, she lost her job. Unable to find another position, she fell behind in her rental payments and was evicted. She was forced to move to another part of town and so lost contact with her few friends. She felt progressively tired. Her limbs ached all the time, and she became depressed.

Several months later, she pulled herself up and found another job. She felt no desire to make new friends at her new position, nor did she look for companionship in her new apartment complex.

From a purely medical standpoint, I didn't think her chemotherapy-induced fatigue and immune dysfunctions were difficult to manage. Indeed, initially she did well with our nutritional plans, nutrient therapies and autoregulation. She regained much of her lost energy, and her depression lifted. Then she relapsed. That didn't surprise me since slow recovery to a general sense of well-being, with peaks and troughs in energy levels, is common. Several months passed, but she showed no improvement. She seemed to follow our management plan well, yet couldn't escape cycles of recovery and relapse. I tried immunotherapy, nutrient and herbal remedies, intramuscular and intravenous injections, treatment for underactive thyroid and adrenal exhaustion, measures for preventing sugar-insulin-adrenaline roller coasters, autoregulation, and slow, sustained exercise. Nothing worked on any sustained basis. Then I tried some other nondrug therapies, each time with limited success. Her symptoms always recurred. Eventually, I became disillusioned. It is hard on a physician to keep seeing a patient who doesn't recover.

After many months of poor clinical outcome, Kim discontinued her visits to our office. Not an illogical decision, I thought. On a few occasions, I asked a nurse to call and inquire about her health. All such follow-up reports were negative for clinical improvement. Then I didn't hear from her for a long period of time. Sometimes I wondered if anyone else had finally found a way to mitigate her suffering and wished I knew what therapies might have turned her case around.

One day Kim returned, looking ghastly pale, disheveled and distraught. She complained of extreme fatigue, severe abdominal bloating, muscle aches and vaginal itching. I thumbed through her thick chart looking for any possible clues and wondered if there was something I had missed, some therapy that I'd neglected to try. There were no clues. She told me she couldn't afford any more diagnostic tests since she had no health insurance. I felt helpless and doubted that similar therapies would work again even if she had the financial resources to stay with the program for several more months.

How does one address such problems? I wondered. Who

could I consult? Where could Kim go to enlist some desperately needed assistance? Groping for an answer, I asked her who else she had seen during the time she didn't come to our Institute. She told me she had been to some clinics and emergency departments.

"You know how it is, don't you?" she spoke with sad eyes. "It's always the same thing. They do some blood tests, take some X-rays, then prescribe antibiotics and antidepressants which make me more sick. My insurance company refuses to pay for the vitamin injections that help me."

"Where do you live now?" I asked to change the subject. "Did you find a suitable apartment?"

"What apartment?" She suddenly broke down and sobbed. "My apartment caught fire. The few belongings I had were burned. I was desperate for a roof over my head. Then an old friend took pity on me and offered me a room. I gratefully accepted. Now I find she is an alcoholic with four unruly children whom she expects me to care for daily in return for the room I sleep in. It doesn't let up, Dr. Ali. I've no money for treatment. I'm just as alone today as ever."

CITADELS OF CORONARY SURGERY

"Why do you think your health care system doesn't reimburse for natural restorative therapies?" Choua asked after Kim left my consultation room.

"Because they don't think nondrug therapies work," I replied.

"Is that because they have tested nondrug therapies and

found them to be ineffective?"

"Of course not! But you know all that. Why do you ask?"

"Your health care system readily shells out hundreds of thousands of dollars for coronary bypass surgery and angioplasty for visiting family members of immigrants, doesn't it?"

"Yes, I have seen that."

"And for illegal immigrants?"

"Yes, that too. But I don't know how all that happens. I sometimes wonder why huge bills for such surgical procedures are paid when the recipients of those services are not insured," I replied as I recalled a case in which a $110,000 bill for a coronary bypass operation, with post-operative complications, was paid by Medicare.

"You use micro-ELISA IgE blood tests for the diagnosis of mold and food allergies in children with recurrent sore throats, ear infections, asthma and eczema."

"Yes, I do."

"How often are the claims for reimbursement of those tests denied?"

"That's a real problem. Unfortunately, that happens only too often. It does cause a lot of stress for the parents of those children."

"Why are those claims denied?"

"I don't know. Maybe the insurers don't think allergy is an issue in those problems."

"Allergy not the central issue in recurrent sore throats, asthma and eczema?" Choua frowned.

"Well, it clearly is, but how else can one understand that?"

"You're so innocent, Mr. Pathologist," he taunted.

"Maybe you know better," I replied, irked by his sarcasm.

"That's not the real reason," he softened.

"Then what is the real reason?"

"The reason that parents of American children with asthma, eczema and recurrent infections are not reimbursed for sorely needed allergy tests has nothing to do with science," Choua chuckled.

"No?" I asked, perplexed.

"Neither does science have anything to do with huge payments for bypass surgery and angioplasty on uninsured visitors and illegal immigrants," he went on somberly.

"Now you have lost me with your flight of ideas," I complained.

"The explanation for such a happening, Dr. Innocent, is quite simple." He laughed out loud.

"And what's that?" I asked, my confusion growing.

"It's simply a question of where the money goes," he winked.

"Speak plainly, will you?"

"Amazing! It's amazing that you don't see something so simple," he grinned. "It's all a question of where the money ends up."

"Explain, Choua, explain," I pleaded.

"It's a question of what that money supports —the great heart surgery centers or the lowly holistic community," he winked again.

"Oh that, but..."

"Your heart-surgery business has an insatiable appetite for money," he interrupted me. "It has a powerful lobby—both inside its great citadels and outside them."

"What do you mean?"

"Inside its citadels, the heart-surgery business feeds all sorts of medical specialists with its surgical complications. You know how it is, don't you? It creates all kinds of work for cardiologists, pulmonologists, gastroenterologists and rheumatologists. Even the lowly psychiatrists get a few bones thrown at them every now and then, don't they?"

"Ah, Choua's venom again," I chided.

"Cardiac surgeons also love to play the secondary gain game, don't they?"

"What's that?" I feigned ignorance of the doctrine of secondary gain.

"When patients continue to be sick after cardiac surgery—and, of course, everyone knows coronary artery bypass surgery does nothing to reverse coronary artery disease —the cardiac surgeons invoke the great doctrine of secondary gain. The surgeons ship their patients to psychiatrists in the belief that the patient isn't recovering because he doesn't want to. He believes the patient has something to gain by remaining sick—some secondary gain."

"Tell me, do you not believe in the concept of secondary gain?"

"Funds flow freely to the citadels of cardiac surgery," Choua continued, without answering my question. "Because that's how people in control of health care dollars make sure the money remains in the family. Why give up any of that?"

"I don't get it."

"What's there to get?" he groused. "Why waste a few hundred dollars on allergy tests?"

"Waste on allergy tests?" I asked in disbelief.

"You don't get it, do you?" he erupted. "It has nothing to do with medical necessity or not. And it has nothing to do with whether the recipient of the medical services is a 93-year-old illegal immigrant or a three-year-old American-born child with asthma."

"So what's the point?" I asked, exasperated.

"The point, Mr. Gullible, is that the booty of $110,000 paid for an unnecessary coronary bypass operation is gleefully divided among the stakeholders of the coronary-surgery citadels, whereas the few hundred dollars reimbursed for an allergic child are considered to be wasted on the holistic community."

"That's a cynical view, if ever I heard one," I reprimanded.

"Cynical?" he scowled. "You say that's cynical. Do you think it would matter whether bypass surgery was performed on a 93-year-old illegal immigrant or some rats imported from Kenya? The concern in the coronary-surgery citadels is not who they operate on, or for what. The issue is simple: how to keep the operating rooms humming, how to keep sending huge medical bills, how to maximize reimbursement. They will operate on people, and if people are not amenable, they will operate on rats. That's the simple truth."

Choua stopped, scratched his head, then walked away.

SISTERHOOD OF LIONESSES AND BISMILLAH SISTERS

A lioness who belongs to a pride lives an altogether different life from one who is on her own. Amiable and loving to their mothers, sisters and daughters, lionesses are militantly intolerant of outsiders —solitary lionesses who might wander into their territory.

Lions are the only feline species in which the females are so militantly sociable... Once a female becomes solitary, she can live in a group only if she rears a daughter. Unlike single males, who readily join unrelated companions, solitary females almost never team up with females from other prides.

Craig Packer
Into Africa

Emigration is traumatic. The old support structures of immigrants are uprooted, and the new ones need time to take root. Even after many years, the new relationships are fragile. For immigrants, the conflict between old and new values is never fully resolved. The children of immigrants grow up in the adopted country with little, if any, understanding of the old traditions. For people in the Judeo-Christian tradition, immigration does not add deep religious schisms to the problems of cultural assimilation. Hindus, Sikhs, Parsis, Buddhists and other Asian peoples who belong to various other religions seem to acclimate readily to American society without serious and prolonged difficulties. But for most Muslim immigrants the conflicts frequently seem beyond resolution.

More than one immigrant Muslim family is torn apart by the deep religious rifts between traditional Islamic values and contemporary American mores. Dating, for example, is explicitly prohibited in Islam. Muslims—especially women—have a great deal of difficulty coming to terms with the idea of their daughters dating before marriage, let alone going out with non-Muslim males. This, of course, makes finding husbands for Muslim women so much more difficult, because Muslim men date women of other religions freely.

A Pakistani woman once consulted me for poor general health and asthma. She lived a very stressed life. She was deeply troubled by the conflict her children faced growing up in the United States. I understood her anguish but had no answer.

"The worst part," she spoke sadly, "is the way my own family treats me here. In Pakistan, we were all simply cousins. We went out together, talked, shopped and ate. We were like sisters. There was no hierarchy. Here, my cousins have become Bismillah sisters—that's their family name. They consider themselves elite Muslims. They live as a tight clan. Everyone else is an outsider. They deride me for not keeping a Muslim home. It's not that they don't want to see me. They invite me to their houses, then make it very clear that they are superior Muslims, and that I am not one of them. I can somewhat understand when Americans discriminate against us, but to receive such treatment from Pakistanis in this country! And from those I knew well in Pakistan! From my own family! Women whom I regarded as my own sisters!"

One Muslim woman told me of her deep hurt when her own brother told her not to invite him to her daughter's wedding if the daughter decided to marry a non-Muslim. Cruelty has many shapes.

BEFORE HE DIED, I TOLD HIM I LOVED HIM. DO YOU THINK HE HEARD ME?

SBG is nearly ten, and she has reared only one cub, a son, past the age of two. He is not with her today, so he has probably died.

Craig Packer
Into Africa

Marie, a thin woman with an intense face, walked into my consultation room and eyed me suspiciously. I stood up to greet her and invited her to sit on a chair. She thanked me nervously and sat at the edge of a chair. She was distraught and obviously depressed. I decided to give her a few moments to compose herself while I read through her clinical questionnaire. After I finished reading, I gently asked her if she wanted to add anything.

"I'm frightened for my job," she blurted. "I'm a senior laboratory technologist. I had a photographic memory. I would read a long procedure for a complex new experiment, then complete the experiment without once looking at the written procedure. Nobody believed my memory. In the laboratory they said I must play some sort of game and memorize the whole procedure the night before without letting anyone know about it."

"And now?" I asked softly.

"Now I read the procedures, but I cannot understand any of it."

"How did this happen?"

"I don't know."

"I mean did it happen suddenly after some chemical exposure or after a severe viral infection, or did the change occur slowly over months?"

"Slowly over months."

"Do you recall the beginning? Is there a specific time to which you can trace this problem?"

"Not really."

As I wrote earlier, such drastic health problems rarely develop suddenly—as bolts from the blue. The exceptions, of course, are cases of sudden massive exposure to chemicals. I then moved to other clinical features of her illness. In the companion volume, *The Canary and Chronic Fatigue,* I describe many such case histories of chronic fatigue sufferers—the human canaries, as I call them. Extensive experience in caring for human canaries convinces me that all their complex case histories can be reduced to one basic element: unrelenting oxidative fires that burn out their digestive-detoxifying-receptor-energy enzymes. The patterns of illness look different only to uninitiated eyes.

I wondered what events might have set Marie's enzyme pathways to oxidative flames. She sat on the edge of the chair, leaning forward, holding herself tight, as if to keep herself from falling on the floor. Her neck and upper torso were stiff. Without touching, I knew her neck muscles were hard as brick. Several moments passed. Yet there was no sign of her softening up. We spoke for about half an hour, mostly with my asking questions and her giving short, cryptic answers. She remained suspicious, yielding no significant clues to the onset of her illness. I began to wonder why she had bothered to come see me if she had decided not to open up to me. I ordered some diagnostic tests and said many things to create and sustain some hope for her recovery, but to no avail.

Weeks turned into months, but she showed no sign of improvement. At the Institute, my colleagues and I are blessed with a large group of extraordinarily compassionate, devoted and diligent nurses. They often tell me when a patient doesn't show satisfactory progress following a reasonable period after beginning our programs. More than one nurse told me that something was holding back Marie's recovery. No matter what therapies we tried, we saw no response. Finally, I asked the staff to schedule an extended visit—a long visit when I spend twice as much time as I usually do—for Marie. I had to learn where the block was.

Between held-back tears and loud sobbing, Marie finally told me the story. Several years before falling sick, she had gone through difficult and prolonged divorce proceedings. She won the custody of their only child, a handsome boy she doted on. With time she recovered from the trauma of divorce and for some years had a good life caring for her little boy. There were some superficial relationships along the way. When her son grew older, his American teenage ways began to clash with her European upbringing. Their conflicts grew in intensity and frequency. Along the way she had troubles with her boyfriend. His insensitive demands for sex, even during her health difficulties, bothered her greatly.

Some time later, trouble began between her son and her

boyfriend, which fanned the flames of her anguish. Her son threatened to leave the house on several occasions. Then came the fateful day. The woman and her son argued intensely. The boy used foul language and repeated his threat to leave the house. Holding a basket of laundry, she angrily told him to go ahead and do what he wanted, then walked upstairs. At the top of the stairs, she stopped and looked back. Her son stood at the door, holding his motorcycle helmet in his hands, his eyes blazing with hatred. "I hate you," he yelled. "I hate you too!" she shot back and entered her bedroom.

Several hours later, she received a call from the police asking her to come to the local hospital. The boy died in her arms a few moments after she reached the hospital.

"I wish someone could answer a question for me," she spoke, holding back her tears.
"What?" I asked.
"Before he died I told him I loved him. Do you think he heard that?"
"Yes, I'm sure he did," I replied, choking on my words.

I managed Marie's case the best I could. I tried therapies that I knew worked, and a few I wasn't so sure about. Nothing seemed to make any difference. She diligently took instruction in autoregulation. Sometimes it seemed it might work, but then she reverted back to her punishing thoughts. Every time I mentioned the subject of bereavement support groups, she recoiled and related her unpleasant experiences there. A year later, Marie still showed no signs of improvement. Once, when her sister visited from Europe, it seemed she might get some relief. But that didn't pan out either.

THE THEORY OF SECONDARY GAINS

"Are there any hidden benefits there?" Choua asked, after she left my office one day.

"What do you mean?" I asked, puzzled.

"Why isn't she getting better?"

"What wouldn't I give to find an answer to that question!"

"Are there reasons why she does not want to get better?"

"Are you crazy?" I asked, angrily. "You don't know her story. There is no reason she does not want to get better. Why would she want to suffer so much?"

"It happens."

"Why would anyone not want to get better?"

"Sometimes there are other aspects to cases, aren't there?"

"That's ludicrous! She has no gains from not getting better."

"Why don't you ask her to see a psychiatrist?"

"I would if I thought it might help. She has done that anyway, and doesn't wish to do it again. Her answer is always the same: 'If you don't want to see me, I'll understand. But I've seen enough specialists and I don't want to see any more.'"

"If you were practicing mainstream medicine, it would have been easy on you."

"What do you mean?"

"When everything else fails, there is always the old standby of psychiatric referral."

"What would that do?" I asked. "After many sessions, he

will declare that she isn't getting better because she doesn't want to. He will invoke the theory of secondary gains, claiming that her pretense of sickness is a ploy for attention. No, I don't think I want to refer her to another psychiatrist. She saw one earlier."

"I know you can't," Choua smiled. "I'm just trying to humor you."

Years earlier I'd promised myself never to fall into the "secondary gains" trap—a clever design that many of my colleagues use to dismiss chronically ill patients. The theory proclaims that such patients don't get better because they don't *want* to. Specifically, their disease creates gains that they loathe to give up, hence the persistence of illness. It's a rather elegant theory!

"Why did some psychologist or psychiatrist concoct the theory of secondary gains?" Choua asked.

"Maybe because there are some people who do not want to get better." This time I went along to humor him.

"What could be the possible benefit for someone not wanting to get better?" he shot back.

"I can think of many," I said calmly. "A child may not want to go to school. A man may not want to go to work. It may be too nice a day for work, or inclement weather may entice him to stay at home."

"You really don't believe that, do you?" Choua frowned. "How much difficulty do you have in differentiating such shirkers from people who suffer from disabling chronic symptoms?"

"Okay, you tell me," I yielded. "Why did some psychiatrist or psychologist invent the theory of secondary gain?"

"Very simple, my friend," Choua grinned. "When

chronically sick people don't get better with drugs, you send them packing to psychiatrists. 'Take him away!' you declare with clinical authority. 'If he had a real disease, why didn't our wonder drugs cure him?'"

"There are difficult problems that..."

"You invoke the theory of psychiatric illness to conveniently explain away your failures," Choua interrupted me, then asked, "What should psychiatrists do when the sick don't get better with their talk therapies?"

"What?"

"Psychiatrists also need some elegant theory to explain away their failures, don't they?"

"I don't know what you're talking about," I replied.

"The theory of secondary gain—that's what bails psychiatrists out."

"How so?" I asked, perplexed.

"What could possibly be more elegant than that? That theory puts the blame squarely on the sick person's shoulders. When that doesn't suffice, it puts the blame on his or her parents. Isn't that a neat way to dismiss a patient?"

"You are being facetious, aren't you?" I asked.

Choua didn't answer. I thought about colleagues who often tell me of patients who they think do not want to recover. But why would anyone want to remain sick? I wondered. Why would anyone want to continue to suffer? Why would anyone not want to get better? Why would anyone not want his suffering to abate?

"It is a fascinating concept, isn't it?" Choua resumed with a squint. Then he added, "Some people write about secondary gain, of people who insist they are sick when they really are not. The pretense of sickness, according to this theory, is a ploy to get attention. What do you think?"

"They're tough problems."

"You see women who tell you they were tomboys as teenagers, then grew up to be energetic young women. When they are hit by chemical sensitivity or chronic fatigue, things fall apart at the seams. Explain how she suddenly became so stupid as to not know what is happening to her."

"You have a point," I agreed. "I have never heard a psychologist or psychiatrist chalk up his own suffering to the notion of secondary gain."

"Have you ever heard a physician tell you he suffers from a psychosomatic illness to win attention from others?"

"I don't recall." I resisted laughing at his words.

"You physicians diagnose all kinds of illnesses in your patients and among yourselves when you fall sick. Indeed, indulging in self-diagnosis is a favorite pastime for many of you. Right?"

"Sometimes we do."

"Why don't you ever diagnose a psychosomatic illness for yourselves? What's good for the goose is good for the gander, so why do you deprive yourselves of such benevolence?" Choua chuckled loudly.

NEURALLY MEDIATED HYPOTENSION

Simple observations lead to simple truths. When a physician has the courage to step beyond the narrow limits defined by drug medicine and make simple observations, unmanageable complex issues are reduced to manageable tasks. Meaningless medical jargon gets unmasked and shows itself for what it really is: an empty play on words. Neurally mediated hypotension elicited by a tilt test is a favorite diagnosis for many fatigue experts today. Experts label their patients with this meaningless medical terminology, then continue their business of prescribing steroids, beta blockers and other drugs that destroy the cholinergic part of the brain and muscle functions in the body. Other chronic fatigue experts are fond of diagnoses like *myoneurogastrointestinal disorder and encephalomyopathy* (MNGIE). For fun I might add one other elegant diagnosis: *mitochondrial encephalomyopathy, lactic acidosis and stroke-like episodes* (MELAS). The humor behind such hollow, tongue-twisting names escapes the champions of drug medicine. I fully expect an ongoing proliferation of such bombastic jargon for people who simply suffer from oxidatively damaged enzymes.

Some fatigue experts might jump at me and say, "Aha! Ali really doesn't understand that these are hereditary disorders with gene point mutations at position 3243 in mitochondrial DNA or gene rearrangements in other locations." Yes, I agree there are point mutations and gene rearrangements. But where do we suppose those types of gene injuries come from? It all comes back to oxidative injury to enzymes that normally repair damaged DNA molecules.

I knew what Marie's problem was. Her agony had exceeded the human limits of tolerance. When she consulted me, I knew she hoped I might be able to make some brilliant diagnosis that had eluded the other physicians she consulted. I continue to see human canaries like Marie who search for rare diagnoses. With the right diagnosis, they fervently hope their anguish can be mitigated. But that's not how it works. There are no drugs—and there will never be any, I am confident that will rejuvenate oxidatively injured enzymes in days or weeks. What is required is deeper, much deeper spiritual work. But sometimes the sufferer is caught in a classical catch 22: Unbearable suffering blocks the way to spiritual growth. And without the spiritual dimension, healing is simply not possible in cases like hers.

****

Truly man is the king of beasts, for his cruelty exceeds them. We live by the death of others.

Leonardo da Vinci

What did the German philosopher, Friedrich Nietzsche, know about women?

When a woman has scholarly inclination there is generally something wrong with her sexual nature.

Beyond Good and Evil

Did Nietzsche even bother to ask what women thought of his philosophy of womanhood? I wonder.

Chapter 4

The Buffalo and Limits of Suffering

No one knows enough to be pessimistic, Norman Cousins wrote. Maybe he was right. But one thing I do know is that there are absolute limits to an animal's ability to endure and a human's capacity for suffering. Beyond that everyone breaks down. Clever thinking is of little help then. And the spiritual dimensions that may keep people from reaching that point of tolerance are not easy to achieve.

A patient related his problems to me as follows:

"Doc, maybe you can explain this. I hire this young woman for office work. She turns out to be very, very good. She learns fast and works efficiently. I'm impressed. I give her some additional assignments and she handles them well. I give her a good raise. She seems to love her job. I offer her a quick promotion and make her a manager. She accepts the new responsibilities with flying colors. I'm more impressed. I often have to be away from my business and need a reliable assistant. So I give her another promotion and another handsome raise. In less than twelve months, I triple her salary.

"Then she begins to come to work distraught. Still, she does her work well. I learn she is having trouble at home. Soon her husband files for divorce. She begins to fall apart. I support her as much as I can. I give her time off to recover. She returns and looks tired. She asks that her hours be reduced. I agree, reduce her responsibilities, yet don't cut her salary. I hope she will fight back and return to her old self. I try to remember how good she once was and bend over backwards to accommodate her. Then I hear she suffers from chronic fatigue. She begins to slip up and leave simple tasks undone, without bothering to tell me. I don't take care of them because I don't know what is being left unattended. I talk to her sometimes about the problems in my business. She acknowledges that things are falling apart and assures me that she will get a handle on things.

"Next, I learn that some checks are missing. One day I enter her office and find old uncashed checks on the floor. As this happens, some payroll checks bounce. I counsel her again. Again she acknowledges her serious mishandling of funds and assures me the problems won't recur. But there's no end to it. Then, another staff member tells me the young woman begins to have interminable meetings with her subordinates, who are always complaining about something. There is no discipline in the place when I'm away. I speak to her and give her a serious warning.

"Now something else happens. She begins to arrive late and leave work early. Next thing, no one at the office knows where she is when she's supposed to be at work. Doc, I have to run a business. I don't want to fire her, but it looks as if she has a death wish. What can I do, Doc? What would you have done?"

Naturalists insist that anthropomorphism —the attribution of human form, characteristics, motivation or behavior to inanimate objects and animals—is bad science. Perhaps they took their lesson from novelists who sometimes express similar beliefs.

The one thing that distinguishes man from the rest of the animal kingdom is his capacity to suffer.

Dostoyevsky

Dostoyevsky's words bring to mind a piece about the limits of suffering written in *The Serengeti Lion* by George B. Schaller, Director for Science at Wildlife Conservation International, a division of the New York Zoological Society. Schaller described the suffering of a cape buffalo bull as follows:

> *At 0800 I find 14 lions of the Magadi pride at the edge of a marshy area about 20m (meters) from a bull buffalo standing up to his belly in mud and water. Deep lacerations cover his muzzle and rump, his hocks are shredded, and his shoulders are full of bites, all the result of an earlier attack this morning. He faces the lions and grunts each time one moves...*

Schaller continued his observation of the scene for one and one-half hour when he observed five nomadic males arrived at the marshy area and chased the lions of the Magdi pride away. Then the newcomers returned to the wounded buffalo, sat 6 to 10 meters from him and resumed the watch. The buffalo stared back at the lions.

Schaller relates what he observed next:

*Fifteen minutes later he walks slowly toward
the lions, a suicidal gesture. One male grabs
his rump, another places a paw over his
back and bites his shoulder. The buffalo
sinks to its knees. A lion then clambers up
on the lower back of the animal, bites him
there and leans to one side as if attempting
to turn him over. Meanwhile, the other lion
first licks blood off the old wound on his
shoulder, then bites there again. The buffalo
bellows, yet makes no attempt to defend
himself...One lion eats the bull's testicles.
After 10 minutes, at 1040, the buffalo dies.*

*Fifteen minutes later he walks slowly toward the lions, a
suicidal gesture!* Was it a gesture? Or did the bull know his
limits of suffering had been exceeded?

Helen Keller observed that the world is full of suffering,
and that it is also full of the overcoming of it. True, but up to
a point.

Your pain is the breaking of the shell that enacloses your understanding.

Kahlil Gibran

Chapter 5

Of
Death

and
Dying

At Lake Baringo—the northernmost section of the big Rift Valley lakes in Kenya—we went for a walk by the lake shore and saw several hippos in the water. The hippos, mostly aggregates of bulbous, bulging eyes, wriggled their piglike ears and snorted through their nostrils. Every now and then, one would yawn with gaping jaws, displaying protuberant, pink flesh in the mouth and gnashing tusks. The hippos looked amiable and acknowledged our presence with occasional friendly looks, or so it seemed to me.

Earlier that evening, a staff member at the Lake Baringo Lodge had cautioned us against being friendly with hippos. He told us about the death of a gardener several months earlier. While watering the shrubs on the lodge grounds, the unfortunate gardener inadvertently approached a calf. The hippo mother misunderstood his intentions, became furious and charged. The poor gardener couldn't outrun the hippo. He was simply run over, then trampled to death by the angry hippo mother.

After telling us this ghastly story, the staff member informed us about the lodge custom of waking the guests at night to view hippos when the beasts come out of the water to graze on the lodge grounds. Later that night, we did get the hippo call. Accompanied by the lodge guard, we quietly walked to the enclosed patio for viewing hippos who grazed on the grounds close to the patio. Even in the safety of the walled patio and close company of armed guards, the globular monsters were intimidating. Silently, we watched them in awe, remembering the gardener's death.

Next morning, Sarah arranged for a boat ride so that we could see the hippos up close in the water. Lolling in shallows, the hippos were placid creatures. Like elephants, hippos practice voluntary birth control when they are out of balance with the environment, we were told. How do they go about that? I wondered. I viewed a large hippo congregation and tried to figure out who might be the top honcho.

Sometime later, I read the following passage:

"When I was collecting in West Africa we once camped on the banks of a river in which lived a hippo herd of moderate size. They seemed a placid and happy group...

But one night, just as it was growing dark, they launched into a series of roars and brays which sounded like a choir of demented donkeys...I decided to go down and see...I sat on that sandbank for two hours, watching these great roly-poly creatures churning up the water and sand as they duelled in the shallows. As far as I could see, the old male was getting the worst of it, and I felt sorry for him. Like some once-great pugilist who had now grown flabby and stiff, he seemed to be fighting a battle which he knew was already lost. The young male, lighter and more agile, seemed

*to dodge him every time, and his teeth
always managed to find their mark in the
shoulder or neck of the old male. In the
background the females watched with
semaphoring ears, occasionally breaking into
a lugubrious chorus...since the fight did not
seem as if it would end for several more
hours, I paddled home to the village...*

*I woke just as the horizon was paling into
dawn and the hippos were quiet. I hoped
that the old male won, but I very much
doubted it...*

*The corpse of the old male...was about two
miles downstream...I went down to examine
it and was horrified at the havoc the young
male's teeth had wrought on the massive
body. The shoulders, the neck, the great
dewlaps that hung under the chin, the flanks
and the belly; all were ripped and tattered,
and the shallows around the carcass were
still tinged with blood.*

Gerald Durrel
Encounters with Animals

Death enlightens in ways life does not. Revelations brought by death, however, are not always enhancing.

I recall many instances when some family members arrived at the hospital after being told of a kin's imminent death. It was evident from their conversations that they hadn't seen nor had cared for the sick person in any sense in years. Yet, the fact that he might die any minute made them intensely interested in the process. Utterly disinterested in the sick man during life, they demanded to be fully informed about minute details of the illness. What clearly intrigued them was the opportunity to witness a death. The life of the sick man wasn't relevant, his dying was.

Durrell's description of the death of an old hippo reminded me of the story of a dying man, related to me by one of my patients —a gentle, sensitive single woman in her forties. Her mother had died many years earlier and she had lived most of her life with her father, whose company she treasured. Some years earlier, she had asked me to look at her dad's colon biopsy that showed a cancer which, as I discovered the next day, had already spread to other organs. Her father's condition deteriorated rapidly. After some initial response, her brothers and sisters flew from different parts of the country to be with him. She told them that she didn't want to live in her father's house after he died and that they should plan on selling the house. She also told them she needed some money to pay for the medical and other unpaid bills. Everyone was most supportive of her. Her siblings understood that each of them would inherit a sizeable sum of money from the sale of the house.

Then a strange thing happened. Her father's condition improved dramatically and the threat of his imminent death disappeared. She felt relieved. Then a major new problem arose: how to pay the accumulated medical bills and plan for the substantial and additional ongoing costs of his care.

"Everything changed," she spoke ruefully. "All of sudden everyone had to return to their jobs and families. All of a sudden I was left alone —without any support for my ailing dad, without any money to pay the bills, without any emotional support. And that wasn't the worst part."

"What was the worst part?" I asked sympathetically.

"Dad understood all. A few days earlier, he seemed so lively with all his children around, so happy, so hopeful. Then he was shattered, his life sapped out of him. I felt abandoned, and he knew that too. I couldn't even pretend I was in control as I'd done while he was deteriorating. It was awful! I didn't know dying could be that awful," she broke down and sobbed.

****

The ancients knew how to pay homage to death, for death is worthy of homage, as the cradle of life, as the womb of palingenesis. Severed from life, it becomes a specter, a distortion, and worse.

Thomas Mann
The Magic Mountain

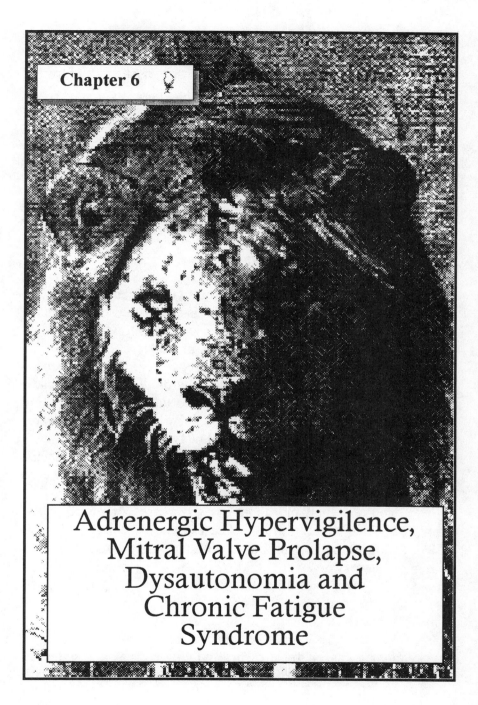

Chapter 6

Adrenergic Hypervigilence,
Mitral Valve Prolapse,
Dysautonomia and
Chronic Fatigue
Syndrome

"Why do doctors prescribe beta blockers?" Choua asked.

"For lots of reasons," I replied.

"Name some."

"For high blood pressure, heart palpitations and coronary heart disease."

"What else?"

"For migraines. Sometimes they're used for anxiety and panic attacks."

"What else?"

"For mitral valve prolapse."

"What's that?"

"The mitral valve separates the two chambers on the left side of the heart. The lower chamber is called the left ventricle, and the upper chamber is called the left atrium. When the left ventricle contracts, the mitral valve prevents a back flow of blood into the left atrium. A prolapsed valve is a weakened valve that fails to close the opening it guards. This allows a back flow of blood. The real cases are due to damage to the mitral valve caused by inflammation of the valve in rheumatic fever."

"How do you diagnose mitral valve prolapse?"

"Clinically, you can hear a clicking sound in the heart with a stethoscope. You can get a picture of the mitral valve with an echocardiogram."

"You're telling me about the *real* cases of mitral valve prolapse. What about the *unreal* cases?" he asked.

"Well, there's a problem with this diagnosis. A lot of young women who were told that they have mitral valve prolapse by their cardiologists and internists. But, it's a false diagnosis. The real problem is some where else."

"Where?" Choua raised his eyebrows.

"What such women really suffer from is adrenergic hypervigilence caused by stressors in their internal and external environments. Their hearts are relentlessly overdriven by sugar-insulin-adrenaline-neurotransmitter   roller coasters. Predictably, their mitral valve come under adrenergic stress. When an echocardiogram is done on these patients, the stress on the mitral valve shows up as mild stretching of the valve flaps. Of course, cardiologist are eager to diagnose the echocardiographic stress on the valve as mitral valve prolapse."

"Are you saying there is nothing wrong with the valve in such conditions?" he asked, frowning.

"Yes. The valve itself is not damaged or diseased. Rather, it flaps a little when the heart is overdriven."

"Like a flag that flutters in wind?" he asked.

"Not a bad analogy, Choua," I replied. "Indeed, what cardiologists diagnose as mitral valve prolapse is, in reality, a functional —and temporary —change in valve function."

SYMPTOMS OF MITRAL VALVE PROLAPSE

"What are the symptoms of mitral valve prolapse?"
"Not all patients suffer from symptoms."
"How many of them do suffer any symptoms?"
"One mitral valve expert published the following figures: mild symptoms, 25%; moderate symptoms, 14%; and severe symptoms, 1%."
"What are the symptoms of those who do suffer?"
"Fatigue, shakiness, jitteryness and anxiety."
"What else?"
"Sleep difficulties."
"What else?"
"Headache and panic attacks."
"And?"

"PMS."

"And?"

"Some patients complain of chest tightness, even pain."

"And?"

"Low blood pressure, especially after standing suddenly from a lying position."

"Aren't those also the symptoms of neurasthenia?" he frowned.

"Yes, they are," I confessed.

"And of dysautonomia?"

"Yes, that too."

"Interesting. Isn't that also the symptom-complex of anxiety neurosis?"

"Yes, it is."

"And of Civil War soldiers who were given the diagnostic label of *soldier's heart*?"

"You're right there too."

"And, of course, of chronic fatigue syndrome?"

"Yes."

"Tell me, how do you clinically differentiate mitral valve prolapse from all those other syndromes?"

"We can't."

"If echocardiograms were performed on people with those disorders, would they have been diagnosed with mitral valve prolapse?"

"I'm afraid so."

"Fascinating stuff, isn't it? The diagnostic labels change, but the symptoms don't. If the patient first consults a neurologist, he gets diagnosed with neurasthenia. If he goes to a rheumatologist, he's labeled with fibromyalgia."

"That does happen," I confessed.

"If he goes to a primary care physician, he's labeled with chronic Epstein Barr syndrome."

"That's a problem too."

"What happens when he sees a clinical ecologist?" he asked.

"He's diagnosed with chemical sensitivity syndrome."

"And if he sees a naturopath?"

"Chronic candidiasis syndrome."

"And what if he consults an infectious disease specialist?"

"Possibly Lyme disease."

"Even if the Lyme antibody tests are negative?"

"Yes, that's an amazing thing. I often see patients who were administered long-term intravenous and oral antibiotics for suspicion of Lyme disease even when repeated tests for Lyme antibodies were negative."

"What do you think of that?"

"I think that's can be a dangerous mistake. Indeed, I have seen patients who were suffered crippling chronic fatigue before their Lyme experts were finished with their multiple courses of broad-spectrum antibiotics."

"Crimes of Lyme, eh?"

"You're not far off the mark there, Choua."

"Isn't it tragic what those Lyme experts do to their unsuspecting and gullible patients??"

"Well, that's..."

"Tell me what happens when the patients is a child?" he cut me off. "What diagnostic label do pediatricians use for children with such a symptom-complex?"

"Usually it's hyperactivity syndrome."

"And with a school psychologist?"

"Attention deficit disorder."

"And if he goes to an internist?"

"Chronic fatigue syndrome."

"And what would be his fate with a cardiologist?"

"Mitral valve prolapse."

"Wow! That's fascinating stuff! Do you think people recognize that their choice of health professional determines how they're labeled?" Choua asked with a chuckle.

"I don't think so. I'm told that some patients are doctor-shoppers. Maybe some of them finally figure it out."

Choua laughed out loud, then fell silent. I didn't realize how amusing our conversation was until we were quiet and I reflected on the words. Perhaps there were some exaggerated nuances, but the essential issue was clear: The diagnostic labels we physicians choose are based on our narrow, reductionistic training. Choua's flurry of questions had crystallized something that I had only vaguely seen before.

"Now, tell me, how is the mitral valve weakened so that the person develops a mitral valve prolapse?" Choua resumed.

"The real cases are caused by rheumatic heart disease that damages the mitral valve," I explained. "Blood clots on the surface of the damaged valve and forms irregular knob-like protrusions called vegetations. Sometimes these vegetations break off, clogging up arteries in the brain and causing strokes."

"Yes, those are serious problems. Fortunately, they're quite rare now."

DRUGS FOR MITRAL VALVE

"You said doctors prescribe beta blocker drugs for mitral valve prolapse. Why do they do that?"

"I guess because it helps the patient."

"You guess?" he grimaced.

"I never use beta blockers for mitral valve prolapse, but I know most cardiologists do use it."

"Why?"

"To slow the heart rate."

"Aha!" Choua became animated. "Are you saying mitral valve prolapse is a disease that can be cured by slowing the heart rate?"

"No. Yes, well, it isn't that..."

"Simple!" Choua flashed a smile. "But it is that simple, isn't it?" He winked mischievously, then continued. "I mean a heart disease that can be cured by simply slowing the heart rate cannot be a *real* disease. Now that's not too complicated to understand, is it? Isn't that what you meant when you made the distinction between a real and unreal mitral valve prolapse?"

"Yes," I confessed.

"Why do you use antibiotics for patients with mitral valve prolapse?"

"I never use antibiotics for mitral valve prolapse unless I know for certain that it is real and was caused by rheumatic heart disease."

"But others do, don't they?" Choua asked.

"Yes, but that's an awful mistake in my view," I replied.

"Why?"

"Because antibiotics are completely unnecessary for the common type of mitral valve prolapse seen in young people without a history of rheumatic fever."

"If that's so, why do doctors prescribe tons of antibiotics for people with mitral valve prolapse?" he frowned.

"They think the mitral valve in prolapse is vulnerable to infection during various types of surgical procedures and dental work. Their putative reason for antibiotic use is to prevent such infection. But in such cases antibiotics only damage the delicate bowel ecosystem and do nothing to protect the heart valve."

"Interesting. Tell me how do beta blocker drugs work?"

"Beta blockers do what their name says: They block beta receptors."

"Why would you want to block beta receptors in mitral valve prolapse?" he went on.

"Well, I don't think it's good to block beta receptors so I don't. I guess those who use it do so to slow the heart rate. That's what beta blockers do."

"What are beta receptors?"

"They're molecules on cell membranes that bind adrenaline and its cousin molecules, catecholamines. In other words, beta receptors are docking sites on the cell surface for adrenaline and other members of this family of molecules."

"Sort of fishing hooks for adrenergic molecules floating in the tissue fluid that bathes the cells."

"Right. Once bound to the cell membrane, adrenaline and related messenger molecules initiate and propagate a host of reactions at the cell membrane as well as within cells. There are two main types of adrenergic receptors: alpha and beta types. Each type has two subtypes: $alpha_1$, $alpha_2$, $beta_1$ and $beta_2$. Stimulation of $alpha_1$ causes the arteries to tighten and the heart muscle to contract; stimulation of $alpha_2$, by contrast, tightens arteries but inhibits the heart. Stimulation of $beta_1$ receptors speeds the heart rate, and stimulation of $beta_2$ receptors causes the opening of the tiny arterioles and bronchial tubes."

"Interesting! So, there are many balancing acts within this system of cell membrane receptors," he added.

"Yes." I agreed. "Adrenaline stimulates all four types of receptors. There are dose-related differences between these receptors, however. For example, with small doses of adrenaline, the beta effects predominate and speed the heart rate but lower the blood pressure by reducing the muscle tone in arteries."

"That makes the checks and balances in autonomic receptors even more interesting, doesn't it?"

"Yes, it does. At higher doses, adrenaline stimulates the alpha receptors to a greater degree, which then raises the blood pressure."

"Since drug metabolism in the body is affected by many variables, how does a doctor know when the drug dose is *lower* or *higher* in a given patient at a given time?" Choua asked, puzzled.

"Precisely! That's the problem. It's often very difficult in any given clinical situation to gauge the sum total of all drug effects."

"Especially when most cardiologists have no understanding of the sugar-insulin-adrenaline roller coasters that their patients live in. Right?"

"Well, that does add to the problems of cardiologists." I admitted.

"Is that why you don't use beta blockers for patients with mitral valve prolapse?"

"Partly, yes."

"If beta blockers help patients by slowing the heart rate, why not simply teach the patient how to slow the heart rate with slow breathing and other meditative techniques?" Choua chuckled.

"It's not that easy in real life," I explained.

"But it is easy to write prescriptions in real life? Is that it?" he scowled.

"Self-regulation requires patient work, and many patients are not prepared for that," I countered.

"Get real!" Choua erupted. "How many cardiologists do you know who are familiar with the potential benefits of self-regulation?"

"There are some," I replied, recovering from his sudden onslaught and holding my ground.

"When the cardiologist tells his patient he has mitral valve prolapse, do you think the patient realizes that the diagnostic label is a sham—an artifact created by an echocardiogram? Do you have any idea what the diagnosis of a heart disease does to a lay person?"

"Those are difficult..."

"First you shock the patient with a phony diagnosis," he cut me off rudely, "then you push a pill. And then you expect the patient to suddenly become enlightened enough to turn down the prescription. Get real, will you?"

We were quiet for a while. I recalled the limp of the patriarch lion along the Mara River and decided to tease Choua.

"How often do lions suffer from mitral valve prolapse?"

"They would suffer frequently if there were echocardiogram clinics in the Serengeti Plains, and if there were reimbursement codes for lion cardiologists," he smirked.

"You're a rascal," I chastised him.

"A lion's heart must flutter frantically to support his ballistic charge during a hunt, right?"

"Probably."

"And if you were to run an echocardiogram, I'm sure many lions would show mitral valve prolapse."

"Probably."

"And if cardiologists were to be reimbursed for such services, no doubt they would diagnose, and treat the mitral valve prolapse with beta blockers, such as Inderal, Lopressor, Tenormin, Corgard and God knows what else. Right?" Choua chimed.

"Only your squinted mind would distort things like that," I replied, suppressing a smile.

"Tell me, why do you use calcium channel blocking drugs for mitral valve prolapse?"

"Didn't I tell you I don't use any drugs for mitral valve prolapse?" I replied, irritated.

"Okay, tell me, why do doctors use calcium channel blockers for this problem?"

"Probably because they help the patients."

"How?"

"By slowing down the speeded up heart."

"Back to slowing the heart rate again, eh?" he grinned.

"Didn't I tell explain that mitral valve prolapse is caused by an overdriven heart?" I asked testily.

"So you use Calan, Cardizem, Isoptin, Procardia and other calcium channel blockers?"

"I don't, although I know that most cardiologists do."

"And why not?" he asked, brimming with sarcasm. "Why not reward the makers of calcium channel blocking drugs? Don't they buy cardiologists and internists doughnuts, cupcakes and coffee for their meetings?"

"That's going too far," I reprimanded.

"What do calcium channel blockers do?" he changed the subject.

"Obviously they block calcium channels."

"Why did Nature create calcium channels in cell membranes?"

"Obviously to facilitate the flow of calcium through the cell membrane —in and out of the cells."

"Why do cardiologists want to block calcium channels in mitral valve prolapse?"

"For the same reason they use beta blockers—to slow the heart rate."

"What happens when you use drugs to block essential healing mechanisms?"

"Then they don't work as well."

"Why?"

"Because the cell membrane receptors and channels become resistant to the drugs."

"Why?"

"Because molecules at the receptors and channels find other ways to do their job."

"Interesting! That's interesting." He shook his head excitedly. "So, do you think those receptors *know* they have jobs to perform even when you block them? Do they figure out how to dodge the drugs used for blocking them?"

"That's an anthropomorphic viewpoint, Choua. And you can do better than that," I counseled. "Assigning human characteristics to molecules is not good science."

"How awkward of me," he posited with sarcasm. "Tell me what other drugs do you use for mitral valve prolapse?"

"Some doctors use antimigraine drugs like Cafegot, Ergostat, Sansert and Wigraine," I replied, ignoring his sarcasm.

"How do those drugs work?"

"Probably the same way. They open tightened arteries —they're vasodilators."

"The end result is the same, isn't it? The heart rate slows down and mitral valve prolapse is cured."

"I don't know if anyone should use the word 'cure' for that," I disagreed.

"Why do you use antianxiety drugs for valve prolapse?"

"I usually don't, but I know some doctors use anxiolytic drugs such as Ativan, Librium, Klonopin, Tranzene, Valium and Xanax for symptomatic relief."

"Why?"

"Evidently because they reduce anxiety and stress."

"How does reducing anxiety cure mitral valve prolapse?"

"Didn't I tell you no drugs cure mitral valve prolapse? Antianxiety drugs relief the symptoms of mitral valve prolapse as they..."

"Relief of symptoms of all other disorders," Choua completed my sentence. "Though we know that happens only for a short time."

"Why do you use antidepressants?" he asked, then hastily added, "I mean why do other doctors use antidepressants like Prozac, Paxil, Zoloft, Serzone and others."

"For the same reason—to relieve symptoms."

"Those doctors must think mitral valve prolapse is caused by depression, otherwise..."

"Not necessarily. Depression is often associated with anxiety, and that can cause the valve to prolapse," I explained.

"Is that a good idea? I mean to use antidepressants to slow the heart?"

"You know my view on that."

"I suppose when you numb a person with mind-numbing drugs, his heart is numbed as well," he mumbled and looked away.

I didn't respond.

ADRENERGIC HYPERVIGILENCE AND DYSAUTONOMIA

"You keep telling me you don't use drugs for mitral valve prolapse. So what else do you do?" Choua asked after a while.

"I look for the elements that overdrive the heart and

stress the mitral valve. Then I address those biochemical issues
so the troubled heart settles down," I replied.

"What issues?"

"Issues of autonomic hypervigilence."

"What is autonomic hypervigilence?"

"The nervous system has two major parts: One is a
somatic nervous system that is under our voluntary control. We
use this part for performing simple tasks, like lifting a glass of
water and drinking. The second part is an autonomic nervous
system that is not under our voluntary control. This system of
nerve cells—neurones, as they are called—and nerve fibers
regulate the heartbeat and activity of other body organs that are
considered beyond voluntary control. When..."

"What causes autonomic hypervigilence?" he cut me off
impatiently.

"Anything that relentlessly pushes the adrenal glands and
brings about adrenaline blasts. Such adrenergic hyperactivity is
then balanced by cholinergic hypervigilence."

"But one type of molecular hypervigilence in biology is
never truly balanced by another compensatory type of
hypervigilence, is it?" Choua's eyes narrowed. "No two storms
ever balance and neutralize each other, do they?"

"No, they don't," I agreed. "Balancing acts in biology are
reciprocal but subtle. We can't really expect adrenergic storms
to exactly counterbalance those arising from cholinergic nerves."

"What happens when adrenergic hypervigilence evokes
cholinergic responses that overshoot their mark?"

"Dysautonomia —a major turbulence."

"What does the word dysautonomia mean?"

"Autonomic refers to the autonomic nervous system and
the prefix 'dys' means dysfunction. So, literally dysautonomia
means functional derangements of the autonomic nervous
system."

"What are the symptoms of patients who suffer dysautonomia?"

"The same as those of mitral valve."

"Are you saying mitral valve prolapse is dysautonomia?" His eyes narrowed.

"Yes. Many people use the two terms interchangeably."

"Do you agree with that?"

"No. I think there is more to dysautonomia than that."

"What?" he pressed.

"In dysautonomia, I'm sure, the autonomic receptor molecules are injured."

"How?"

"By environmental pollutants."

"What kind?"

"The most dangerous are pesticides."

"Oh yes," he wrinkled his forehead. "That's entirely predictable, isn't it? After all, pesticides are designed to kill insects by poisoning the enzymes of their autonomic nervous system. The choline esterase of insects, for example, is identical to human choline esterase. It's essential for breathing. Right?"

"Right."

"Is that why so many young people have cold hands and feet, and when you take their body temperature it's usually a degree or two lower than normal?"

"Right again."

"You teach your patients stress control and call that autoregulation. Where did that term come from?"

"I once called it autonomic regulation. We abbreviated the term to autoregulation, then to autoreg."

"So you believe the autonomic nervous system can be regulated, do you? After all it isn't beyond human voluntary control, is it?" Choua winked.

"I won't go that far," I replied. "I think the autonomic

nervous system regulates itself if it is allowed to revert back to its natural balancing acts," I elaborated.

"Ah! I get it now. The autonomic system autoregulates when the thinking mind—your cortical monkey—is kept off its back. Right?"

"Now you've got that right," I laughed.

"Right." He smiled knowingly. "Now, tell me, what other elements cause autonomic hypervigilence?" he asked.

"Sugar-insulin-adrenaline roller coasters, and those of neurotransmitter turbulence," I answered.

"And?"

"Food incompatibilities, chemical sensitivities, and mold allergy."

"And?"

"And?"

"And stress of sad thoughts, such as recycled past misery and..."

"Feared future misery, right?" he completed my sentence.

"Yes, that too," I agreed.

"The oxidative fireworks, your Fourth-of-July chemistry, the whole ball of wax," Choua laughed.

"Yes, yes," I said, irritated by his unending questions.

"Does the nondrug approach work?"

"Of course, it does. Why else would we do those things if they didn't work?"

"Why don't internists and cardiologists use any of those nondrug approaches?"

"I don't know."

"*You* don't!" he pouted, stared at me for several moments, then beamed knowingly. "Because none of them understands clinical nutrition or clinical ecology. If they don't prescribe drugs to slow down a racing heart, they won't know what else to do, right?"

"You're a rascal," I rebuked him.

"I'm a rascal?" he groused, then his face softened and he asked, "Where does physical exercise fit into your scheme of things?"

"Slow, sustained exercise fits everywhere," I replied. "That's the only way anyone can keep his fat-burning enzymes up-regulated. And..."

"No one can keep a heart healthy without up-regulated fat-burning enzymes." Choua interrupted me, the asked, "Right?"

"Right." I laughed at his impetuousness.

ANTIBIOTICS FOR MITRAL VALVE PROLAPSE

"Why do you use antibiotics for mitral valve prolapse?" Choua asked.

"I don't," I replied emphatically. "Unless there is clear evidence of structural damage to the mitral valve caused by rheumatic heart valve disease or other uncommon diseases that damage the valve structure."

"Do other doctors use them?"

"Yes."

"Why y

"Good! Tell me, why do other doctors use antibiotics?"

"To prevent the development of superimposed bacterial endocarditis during periods of high risk."

"What are those periods of high risk?" he groused.

"Dental procedures, tonsillectomy, adenoidectomy, bronchoscopy."

"What else?"

"Surgery of the respiratory tract."

"And?"

"Incision and the drainage of abscesses."

"And?"

"Gastrointestinal surgery."

"And?"

"Gynecologic and urinary surgery."

"And?"

"Brain surgery."

"Why don't you say all kinds of surgery? Why make such a long list of operations that increase the risk of infecting the mitral valve in mitral valve prolapse?"

"You're right," I confessed. "Those who prescribe antibiotics for mitral valve prolapse do so regardless of the type of surgery."

"Do you think any of that is necessary?"

"Didn't I tell you I don't prescribe antibiotics for my patients who have mitral valve prolapse and require surgery?" I asked, irritated.

"Why?"

"Because the mitral valve prolapse that I commonly see in my patients isn't structurally damaged. That's the whole problem. Why would I use drugs to calm down the heart and protect the valve from unnecessary turbulence when I can do that with autoregulation and nutritional and herbal therapies?"

"Huh!" Choua chuckled. "Why don't cardiologists and internists do that?"

"I don't know. I don't know," I nearly yelled, exasperated.

Choua stiffened, looked at me with baffled eyes for several moments, then turned his face away.

LIONS AND BETA BLOCKADE

"Is the chemistry of the predator different from that of the prey?" he resumed.

"It should be different," I replied.

"Why?"

"Because the flight of the prey is for saving its life while the predator merely sprints for a meal. The predator clearly doesn't suffer from the fear of death that consumes the prey."

"When a lion attacks an impala, do you think he knows the distinction between the chemistry of the hunter and that of the hunted?"

"Probably, at some level."

"When an impala flees the lion, do you think he intellectualizes about the chemistry of fear?"

"Probably not." I suppressed a smile. "But I don't know if impalas intellectualize about anything."

"Do you think a lion in the midst of his fast, flat gallop thinks about the chemistry of his state?" Choua pressed.

"Maybe. Well, I really don't know."

"So fear doesn't drive either of them once the life-and-death dance begins, does?"

"I still think it does," I held my ground. "Just because a fleeing impala doesn't express fear in terms that we understand, it doesn't mean the fear of death won't change his chemistry."

"The adrenaline blasts of the impala and the lion are the same—the adrenal glands in both flush out—releasing all their adrenaline. Their adrenergic hypervigilence in both is identical.

In those moments, the cat is but a zooming pulse of killing energy. The impala is mere leaping energy. The adrenergic blasts in both are..."

"Oxidative explosions, igniting the chemistry in both," I completed the sentence.

"Yeah," Choua grinned. "That's it. Oxidative explosions ignite the enzyme fireworks. Adrenaline is one of the most powerful, if not the most potent, oxidizing molecule in biology. Adrenaline blasts set off a frenzy of oxyradicals; turning, twisting and bumping into each other, triggering oxidant chain reactions and lacerating and mutilating other molecules. It evokes powerful cholinergic responses and revs up neurotransmitters, firing up the neurones and muscles."

"Not a bad description of the fight-or-flight response."

"The lion's lips curl, baring his fangs," he continued, ignoring my comment, "His mouth froths and pupils widen. The cat in those moments is a mass of killing energy, the impala a speck disappearing in dust. There is no room for analysis, no attempt to understand —just the lion's destructive energy and the impala's quest for escape. There is the Fourth-of-July chemistry in both."

"And if we were to run a echocardiogram, lions in their charges will also show mitral valve prolapse. Is that it?"

"And if you block their beta receptors, they will turn into zombies just as people do," I chided.

"Not too far off the mark," he grinned.

LIFE IS A CONTINUUM

"What about dopamine activity? While we're at it, we

might include that in your poetry of chemistry?" I teased. "What about the activity in the mesocortex? And that of nerve cells in the frontal cortex of the brain that produce dopamine? Why should we leave them out while we're at it?" I provoked him.

"As far as the chemistry of fireworks is concerned," he frowned, "a lion's brain is not much different from that of a human, nor is the mesocortex of an impala different from that of a lamb."

"And hypothalamic-pituitary-adrenal axis activity?"

"The same."

"And endorphin and other opiate production?"

"Why should they be any different?" Choua's eyes narrowed. "Perceptions of danger in man and lion evolved over eons. The basic cortical and limbic structures are the same in both. That premise holds for their functions as well."

"What about the chemistry of stress in the impala?"

"You don't understand, do you?" he showed irritation. "The same! It's all the same! It doesn't much matter whether adrenergic hypervigilence is triggered by a desire for a hamburger in one species or by the need to avoid becoming a hamburger in another. It's all the same."

"Do animals suffer from post traumatic stress syndrome, as people do after intense war experiences?" I asked.

"What do you think?" he scowled.

"Do animals suffer from fear-potentiated neurosis?" I ignored his ill temper. "I mean the type that stress experts talk about? Do animals have neurochemical information systems for the regulation of neurotransmitters as humans do? I mean the mediators that orchestrate activities of steroids, adrenaline, serotonin, dopamine, GABA and others?"

"Didn't I just tell you that humans share neurochemistry evolution with other living beings? It's all one and the same thing. Like a kaleidoscope, everything is related to everything else. Each molecular piece relates to every other piece, although some inter-relationships may not be as transparent as others."

"But, wait," I countered. "That's not what stress experts teach us. They insist that the chemistry of fear and anxiety is quite distinct from that of fight-or-flight readiness. They rigidly differentiate fear conditioning from the encoding of traumatic memories."

"Ah! Those stress experts," he waved his arm contemptuously. "Don't I know. They thrive on classifications."

"The stress experts hold that combat fatigue and war neuroses are discrete diagnoses. They are obsessed with notions of long-term potentiation in amygdala in brain. They are infatuated with ideas of encoding of traumatic memories. They're..."

"But, wait!" I interrupted. "What's wrong with the concept that impulses are generated in the encoded nerve cells that create disturbing war images—the so-called post traumatic stress syndrome. You know what I mean, don't you?"

"Its all the same, isn't it?" he asked with a disarming smile.

"No, it isn't," I protested vigorously. "You can't have the same neurochemical machinery elicit so many different biochemical responses! Things in real life are not that simple. Fear conditioning is not the same as experiential extinction nor is it the same as behavioral sensitization. And experiential extinctions are thought to be distinct from behavioral sensitization. All those conditions cannot simply be parts of your simple plan of neurochemistry."

"Oh, no?" Choua tilted his neck and stared at me. "

We were quiet for several minutes.

"Life is a continuum, a seamless mosaic," he resumed after a few moments. "In biology, if you change one thing in one way, you change everything in some way. Remember, you wrote that."

"I *know* I wrote that." I controlled my irritation. "But you can't disregard all the ideas of stress physiology that have evolved over decades of intensive research. Even now, geneticists describe genes that are activated by chronic stress and illustrate how such activated genes change neurochemistry patterns."

"I have no doubt we will see an avalanche of stress gene experts now that public funds are available for that research. But that's not what we're talking about. I'm talking about the continuum of life—the essential molecular relatedness in biology. Didn't you just tell me adrenergic impulses are balanced by opposing cholinergic responses and vice versa?"

"Yes, but..."

"But what?" he interrupted me. "I'm asking you a simple question about whether or not the chemistry of a charging lion differs from that of a fleeing impala."

"Are you saying that the human stress research findings are not valuable?" I asked, utterly confused.

"No, I'm not saying that at all." Choua suddenly broke into an impish laugh.

"Then, I'm afraid I don't follow you. I'm confused," I complained.

"The chemistry of a lion's charge and an impala's escape is true to life. It isn't the same as that of rats that are poked, probed, shocked with electrodes and dissected in the laboratory. That's all!" he grinned broadly.

"Get real," I threw up my hands. "We can't live in the African savannah."

"Now that's a pity, isn't it?" Choua snapped, then raised

his arms, pointing his hands upwards and added with a gentle smile, "Look at the heavenly paradise here. A heaven that is pure and pristine! A heaven that comforts and liberates and sustains! An unpolluted and uncontaminated heaven! A heaven so different from the heaven you left back in New York."

"It is not that bad back there," I disagreed. "If you drive a few dozen miles out of New York City the heaven there is as unpolluted, pure and pristine as it is here."

Choua studied my face for some moments, looked up to the sky for several more, then mumbled, "Can't tell the difference between the Serengeti heaven and the New York heaven, eh!" Then he looked away and fell silent.

I pondered Choua's words about the Serengeti heaven and the one back in New York. I remembered patients who insisted that fluorescent lighting drained their energy. I had considerable difficulty believing the first few such patients, but then there were many more. What fascinated me most about their light sensitivity was that it was limited to fluorescent light. They had no difficulty with common incandescent light bulbs.

I recalled the many times when my plane was engulfed in clouds of pollution as it approached the Newark runways. I thought about the 'cancer corridor' along the Louisiana coast where the highway is lined with smokestacks billowing pollutants. The incidence of lung cancer is reported to be three times as high as that in other parts of Louisiana. My thoughts then drifted to reports of children dying of cancer of the lymph nodes caused by the radiation emanating from power line grids. 'A heaven that is pure and pristine,' Choua's words returned to me.

OVERWORKED   ADRENALS   GET   EXHAUSTED

"How much do adrenal glands weigh?" Choua asked.

"Usually between seven and ten grams," I replied.

"That's roughly equivalent to the weight of two to three teaspoons of sugar," he computed. "Tell me, how much do adrenal glands weigh after sudden death?"

"Slightly more than that—between eight and eleven grams."

"So, the glands are enlarged somewhat in patients who die suddenly. Tell me, what do you find in the adrenal glands at autopsy in people who die after chronic illness?" Choua asked.

"The glands show irregular enlargement," I replied.

"What do you find microscopically?"

"The layer of the gland substance called zona fasciculata is thinned out, and its cells look pale and empty—like ghosts of healthy cells."

"And those who die after massive burns, toxemia and severe infections?"

"The same."

"And in those are given radiotherapy?"

"The glands are shriveled."

"What do you in patients given steroid therapies?"

"The adrenal glands show cytolysis."

"What's that?"

"Cell death."

"What do you see in people who die after long-term treatment with ACTH?"

"ACTH—the adrenocortical stimulating hormone of the

pituitary gland—stimulates the adrenal gland, but later on..."

"ACTH beats on a dead horse. The exhausted adrenals simply cannot respond, right?"

"Right."

"What's cortical adrenal hyperplasia?" Choua now picked up the other side of the adrenal story.

"It is an irregular enlargement of the gland."

"How often do you see in autopsies?"

"In approximately half of all patients over 50 years of age."

"What is its significance?"

"It's not known."

"Not known?" His eyes narrowed.

"That's what textbooks of pathology say," I gave the standard answer.

"What hormones does zona fasciculata synthesize?"

"Hydrocortisone, also called cortisol."

"And you say the significance of structural changes in the adrenal glands is not known?" he frowned.

"Well, it's not..."

"Known," he cut me off curtly. "I'm not asking what your textbooks tell you. I'm asking what your patients tell you about their adrenal gland."

"It's hard," I replied, flustered. "It's hard to know what my patients' adrenal glands tell me when so many things are taking place all at one time."

"Com'n, you can do better than that," he scowled. "What do the laboratory reports tell you when you order 24-hour urinary steroid tests for your patients with debilitating chronic fatigue? And in other patients with sever immune disorders."

"Oh that," I recovered. "In the early stages, some urinary steroids are increased while others are in the normal range."

"And then?"

"In the intermediate stages, some hormones are increased and the levels of some others begin to decrease."

"And then?"

"Some are low, and others within the normal range. But I don't see any that are abnormally high."

"And in the final stages?" he pressed.

"Everything is low, sometimes there is total depletion," I replied.

"You mean the adrenal glands are totally exhausted."

"Yes."

"Amazing! That's amazing!" Choua waved his right arm.

"What's amazing?" I asked, perplexed.

"It's amazing how you look at thousands of adrenal glands as a pathologist. You do thousands of adrenal gland tests. You study all that. Yet, when I ask you what's the significance of structural changes you tell me it's unknown. Now, isn't that amazing?" he laughed derisively.

"Well, I...I told you what pathology textbooks say," I fumbled.

"I know. I know. Isn't that the problem with you doctors. Once you learn anything from your medical texts, you cannot unlearn it no matter how many true-to-life observations invalidate what the textbooks say. Now, isn't that a riot?" he shook his head and looked away.

Choua can be abrasive, but he does a way of sinking his message in. In late 1960s, during my pathology residency training I observed irregularly enlarged adrenal glands at autopsy almost every week. Whenever I asked my professors about the significance of the so-called adrenal nodular hyperplasia, they always muttered something that being poorly understood. And now, years later I still gave Choua the party line answers—meaningless but consistent with my pathology textbooks. I wondered why but decided not to ask Choua about it. I knew he would be yet more sarcastic.

LIONS, DYSAUTONOMIA, NEURALLY MEDIATED HYPOTENSION AND CHRONIC FATIGUE SYNDROME

"What is neurally-mediated hypotension?" Choua asked.

"It is a condition in which the blood pressure suddenly drops when a person stands up quickly from a lying position. Usually it is diagnosed with a tilt test, whereby the patient lies on a board that is tilted to 70 degrees and changes in blood pressure are recorded."

"Why does the blood pressure drop in such people?"

"Because their autonomic nervous system is unstable."

"How do you distinguish dysautonomia from neurally mediated hypotension?"

"You can't. Dysautonomia is the same thing as neurally mediated hypotension."

"Is neurally mediated hypotension the cause of the chronic fatigue syndrome?"

"No, I don't think so."

"Isn't that what that famous Johns Hopkins study concluded?"

"That's not quite right. The Johns Hopkins group was careful to point out that they observed an *association* between chronic fatigue syndrome and neurally mediated hypotension. They didn't say either is caused by the other."

"What do you think is the nature of that association?" he asked.

"I don't think there's any mystery about it," I replied. "The common link between the two is evidently injured autonomic receptors."

"What drug regimens did the Johns Hopkins researchers recommend for chronic fatigue syndrome?"

"Flurinol, Inderal and Norpace."

"Flurinol is a steroid and Inderal a beta blocker. What's Norpace?"

"A drug that blocks cholinergic receptors."

"Wow! What a triple whammy!" Choua swung his arm. "Blockade their adrenergic nervous system. Blockade their cholinergic nervous system. Then give them potent steroids. What a game plan! I tell you I'm impressed."

"They said it works and..."

"Do you agree with that drug therapies for your human canaries?"

"No."

"No?" Choua's eyebrows lifted. "You dare to disagree with Johns Hopkins?"

"Yes, I do. Their drug regimens may be helpful for some people during short periods, but those regimens don't address the real problems."

"What real problems?"

"Chronic fatigue is caused by oxidatively damaged enzymes—of energy, detoxification, absorptive-digestive and neurotransmitter systems. The notion that you can restore damaged enzymes with drugs is absurd."

"Strong words for Johns Hopkins, eh!" Choua's eyes widened.

"Hopkins is a prestigious institution. The folks there have made tremendous contributions to medicine. But this time, I'm afraid they are wrong. I'm certain of that."

"How so?"

"Because you can't facilitate healing by blocking the essential healing mechanisms of the human body," I replied testily.

"Because it's silly to try to mend a broken autonomic nervous system by using drugs that block the autonomic receptors. Is that it?" Choua asked calmly.

"Yes."

"Tell me, then, why did the patients taking their drugs get better?"

"Anybody can feel better for some time if you block his overstimulated and irritated autonomic receptors. That's not the issue."

"What is the issue?" he pressed.

"Long-term restoration of autonomic health. No drugs can ever do that. Facilitation of the enzyme recovery process is like facilitating the growth of a sapling or a houseplant. If you try to speed plant growth with excess water, you'll kill the plant with waterlogging, and..."

"If you try to accelerate plant growth with too much fertilizer, you'll burn the plant's root system," he completed my sentence, then asked, "Right?"

"Right!" I responded.

"What led you to your theory that chronic fatigue is caused by accelerated oxidative damage to energy enzymes?"

"It simply evolved as a part of my larger theory that all illness, at an energetic-molecular level, is caused by oxidative injury to life span enzymes."

"When did you first recognize that?"

"Back in the early 1980s, when I published it in the *Course Syllabus* of the *American Academy of Environmental Medicine.*"

"When did you published your oxidative theory of the chronic fatigue syndrome?"

"In 1993, in the *Journal of Advancement in Medicine.* But that wasn't my first publication on that subject."

"When did you first recognize that chronic fatigue was caused by accelerated oxidative injury?"

"Sometime during 1987. It was then that I began to see clear evidence of oxidative injury to red blood cells in chronic fatigue sufferers. I actually published my microscopic findings of the oxidatively damaged red blood cells in chronic fatigue in the *American Journal of Clinical Pathology* in 1990. In that study I demonstrated how vitamin C, an antioxidant, can help reverse oxidative cell damage. Next year, in 1991, I published my observations about the ability of vitamin C to break up blood platelet clots in the *American Journal of Clinical Pathology.*"

"You should feel gratified," Choua spoke with a grin. "Your oxidative theory of chronic fatigue syndrome is now being accepted."

"I don't think so," I replied. "Every month I see a flurry of medical articles about chronic fatigue syndrome, but all the fatigue researchers are interested is in different drug combinations to cure fatigue."

"Well, your oxidative theory is now being accepted." He smiled again.

"By whom?"

"Well, there's Paul Cheney, probably the foremost researcher in the chronic fatigue community. He now focuses heavily on the oxidative injury in patients with chronic fatigue."

"That is gratifying."

"But you knew all along that unbiased researchers would validate your observations as well as your theory, didn't you? You didn't think it would happen so soon, did you?"

"No, that's a pleasant surprise."

"Maybe some day the groups at Johns Hopkins will also see the obvious," Choua said with a naughty smile.

Dr. Ali is a relatively new player in the field of chronic fatigue (M.E.). His research and success with nutritional protocols has obviously influenced Dr. Paul Cheney who recently commented on the debt he owes to him. That Cheney has now switched to nutritional therapies with particular emphasis on antioxidants is sufficient tribute.

Jacqueline Steincamp
Hauora Open Forum 9:43; 1995

The core clinical value of my oxidative theory of chronic fatigue syndrome, I wrote in my original article published in the *Journal of Advancement in Medicine* (6:83-96; 1993), is that it provides a unifying theory to provide scientific basis of the efficiency of nondrug, antioxidant therapies. I suggest the companion volume, *The Canary and Chronic Fatigue,* to readers who might suffer from debilitating chronic fatigue and need detailed information about natural therapies to reverse chronic fatigue.

For the readers' interest, the table on the next page provides a partial listing of drugs that have been prescribed for chronic fatigue syndrome as well as mitral valve prolapse.

DRUGS FOR MITRAL VALVE SYNDROME	
Beta Blockers	Inderal, Lopressor, Corgard, Tenormin, Tenoretic, Corzide, Inderide, Timolide, Kerlone, Visken
Calcium Channel Blockers	Calan, Cardizem, Procardia, Isoptic
Antimigraine Drugs	Cafegot, Ergostat, Midrin, Sansert and Wigraine
Antidepressants	Paxil, Prozac, Zoloft, Elavil, Pamelor, Amitryptaline, Doxepin, Parnate, Tofranil, Norpramine, Adapin, Asendin, Serzone
Antianxiety	Ativan, Zanax, Valium, Librium, Searx, Klonopin, Tranzene
Miscellaneous	Clonodine, Zantac, Pepcid

Any of the above drugs may relieve the symptoms of adrenergic hypervigilence caused by accelerated oxidative injury in patients with chronic fatigue syndrome with or without the diagnostic label of mitral valve prolapse. However, none of them addresses any of the real underlying causes of their suffering. The problems of adrenergic hypervigilence and accelerated oxidative stress can only resolved with a broad, integrated holistic approach. Such an approach must address all of the following issues: functional nutritional deficiencies; sugar-insulin-adrenaline roller coasters; undiagnosed mold allergy and food incompatibilities; chemical sensitivities; overload of toxic metals and environmental pollutants; problems of fitness; and the Fourth-of-July Chemistry fueled by recycled past pain and recycled feared, future misery. Needless to say, none of the above issues can be resolved with any drugs.

Waiting for Godot

The CDC definition of chronic fatigue syndrome is eminently suited to those who believe drugs are the only legitimate therapies for all diseases. They are quite clear in their heads. They have named the syndrome. That means they understand the problem. That also means that all that is required now is for some drug company to come up with a drug to cure this dreadful syndrome. Waiting for another triumph of synthetic chemistry! Waiting for another miracle drug! Waiting for Godot!

The Canary and Chronic Fatigue

No shrine is holier than the human frame, for it houses the human spirit.

Caring for this shrine is a scared trust— sacred for the patient and sacred for the physician. It is this trust that sets medicine apart from other professions.

Physical disrobing of a patient for examination by his physician is symbolic of a deeper personal and emotional disrobing for the patient. And so it is that the simple act of a physician touching his patient establishes a unique bond between the two. This bond must not be breached by any expediency.

Molecular medicine is not an easy way out for the poorly informed physician...Nor is it an easy way for the patient. It asks for an ongoing pursuit of the knowledge of a patient's own biology.

The Cortical Monkey and Healing

Chapter 7

Lions, Hypoglycemia and Insulin Roller Coasters

Choua suffers from squint of the mind. He looks at the same things others do, but he sees them differently. Or maybe he sees the same things but thinks differently. At one point during our safari, my thoughts wandered to my patients who suffer from dysfunctional sugar metabolism.

"Do lions suffer from low blood sugar levels?" I teased Choua.

"They do, but not the way people do," he replied.

"Are you saying there are differences in the chemistry of sugar metabolism between humans and lions?"

"Not really," he posited. "If lions ate as many cookies, candy and cakes as people do, they would suffer from sugar roller coasters and hypoglycemia too."

"But they do get hungry, don't they? And hungry lions are thought to be mean and dangerous, ready to eat anything that moves and even things that don't move. Didn't George Schaller write about hungry lions who eat decomposing meat?"

"Yes, but there is more to hypoglycemia than simple hunger."

"Do you mean the blood glucose levels in a hungry lion do not fall as low as in people?"

"Blood sugar levels probably fall quite low in lions, but that's not the key issue in hypoglycemia. The real issue is the rate at which blood sugar levels change —sudden rises and sharp drops, the sugar roller coasters as you call them."

"Do lions develop insulin roller coasters?" I asked, then hurried to correct myself. "They probably don't. I mean lions eat the whole animal, meat, skin, fat and all. And proteins and fats do not cause roller coaster effects."

"Right," Choua nodded. "Hypoglycemic-hyperglycemic shifts—sugar roller coasters —are problems caused by SAD, the Standard American Diet. That's your stuff."

The term hypoglycemia means low blood sugar level; hyperglycemia is opposite of that—high blood sugar level. Blood sugar levels reflect the amount of sugar in food and the rate of its absorption in the stomach and upper bowel. In health, the blood sugar level rises gradually as a wholesome meal—low in simple sugars and rich in fiber and undigested foods—is slowly digested and absorbed. In response to a gradually rising blood sugar, the pancreas secretes its hormone, insulin, in a slow, sustained fashion. Insulin, in turn, gently brings down the raised blood sugar level—regulating the sugar level within the normal range of 75 to 150 milligrams of sugar per deciliter of blood. (A deciliter is one-tenth of a liter, or equal to approximately six tablespoons of fluid.)

While insulin is the principal regulatory hormone, there are other hormones that oppose its actions and serve as counter regulatory hormones. These include adrenaline, cortisone, glucagon and growth hormone. Excessive stimulation of the vagus nerve is also considered to play a role, and some physicians use an anticholinergic drug (propantheline bromide, 7.5 mg 30 minutes before meals) to control symptoms of hypoglycemia. The blood glucose also "autoregulates" itself in the sense that it undergoes spontaneous nonenzymatic oxidation.

Eating sugary foods—such as sodas, orange juice, candy, cakes and cookies—unaccompanied by whole undigested foods and fiber causes sudden rises in blood sugar levels. Such a hyperglycemic response to sugar intake is rapidly followed by a sudden release of insulin from the pancreas. Insulin drives sugar into cells and lowers blood sugar level.

"In your hospital laboratory, you give narrative reports of

glucose tolerance tests and try to emphasize the role of hyperglycemic-hypoglycemic shifts, don't you?" Choua asked.

"Yes, I do," I replied.

"Do the doctors pay any attention to your emphasis on sugar shifts?"

"To be frank, I'm not sure they ever do."

"Why?"

"I guess because mainstream notions of sugar metabolism, hypoglycemia and diabetes are oriented to absolute numbers of blood glucose values," I explained.

"Not oriented, fixated," he scowled.

"I wouldn't go that far."

"But the doctors who read your reports rarely use the sugar shifts information to manage their patients. When the blood sugar levels are high, they simply use the labels of diabetes, pre-diabetes or chemical diabetes and prescribe blood glucose-lowering drugs. They rarely, if ever, manage sugar roller coasters as a dysregulation of sugar metabolism."

"Why?"

"Because they aren't trained to diagnose sugar-insulin shifts as metabolic dysregulation. And those few who are aware of the problem just don't know how to manage those shifts. Rarely is an internist's office organized to provide the necessary nutritional education and nutrient therapies to successfully manage those cases."

"What do lions know about hypoglycemia, Choua?" I asked.

"What is hypoglycemia?" he frowned.

"Low blood glucose level."

"How is it diagnosed?"

"There are two standard criteria for the diagnosis of hypoglycemia: 1) the blood sugar level has to be 50 mg/dL or lower and 2) the low blood sugar level must be associated with hypoglycemic symptoms," I explained.

"What diagnostic tests do you perform?"

"We do three-hour or four-hour glucose tolerance tests. During the test, we ask the patients to carefully record the development of any hypoglycemic symptoms. If the blood glucose level dips to 50 mg/dL or lower *and* the patient experiences any symptoms, we establish the diagnosis of reactive hypoglycemia."

"You run a hospital laboratory and read most of the glucose tolerance tests. You must have signed out more than a few thousand glucose tolerance tests. Tell me, how often does that happen?"

"Actually, Choua, it's not that common. Blood sugar infrequently falls below 50 mg/dL at our laboratory."

"How often do nutritionist-physicians diagnose hypoglycemia?"

"Frequently."

"And how many of your patients suffering from food and mold allergies, disabling fatigue and chronic immune disorders tell you they've been diagnosed with hypoglycemia by previous nutritionist-physicians?"

"That's common."

"Do you think those patients suffer from hypoglycemia or not?"

"Well, that's a problem," I confessed. "When I repeat their glucose tolerance tests, they often don't meet the numerical criterion for hypoglycemia. And even when they do, the lowest blood sugar level is not accompanied by typical hypoglycemic symptoms."

"What do you make of that?"

"Nutritionist-physicians diagnose hypoglycemia largely on an empirical basis when patients complain of hypoglycemic symptoms. Then they treat their patients by prescribing low-carbohydrate diets and frequent small meals. Many think hypoglycemia is caused by yeast overgrowth and prescribe antiyeast herbs and drugs."

"Does that work?"

"That's the thing. Such management plans do work—not always though."

"What do mainstream doctors think about that?"

"They think symptoms that can be relieved by low-carbohydrate diets; small, frequent meals; and antiyeast agents are psychosomatic problems."

"In other words, it's the old all-in-the-head theory. Right?"

"Right. And that's tough for patients. The disagreement between mainstream physicians and holistic physicians causes much confusion among patients who are caught between two very different viewpoints. They go from one professional to another, encountering contradictions at each step. That's a difficult problem."

"Do you want to know what lions think of hypoglycemia?" he asked me with a wink.

"Yes." I felt relieved.

"Lions don't agree with either group. They simply sense things and act accordingly. When they feel hungry, they go looking for food. Their meals contain complete foods, with high-grade proteins and essential, unoxidized fats. There is no sugar and little starch, if any, in lions' meals. Lions usually go for the gut of their kill first."

"Why?"

"Because that's where live enzymes, vitamins, minerals and digestive juices are. Lions, unlike your university internists, have a gut sense of good nutrition."

"And, tell me, what do lions think of hypoglycemia?"

"Lions have no compulsion to fit their sensory perceptions into someone else's frivolous numerical model the way mainstream doctors do. Nor do they have any desire to make things up just to satisfy their patients as nutritionist-physicians do."

"You're an equal opportunity abuser, aren't you?" I laughed.

"Lions know an individual's metabolism is for him to know, and each of them must learn to sense his own metabolic regulations —and dysregulations—and respond to them accordingly."

"Tell me, what do lions think about the nutritionists' take on hypoglycemia?" I pushed him.

"Why don't you tell me what nutritionists do after they diagnose hypoglycemia?"

"They confirm their diagnosis by prescribing food plans that assure steady-state sugar metabolism. They look for adverse food reactions and teach their patients how to avoid them."

"What do mainstream doctors think of that?" he asked mischievously.

"Didn't I tell you they think it's quackery? They laughingly dismiss the nutritionist's diagnosis."

"Mainstream physicians like to think that what their blessed tests cannot detect doesn't exist, don't they?"

"Yes. They cling to their view that symptoms experienced by patients are imaginary, and they contemptuously accuse nutritionists of reinforcing pathologic belief systems."

"Have you ever heard a cardiologist attribute an episode of heart rhythm irregularity to sudden shifts in blood glucose?" he asked.

"No, I haven't," I replied.

"Or to sudden surges in insulin and adrenaline levels?"

"No."

"Have you ever heard a gastroenterologist blame abdominal symptoms on yeast overgrowth in the gut?"

"No."

"Or a neurologist ascribe a headache to chemical sensitivity reaction?"

"No."

"Or a pulmonologist think of mold allergy when treating an asthma attack?"

"No."

"Or a rheumatologist blame joint pains on food allergy?"

"Not that either."

"And, of course, psychiatrists are rarely burdened by any knowledge of nutritional and metabolic dysregulations when they prescribe drugs for mood disorders."

"What's the point of all this?" I asked, exasperated.

"Tell me, how do mainstream doctors think patients with hypoglycemic symptoms should be managed?"

"For one thing, they certainly don't think that legitimate psychiatric symptoms should be chalked up to quackish notions of hypoglycemia."

"Tell me, what do you think of problems caused by low blood sugar? Are they real or imaginary?"

"Real. If they weren't real, why would patients get better? That much I can assert from my own clinical experience."

"Clinical experience?" Choua grimaced. "Tell me, what's clinical experience?"

"Clinical experience is that intuitive-visceral sense a clinician develops after long periods of close observation."

"Now that's different!" His eyes brightened. "I can understand that. Indeed, that's what my Serengeti lions also know."

"How so?" I asked.

"The lions follow their instincts. Low blood sugar signals a time to get up and look around for food."

"So, do your lions agree with nutritionists? Do they also know that problems of low blood sugar are real?"

"No."

"No?"

"Lions know it's not about how low the blood sugar gets—whether it reaches 50 mg/dL or not."

"Well, we really don't know whether 50 mg/dL is the right number for lions, do we? Do the lions know that?" I teased.

"Precisely!" Choua's eyes lit up. "That's precisely the point!"

"What point?" I asked, perplexed.

"Serengeti lions don't play the numbers game. They just follow their instincts, which guide them to their next meal."

FIVE FACES OF SUGAR-INSULIN DYSREGULATION

"Sugar is the primary villain in human metabolism," Choua went on. "Excess sugar in food stresses human energy systems in many ways and causes the dysregulation of carbohydrate metabolism. Sugar-insulin dysregulation has five faces."

"What are those faces?" I asked.

"First, it creates sudden surges in blood glucose levels—a condition called hyperglycemia. Second, sudden hyperglycemia triggers the rapid release of large amounts of insulin from the pancreas —a condition called hyperinsulinemia. Third, the insulin response to high blood sugar overshoots its mark and drives the blood sugar level below the normal range—a state of low blood sugar called hypoglycemia. The fourth face of glucose-insulin dysregulation is the insensitivity of insulin receptors at cell membranes. Such receptors are overwhelmed and literally numbed by excesses of insulin."

"Do you mean peripheral insulin resistance?" I asked.

"You aren't comfortable with simple language, are you?" he retorted. "Why do you turn simple things into complicated medicalese?"

"Okay! Okay!" I replied, annoyed. "What's the fifth face?"

"The fifth face of glucose-insulin dysregulation is too much adrenaline —a state you may call adrenergic hypervigilance. When an insulin surge drives sugar below the desirable range, the adrenal glands kick in and dispense blasts of adrenaline to counter the insulin. Adrenaline is one of the most—if not *the* most—potent oxidant in the human body. The oxidative fires lit by adrenaline overdrive the heart causing palpitations, tighten arteries producing high blood pressure, rev up nerve-muscle conduction sites causing stiff muscles, jitters and sweating. And that sugar-insulin-adrenergic dysregulation is what the stress specialists call the stress response. Right?"

"Right."

"What are the symptoms of hypoglycemia?" Choua continued.

"The main symptoms include the jitters, sudden weakness, mood swings, nausea, abdominal discomfort, sweating, heart palpitations and brain fog."

"What's brain fog?"

"Confusion, haziness and concentration problems."

"Now, tell me, what are the symptoms of adrenergic hypervigilance? Of adrenaline rush?"

"It causes jitters, sweating and heart palpitations."

"And what else?" he pressed.

"Nausea, abdominal discomfort, sudden-onset weakness and mood swings." I found myself enumerating the symptoms of hypoglycemia.

"Huh!" Choua beamed with satisfaction. "I was hoping you'd count the symptoms of hypoglycemia in the same exact order as you would those of an adrenaline rush. But that was pretty close."

"Of course, symptoms of glucose-insulin roller coasters and adrenaline rushes show a large overlap because..."

"It isn't an overlap," he interrupted me. "It's a continuum. All of biology is a continuum, not a bunch of overlaps. Your classifications of diseases and syndromes are mere artifacts."

"That's absurd," I protested. "Disease classification is essential if we are to make any sense of the enormous number of diseases that we see."

"I'm not saying your disease classifications don't make your life easier for you. I am saying nature is a continuum, and so is biology. Tell me, what blood tests and scans do you use to diagnose sugar-insulin-adrenaline dysregulation?"

"That's not an easy thing. Glucose studies are simple enough to perform and three- or four-hour tolerance tests are frequently done, but insulin and adrenaline activities are rarely, if ever, evaluated in clinical medicine."

"It's far easier to chalk up the symptoms of glucose-insulin-adrenaline dysregulation to hypochondria, anxiety-neurosis or the all-time favorite, the all-in-the-head label. Isn't that the way it works in real life?" he asked sarcastically.

"No. Yes, well it isn't that..."

"Simple," he completed the sentence.

"Why do you ask me questions if you don't have the patience to hear the answers?" I complained.

"The poor patients are dismissed as doctor-shoppers or,

worse, pests by their doctors, right?"

"Regrettably that does happen sometimes," I confessed.

CHOLESTEROL: AN INNOCENT MOLECULE TAKES A BUM RAP

"Sugar and insulin are the real molecular culprits in the cause of coronary heart disease," Choua resumed.

"What?" I asked, surprised. "Not cholesterol?"

"The cholesterol story is phony. Sugar and insulin are the real molecular villains in coronary heart disease," he groused.

"Now that's a switch, isn't it? The whole world thinks heart attacks are caused by cholesterol. Where did you..."

"Not the whole world," he cut me off curtly. "Only the cholesterol cats—the fat cats who make money by promoting cholesterol tests and the fatter cats who pile up riches in selling worthless drugs to lower blood cholesterol levels."

"Let's keep cheap sensationalism out of it, Choua. Do you have any evidence that excess sugar and insulin cause coronary artery disease?"

"Evidence!" he shot back. "Why don't you first tell me about the evidence that cholesterol causes heart disease?"

"That's ludicrous," I replied, irritated. "There are dozens of large studies that show reduced risk rates of heart attacks with lower cholesterol levels."

"You should know better than to speak so frivolously, Mr. Pathologist," his voice rose sharply. "All those studies report bloated *risk* reduction figures while the true *rate* reduction numbers are dismally poor. When they gloat about forty-four percent risk reduction, the real rate reduction is actually less than *two* percent."

"You look at everything through your squinty eyes," I taunted.

"Don't be fooled by the distortion of high-risk reduction figures," he continued. "Suppose two persons out of one thousand people with high blood cholesterol levels suffered a heart attack in 1985. Then all one thousand people were given a cholesterol-lowering drug. Ten years later, in 1995, only one person out of those thousand suffered a heart attack. You could rightly say that the drug had reduced the risk of heart attack by fifty percent —from two persons to one. While one out of two evidently means fifty percent, that statement would be patently absurd. Don't you see that the risk reduction of fifty percent is a meaningless number until you know something about the total number of people studied?"

"Okay, you made your point," I conceded. "Now, tell me about rate reduction."

"Rate is an accurate mathematical expression. For example, a two percent rate reduction in heart-attack patients taking a drug means that two out of one hundred people were saved from a heart attack by that drug. The remaining ninety-eight persons received no benefits from the drug. Now, if you take the raw data from the published cholesterol studies and calculate the real rate reduction number, you'll readily see the deception in bloated risk reduction numbers. You'll find that the actual rate reduction numbers are well below two percent in all those studies."

"I think you're confused, Choua," I countered. "Obviously the purpose of a drug is to help those two percent who might suffer a heart attack. Why confuse the picture with the remaining ninety-eight healthy persons?"

"I'm confused?" he scowled, then added sarcastically, "Sometimes you're maddeningly slow to catch on."

"Don't insult me," I retorted angrily.

"Don't you see the absurdity of your logic?" he asked, his face softening a bit.

"No, I don't!" I replied tersely.

Choua looked at me intently for several moments but said nothing. As my angst subsided, I wondered what that was all about but decided not to ask any questions.

POISONING NINETY-EIGHT TO HELP TWO

"Why do you conduct drug research?" he asked after a while.

"To assess drug efficacy for clinical use," I replied evenly.

"When a drug passes the research efficacy test, it is released for use by the general public, right?"

"Right."

"If the drug benefits only two out of a hundred patients in a research setting and you prescribe it for a single patient, how do you know whether that patient is among the two who will benefit from the drug or he is among the ninety-eight who won't?"

"I won't," I confessed.

"That's precisely the problem, isn't it?" he gored. "And this, indeed, is what happens in real life. You put in jeopardy the health of ninety-eight persons with a toxic drug to cover those two who might benefit from it. When the true rates of rate reduction are dismally low, their royal highnesses, the cholesterol cats, hoke it up with phony bloated risk reduction numbers. Don't you see something that simple?"

"That's a problem with all therapies for the prevention of disease, isn't it?" I asked.

"*All* therapies?" he cocked his head and asked, a shade away from anger. "You don't hurt *all* persons when you prevent heart attacks with nutrients, such as essential oils, magnesium, pantothenic acid and taurine! You don't hurt *anyone* when you prescribe ginger root and garlic for a healthy heart. Do you? Or when you teach your patients limbic breathing to slow down a racing heart."

"Natural therapies are different from drug therapies," I protested.

"*Exactly*! That's the point!" he added sharply. "With natural therapy you don't hurt the ninety-eight when you try to help the two."

"At least two percent are helped by cholesterol drugs. You have to grant that." I returned to cholesterol drugs.

"Nonsense!" Choua erupted. "Are you really that naïve? Do you think people are robots who mindlessly take pills pushed by cholesterol cats? Nobody takes those drugs unless they are scared into doing so with dire predictions of sudden death from heart attack. You show coronary angiograms to frightened patients and tell them those arteries are widow makers, don't you?"

"You know I don't do those things," I protested.

"Do you know of anyone who knowingly would take a toxic drug for years to prevent a heart attack without thinking about it at some deeper intuitive-visceral level? Without changing his eating habits in some way? Without doing some exercise? Without finding ways to reduce stress and anger? Your drug researchers blissfully ignore such questions, don't they?"

"Are you saying the observed two percent rate reduction is not due to cholesterol drugs?" I asked incredulously.

"Do you know something I don't?" he groused. "Tell me, who would ever take an investigational drug without making some lifestyle changes?"

"All people don't take investigational drugs," I challenged.

"Each drug use is an experiment in biology. All drugs are investigational for a given individual. Don't you see each person is unique in his biologic responsiveness to a synthetic chemical?"

"You're way off base," I replied harshly. "The whole idea behind blinded studies to scientifically prove the clinical efficacy of new drugs and to..."

"I know! I know!" he interrupted me sarcastically. "You doctors love to be blinded, don't you? And when that's not enough, you want someone to double-blind you, don't you?"

"You're incorrigible. If that's all true, why doesn't anyone expose that deception?" I asked.

"Because there is no money in disease prevention. The money is in procedures —in angioplasties and coronary bypasses."

"You exaggerate," I admonished.

"Why would any angioplasterer bother to teach his patients meditation for a few dollars when he can earn thousands doing angioplasties? Why would a cardiac surgeon let a holistic physician reverse coronary artery disease with inexpensive EDTA chelation therapy when he can make thousands of dollars for a few hours of work doing bypass surgery?"

"Most people aren't convinced that EDTA chelation therapy reverses coronary artery disease," I held my ground.

"Aren't you convinced?" he shot back.

"Yes, I am. And there are a small number of other physicians who know that, but..."

"But folks who control the health care largesse don't," he cut me off rudely.

"Do you think cholesterol plays *any* role in the cause of heart attacks?"

"Yes, in rare hereditary cases of hypercholesterolemia, when the cholesterol level is in the three- or four-hundred range—or even higher."

"What about the general public, those with cholesterol levels below three hundred?"

"Native, unoxidized and nontoxic cholesterol is an innocent molecule. The real issue is how oxidized and denatured cholesterols cause tissue damage."

"How do you know that?"

"Back to basics, Mr. Pathologist," he jeered. "The lining cells in the arteries have no receptors for natural, unoxidized cholesterol; they do for oxidized, denatured cholesterol. You don't find healthy, unoxidized cholesterol in plaques —but you do find oxidized, denatured cholesterol there. In circulating blood, there are no anticholesterol antibodies against healthy, unoxidized cholesterol; there are antibodies against oxidized, denatured cholesterol. Tell me, why would nature make the cholesterol molecule essential for all cell membranes and yet make it so toxic to the heart?" he scowled.

"The same way it gave oxygen opposing roles in biology," I shot back. "Oxygen ushers life in. Oxygen terminates life. Oxygen is the great molecular Dr. Jekyll and Mr.Hyde, isn't it?"

It isn't often that I corner Choua like that. I was certain he would have no comeback, and he didn't. He looked at me for several moments in silence. For once he had no answer and that amused me. I looked back at him, savoring the moment. Finally, he broke out laughing, "Good! That was good!"

GLUCOSE, INSULIN AND ADRENALINE ROLLER COASTERS: A TROUBLESOME TRIO

"You're a contrarian, Choua," I chided. "You've a squint of the mind. You see everything differently. Let's move on to sugar and insulin. What evidence do you have that an excess of these substances causes heart attacks?"

"For one thing, Eskimos in Alaska didn't suffer heart attacks when they lived on pure blubber containing huge amounts of cholesterol. Then you took sugar, alcohol and television to Alaska and ruined their health. Now coronary artery disease and heart attacks are rampant among the Alaskan natives."

"That could mean many things," I contested. "You can't blame excess sugar and insulin for heart attacks simply with that reason," I protested.

"Before the turn of the century, heart attack was unknown as a diagnosis in Europe or the United States. Yet, at that time, the people of both continents consumed diets rich in cholesterol."

"Is that true?" I was surprised.

"Did you see a single pathology specimen of the heart showing changes of an infarction dating to the eighteenth or nineteenth century at the Museum of the Royal College of Surgeons of England in London?"

"No."

"Is there such a heart specimen at the pathology museums in the United States?"

"I don't recall seeing any."

"At the turn of this century, the average American child consumed between five and ten pounds of sugar each year. Now many children ingest between one hundred and one hundred and fifty pounds of sugar each year."

"How does that prove sugar causes heart attacks?" I asked.

"What beats up on a tired heart, cholesterol or adrenaline?"

"Adrenaline."

"What triggers heart palpitations? Excess of cholesterol or of adrenaline?" Choua was unrelenting.

"Adrenaline."

"What drives the adrenal glands to pour out adrenaline, the excess of cholesterol or insulin?" he groused.

"Insulin," I confessed.

"What drives the pancreas glands to pour out insulin, the excess of cholesterol or sugar?" he nearly yelled.

"Sugar," I replied.

"Let's talk about your patients at the Institute. What do you see in them every day? Are their hearts tormented by cholesterol roller coasters or by sugar-insulin roller coasters?"

"Sugar-insulin roller coasters," I admitted, then added, "I don't think anyone ever suffers from cholesterol roller coasters."

"Precisely! There is no such nonsense as cholesterol roller coasters. At autopsy, do you ever see coronary arteries that aren't blocked in people who die of heart attacks?"

"Yes, I do. Actually, that's not all that uncommon."

"What is the cause of heart attack in such cases?"

"A spasm of the coronary arteries, which suffocates the heart muscle and causes its death."

"Would you agree that the real cause of heart attacks in such cases is stress?"

"Yes."

"Does that stress come from high cholesterol?"

"No."

"Except, of course, when you doctors keep hammering the cholesterol number into the heads of your poor, gullible patients," he added impishly.

"Now you're being Choua," I chastised him.

"At autopsy, how frequently do you find blood clots occluding the coronary arteries in persons who die soon after suffering a heart attack—in less than six or eight hours?" he asked.

"Not often. Maybe in less than one out of five cases," I replied.

"Interesting! And what do you find in persons who die much later, say, forty-eight or seventy-two hours after the heart attack?"

"Coronary occlusions are seen in almost all such cases."

"What conclusions do you draw from those data?"

"That the spasm of the coronary arteries occurs first and occlusion of the vessels with blood clots develops later in most cases of heart attacks."

"In other words, blockage of coronary arteries occurs as the consequence rather than the cause of heart attacks in most cases. Right?" he pressed.

"Yes," I conceded.

"Now tell me, what role does natural, unoxidized cholesterol play in the causation of coronary artery spasm?"

"No direct role that I know of."

"Any indirect role?"

"I don't know," I admitted.

"Does adrenaline cause coronary artery spasm?"

"Of course it does," I replied, irritated. "Didn't we cover that before?"

"Do sudden increases in blood insulin levels trigger adrenaline blasts?"

"Of course they do."

"Do sudden shifts in blood sugar—your sugar roller coasters —cause sudden bursts of insulin?"

"Of course they do. But why are you repeating yourself?" I asked, exasperated.

"Sugar, insulin and adrenaline —that's the troublesome trio."

SYNDROME X

"What is Syndrome X?" Choua shifted suddenly.

"It is a syndrome of recurrent episodes of chest pain characterized by three elements," I replied. "First, the chest pain is stress-related and clinically suggests heart ischemia; second, the cardiogram taken during attacks shows evidence of insufficient blood supply to the heart muscle; and third, the coronary angiogram shows a normal structure of the arteries without any evidence of blockage."

"If coronary arteries are structurally normal, what causes angina and associated abnormalities in the cardiogram?"

"Obviously there is a coronary arterial dysfunction. Something is provoking those arteries into spasms. And that must occur at the level of smaller arteries."

"What about blood glucose levels in Syndrome X?" he asked.

"The fasting glucose levels and the glucose tolerance patterns are usually within normal limits."

"And insulin levels?"

"That's interesting. Patients with the syndrome show normal fasting blood insulin levels, but the insulin levels after a glucose load are higher."

"Is that common—a normal blood glucose tolerance curve and an abnormal insulin response?"

"Actually, Choua, it's not uncommon at all. That's exactly why I always insist that we perform a four-hour insulin study every time I do a four-hour glucose tolerance test."

"What do you make of that finding?" he asked.

"Evidently, excess insulin has something to do with coronary arterial dysfunction," I replied, then asked, "But isn't Syndrome X usually seen in patients with high blood pressure, heart valve diseases, and autoimmune disorders that injure the small vessels of the heart?"

"Not so. It is also frequently seen in people without high blood pressure and heart valve disease."

"What about immune disorders?"

"That's an interesting point. Since most cardiologists do not believe mold allergy and food sensitivity can play a role in the cause of heart disease, they never test for the presence of immune injury in patients with Syndrome X."

"But didn't you just tell me this syndrome is often associated with autoimmune disorders?" I asked.

"They mean disorders such as lupus, scleroderma and vasculitis," re replied, then continued. "Most cardiologists don't believe food sensitivity or mold allergy can have anything to do with lupus and vasculitis either. Do they?"

"Not really. That's amazing! Tell me, Choua, what metabolic derangements occur in Syndrome X?"

"For one thing, production of lactic acid in the heart muscle is increased in these patients. That interferes with the ability of the heart to contract properly and eject blood into the aorta, then into the large arteries. Biopsies of the heart show the normal structure of small arteries and smaller arterioles. Muscle fibers in the heart show swelling of mitochondria —sausage-like minute structures in the cells that function as cell batteries. What does that all mean?" he asked.

"All these changes indicate metabolic derangements related to sugar-insulin dysregulation," I replied.

"What about adrenaline?"

"You're right. I should have said glucose-insulin-adrenaline dysregulation."

"Eventually, the heart muscle suffers and gets damaged."

"That's not quite true," I corrected. "Syndrome X is supposed to be a benign disorder. It is not supposed to cause significant damage to the heart."

"I don't know whether it is supposed to or not, but it does," he bellowed. "In 1989, *Circulation* published an article by Dieter Opherk and colleagues at the University of Heidelberg. The article presented evidence for injury to the heart muscle in Syndrome X. It's not all that benign."

"What do you think is the basic problem in the syndrome?" I asked.

"Sugar-insulin-adrenaline dysregulation," he smiled.

"Is that a fact or a factoid?" I provoked.

"Fundamentally, Syndrome X is no different from other cases of coronary artery spasm that cause angina," he frowned.

"If that were so, wouldn't we see thousands of cases of Syndrome X?" I persisted.

"Think, professor, think," he spoke with biting sarcasm. "What is Syndrome X? Didn't you just tell me it is a syndrome of angina with an abnormal cardiogram but without coronary artery blockage?"

"Yes, I did," I replied timidly.

"So, tell me, professor, how on God's green earth can anyone separate such cases of Syndrome X from patients who develop angina due to coronary artery spasms and show positive cardiograms but negative angiograms conducted days or weeks later?"

"I don't know. To tell you the truth, Choua, I never thought about it."

Could it be *that* simple? I wondered. What am I missing? The whole world of cardiology is sure that Syndrome X is a distinct and uncommon syndrome. They have carefully defined diagnostic criteria for it. There have been so many papers written about it. Yet Choua is mocking the very concept of this syndrome. What exasperated me most was my utter inability to provide a counterpoint to the position he so adamantly held.

"Why do cardiologists call this condition Syndrome X?" I finally asked.

"I suppose because they do not know the cause of this syndrome," he mumbled absent-mindedly, then suddenly perked up and asked with a wink, "But, then, is there a disease that they really know the cause of?"

"Why are cardiologists so sure of the role of cholesterol and totally ignore the role of sugar-insulin-adrenaline dysregulation in the cause of heart attacks?" I prodded, ignoring his cheap shot at cardiology.

CHOLESTEROL CATS AND SUGAR CATS

"Because cholesterol cats pay the cardiologists to keep blubbering about cholesterol. Meanwhile, the cats rake in bundles of money by selling cholesterol tests and worthless cholesterol drugs," he replied angrily.

"Cholesterol cats, eh?" I jeered.

"Those cholesterol cats keep cholesterol commercials on TV to keep people scared. Kept sufficiently in fear, people continue to take cholesterol tests every six months. There is a lot of money in that."

"You see evil in everything with your Cyclopean eye," I chastised him.

"There are richer cholesterol cats who make yet more money selling worthless cholesterol drugs."

"I have to hand it to you, Choua, you do have a unique perspective on things. I don't know if you're right, but certainly your thinking is different."

"Then there are the sugar cats," he went on, ignoring my sarcasm, "who throw a few bucks to doctors on their payroll and tell them to make pretty little speeches about the safety of sugar for children. Next, they denounce holistic physicians as quacks because the holistic physicians audaciously warn mothers about the health hazards of sugar." Choua smirked.

"Go on," I prodded.

"The sugar cats also make enormous profits by keeping such information about sugar and insulin from being aired on television. Instead, they show clever ads that compare the sugar content of their highly sugared cereals with that of apples. Now, isn't that responsible advertising?"

"That's awful, if that really happens," I replied.

"Haven't you seen them?" he asked indignantly.

"I vaguely remember something like that. Tell me, if things are the way you think they are, why does the main body of physicians keep silent?" I provoked.

"Because you doctors learn only what your drug czars want you to learn," he replied acidly. "Have you ever heard a visiting speaker at your hospital speak about the relationship between sugar excess and heart disease?"

Choua finished and fell silent. I tried to recall if any visiting cardiology speaker at the hospital had indeed ever spoken about a relationship between sugar and heart disease. I couldn't recall one. Cardiologists simply are not interested in human nutrition —except when talking about low-fat diets as a prelude to their scholarly discussion of drug therapies. I then tried to think of some other weakness in Choua's arguments, more to provoke him than to actually challenge his assertions. I wondered how a cardiologist might rebut him.

"How does coronary artery disease fit into your theory that the spontaneity of oxidation in nature is the root cause of aging and of all degenerative diseases?" Choua spoke after a while.

"It's consistent with my theory," I replied.

"How?"

"Because the spasm of coronary arteries is provoked by oxidative stress. Natural, nontoxic cholesterol is turned into toxic oxidized cholesterol by oxidative stress—and so are other healthy fats oxidized and made unhealthy. Such oxidized fats injure the lining cells of coronary arteries and begin the process of plaque formation."

"So, you do agree that native, unoxidized cholesterol is an innocent bystander molecule that has nothing to do with coronary artery disease?"

"No. Yes, well, I'm not..."

"How does sugar-insulin-adrenaline fit into your oxidative theory of coronary heart disease?"

"I never really thought about it, Choua. Do you have any idea?"

"It's quite simple," he grinned.

"How?" I asked, my curiosity piqued.

"Glucose generates oxidant molecules during its metabolism. Furthermore, it undergoes spontaneous autoxidation creating additional oxidant species."

"That's some stretch of the imagination," I smiled.

"Sudden and sharp glucose shifts trigger insulin roller coasters that lead to adrenaline blasts. Now you have to agree that adrenaline is one of the most—if not the most—potent oxidant in the body. It shocks the heart in many ways and also causes the spasms of coronary arteries that lead to heart attacks."

"To be honest, I never thought of these relationships. Are those relationships really true?" I asked, doubts rising in my mind about the simplicity of his theory.

"What is the primary source of energy for cells—cholesterol or glucose?" he asked, without answering my question.

"Glucose, of course."

"Metabolically, which one is a more active molecule—cholesterol or glucose?"

"Glucose."

"What molecule creates more oxidative stress during its metabolism, cholesterol or glucose?"

"Glucose."

"So?" he grinned and winked.

"So what?" I asked, perplexed.

"So, what do you think?" he laughed churlishly and walked away.

JAMA DEFENDS SUGAR

"How prevalent are clinical problems caused by sugar-insulin roller coasters?"

"Quite common."

"Most internists and family practitioners are indoctrinated to think that only quacks diagnose clinical hypoglycemia."

"That's a problem."

"They fail to see the obvious, but I don't blame them."

"No?" Choua took me by surprise.

"How can you blame mainstream doctors for not buying what their gurus sell?"

"What?" I asked, baffled.

"That sugar isn't bad at all. Wasn't that the conclusion of the meta-analysis study published in the *Journal of the American Medical Association* in its November 22-29, 1995, issue?"

"I must have missed that. What did the article say?" I asked, taken by surprise. "I don't believe anyone would have defended sugar in 1995."

"You're not a good judge of those things, are you?" Choua laughed. "You underestimate the ingenuity of docs on the sugar industry's payroll. They've been eloquently defending sugar for decades."

"I know they've done it in the past, but you're talking about 1995," I expressed doubt.

"Why should 1995 sugar dollars buy less than 1965 sugar dollars?"

I recognized his reference to studies published in prestigious American medical journals repudiating a handful of nutritionist-physicians who warned against the hazards of sugar, especially for children. It was later revealed that doctors who wrote in defense of sugar were funded by the sugar industry.

"But, Choua, I don't understand one thing. In meta-analysis, the data obtained with several studies are analyzed to enhance the statistical power of the results. Such studies are scientifically valid. How could *JAMA* make such a glaring mistake? If there's one thing that all nutritionist-physicians agree on, it's the harmful effects of excess sugar."

"Do you understand, Dr. Innocent? Do you?" he laughed. "If you select only previous papers published by sugar defenders and do a meta-analysis, what's the probable outcome?"

"Of course! The conclusions drawn from a bunch of studies that defend sugar would be no different from those of a single study extolling sugar."

"Not bad for a pathologist!" Choua chimed.

We rode in silence. I thought about the kids with attention deficit disorder (ADD), hyperactivity syndrome and Tourette's syndrome that my associates and I see at the Institute. Invariably, focus on sugar dysregulation, food sensitivities and mold allergy brings about a positive change. In over eighty percent of children with ADD, we are able to discontinue Ritalin and other drugs that were prescribed for them before we saw them.

Abrupt changes in blood glucose levels are caused by the intake of large amounts of sugar that is readily absorbed. Eating candy, cakes, cookies, and other sugary foods causes sudden increases in blood sugar levels which, in turn, evoke strong pancreatic responses with rapid release of insulin. The insulin bursts quickly drive the sugar level down to lower levels than normal. This sequence of events creates sudden hyperglycemic-hypoglycemic shifts which I call glucose-insulin roller coasters. The more sugar a person consumes, the more vulnerable he becomes to those sugar-insulin roller coasters.

The adverse effects of sugar on mood, behavior and school performance, of course, are well known among experienced, knowledgeable nutritionists. The *JAMA* paper was patently deceptive, a brazen attempt to promote the interest of, as Choua says, those who profit from sugar addiction among children and adults. Excess sugar is an immunodepressant. The Russian endocrinologist, Professor Vladimir Dillman, proposed that theory and the New York physician, Pavel Yutsis, M.D., among others, validated it. They demonstrated adverse effects on the immune functions of human immune blood cells. But why did Choua bring hypertension and coronary heart disease into the picture? I wondered. What was the link between the two? Perhaps it was adrenaline, as he stated. But it was his strong statement against the role of cholesterol that concerned me.

Could there be another area of medical controversy where mainstream physicians and nutritionist-physicians are further apart? Sugar-insulin dysregulation is clearly one of the most fundamental —if not the *most* fundamental —metabolic derangement of our time. Yet mainstream physicians never pay attention to sugar-insulin-adrenaline roller coasters. The community of nutritionist-physicians, by contrast, is only too happy to ascribe all sorts of symptoms to real or imagined hypoglycemia. Many nutritionists blame yeast for everything—and hypoglycemia is no exception. The *Candida* yeast organism is the new dragon, and Nystatin is the new dragon-killer. One would think the gulf between the two schools of medicine would narrow as our knowledge about glucose-insulin dysregulation increases. But it seems the exact opposite is taking place—and the positions of both groups only harden with time.

SUGAR-INSULIN ROLLER COASTERS

My thoughts eventually drifted to Robert K., a successful corporate attorney. Robert initially saw me for weight control and allergy treatment. Like many patients in this predicament, he wanted to know if I had an exotic potion or secret formula that might speed his metabolism and melt his unwanted pounds. I told him he was out of luck. All we had was rational and scientifically sound advice about some food choices that would prevent the clogging of his fat-burning enzymes and some recommendations for slow, sustained, nongoal-oriented, noncompetitive exercise that would up-regulate those enzymes. I advised him to read some chapters of *The Butterfly and Life Span Nutrition* and *The Ghoraa and Limbic Exercise*. He listened to me with interest, promising to finish his reading assignments and follow our program carefully.

Not surprisingly, he didn't lose any weight, but his allergy symptoms improved markedly with immunotherapy injections. Several months later he returned and said the following:

What's happening to me is incredible. I was always a very high-energy-level person. I would meet with clients, discuss complex issues for hours, stay very focused, then return to my office to quickly dictate a brief and finish the matter. Now I listen to clients, thinking I'm focused the whole time, but when I return to my office, I find my mind is utterly blank. There's nothing there! Nothing at all. I can't get anything done. I'm irritable, confused and terribly scared. All my tests come back normal. What kind of a disease is this? It couldn't be a hidden cancer somewhere, could it?

One important aspect of his case history, which I discovered during that visit, was his deep involvement in a Holocaust survival group. Robert lost both his parents and other family members in concentration camps. Several days before his office visit, Robert had presided over some Holocaust memorial functions. His wife told me he spoke eloquently and with emotion. At an intellectual level, he seemed to have carried his responsibilities admirably. But his work exacted a heavy toll he didn't consciously acknowledge.

"What did you have for breakfast today?" I asked.

"It's not that," he snapped, then softened. "I don't eat breakfast."

"Why?"

"Why?" he was taken aback. "Because I never do. I never

have."

"I thought I emphasized the importance of a good breakfast when we started our program."

"Doc, that's not the issue. I don't have breakfast because I'm not hungry then. Besides, something this serious couldn't possibly be due to missing breakfast."

"It's not that simple, Robert. It's imperative that we focus on..."

"I never ate breakfast before, and I never had this problem," he interrupted me. "We have to look elsewhere for the root of this problem," he said emphatically.

"Let's do a four- or five-hour glucose and insulin tolerance test," I countered, equally emphatic.

"Do it if you must, but I'm telling you that's not where the problem is," he sighed.

Robert's four-hour insulin profiles after a 75-gram sugar load are shown on the next page (R). That profile is contrasted with a normal insulin profile (N). Note the sharp rise followed by rapid fall in Robert's blood insulin levels—a typical insulin roller coaster that evokes powerful and distressing adrenergic rushes followed by symptoms of hypoglycemia. Such insulin roller coasters also set into motion cholinergic and neurotransmitter roller coasters. Human metabolism can cope well with an occasional insulin roller coaster, but does poorly when one roller coaster is followed by another in quick succession due to massive boluses of sugar.

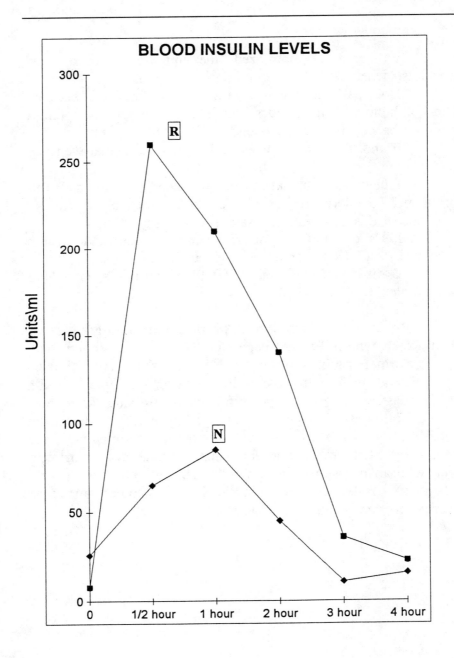

Serendipity taught me the next important lesson in sugar-insulin dysregulation: Optimally designed protein formulas (90% or more in protein content) have a desirable effect on an individual's sugar-insulin profiles. A man consulted me for severe fatigue, sugar craving and hypoglycemic symptoms. As a part of my diagnostic work-up, I ordered glucose and insulin tolerance tests. The man misunderstood my instructions and reported to the laboratory after drinking a protein formula that I had prescribed for breakfast. Unable to reach me, the laboratory staff proceeded with the glucose and insulin tolerance tests. When I saw the results, I was utterly surprised by his insulin profile.   Until then, I had never seen a gentle slope of rising insulin levels after breakfast. Of course, the slow, sustained rise in blood insulin level was followed by a slow and steady fall.

An example of a four-hour insulin curve idealized by taking a protein and vegetable juice drink is shown on the next page (P). This health-promoting insulin curve is contrasted with an abnormal health-threatening insulin profile of a patient with high blood pressure and a history of heart attack.

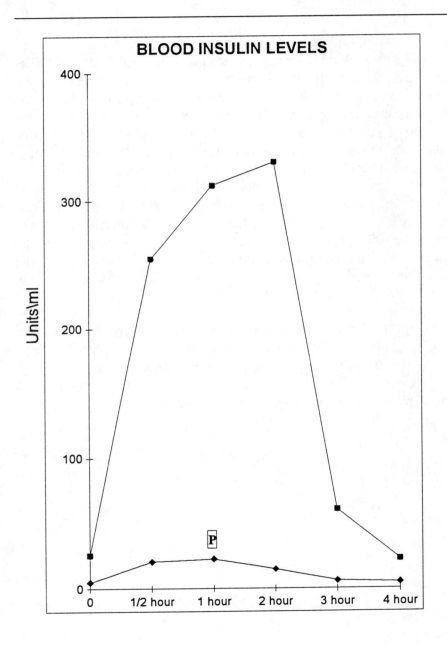

When evaluating patients for the existence of glucose-insulin dysregulation, most patients limit laboratory tests to a three- or four-hour glucose tolerance test. This is a mistake. I have seen many patients with clear and strong histories of clinically significant sugar roller coasters. Yet their glucose tolerance studies disclosed unimpressive deviations from normal profiles. However, when I examined their insulin curves ordered at the same time as glucose tolerance tests, objective laboratory evidence for their symptomatology became abundantly clear. Below, I give the values for blood glucose and insulin levels of one such patient. Corresponding graphs appear on the following page.

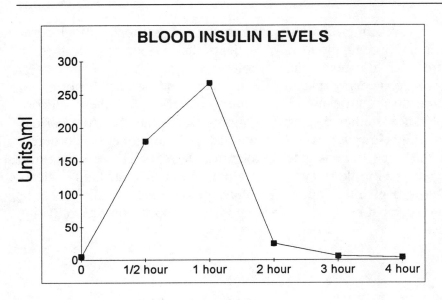

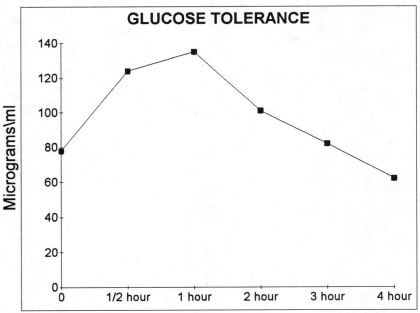

I DON'T WAKE UP SHAKY, SWEATY, DIZZY AND ANXIOUS ANYMORE

Some weeks after we returned from Kenya, Choua walked into my office holding a canary folder. The staff keeps charts of male patients in blue and those of females in canary folders.

"This is Catherine D.'s chart. You remember her, don't you?" he asked.

"How could I forget her?" I replied.

"She's a 44-year-old nurse."

"Yes, I know."

"You would think a nurse devastated by a chronic, unrelenting illness who sees many doctors and gets no relief would keep good records, wouldn't you?"

"Yes, I'd think so."

"Here, I'll read the typed clinical history sheet she brought with her when she consulted you."

"You really don't need to read that sheet. I remember every detail." I tried to save time.

"Listen," Choua began, ignoring my plea.

'74   *Hypoglycemia-like symptoms brought under control with diet changes.*

'77   *Kidney stone removed from right kidney, nephropexy.*

'79   *Hysterectomy and left ovary removed for fibroid.*

'88-89   *Repeated bladder infections.*

'90   *Premarin discontinued after two weeks due to blood sugar drop.*

'90   *Flu. Bowel pattern change, anal irritation Progressiveweight loss: 6-8 pounds.*

'91   *Severe irritability and hypersensitivity to sound, periods of dizziness and apprehensiveness. Flu*

6/92   *Sore throat, headache, achiness, fatigue for 3 days, recurs in two weeks along with episodes of dizziness, anxiety and sense of impending doom.*
One week of severe fatigue, dizziness, in bed for 1 wk.

8/92   *Severe symptoms upon awakening in a.m.- hunger, severe anxiety, faintness, tingling in fingers. Periodic chills, sweating esecially at night—anxiety, shakiness, weakness, dizziness, wooziness, severe irritability, heart palpitations, problems with balance, visual changes, hypersensitivity to sound.*
Hungry every two hours around the clock, diarrhea, loose, light-colored stools, gas, intestinal gurgling, cool sensation in esophagus, stomach pain and acidity, achiness, migraines

10/92   *Occasional 3-4 hours stretches before*

needing to eat; severe bladder infections

11/92   *Some general improvement in all areas; still occasional shakiness, sweating, very bad nightmares. Sore gums, fatigue, achiness, diarrhea, foot cramps at night, irritability to touch on left side of face (lasted two weeks). Still occasional dizziness, shakiness, chills, sweating, achiness in joints and muscles*

2/93   *General improvement.*

3/93   *Slight sore throat, periods of achiness and fatigue.*

6/93   *One week of diarrhea (virus going around)*

8/93   *Dizziness, fatigue, hunger increasing every two hours. Still have fatigue, light-colored stools, diarrhea, need to eat every three hours, sometimes more frequently, occasional periods of shakiness, weakness if food is delayed (especially mid-morning), occasional dizziness, blurred vision, sweating (especially at night), migraines, palpitations*

"I defy any mainstream physician to make sense of this case," Choua said to me after he finished reading the sheet. "The only thing any internist, cardiologist, gastroenterologist, neurologist, endocrinologist or rheumatologist can do for her is refer her to a psychiatrist, right?"

"I'm afraid so," I confessed.

"And that's exactly what they did."

"Yes."

"What did the psychiatrist do?" he groused.

"Prescribe antidepressants and antianxiety drugs," I replied.

"Did she get better?"

"Not really."

"What else did the psychiatrist do? Invoke his grand theory of secondary gains? Tell her she wasn't getting better because she doesn't *want* to?"

"That was hard on her."

"Now let me read from your notes what she said in the spring of 1995. 'I don't wake up shaky, sweaty, dizzy, and anxious anymore.'"

"I remember that," I said.

"How did she get better?"

"You know how, don't you?"

"I really do," he smiled. "You went the full nine yards —frequent small meals; liberal protein and essential oil supplements; vitamin, mineral, and herbal therapies; intramuscular and intravenous nutrient therapies; food sensitivity, mold and pollen allergy tests; immunotherapy; chelation for toxic metals; gentle support for her sagging thyroid, adrenals and ovaries; DHEA tests and therapy; protein protocols; lot of meditation; and slow and sustained incremental exercise. Then, slowly and with many relapses, her symptoms improved. What made you think her problems were not all in her head?" he asked with a wink.

"Because they weren't," I replied firmly. "She's an intelligent woman. She is a professional —a nurse. She recorded her case history carefully. She never suffered any psychiatric disorders before she came down with debilitating hypoglycemia. Why would I think she suffers some psychiatric disease?"

"You need to take some psychiatry classes, don't you?" he laughed impishly, then shuffled some papers in his hands.

NON-HYPOGLYCEMIA
IS AN EPIDEMIC CONDITION

"Do you know non-hypoglycemia is an epidemic?" Choua asked.

"That's a ludicrous statement. Who said that?" I asked.

"*The New England Journal of Medicine*—on page 907, volume 291, 1974," he beamed.

"How can anything be an epidemic when it doesn't exist?" I asked, astonished. "What does the *Journal* mean?"

"Who knows what it means?" he waved his arm contemptuously, then continued, "Here, listen to this:

They are usually physically healthy persons with various forms of anxiety or emotional disturbance...studies have shown that "reactive hypoglycemia" is strongly associated with a variety of anxiety states, with certain psychiatric disorders, especially depression, and with certain personality types and neurotic behaviors (which tend to be associated with high scores for somatization hypochondriasis and hysteria...The majority of patients are women (the reported proportion varies from 65% to 90%).

That's the March 30, 1989, issue of *Hospital Practice.*
Illuminating, isn't it?" he asked with a smirk.

"I don't know what's illuminating about it," I replied,
ignoring his sarcasm.

"The journal says hypoglycemia is neurosis."

"That's absurd."

"When it isn't neurosis, it's hypochondria. Isn't that
brilliant?" he groused.

"A bad mistake."

"Do you know what somatization hypochondriasis is?"

"No," I replied.

"It's when the doctor thinks he knows everything there is
to know and the patient is too stupid to know anything," Choua
chuckled.

"Now you're being Choua," I chastised.

"Being Choua?" he frowned. "What is hypochondria?"

"When a patient imagines she has a health disorder when
in truth she doesn't," I explained.

"How do you diagnose it?"

"By ruling out the existence of various diseases."

"How?"

"With appropriate tests and scans."

"When a patient tells yous he is suffering but your test
results are negatives, do you think you're entitled to call her a
liar?" he asked with piercing eyes.

"No, it's not that simple," I protested.

"Is your diagnostic technology improving with time?" he
pressed.

"Of course! Why do you ask?"

"Are there disorders which you can diagnose with your
tests today that you couldn't twenty years ago?"

"Yes, but..."

"So you confess," Choua cut me off curtly, "it's possible

for people to be sick even though their doctors' tests can't define the molecular basis of a patient's suffering, right?"

"Right, but..."

"That's what folks who write for *The New England Journal of Medicine* and *Hospital Practice* don't understand," he snarled. "A patient's suffering doesn't become any less just because his doctor doesn't know enough. People who suffer from hypoglycemia know that their symptoms can be relieved by dietary measures that stabilize their blood sugar levels. Whether your academicians know that or not isn't relevant to them. That's the blunt truth about somatization hypochondriasis —it's a diagnosis of ignorance," Choua gored.

"You exaggerate," I complained.

"Exaggerate?" He suddenly stiffened, stared at me intensely for several moments, then asked, "Did Catherine's doctors tell her she didn't suffer from hypochondria?"

"That was bad, I agree. They should have coomforted her."

"Listen to this," he suddenly laughed, leafing through several articles he was holding:

Patients should be told that they do not have hypoglycemia...should be given reassurance that their disorder is benign...This approach gives patients some insight into their condition and enables them to save face.

This is from the end of the editorial in *Hospital Practice*. How noble of the doctor!" Choua waved his arm scornfully, then resumed. "He is so deeply concerned about his patient saving her face. Tell me, whose face needs to be saved? The patient who suffers from symptoms of hyperglycemic-hypoglycemic shifts or her ignorant doctor?"

"Things are changing," I replied lamely.

"Changing?" he growled. "When did you see Catherine first?"

"Fall of 1993."

"Did you note that the writer used figures of 65% to 90% for the incidence of hypoglycemia in females to support his view that hypoglycemia is a psychiatric disorder?" he shifted from Catherine's case.

"That's not uncommon. Most medical texts describe hypochondria primarily as a female psychiatric disorder," I replied.

"Why?" he pressed.

"I never really thought about it, Choua. Do you know?"

"What you dismiss as hypochondria are feminine qualities of sensitivity and nurturing. Women sense things earlier and to greater degrees than men. They can feel their pain—as well as that of their kin and friends—more than men. They're more aware of their needs—and the needs of their offspring. When a lioness senses the hunger of her cubs, she goes hunting. She doesn't idle around, infatuated with her stately bearing, the way a patriarch male does. When women experience abrupt metabolic and hormonal shifts, they don't play macho games the way men do. What does a father really know about the anguish of his child with hyperactivity syndrome if all he sees him is on the basketball court? Hyperactive Johnny thrives on the court—his hyperactivity helps him outperform other boys. The dad is so proud. But does the dad know—or care—how many times little Johnny kicks his mom's shins when she insists he finish his homework? Biology has set different biologic priorities for females and males. Life is a cliff, and women have a sharper depth perception. The male psychiatrist who freely doles out his pseudo-wisdom of psychiatric diagnoses for women suffering from hyperglycemic-hypoglycemic shifts should know that." Choua heaved as he finished his last sentences, then walked out without caring to hear my response.

Some days later, I read the following passages in *The Diary of William Harvey:*

> *A long time ago I was asked to go to St. Thomas Hospital to see an eighteen-year-old girl called Mary. She too had lost the sense of pain...Needles could be stuck into all parts of her body without causing her any pain...All the women I have seen behaving in this way were single women who had no man in their life, and as if their uterus, indignant at being deprived of its due sustenance of relations with the masculine sex, were responsible for the paroxysm in the brain. I believe we could talk of uterine melancholy. These women are not fabricating their feelings, they are not simulators, their morbid symptoms are genuine. They have a deranged mind, and it creates some bizarre disturbances that resemble no known disease.*

William Harvey, one of the most famous English physicians of all time, was physician to King Charles I of England. He is known for his discovery of blood circulation in the human body—a discovery that had actually been noted earlier by the Italian anatomist, Michel Servet. Things haven't changed much since Harvey's days, have they? I imagined Choua saying. (In addition to penning the above lines, William Harvey also wrote what I consider one of the most moving accounts of why many physicians feel compelled to record their clinical and research observations.)

FRIENDS OF SUGARS

"Sugar industry is very resourceful and it has powerful friends," Choua asked me some weeks later in my New York office. "Consider the following quote from the April 8, 1996 issue of *Time* magazine:

SUGAR'S SWEETEST DEAL

Agricultural socialism was supposed to end this week with the signing by President Clinton of the landmark Federal Agriculture Improvement and Reform Act (FAIR). Touted as the most ambitious effort to bring free enterprise to the farm..., the overall slashes price supports for staples from wheat to cotton...But for America's sugar growers, how sweet it still is...The (sugar) growers outfoxed not only congressional reformers but also a high-powered coalition of sugar and sweetener users.

"Interesting, isn't?" he winked.

"That's amazing," I replied.

"Why should it amaze you? Why should it amaze anyone? What do you think it will take them to persuade the *Journal of the American Medical Association* to publish a piece in defense of sugar?"

"I don't think the editors of the Journal would fall for such browbeating," I countered.

"Mr. Innocent, you understand neither the sugar industry nor the editors of the *Journal*," he growled. "Considering the sweet persuasive power of the sugar industry, why should it surprise anyone to see the *Journal of the American Medical Association* march to their drums? How difficult it would be for them to persuade a few writers to prepare for publication a super study in eloquent defense of sugar. Consider the following quote:

The meta-analysis synthesis of the studies to date found that sugar does not affect the behavior or cognitive performance of children.

Journal of the American Medical Association
274:1617; 1995

Medical science is malleable, isn't it?" Choua asked with a grin as he looked up from the pages of the *Journal.*

"Rascal!" I suppressed a smile.

"Right amounts of money can always order the *Journal* to deliver the right medical *science* on any subject, at any time. Right?" he winked.

"You're a rascal!" I laughed and left the room.

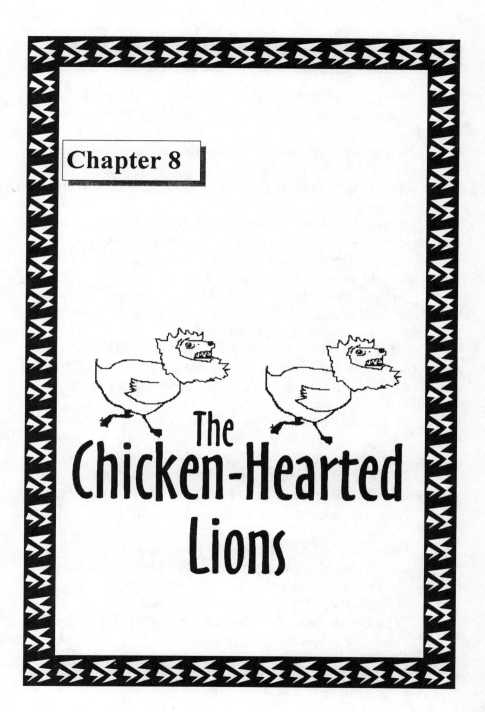

Chapter 8

The
Chicken-Hearted
Lions

"Why has man been obsessed with lions?" Choua asked.

"Lions are majestic animals, and they inspire awe," I replied.

"There are other majestic animals that inspire awe. Why single out the lion species?"

"The lion is king of the jungle—the most powerful and fastest of all cats."

"It's not the most powerful—the Indian tiger is. And it's not the fastest—the African cheetah is," he countered.

"Those claims about tigers and cheetahs may be true, but the lion is still king of the jungle," I held my ground.

"What happened when a pride of lions moved too close to the black elephant bull?" he asked, referring to a scene we had seen in a *National Geographic* video.

"That was totally unexpected," I replied. "The huge bull charged when it was angered by the lions coming too close to her herd. The lions scurried away in different directions, as mice do when they see a cat."

"Some king of the jungle!" Choua mocked.

"Okay, you tell me why the lion is called king of jungle?" I asked, a trifle confused.

"Because man cannot live without heroes. And, when none are forthcoming, he invents them," Choua grinned broadly.

"Are you saying man created a mythical king of the jungle?"

"Who else do you think has lionized lions?" he asked back, then continued. "Certainly lions didn't lionize themselves. They didn't create lion myths, did they?"

"I guess not. Who do you think created them?"

"Those who benefitted from those myths. Who else?"

"Who?" I repeated my question.

"Tribal chiefs, princes, kings and emperors, or their story-tellers."

"Why would they do that?" I asked.

"If they didn't first assign supernatural powers to the beasts, how could they claim supernatural powers for themselves by killing the animals? If their bards didn't first sing the songs of mighty lions, how could they sing the songs of the mightier lords who slew the beasts?"

"Choua, that's a new one for me. I never heard of that before," I replied in mock admiration.

"In the conquest of lions, man searches for his own manhood," Choua continued.

"Since when have you become interested in psychology and hidden human motives?" I teased.

"Do you think those princes and kings killed lions simply because they inspire awe?" His forehead wrinkled a little.

"I'm sure they didn't hunt lions just for that," I replied.

"Of course not. Lions are idolized. Don't you see how many ways we use their symbols?"

"That's true," I agreed as I thought about the hundreds of palaces I had visited in Pakistan, India, Europe, Central America, Japan and China.

"I doubt you can visit any major palace in any country without seeing lions everywhere." Choua seemed to sense my thoughts. "Lions guard the palace gates and look down from the roofs of guard houses. They swarm the palace gardens. They are in palace courts. And of course, they adorn the court-of-arms."

"True," I agreed again.

"Some lions are there to add to the might of their keepers," he continued. "They hold shields and swords in their paws. Others rest their paws on marble and granite globes, symbolizing their mastery of the planet."

I remembered a visit to the royal palace in Copenhagen. There were lions everywhere inside the palace buildings, as well

as in the surrounding gardens. Sitting on either side of the
throne that rose at one end of an enormous ballroom stood two
huge silver lions. A guidebook told the story of a king who
wanted to embellish his throne with four lions made of pure
silver. Alas! His subjects ran out of tax money.

I remembered the Mogul palaces in Lahore, Pakistan,
where I grew up. I recalled lions symbols in Lal Quilla, Delhi,
India where Bahadar Shah Zafar, the last Mogul emperor, was
incarcerated by the British before they exiled him to Rangoon,
Burma to die. Next, I remembered a walk through the
Forbidden Palace in Beijing. The Chinese Emperors were no
less obsessed with lions than the Mogul emperors of India. They
adorned their dragons with lion heads in equally ingenious ways.
They put their royal motifs everywhere—on roofs, walls,
fountainheads, patios, even their robes.

But nowhere was royal infatuation with the lion torso
more compelling than on the Avenue of Sphinxes at Karnak.
Ramses II, the pharaoh often associated with Moses, who
proclaimed himself to be the world's greatest builder. He was
one megalomaniac who called his shot right. Who would deny
his claim today? Not anyone who ever saw the Temples of
Karnak and Abu Simbal. The broad avenue is lined on two
sides by motionless lion-sphinxes, waiting obediently for the
pharaoh's procession to pass or squatting on their haunches as
if threatening those who might question the pharaoh's divinity.

"Homer's chimera was a lion-headed beast with a goat's
body and a dragon's tail," Choua spoke and brought me back
from my wandering thoughts. "If the dragons are not much of
dragons, dragon-killers cannot be much of dragon-killers either,"
he laughed.

"What's the point of all this?" I asked.

"Lions are the latest of the fallen hero." he went on. "The legends of lion-hearted lions are now being contaminated with stories of chicken-hearted lions."

"Chicken-hearted lions?" I asked, amused and baffled. "Who are chicken-hearted lions?"

"Cowardly lions who don't stick to the script written for them," Choua chuckled.

"What do you mean?"

"They don't act like lion-hearted lions. They shy away from turf battles. When called, they lag behind."

"Is that true?"

"It's not that the lion-hearted lions don't understand the consequences of the cowardly behavior of the nonlion-hearted lions," he went on, ignoring my question. "They know territorial battles are serious business. When they charge the invading lions, they go for the kill. And so do the invaders. They know when their chicken-hearted comrades lag behind, it strengthens the invaders who fight more ferociously."

"Why do the laggards stay behind?" I asked.

"Why?" he frowned. "Because they what the fighting is all about. That's precisely the reason the laggards dawdle behind. They hope to escape mutilation and death."

"And their lagging behind puts their stout-hearted comrades at greater risk of injury and death," I guessed.

"Exactly. In turf battles, lions know their chances to survive depend on their number. Grossly outnumbered cats have no staying power. Forced into isolation, a lioness knows that she has no chance of a decent life—it's solitary death."

"So chicken-hearted lions jeopardize the lives of lion-hearted lions."

"Right."

"What happens when the conflict is over?" I asked. "How

do the leaders deal with laggards?"

"That's the surprise. The laggards go unpunished."

"Then how do lions maintain order in the pride?"

"Lions do not share your anthropomorphic sense of social order in animals."

"What's your point?" I asked, frustrated.

"When the fittest among lions fight off the intruders, they don't intellectualize about your notions of survival of the fittest. They don't lead the charge because they think they are the fittest and hence must lead the charge. They lead the charge for the same reason the chicken-hearted lions do not—they follow the impulses fired by their neurons."

"The stout-hearted lionesses tolerate their soft-hearted sisters without protest. That's astonishing! Tell me, how do you know there are leader and laggard lions?"

"*Science* magazine, in its September 1, 1995, issue, carried an interesting report about Serengeti lions by Robert Heinsohn of the Australian National University and Craig Packer of the University of Minnesota. They used recorded sounds of intruding lions to provoke prides of lions, then observed their responses."

We were quiet for a while. I had no reason to question the research observations of Heinsohn and Packer. But their finding that leadership lions readily forgive laggard lions intrigued me. The leaders must know the cost of their charge against the intruders: Strangers kill strangers. The laggards must also know that. Wouldn't that be the only reason why they lag behind? Why wouldn't the lion-hearted shun the chicken-hearted after a few skirmishes, after the stout were let down by the meek? It just didn't make sense.

"You would think the fearless lions would recognize the

cowardly lions and shun them in future skirmishes," I said after some minutes.

"Why should they?" Choua asked back.

"For one, it flies against the accepted theories of social cooperation among animals."

"What theories?" he grimaced.

"The standard theories of Tit-for-Tat Cooperation and Prisoner's Dilemma."

"Tit-for-Tat meaning that leaders should punish the laggards after the conflict is over. Tell me what's Prisoner's Dilemma?" he asked.

"According to Prisoner's Dilemma theory," I explained, "if two prisoners are incarcerated in separate cells and are charged with the same crime, the length of their sentences depends on whether they cooperate with each other or try to implicate each other. The one who defects might go free or receive a shorter prison term while the second who remains faithful to the defector would likely get a longer sentence. If animals do the same for food or sex, it's hard to see how they can be altruistic. Those are the accepted theories."

"Accepted?," he groused. "Accepted by whom?"

"It is generally accepted among behavioral ecologists," I held my ground.

"Do you think lions calculate the odds of mutilation or death?"

"They may not do so in our terms but they must have some sense of such things."

"They are what they are. In nature, living beings are what they are."

"What does that mean?" I asked, irritated.

"It means just what it says," he posited. "You can observe biology but you cannot rationalize it. You can witness the struggle for life and death —call it fight-or-flight stress response or relaxation response or whatever else you will—but naming things doesn't change their nature. Nor do you understand things better just because you classify them. That's the point."

"You have to classify things in science," I countered.

"Humans need heroes —larger-than-life beings that they can idolize," he went on. "But, nature has no respect for man's need of heroes, does it?"

"It's not a question of whether nature has or doesn't have respect. There are some clear patterns of leadership, not only among men but also among lions. In periods of turmoil and stress, the animals support and sustain each other. At least that's what behavioral ecologists tell us."

"Notions of behavioral ecology are human inventions, as are those of stress."

"But the concept of behavioral ecology and stress in animals is based on the extended observation of animal behavior in nature," I challenged.

"The concepts of cooperation among animals are as much artifacts of the human mind as those of stress," he countered.

"Why would an animal do something that benefits another but is a cost to him?" I asked. "Everyone is stumped by such questions."

"Lions evidently don't care whether human observers ask the right questions or find the right answers."

"Are you saying that when a lion jumps to defend its pride's turf and risks being mauled —even killed—by the intruder, it's all premeditated selflessness?"

"Selflessness is another human concept. I don't know if lions care much about that."

"You don't believe in altruism?" I asked in disbelief. "How can you deny the established tenets of sociobiology—the science that deals with the altruism that governs animal behavior?"

"Does altruism govern human behavior?" he asked, ignoring my questions.

"Yes! Well, no! I mean people do care for each other," I stammered.

"Some lions dislike fighting with other lions. Are they really bums? Are those lions chicken-hearted because they aren't quick to attack?" he asked, grinned impishly, then continued. "Or, shall we wait for a future lion study to show that bum lionesses make better communal mothers? Or that chicken-hearted lionesses might be more generous with their milk, freely sharing it with other lionesses' cubs? Or that cowardly lionesses might be better strategists in stalking prey and driving it to the lion-hearted hunters?"

"Science is self-correcting," I replied. "If any of that is true, it will be proven with future research."

"I don't know why that troubles you so," Choua frowned. "Some lions thrive on charging at intruders. Others find it stressful. After the posturing for defense or fighting is over, both groups take that in stride. The chargers and non-chargers of the pride get together and go on with the business of living together. That's all. What is there to understand?"

"Still, I find it baffling that..."

"Some lions can cope well with the Fourth-of-July chemistry of fighting while others can't," Choua completed my sentence, gazed at me for some moments, then walked away.

Roosters flutter their wings to announce their morning. Canaries flap their feathers before they fly off their nests. Dogs stretch before they take their first steps. So do cats. We humans wake up to our coffee and begin to recyclethe misery of our yesterdaysand map out the feared future misery of our tomorrows.

The Ghoraa and Limbic Exercise

Chapter 9

Anxiety, Lactic Acid and Limbic Lions

"What do lions know about lactic acid?" Choua asked me later during the safari.

"I thought we were through with chemistry," I replied.

"Lactic acid is the guardian angel molecule for antelopes," he murmured.

"I thought you asked me about lions and lactic acid. Are we on to antelopes now? Tell me, what makes lactic acid a guardian angel molecule for antelopes?"

"Lactic acid is a guardian angel molecule for lions," he mumbled.

"Will you make up your mind?" I asked, perplexed, "Are you talking about lions or antelopes?"

"It's the same thing, isn't it?" he grinned.

"Lions are not antelopes, nor antelopes lions," I countered. "Is lactic acid a guardian molecule for lions or for antelopes?"

"For both," he replied calmly. "It saves antelopes from lions and lions from themselves."

"Saves lions from lions?" I asked, irked by his cryptic words. "What do you mean it saves lions from lions?"

"Just as it saves antelopes from lions."

"Speak plainly, will you? How does lactic acid save antelopes from lions and lions from themselves?"

"It's simple," he grinned. "Think about it. What does lactic acid do in muscles?"

Lactic acid is an interesting molecule of human energy pathways. It is produced from its precursor, pyruvic acid, during the metabolism of carbohydrates, fats and proteins. It is a cul-de-sac molecule—once produced in tissues, it cannot be metabolized further.

All food substances are metabolized to release chemical

bond energy contained in them for various body functions. After initial breakdown is completed, partially digested fat, protein and carbohydrate molecules enter a metabolic cycle called the Krebs cycle. Next, the enzymes of this cycle break down those food molecules into pyruvic acid, and finally into water and carbon dioxide.

When one is healthy, sufficient oxygen is available during rest to completely break down pyruvic acid. Under those conditions, only minute quantities of pyruvic acid is anaerobically (without oxygen) converted into lactic acid. Whatever amounts of lactic acid are so produced eventually get converted back into pyruvic acid, then broken down further into water and carbon dioxide.

In many acute disease states and other conditions such as heart failure, sufficient oxygen is not available for the complete metabolism of food molecules in the Krebs cycle. Metabolism is then arrested at the pyruvic acid level. Excess pyruvic acid is then turned into lactic acid that accumulates in the tissues, producing a condition called lactic acidosis. Acidosis, a condition of excess acidity, inhibits many essential energy and detoxification enzyme systems.

When a sprinter sprints, muscle tissue burns sugar rapidly to release the required energy for the sprint. When oxygen in the tissues has been used up, pyruvic acid cannot be broken down further, and instead is converted into lactic acid. Excess lactic acid, in turn, shuts off energy and detoxification, forcing the sprinter to break his sprint. *Thus, lactic acid may be considered a limiting factor in intense physical activity.*

But, why did Choua bring up the subject of lactic acid in

a discussion about stress? I wondered. I looked at him. He looked at the distant horizon, deep in thought.

"How does lactic acid save an antelope from a lion?" I asked after a while.

"Lions have everything going for them, antelopes nothing —except for lactic acid in the lions' muscles," he replied without turning to face me.

"Ah, I get it now. Lactic acid is a fatigue molecule. Its accumulation in the lion's muscles turns off the energy enzymes in those muscles."

"Yes," Choua continued. "The mitochondria —cellular powerhouses —in lions' muscles need oxygen to keep humming. Why do you think lions often stop midway in their hunts?"

"Because lactic acid buildup inactivates energy enzymes in the lion's legs and stops the lion dead. That gives the poor antelope has a chance to escape. Right?" I asked.

"Right," Choua replied.

"Lactic acid accumulation —or lactic acid debt, as it is called—switches off enzymes that oxidize foods for release of energy. Thus, the oxidative breakdown of foods in Krebs's energy cycle is halted," I elaborated.

"Right!" Choua's eyes lit up. "That's what happens in the lion muscle cells. Wouldn't it be nice if things were that simple for humans?" he murmured, raised his eyebrows, then turned his gaze to the distant hills again.

Nearly four decades earlier in physiology class, I was taught that the blood and tissue fluids in the human body are maintained in a slight state of alkalinity. Optimal function of enzymes (catalysts) in the body depends on this alkalinity. The body spends considerable energy to prevent build-up of acids such as lactic acid in tissues and blood that would put in jeopardy the physiologic functions of many energy and detoxification enzymes.

Lactic acid accumulation exhausts the acid-alkali buffering capacity of the blood and the tissue fluid that bathes cells. If not corrected expediently, lactic acidosis impedes the function of enzymes of the energy, detoxification and antioxidant systems of the body. Hence, the importance of preventing lactic acidosis in patients with massive trauma and acute medical emergencies.

Oxygen-starved cells produce lactic acid in large quantities. The result may be irregular heart rhythm, which, unless reversed expediently, can lead to cardiac arrest and death. Indeed, the occurrence of lactic acidosis during surgery is so feared by surgeons that they are ever so watchful of it. This is also the reason why it is frequently the subject of questions in their certification examinations. In 1964, when I sat in the examination for the diploma of the fellow of the Royal College of Surgeons of England, I remember I was asked questions about lactic acidosis.

Similar risks are encountered by cardiologists in the care of patients with congestive heart failure. The heart fails to pump enough blood—and oxygen—to tissues for oxidative metabolism. Tissues then struggle to function without oxygen, or anaerobically. This type of metabolic insufficiency is diagnosed in clinical practice by measuring blood levels of lactic acid or lactate-pyruvate ratio. The higher the values, the more severe the heart failure.

I learned all those things about lactic acid in medical school, and again during my surgical and pathology training. But it was of little use once I began my pathology and clinical work. With time, lactic acid faded away from my working knowledge of clinical medicine. And then, in the Serengeti Plains, Choua fired all those questions at me. Why? I wondered. And what did he mean by lactic acid metabolism not being as simple for humans as it is for lions?

"Why isn't lactic acid as simple for humans as it is for lions?" I finally asked Choua.

"Because you humans are humans, and lions are lions. That's why?" he glowered. "You can't let go. You brood and sulk, and keep the oxidative coals simmering even when the metabolic digestive fires are out. The cortical monkey simply doesn't let up."

"What does the cortical monkey have to do with lactic acid?" I asked, baffled.

"What would happen if you injected lactic acid into the veins of those lions?" he asked, without acknowledging my question.

"I am not about to try that. Tell me what would happen?"

"Some lions would suffer from anxiety attacks," he continued evenly.

"Really?" I was surprised. "Has that ever been done, or are you just making it up?"

Choua grinned but didn't say anything. I didn't follow through. We rode in silence for a while.

"Exercise requires energy," Choua spoke finally. "Where does such energy come from?"

"From oxidative metabolism of food substances that releases chemical bond energy," I replied. "Didn't we just cover that subject?"

"So, the increased demands for energy during exercise can only be met by increased oxidative breakdown of food, and of starches, fats and proteins stored in tissues. In other words, during exercise, tissues come under greater oxidative stress. Right?" he asked.

"Right," I replied, not knowing where that might lead me.

"You would expect that toxic molecular species—aging-oxidant molecules, as you call them—would be produced in greater quantities during exercise."

"I agree."

"What kinds of toxic oxidative species might those be?"

"Hydrogen peroxide, superoxide radicals, singlet oxygen, hydroperoxides, hydroxyl radicals, and aldehyde, such as malonaldehyde," I named some commonly known oxidants.

"How does the body cope with them?" he asked.

"By neutralizing them with antioxidants," I replied.

"What would happen if there were an excesses of lactic acid in tissues when there was also an excess of toxic oxidative species?"

"The body's antioxidant systems would be overwhelmed. Indeed, that's the reason I recommend the use of antioxidants, such as vitamins A, E and C and other plant-derived antioxidants such as pycnogenol for my patients who engage in endurance training."

"Now, tell me, what would happen if you injected lactic acid into lions?"

"I don't know."

"Didn't you cite the lactic acid study of Pitts and McLure in *The Cortical Monkey and Healing?*"

"The one published in the *New England Journal of Medicine* in 1967?"

"Yeah."

"But, Choua, that wasn't about injecting lactic acid into lions' veins. It was about people who suffered from anxiety."

"What happened to anxiety sufferers when they were injected with lactic acid?" he asked.

"About one half of the subjects with anxiety developed acute anxiety reactions, while one out of five volunteers who served as control subjects suffered similar symptoms," I replied, then asked, "Are you saying injections of lactic acid would cause anxiety reactions in lions as well?"

"Yeah. Some lions would suffer anxiety attacks just as some people do."

"You're just guessing, aren't you?" I expressed doubt.

"Lactic acid doesn't differentiate between the oxidative energy enzymes of humans and lions. If there are differences between the lactic biochemistry of humans and lions, they are quantitative, not qualitative."

"There must be species differences," I countered.

"When enough lactic acid accumulates in the tissues, its effects are the same," he went on, ignoring my objection. "Lions, of course, may express their anxiety somewhat differently."

"Do lions suffer anxiety attacks the way my patients do?" I asked. "Do they also sweat, develop the jitters, hyperventilate and suffer heart palpitations?"

"Lions would if they carried cortical monkeys on their backs as humans do," Choua snapped.

"Okay, let's agree that lactic acid plays the same role in lions as it does in humans. So what?"

"Lions are straight shooters. Their charge is ballistic in speed. Once begun, it has no strategy. A lion's prey can often outrun him. If the prey escapes the charge, a lion stops but doesn't dwell on his failure. When a lion breaks his sprint, it soon settles down. His lactic acid-producing chemistry returns rapidly to a pyruvic-burning state. And..."

"And the accumulated lactic acid is converted back into pyruvic acid, then pulled back into Krebs's oxidative cycle and oxidized," I completed his sentence.

"Right. When the opportunity arises again, the limbic lion strikes again, fresh and without any lactic acid debt. Lions don't sulk the way people do. You know how it is with humans, don't you?"

"When humans fail, they brood and sulk and..."

"The cortical monkey doesn't let up, does it?" he interrupted me. "It loves to recycle misery. And when that's not enough, it pre-cycles feared, future misery. Those are your words, right?"

"Right," I replied, irritated.

"The monkey keeps the blood and tissue lactic acid levels raised—tightening muscles everywhere in the body and raising blood pressure."

"Do lions suffer from high blood pressure?" I asked.

"Who knows?" he shrugged, then continued, "But the cortical monkey stays revved up, keeping arteries clamped, hands and feet cold."

CANCER CELL: AN OXYGEN HATER

"How does a cancer cell differ from a noncancerous cell?" Choua asked.

"That's some schizophrenic flight of ideas," I chided. "What does lactic acid accumulation in lions' muscles have to do with cancer cells in humans?"

"How does a cancer cell differ from a noncancerous cell?" he repeated.

"A cancer cell continues to multiply. Its multiplication serves no useful function, but robs healthy cells of nutrition," I answered.

"How does it differ from a healthy cell in its energy utilization patterns?"

"Oh, that!" I saw where he was leading me. "A cancer cell is an oxyphobe—it abhors oxygen."

"It does its dirty work without oxygen," he added.

"Yes," I agreed, then continued, "Metabolism in a cancer cell is anaerobic."

"What are the chemical consequences of that?"

"A cancer cell accumulates lactic acid."

"Lactic acid, again," he grinned broadly.

"So?" I asked, baffled.

"Where ever you see trouble, you'll find lactic acid behind it," he winked.

BRICKS IN THE NECK

"How often do you see patients with stiff necks?" Choua resumed after a while.

"That's not uncommon at all," I replied. "Why do you ask?"

"Sometimes their neck and shoulder muscles are hard like bricks."

"Yes."

"Where do those bricks come from?"

"Obviously what makes neck and shoulder tissues hard are spastic muscles."

"What causes the muscle spasm?" he pressed.

"Muscles go into spasm when they are injured," I offered the standard answer.

"But isn't it actually more common for muscles to go into spasm to protect injured ligaments and tendons that lie beneath them?" he asked.

"Well, that's true." As usual Choua was closer to the truth than I.

"So?" I asked, a bit flustered.

"Why don't injured ligaments and tendons heal as fast as other soft tissues?"

"Because those tissues are poor in blood supply—and in the healing nutrients transported by blood."

"Right! What else?"

"Spastic muscles that protect injured ligaments make things worse by clamping down on the very injured ligaments and tendons they are designed to guard, further reducing their limited blood supply."

"Why don't the spastic muscles relax?"

"People with chronically stiff necks and shoulders are often angry." Words simply escaped my lips, then I recovered. "Your schizophrenia is rubbing off on me."

"Aha! Anger produces lactic acid! Mighty fine words from a pathologist," Choua chirped. "Psychiatrists are turning into neurobiologists. Why shouldn't pathologists also change colors? Why not turn into psychiatrists?"

"I don't know if anger produces lactic acid in muscles," I retrenched. "But I know angry people don't heal."

"Same thing! same thing!" He grinned impishly. "Tell me, what is the biochemical basis of anger feeding muscle spasms?" he pressed.

"Anger causes the muscles to go into spasm and leads to lactic acid overproduction. Excess lactic acid, in turn, further irritates the spastic muscles, so perpetuating the muscle spasm-lactic acidosis-muscle spasm cycle."The words again slipped my lips before I recognized I had obviously contradicted myself.

"Lactic acid, again, eh?" he grinned, then looked away—to save me embarrassment of contradiction, I thought.

LIONS PREFER LIMBIC TO LACTIC

"Humans sulk, lions don't," Choua continued.

"Lions don't have much to sulk about," I replied.

"Humans carry bricks in their shoulders, lions don't."

"Do you mean bricks *on* their shoulders, don't you?" I corrected him.

"Bricks *in* their shoulders," he repeated with emphasis. "Bricks are the frozen stiff muscles *in* their shoulders."

"Oh that," I recovered quickly, then added. "Lions don't have to report to work on time, nor do they have to cope with phones that never seem to stop ringing."

"Humans keep their neck muscles stiff and frozen, lions don't."

"The lions don't have any bills to pay, nor any real estate taxes," I went along.

"Quite right," he smiled, then added, "Humans love to build walls, don't they?"

"Walls? For houses?" I asked, puzzled.

"Wall of prisons in which they are ever so eager to incarcerate themselves. Lions don't like walls."

"Not wholly true," I countered. "Lions rigorously map out their pride's territory, only the walls they erect are of scent of their glandular secretions sprayed on tree trunks and low shrubs."

"Humans love to recycle past misery, lions don't."

"How do we know lions don't remember past misery?" I asked.

"Humans thrive on precycling feared future pain," he continued, without answering my question.

"I don't think lions have any feared future pain," I countered.

"Humans nurse their resentments for a long time; lions don't."

"How do you know?" I asked.

"When lion-hearted lionesses return to their chicken-hearted sisters after fighting off invaders, they're limbic about the whole thing. You'd think they'd hold a grudge, but they don't."

"What do you make of that?" I asked.

"There is no lactic acidosis in lions' limbic limbs," he grinned, baring his teeth.

"How do you know?" I asked, a trifle annoyed.

"Nor any bricks in their limbic haunches."

"Are you saying holding grudges causes lactic acidosis in shoulder muscles?"

"How else do you think folks bake those bricks in their neck and shoulder muscles?" he laughed out loud and walked away.

It is sad to see anyone waste away the present trying to return to the past or wanting to live in the future.

Chapter 10

Stress and the
Fourth-of-July Chemistry

"Your Serengeti lions know so much about stress chemistry. Tell me, what do they know about nitric oxide?" I teased Choua.

"You mean laughing gas?" Choua raised his eyebrows.

"No, silly,"I laughed. "Laughing gas is nit*rous* oxide. I'm talking about nit*ric* oxide."

"Hmm!" he mumbled. "Why are you interested in nitric oxide?"

"It's an important molecule. I figure it must play some role in the stress response," I replied.

"The stress response again, eh?" he grimaced.

"Tell me, what do your lions know about nitric oxide?" I pressed.

"Why do you think nitric oxide is important?" he asked, ignoring my question.

"It's an oxidant. It has free radical properties that light up many a molecular fire,"I replied.

"Light up a molecular fire!" he grinned, then added, "So it's bad player."

"Not quite. It's an oxidant but it also has many positive effects."

"For example?"

"It relaxes the blood vessel wall and that improves circulation."

"Where does it come from?"

"From the cells that line the blood vessels—the endothelial cells. An enzyme, nitric oxide synthetase, produces nitric oxide whenever the vessel wall goes into spasm. This enzyme breaks down the amino acid arginine into nitric oxide and citrulline."

"What else does nitric acid do?"

"It provides a counterbalance to adrenaline, the primary stress hormone. Adrenaline causes spasm of the arteries, and nitric oxide relieves that spasm. So oxygen-starved tissues get a breather."

"Anything that protects tissues from adrenergic hypervigilence can't be all that bad," he nodded.

"Nitric acid has other roles," I added. "It normalizes raised blood pressure. But that's not where the story ends."

"What else does it do?"

"It's truly a miracle molecule. In the brain, it influences several neurotransmitters. Specifically, it regulates the activities of two essential messenger molecules: cyclic GMP and glutamate, which is a major excitatory neurotransmitter molecule."

"Heady stuff!" Choua shook his head, then asked, "What else?"

"Nitric oxide facilitates conversations among neurones as well as among those between those nerve cells and immune cells."

"Impressive rogue, this nitric oxide! Isn't it?" Choua asked.

"It blocks platelet aggregation—makes them less sticky and so prevents clot formation within blood vessels," I added. "It inhibits adhesiveness of white blood cells and so protects the inner lining of blood vessels from injury. It scavenges free radicals and so protects cells from oxidant injury. It kills microbes directly."

"Wow!" he grinned.

"It modulates immune response by regulating the production of a substance called tumor necrosis factor."

"What else?"

"There is much more to this amazing molecule. It rises to the occasion in yet other ways."

"How?" he asked, his eyes narrowing.

"It is present in large amounts in nerve plexuses in the

penis, and has some special assignments there."

"What special assignments?"

"It is *the* molecular messenger for the erection of the penis."

"That should raise some eyebrows, shouldn't it?" he smirked.

"I don't think many folks know that yet," I boasted.

"What else?" Choua wasn't impressed by my knowledge.

"Nitric oxide also has some anticancer properties —it goads killer immune cells to attack and destroy tumor cells."

"Wow! That's impressive." He nodded.

"It detoxifies microbial toxins."

"How?"

"By oxidation."

"Hmm!" he rubbed his forehead. "How do you know nitric acid does all those things?" Choua asked.

"Experiments have proved it," I replied. "If you take arginine out of the nitric oxide experimental system, scavenger cells cannot kill cancer cells. This procedure proves the important role of nitric oxide in killing tumor cells."

"Fascinating stuff! Tell me, what's wrong with your nitric oxide story?"

"Wrong?" I was taken aback. "Nothing! There's nothing wrong with the nitric oxide story. It's nature's master stroke —a marvel of molecular engineering. This simple molecule —composed of one atom of oxygen and nitrogen each—can perform so many useful functions in so many molecular tribes. Can you name another molecule that can outdo nitric oxide in a diversity of roles?"

"That's where these Serengeti lions have a better sense of the natural order of things than you do," he smiled impishly.

"What?" I blurted, utterly unprepared for his response.

"Lions know there are no untainted molecular heroes in

nature," he grinned.

"No?" I was incredulous.

"And there are no pure molecular villains either," he went on.

"Are you saying there is an evil dimension to nitric oxide that I am unaware of?" I asked.

"What happens in shock states in which blood vessels lose their tone and go limp? How is the blood flow regulated then?"

"How?"

"Not by nitric oxide," he pouted, then continued. "Tell me, what does nitric oxide do in such a circumstance?"

"If it were to relax the muscles any further, it would make matters worse—exaggerate the shock state," I replied tentatively, then asked, "Does that really happen?"

"Right!" he beamed. "Nitric oxide adds fuel to the oxidative flames of shock. Do you get the picture now?"

"I never thought of that," I confessed. "But, is that true?"

"*Nature Medicine* published an interesting article in its August, 1995 issue."

"About nitric oxide?" I asked, my interest rising.

"No, about nitrates in bacon," he said sarcastically. "We are talking about nitric oxide, aren't we?"

"Yes. Yes," I replied, flustered. "What did *Nature Medicine* say?"

"Researchers from Johns Hopkins showed that nitric oxide damages the heart muscle in shock states."

"The heart muscle?" I was incredulous. "How did they know the culprit was nitric oxide?"

"They measured nitric oxide in injured hearts with a technique called electron paramagnetic resonance spectroscopy."

"What did they find?"

"They found that nitric oxide is produced directly from

nitrite without the involvement of any enzymes in the injured heart. Next, they found that nitric oxide so produced directly damages the heart muscle."

"That's surprising."

"Surprising! Why?" he groused. "Didn't you tell me nitric oxide is an oxidant? Doesn't that mean it lights up many an oxidative fire?"

"Yes, but generally people only talk about its good effects," I replied.

"Don't I know that?" Choua chuckled. "That's what the Serengeti lions know about nitric oxide."

"Get serious, Choua," I admonished.

"Notwithstanding their benefits, all oxidant molecular species are toxic in the sense that they ignite oxidative fires. Then they fan those fires by setting off chain reactions with other oxidant molecules in their vicinity. Why should nitric oxide be an exception?"

"I know that but..."

"But what?" he brusquely cut me off. "You write books about the molecular duality of oxygen. You fill pages with your molecular Dr. Jekyll-Mr. Hyde stories. And yet you can't see something that elementary."

"Yes, but..."

"An injured heart has an excess of free radicals including superoxide," he interrupted me again. "Nitric oxide reacts with superoxide to spawn toxic peroxynitrite molecules. All three molecules individually—as well as in consort—further fan the oxidative flames in the damaged heart muscle."

"How do you know those Serengeti lions know all that?" I asked sarcastically.

"Lions aren't reductionistic. You doctors are," he replied condescendingly. "There are no molecular good guys and bad guys out there in the Serengeti Plains. Nature weaves seamless molecular mosaics. Each molecule plays diverse roles, supporting and opposing others as it is called upon to do."

"And nitric oxide?" I asked.

"Nitric oxide also has its own sense of order. It preserves life in one way and terminates it in another. It can light up oxidative fires under one set of conditions and extinguish oxidative coals fanned by other oxidants in another."

"How so?"

"Up to a point, it opens tightened vessels to facilitate blood flow within them, but when the heart is damaged beyond a certain point, it tries to kill the remaining heart muscle."

"But how does it *know* so much?" I asked. "How can a simple molecule like that know so much?"

"Nature's economy. When nature can get one molecule to play both sides of the field, why wouldn't it? It's the same way with many other molecules. Don't you see hydrogen peroxide —another simple molecule—also plays both sides of the field? It is good—and it is evil. Ozone is good—and it is evil. And so are iron, copper and vitamins C and E. Every oxidant becomes an antioxidant when it is used up. And every antioxidant turns into an oxidant when it scavenges free radicals. That's the natural order of things. You see the molecular duality of oxygen in everything. You see molecular Dr. Jekylls and Mr. Hydes everywhere. It's the same way with nitric oxide, hydrogen peroxide and ozone. You shouldn't have any difficulty with that, should you?"

"You're right," I confessed.

LIONS AND ETS

"What do your Serengeti lions think of ETs?" I asked Choua after a while.

"Extra-terrestrial beings?" he asked.

"Not extra-terrestrials, silly,"I chided. "I don't mean the ETs of movies. I mean the ETs of blood vessels."

"What are ETs of blood vessels?"

"ETs are endothelins, the molecules that are produced in endothelial cells that line the inside of blood vessels."

"Oh that!" he shook his head. "Didn't *Science* and *Nature* run some articles about them recently? Tell me, what do ETs do?"

"ETs save people from cold hands and feet," I replied, then baited him, "Do you think lions ever suffer from cold paws?"

"Lions with cold paws! Now that's an interesting thought, isn't it?" He grinned, then continued, "How often do your patients complain of cold hands and feet?"

"Not infrequently," I replied.

"What kinds of patients complain of cold sensitivity?"

"Those with chronic stress states, anxiety, panic attacks and depression."

"What about those suffering from immune disorders?"

"Yes, they also often complain of cold sensitivity. The same holds for patients with food and mold allergy, chemical sensitivity, chronic fatigue syndrome, fibromylagia and other severe autoimmune disorders."

CAUSES OF COLD SENSITIVITY

"What are the causes of cold sensitivity?" Choua asked.

"There are four main causes in my view," I replied. "First, there is the possibility of an underactive thyroid gland caused by oxidative injury to thyroid gland cells, enzymes and hormones. Second, there is the tightening of arteries due to the oxidative stress of excess adrenaline produced by stress. Third, there's the direct oxidative injury to receptors of the autonomic nervous systems that regulate blood flow. Finally, the clumping of blood cells due to oxidative injury to cell walls can clog tiny blood capillaries, cutting off the blood supply and leaving hands and feet cold."

"How do you know the clumping of blood cells causes cold sensitivity? That's not in medical textbooks, is it?" he asked.

"No. That's my personal observation," I replied, a trifle self-consciously. "It became obvious to me during my microscopic studies on the blood samples of patients with accelerated oxidative stress, chronic fatigue syndrome and immune disorders."

"What do endothelins do?" he returned to the question.

"Like nitric acid, endothelins are nature's prescription for normalizing the blood flow in small blood vessels. These molecules provide a natural counterbalance to nitric oxide."

"Do they open up arteries or tighten them?" he asked. "Didn't you tell me nitric oxide can play both sides of the field?"

"You learn fast," I teased. "Endothelins, like nitric oxide, also play both sides of the field. They are composed of short chains of amino acids and influence the muscle in the vessel wall. "

"What do they do?" he pressed.

"Some raise blood pressure. "

"And others?"

"Others produce certain growth hormones. There are three types of endothelins: ET1, ET2 and ET3. These molecules regulate many other body functions such as multiplication of cells. Some influence the production of some hormones. "

"What else do endothelins do?"

"Some of them have crucial roles in the development of unborn babies," I replied. "Strange things happen in gene targeting research, when mice are bred to be endothelin-deficient, and some others to be deficient in endothelin receptors. "

"What?" Choua asked.

"ET1-deficient mice are born with heart defects and die of respiratory problems soon after birth. Mice with lower ET1 blood and tissue levels have high blood pressure. Other ETs influence the development of some brain structures, and their deficiency leads to congenital malformations. "

"How does anyone know what endothelins do in real life?" he enquired. "I mean when a family of molecules plays so many roles, how can anyone know what the sum total of all the effects might be in a given individual and in a given clinical text?"

"Well, that's a..."

"A problem," he completed my sentence, "isn't it?"

"Yes," I confessed, a trifle flustered.

"No molecule is a loner, and molecular conversations cover a larger range of topics than your philosophy or politics."

"Or poetry," I mocked.

"Biology is a kaleidoscope," he went on without taking notice of my sarcasm. "When you change something in one way, you change everything in some way."

"Are you saying we shouldn't study individual molecules? We shouldn't characterize any of them?"

"On the contrary, that's essential for recognizing their versatility—the breadth of their structural and functional reach."

"So, what's your point?" I asked, exasperated.

"You asked me the question about nitric oxide, I didn't. Then, you asked me about ETs," he replied with a smirk.

THE FOURTH-OF-JULY CHEMISTRY

"This is Sylvia's chart," Choua announced some weeks later, as he entered my New York office carrying a thick chart. "Do you remember her?"

"Sylvia who?" I asked.

"I'll will read the summary of her illness written by her fiancé. It will help you remember who Sylvia is," he continued. Pulling two sheets from the folder, he began reading:

Sylvia has had few health problems in the past and has always been active. She's an office worker, involved with purchasing for a large New York publishing firm. She does not smoke or drink and did aerobic exercise three to four times a week. She has a hypothyroid problem, is asthmatic and takes Synthyroid and Serevent.

"I think I know who Sylvia is," I interrupted him. "Isn't she the young woman who cried several times during the initial consultation?"

"Yes. She told you she would end her life if she didn't get better," he replied and resumed reading:

> *One day in mid-August 1995, Sylvia felt flu-like symptoms and stayed home. She later felt dizzy, light-headed and nauseous. She has not returned to work since then and has been on disability for what is believed to be some form of CFS. Her primary symptoms have been weakness, muscle aches and pains, nausea, fatigue, insomnia, heavy headedness, lightheadedness, confusion and poor memory. These symptoms have remained prominent and recurring.*

"Viruses incite inflammation in muscles and so cause muscle spasms and pain. All of those cause muscle weakness. But what do you make of confusion and poor memory? How do viruses cause mental impairment?" he asked.

"Viruses cause inflammation in muscles by oxidative injury. I'm sure viruses cause problems of memory, mood and mentation the same way—by oxidative injury to neurotransmitters and neurones. Why do you ask?"

"When you left medical school, did you recall patients with viral infections who complained of persistent cerebral fogging months and years after their acute symptoms cleared up?"

"I don't, but some patients must have suffered those symptoms, though it wasn't as common then as now."

"Why is that? Have the victims become more vulnerable or have the invading viruses become more virulent?"

"Probably both," I ventured a guess.

"I agree that human immune defenses have been weakened by antibiotic and hormone abuse, and by the chemical avalanches unleashed by technology. But do you have any direct evidence for the latter? For viruses becoming more virulent?"

"Well..."

Choua didn't let me finish my sentence and resumed reading from the sheet:

Sylvia had numerous blood tests performed, and has shown consistent elevations of Epstein-Barr antibody titers and evidence of herpes virus 6. On two occasions, Sylvia had to visit the emergency room for severe abdominal and back pains. No problems were found. On the second visit to the hospital, Sylvia had severe nausea, vomiting, weakness, loss of appetite and diarrhea. She improved with Ringer's lactate and Compazine. Immediate improvement specifically included less fatigue, less fogginess, less anxiety, fewer muscle pains, less nausea and increased energy, strength. Sleep continues to be a problem.

"Those viruses can be killers—just when you think a patient begins to heal, they suffer a relapse of symptoms," I commented.

"That's not a relapse. That's a free fall," he countered.

"What do you think is the reason?"

"Oxidative fires feed upon each other, that's why."

"Do you mean depleted antioxidant defenses?"

"Yes, if that seems scientifically authentic to you," he taunted, then began to read again:

After four days, the original symptoms re-appeared, although not as severely. Eventually her symptoms were as bad as ever. Her asthma symptoms worsened. An endoscopy revealed evidence of a moderate form of gastritisand mild duodenitis. X-rays showed gas in the mid small bowel loops and in the right transverse colon. After hospitalization, she consulted several physicians.

The stomach and duodenum get into the picture now. Why do you think that is so?" he asked.

"Viruses can affect any organs," I replied.

"Does stress cause gastritis and duodenitis?"

"Of course."

"How?"

"By oxidative injury, how else?"

"What's your take on gas in the small bowel and colon on

X-ray pictures?"

"Nothing unusual there either. Viruses often cause inflammation of the small bowel and colon. That leads to yeast overgrowth and increased fermentation of sugars with excessive production of gas."

"That's your disrupted bowel ecosystem," he said, then read again:

MDs Consulted

Sylvia's primary care physician wasn't sure what she had. Additional tests disclosed an abnormal liver function, which returned to normal after vitamin therapy. A second physician reviewed the entire case and ran many tests. The physician couldn't find anything specific and recommended antidepressants. Sylvia didn't accept that view. She went to a psychiatrist who believes in CFS and recommended high doses of vitamins.

Never fails, does it?" he frowned.

"What?" I asked, puzzled.

"Those doctors, they never blink an eye before doling out prescriptions for antidepressants."

"Antidepressants are necessary sometimes," I countered.

"Intellectual bankruptcy, isn't that what you called antidepressant therapy for chronic fatigue in *Canary?*"

"Choua, you don't practice medicine. You don't care for sick people. You have no sense of clinical urgencies. You ride your high horse and are quick to ridicule others," I rebuked him. Then I asked, "What would you do if you were caring for her and nothing worked?"

"Sylvia's primary care physician played at psychiatry. Fortunately her psychiatrist turned out to be a quack," Choua went on, ignoring my question. "The psychiatrist prescribed high doses of vitamins. I mean there is a psychiatrist who thought his patient's problems were all in the body. Fascinating, isn't it?" Choua chuckled.

"Let's not call him a quack, Choua. Let's say he is a closet nutritionist."

Choua grinned, then read:

Endocrinologist: Prescribed 125 mcg of Synthyroid, Prozac and Ativan.

"A psychiatrist becomes a closet nutritionist and an endocrinologist becomes a psychiatrist. He gave her Synthyroid and Ativan, then threw in a prescription for Prozac as a sweetener. How very charitable of him," Choua's lips curled.

"You're going too far," I chastised him. "What's an endocrinologist to do if his patient continues to suffer despite all efforts?"

"Despite all efforts?" he frowned. "What *all* efforts? What did this endocrinologist do to figure out how a viral infection could wreak such oxidative havoc upon a vigorous young woman? What did he ever do to cool down her oxidative metabolic plate?"

"What do you mean?" I asked, puzzled.

"He simply performed some tests on her thyroid function and prescribed Synthyroid. He did nothing to figure out what was keeping her body inflamed."

"Oh, that!"

"What did he think was the basic problem? Did he really think her previously healthy thyroid gland was suddenly smitten by Olympian gods?" Choua asked harshly.

"What do you think the problem was?" I asked, irritated. "What do you think set her body in flames?"

Choua didn't answer. He looked at the sheets of paper in his hands, then read:

Neurologist: No problems found. MRI and EEG neg. Cardiologist: No problems found. Slight murmur noted.

"At least those guys admitted they knew nothing about the cause of the problem."

"There was that heart murmur. What about that?" I prodded, remembering his tirade about mitral valve prolapse.

Choua opened his mouth to say something. Then, as if sensing the thought behind my question, he smiled knowingly, looked at the sheets and read:

Infectious Disease: The doctor believed symptoms due to past viral infection, not CFS.

"Now, that's a riot, isn't it?" he smirked.

"Do you mean an oxidative riot?" I teased.

"I wonder what led him to conclude that she didn't suffer from chronic fatigue syndrome." He sidestepped my question. "What difference does it make what he or someone else might or might not call it?"

"To each his own." I knew what he was aiming at but decided not to engage in that subject.

"It amazes me how silly thinking—or, shall I say, robotic nonthinking—persists among many infectious disease specialists," Choua railed, unsatisfied with my answer. "No one can define what chronic fatigue syndrome is. The definition offered by the Centers for Disease Control is a sham. What they really believe is that chronic fatigue is a malady that Olympian gods cast upon hapless mortals. No one can define fatigue caused by a past virus infection. Yet, this infectious disease *expert* doles out his wisdom with full clinical authority. While chronic fatigue sufferers—your human canaries—continue to live severely diminished lives, the infectious disease experts are busy inventing clever diagnostic labels for them."

"That's unfortunate, but I think it's changing."

Choua looked at me, then through me, for several moments. I waited for what I thought was going to be one of his attacks against my profession. Instead he lowered his eyes and resumed reading from the sheets held in his hands.

Eye, Nose Throat: No problems found.
Allergist: Tested for food allergy. No
significant finding.
Gastroenterologist: No problems found.
Psychiatrist: Prescribed antidepressants.

"Quite a case history, isn't it?" he asked, putting the sheets of paper back and removing my pink progress sheet from the chart folder.

"I remember her case vividly,"I replied.

"Muscle twitching. Needles in skin. Electrical sparks in face and head. That's what you wrote in your progress sheet."

"I remember her well."

"How could you not?" he waved the sheet in his hand testily. "She told you she had begged her fiancé to help her kill herself if she didn't get better because she couldn't bear the thought of suffering like that for long."

"That's tough."

"Do you remember that her fiancé nodded when you looked at him to corroborate her story."

"I do," I replied. "What do you think her problem was?"

"The Fourth-of-July chemistry syndrome," he replied.

"The Fourth-of-July chemistry syndrome?" I asked. "That's not a valid diagnosis. There is no CPT reimbursement code for it. You can't make up things as you go along," I taunted, then added, sarcastically, "But, Choua, you can. You don't see patients. You've no clinical responsibilities. I guess you can. Yes, you do have the freedom to concoct new diagnoses."

"What better analogy can you give to illustrate the randomness and unpredictability of energetic-molecular events in Sylvia's unremitting agony? What better way to explain the nature of oxidative flyballs in Sylvia's acute illness than the Fourth-of-July fireworks? The only way you can understand her intense suffering is if you can visualize the oxidative fireworks under her skin—if you can see the electrons turning, twisting and leaping in her tissues. Her antioxidant enzymes are overwhelmed, and are no longer able to extinguish the oxidative fires. Her blood boils, figuratively as well as literally. The surface membranes of Sylvia's blood cells are abraded by oxidants which poke holes in them. What's within the cell hemorrhages out, and what's outside them floods the cell innards. Her cell membranes become crooked, crumpled and shredded —then the cells stick to each other the way cherries do after their skins are abraded. The clumped cells clog tiny capillaries and suffocate tissues—in the bowel, liver, kidneys, muscles, brain and everywhere else."

"So that's the Fourth-of-July chemistry," I interjected.

"Sylvia's blood plasma proteins are cooked, just as the white of an egg is cooked when it is boiled," he went on, ignoring my comment. "Her enzymes, plasma proteins and messenger molecules turn into tiny flakes of worthless coagulum that stick to the lining cells of capillaries. Isn't that what you saw in her blood with your microscope?"

"Yes, That's a fair description of what I saw in Sylvia's blood as well as in the blood of patients with disabling chronic fatigue, cancer and chemical sensitivities," I agreed.

"Now, the electrical surface charge of Sylvia's damaged cell membranes are disrupted and membranes lose their normal polarity," he resumed. "Now, her cell membranes go into a frenzy of misfiring. In her limbs and torso, the muscles fibers twitch and cause painful spasm. Now, in her heart, abraded membranes of the conducting system misfire and cause her heart to palpitate and skip beats. Now, the overdriven nerve cell synapses in her head generate confounding signals causing headache, anxiety, fogginess and spaciness —sometimes culminating in electrical shocks. Now, the battered cells in her bowel cause it to bloat, blister and bleed. Now, the skin surface cells erupt in rashes, the cells lining her nose weep and those in the eyes sear. And now, her synovial cells layered on her joint bones get inflamed making the joints stiff, swollen and painful." Choua stopped, his eyes glazing.

"Go on," I prodded, amused at his description of Sylvia's problems.

"Her agony is unrelenting," he went on. "Fanned by the frenzy of oxidants, oxidative flames in her tissues continue to consume her from within. She desperately searches for help. The medical specialists she consults one after the other are interested in their diagnostic labels—not in mitigating her suffering. All her..."

"That's preposterous," I reprimanded. "They tried different drugs but none of the drugs worked. Now, you can't blame them for it, can you?"

"All her infectious disease specialist could do was to see her as a challenge to his diagnostic acumen. 'It isn't chronic fatigue syndrome, it's a past viral infection', he pronounced. How absurd? How stupid? Does he really think it matters how he labels her unrelenting suffering?"

"He had to make some diagnosis, Choua," I said, irritated. "He had to establish a diagnosis before he could treat Sylvia."

"You don't see the utter stupidity of that either, do you?" He growled, his eyes turning intense and piercing. "You're a pathologist. You've spent a lifetime making diagnoses. Tell me, what does the diagnosis of chronic fatigue syndrome mean to you? What does that tell you about the true nature of her suffering?"

"That's a..."

"A difficult problem," Choua testily completed my sentence. "Now tell me, what does the diagnosis of postviral syndrome mean? What does that tell you about Sylvia's anguish? Don't you see the sheer stupidity of that?"

"That does happen sometimes," I protested.

"Is there a person alive anywhere in the world who didn't have some viral infection at one time or the other? Does anyone ever get as sick as Sylvia without evidence of activation of one virus or the other? Do you see how frivolous your arguments are? Don't you see how intellectually bankrupt that infectious disease specialist was?" he growled."

"Hold it!" I shouted. "That's not..."

"Fair!" he interrupted me angrily. "This isn't about fairness. Don't you see it's about Sylvia's unbearable pain. When the limit of her suffering is exceeded, she seeks refuge in death. She looks around and the only helpful person there is her fiancé. So she begs him to help her end her life. Now tell me, Mr. Pathologist, what diagnostic label would you put on her?" he gored.

"You're always rambling against diagnostic categories," I replied exasperated, then asked. "But, do you realize it would be impossible for physicians to communicate among themselves and with patients about diseases and treatment plans without precise disease classifications?"

"Precise disease classifications, eh?" he snarled. "Will you tell me what precise disease classification you would use for Sylvia? What diagnostic category, Mr. Diagnostician?"

"She's manifestly depressed. There's nothing unusual about depressed people thinking of ending their lives, is there?"

"Depressed!" he waved his hand contemptuously Who in

Sylvia's place wouldn't be depressed, Mr. Psychologist?" Choua
bristled. "If your disease classifications were really as great as
you make them out to be, tell me, how is it that no two doctors
among the dozen she saw agreed on a single diagnosis?"

"Because her clinical problems are very complex."

"What's your diagnosis for her?" he shot back.

"Well, well, that's tough," I stammered. "She really
doesn't fit into any disease names that I know," I answered,
before I realized I had fully validated Choua's argument.

Choua turned his faces away, then looked at the floor
and fell silent. He often does that when he knows he has clearly
won his point—as if to mitigate my distress at losing. My
thoughts wandered to hundreds of other patients who, like
Sylvia, were also healthy and vigorous young men and women
until they came down with Sylvia's condition—whatever we
choose to call it, the Fourth-of-July or any other syndrome.
They had also literally melted away right before the eyes of
their medical specialists who diagnosed one disease after the
other—and prescribed one drug after another—until the patients
were totally disabled. Then they were sent to psychiatrists who
had their fill using their favorite psychiatric labels. But the
patients continued to deteriorate until—as one of them put it—'I
try hard to pull myself out of coma each morning, but honest,
Dr. Ali, it's impossible'.

What are these new diseases that have not been written
up in medical texts? Choua exaggerates to the point of
absurdity, but how does a physician explain to the Sylvias of our
time what's wrong with them? How does a physician
communicate with other physicians about what is killing Sylvia?
What diagnostic category label do I give her and other hundreds
of other patients like her I see every week? Label! I suppressed

a smile as I glanced quickly at Choua. He was lost in thought.
How can I spend so much time with Choua and not fall into his
quirks of language? Of course, diagnostic labels was not a term
that I was taught to use in my pathology residency. Pathologists
must be precise in their use of pathologic terms, I remembered
the advice Michael Tracht, M.D., my mentor had given me
tome thirty years earlier.

Choua's description of oxidative storms in acute illness
was rather apt, I thought. One may or may not call it the
Fourth-of-July-chemistry syndrome, but wasn't that what really
happened to Sylvia? How else did her steady, even-state energy
dynamic of health turn into the tumultuous chemistry of
insufferable pain and mental anguish? And once initiated, how
does one terminate it?

BUCKETS OF WATER FOR A HOUSE ON FIRE

"Intense suffering calls for intense measures," Choua
resumed. "Sick people like Sylvia need a holistic viewpoint of
health and disease. They require sound aggressive global
management plans to put out their metabolic oxidative fires," he
continued."
"What might those plans be?"
"Intravenous infusions and intramuscular injections of
vitamins and minerals! They need their battered bowel
ecosystems restored with effective and safe herbal protocols.
They need their flaming blood ecosystems cooled off. They need
loads of antioxidants to protects their vulnerable enzymes,
hormones and plasma proteins. They need the simmering

oxidative coals in their liver ecosystems extinguished with sound detoxification protocols. Their dried up kidney ecosystems need to be flushed with healing liquids. Their boiling brain ecosystems need the balms of hope and spirituality. Do you understand any of that?"

"Yes, but..."

"But what?" he frowned as he interrupted me.

"But I can't use the diagnosis of the Fourth-of-July chemistry."

"Why not?"

"Because it isn't an accepted diagnosis."

"What is an acceptable diagnosis for her?" he leaned forward and looked me with intense, piercing eyes.

"I don't know! I don't know!" I blurted in frustration. "But the Fourth-of-July chemistry isn't an acceptable diagnosis for her. For one thing there isn't any insurance code for it. She wouldn't be reimbursed if I were naive enough to use that diagnosis."

"Ah, the reimbursement code! Isn't that how men of money control things in medicine. Damn the patient's suffering! Damn the basic cause of that suffering! Damn her battered bowel ecosystem! Damn her boiling blood ecosystem! Damn her blistering brain ecosystem! Damn the possibility of healing with natural therapies! Just make sure that there are codes that pay well for drugs and scalpels. What better way to do that than by controlling the doctor's paycheck?"

"Hold it! Hold it, Choua!" I shouted. "What are you ranting about? Are we talking about science or money?"

NITRIC OXIDE, ENDOTHELINS AND DRUGS

"Why did you ask me what lions know about nitric oxide?" Choua asked, a sudden mysterious smile spreading on his face.

"Oh God!" I groaned and shook my head in dismay. "Not nitric oxide again!"

"What do lions know about nitric oxide?" he jabbed me again.

"Because it's a hot molecule these days," I replied, the ring of exasperation in my voice turning into a low laugh at his schizophrenic flight of ideas from Sylvia in my New York office back to the lions in Serengeti.

"Hot for whom?"

"Cardiologists love it, so do neurologists. One can hardly attend a medical conference these days without hearing a lot about it."

"What do cardiologists and neurologists talk about after they have discussed nitric oxide?"

"Drugs."

"Why do they discuss the chemistry of nitric oxide and endothelins before they pimp drugs?"

"To establish the scientific basis for the cause of a disease before tackling the issue of therapies," I ignored his obscene reference to the lecture fees paid by drug companies.

"*Scientific basis*, eh?" Choua's eyes narrowed.

"Didn't we talk about the several roles of nitric oxide and endothelins?"

"Molecules don't work in a vacuum," he countered.

"Nothing does in biology. You doctors talk about nitric oxide to make your drug therapies look scientific. Now, isn't that a laugh? Do you really believe talking about nitric oxide makes your drug medicines scientific? Some of you even bring endothelins into your discourses to reaffirm your belief that drug medicine is scientific."

"That's ludicrous, Choua," I complained.

"You seem to think sick people are hollow, tin dolls," he went on. "You assume that nitric oxide and endothelins turn, twist and bump into each other in people's bodies—as if there is nothing but a vacuum under their skin. But people aren't malfunctioning mechanical devices. They're living, breathing beings. And nitric oxide and endothelins don't merely exist in their bodies to provide you with a rationale for your drug therapies."

"What are you ranting about?" I asked angrily.

"It's disingenuous to use nitric oxide or endothelins as a rationale for using drugs," he posited. "Those molecules work in far too many ways to be simple-mindedly used as the *scientific* basis for using this or that drug."

"So what do you propose? Should we abandon research in nitric oxide and endothelin metabolism?"

"Clinical medicine isn't a science," he went on, ignoring my comment. "Without a holistic understanding of the essential molecular relatedness in biology, touting drug medicine as science is a farce."

"Are you saying we shouldn't use drugs for sick people?" I asked.

"Use drugs when they help—empirically, just as the ancients used their herbs and potions. Just don't call it science," he admonished. "Nitric oxide and endothelins play many sides of cellular fields. Don't pick up a role that seems to support the use of this or that drug and call it valid scientific evidence for your therapeutic decision. Isn't that what you do?" He looked at me sternly.

"No. Well, maybe sometimes..."

"That's what your professors do all the time, don't they?" he interrupted me. "Clinical medicine is not science. Those who claim it is aren't scientists. There are no absolutes in biology. Facts in biology are changed everyday by the environment, right?"

"Right, but..."

"What were *facts* of biological science fifty years ago are mere *factoids* today—a roadkill of pesticides and pollutants. If you want to search for truth in biology, look for it in this savannah —see how the chemistry of a lion's ballistic charge ebbs into that of a lion snoozing in the sun. You'll learn more about the balancing acts of nitric oxide and endothelins here."

"What a schizophrenic flight of ideas!" I couldn't help myself.

"Schizophrenic flight?" Choua stiffened, then recovered. "Don't you recognize pseudoscience when you see it? When mice are drowned in ice-cold water to conduct drug research, that's not science. When physicians on the payroll of drug makers talk about the science of blinded drug studies, that's not science."

"Why isn't it science?" I protested.

"Because biology can't be blinded," he asserted.

"I don't know if I agree with that," I countered.

"When drug companies do controlled and blinded drug studies for one drug at a time, then sell it to be used concurrently with several other drugs, that's not science," he continued.

"Those are difficult problems, but..."

"But nothing," he cut me off curtly. "When drugs ads promise cures for degenerative disorders, you should see them for what they are: pure deceptions. Synthetic chemicals do not cure any degenerative diseases, nor do they reverse ecologic, nutritional or immune disorders. Disease reversal is possible only when therapies are based on a sound understanding of the energetic-molecular relationships in biology. There is no free lunch in biology. Every synthetic chemical carries a cost."

"Is there anything scientific in medicine?" I asked, exasperated.

"Good medicine is an artful application of the knowledge of biology. That's it! The less you boast about your knowledge of nitric oxide and endothelins, the better. The only truths in biology are truths of molecular and ecologic relationships —and the empirical observations based on them. But, ecologic thinking is hard for you physicians, isn't it?"

"What ecologic relationships?" I asked.

"The bowel ecosystem separates the internal order of the human frame from the external disorder, just as the cell membrane separates its internal order from the external disorder. The bowel ecosystem interfaces with the blood ecosystem, the blood ecosystem with the liver ecosystem, and the liver ecosystem with the brain ecosystem."

"Do you realize what you're asking us to do?" I asked, shaking my head.

"I know *unlearning* is much harder than learning," he replied somberly. "But, you really don't have any choice. Don't you see your nineteenth-century idea of diseases and drugs are utterly irrelevant to the twenty-first century's problem of environment, nutrition and stress? Don't you see how utterly frivolous your notions of disease classification are to Sylvia's unbearable agony? And to the unremitting agony of hundreds of thousands of Sylvias all over the world?"

"You're a dreamer and a schizoid," I taunted.

Just then a staff nurse asked me to walk over to the treatment room and start an EDTA chelation infusion for a patient with coronary heart disease. When I returned, Choua was gone.

WHAT DO LIONS KNOW ABOUT STRESS?

"Lions know something about the Fourth-of-July chemistry, don't they?" Choua asked when he returned the next day.

"What?"

"Those few brief moments of the life-and-death dance, that's the Fourth-of-July chemistry, isn't it?"

"Those are amazing sights, the moments when the crouched cats know they can't hide behind the bush anymore and must reveal themselves to the prey—those instants when they break loose from their formations, when they lunge with the speed of lightning."

"What happens when the gazelle literally disappears in the dust?" Choua asked.

"The cats wander back to their cubs, hungry and exhausted, but they don't seem to sulk—rather, they become limbic."

"How does their Fourth-of-July chemistry revert back to the chemistry of limbic *being*?"

"How?" I asked.

"How do lions extinguish the oxidative fires that are lit during the hunt?"

"How?" I repeated. "I don't know if the lions know about those oxidative fires, let alone how to put them out."

"And when the gazelle escapes the killing machines, what state of energy is it in?"

"I guess the same as in the lion that chases it. The gazelle is also in a Fourth-of-July state."

"Quite right!" Choua nodded. "How does the gazelle normalize its chemistry?"

"I guess it's normalized in the prey just as it in the predator."

"How long do you think it takes them?"

"Who knows?" I asked back indifferently.

"What kind of chemistry does a woman have while sitting in her car during a traffic jam?" Choua abruptly changed the subject. "The one who is late in picking her toddler up from nursery school."

"Not the Fourth-of-July type, I hope."

"Why not?"

"C'mon Choua, be reasonable. The state of energy of a woman caught in a traffic jam has nothing to do with that of a lion in a hunt or a gazelle dodging the predator," I countered.

"The woman has been yelled at several times before for arriving late. Now the highway is a parking lot and there is no way for the poor thing to fly over the unending streak of cars and trucks ahead of her."

"It's not the same thing," I shook my head.

"In a way you're right," Choua relented. "The lion and the gazelle are back to status quo in some minutes but the poor woman who is incarcerated in the traffic jam is there for hours. You're right, there is a difference. Her raw nerves are jarred for hours—free radical flyballs in her tissues continue to cook her plasma proteins for hours after she finally escapes her moving prison."

"You imagine things," I chastised Choua.

"Imagine things, eh!" Choua scowled. "Why don't you

wire someone like that to your autoreg machine sometime and
see for yourself what I imagine."

"Are you saying you don't agree with Hans Selye's fight-
or-flight response?" I asked after several moments.

"He was only partially right," Choua replied, still looking
out the window.

"Where did he go wrong?"

"Stress is not about fight or flight. *Stress simply is.* It's not
a response to demand for change. It's an integral part of the
injury-healing-injury cycle of life."

"What about his general adaptation response?"

"No one ever adapts to stress—to a Fourth-of-July state.
No one ever adapts to the tyranny of the thinking mind—the
cruelty of the cortical monkey," he replied somberly.

"So, what's the answer?" I asked.

"The Fourth-of-July chemistry is fired up by perceptions.
One can learn to dissolve perceptions." Choua slowly closed his
eyes, then whispered, "All suffering is perception. One can learn
to dissolve all perceptions and, thus, all suffering. That's what
the ancient Africans understood. That's what the ancient Jains
wrote about. But psychologist today don't see that. They
continue to focus how people can be *realized, individuated or
actualized.*"

NOS INHIBITORS

Nitric oxide synthetases (NOSs) are enzymes that
produce nitric oxide from amino acid arginine. There are four
distinct—and probably other uncharacterized —types of these
enzymes. Since nitric oxide is involved in so many of the

essential physiologic —and natural healing—processes, one can easily predict that there will soon be a plethora of new drugs designed to block these enzymes. While some such drugs will no doubt prove to be valuable for lifethreatening conditions, I am afraid many such drugs will also be used to treat chronic ecologic, nutritional and immune disorders. Of course, long-term blockade of essential enzymes such as NOSs always leads to serious adverse long-term consequences in many patients. I make this prediction safely because that has been the sad history of drug medicine.

For the reader's general information, I list below the four recognized forms of NOSs along with their cells of origins.

cNOS	Constitutionally present in cells
eNOS	Present in cells lining the blood vessels called endothelial cells.
nNOS	Present in brain tissue (neuronal)
iNOS	Produced by some mediator molecules of inflammation

I can also safely predict that much overlap between the functions and cell of origin of these enzymes will be found with future research. Nature shows no respect for mankind's need for reductionism and neat classifications.

There must be something strangely sacred in salt. It is in our tears and in the sea.

Kahlil Gibran

Chapter 11

Directed Pulses

I teach all my patients stress control with effective self-regulatory methods. These methods are based on energy perception is tissues. I begin training with a specific method I call "pulses." In this chapter, I reproduce some text from the companion volume, *The Dog, Directed pulses and Energy Healing* as a frame of reference for some text included in the chapters that follow.

The heart beats to pump blood into the arteries. Then it relaxes and its chambers open up to receive blood from the veins. During systole (the contraction phase of the heart), the pressure of the blood in the arteries rises suddenly, creating a peak pressure. During diastole (the relaxation phase of the heart), the pressure of the blood within the arteries falls, creating a trough. The difference between the high (systolic) and low (diastolic) pressures creates a wave effect in the arteries that can be palpated at the wrist, feet, neck and other areas in the body.

Under ordinary conditions, we are not aware of pulses in our arteries. I coined the term *directed pulses* (the "pulses") to describe a method by which a person can sense pulses in the arteries in any given part of his body. I use this as the first step in my autoregulation training for all patients.

What do pulses feel like? Most people have experienced the throbbing sensation with headaches, tooth abscesses or in inflamed tissues. Of course, in such circumstances the throbbing sensation is associated with pain of varying degrees. The pulses are also felt as a throbbing sensation that follows the rhythm of the heart but is not uncomfortable. Indeed, the experience of the pulses is very calming for the novice and deeply comforting for the experienced.

Autoregulation, as I define it earlier is this volume, is a process by which a person enters the natural state of healing energy. Once the energy of the pulses—or tissue energy in other forms—is perceived, one simply allows oneself to be guided by that energy. Perception of tissue energy might seem improbable to those who have never practiced self-regulation. In fact, it can be experienced physically, not merely understood intellectually, and it is easy to learn and simple to understand once one learns effective methods of self-regulation. Indeed, it is rare for me to see a patient who does not succeed in sensing the essential energy of his living tissues in the very first training session.

For more than 10 years, I have taught self-regulation to all my patients regardless of the nature of their illness. In these sessions, I introduce the principles and practices of self-regulation in basic terms. In my autoregulation laboratory, I use electrodes to monitor the energy levels and functions of the various body organs. The data are then fed into a computer that formats the information into easily understandable, multicolored, moving graphs on the computer screen. Extensive clinical experience has convinced me that this training is the most valuable method for teaching patients to become aware of the energy patterns of living tissues. I advise my patients to follow up on the training with autoregulation, using tapes that I prepared specifically for this purpose. (The text of the basic autoregulation tape appears at the end of this chapter.) After initial training, the use of the tapes becomes unnecessary.

VISCERAL RESISTANCE

Earlier in my autoregulation work, I observed some

patients slide effortlessly into deep meditative states. These patients showed clear electrophysiological evidence of profound and demonstrable changes in the function of various body organs. Others found autoregulation hard to understand and its practice difficult. It appears the patients in the second group had some "visceral" resistance, an internal impediment to the practice of autoregulation that they could neither explain nor overcome.

Whereas the first group succeeded in regulating some of their biologic functions with just one or two training sessions, those in the second group required extensive training with several sessions to learn even the basic steps. After several unsuccessful attempts, some of them gave up autoregulation. The reason why some succeeded so readily while others failed, even after considerable effort, puzzled me. I searched for some simple method of teaching patients how to dissolve their internal, visceral resistance in order to perceive their tissue energy, an essential step if autoregulation is to succeed.

Intellectually, sensing tissue energy with autoregulation is a simple concept. However, it is unsettling for most physicians who have no real sense of the energy of living tissues. Often they contemptuously dismiss all references to energy in healing as witchcraft and sorcery. This is regrettable. All matter is condensed energy. This is elementary physics, not an abstract metaphysical notion. Living tissues are energy beings. (Indeed, from such a perspective of energy dynamics, non-living entities such as stones are also energy entities—there is no difference between a grain of sand and a sandfly—both are energy beings.) Thus, whether a person can or cannot sense energy in his tissues is a matter of knowledge and training, and not that of witchcraft or sorcery.

HAND WARMING

Hand warming is one of the oldest, simplest, and most widely practiced methods of self-regulation. It is especially suitable for beginners. The warming of hands is easily sensed by the subject. The changed skin temperature of hands can be monitored and documented readily with inexpensive thermometers or suitable electronic devices. Beginners often have initial self-doubts. But the objective evidence of significant temperature changes effectively dispels any doubt about whether the beginner is really witnessing a true change or simply imagining it.

The hand-warming method generally worked well for most of my patients during the early years of my work with autoregulation. The computerized autoregulation equipment graphically demonstrates such changes. However, some patients face much difficulty in learning this simple skill. The absence of a response in their skin temperature—sharply contrasted by the changes seen in other patients during the training sessions—seems to intimidate and discourage them. How might I help such patients overcome this hurdle? I wondered. Rather than being instruments of enlightenment about the inner workings of the human frame, the moving graphs of their biologic functions on the computer screen became obstacles for them. The electrophysiologic sensors were a hindrance—cold, intimidating electronic devices adding to the suffering of the sick. I became increasingly doubtful about the relevance of my work to such patients—the very people who I knew needed self-regulation most.

A BREAK IN THE SHOWER

One day, it occurred to me that I might try to break the visceral resistance to hand warming by incorporating a simple procedure that the patient can try at home. Patients with strong visceral resistance almost always have cold hands. Could a warm bath or a hot shower help dissipate an individual's visceral resistance? I wondered. I decided to test the idea.

After standing under a hot shower for several minutes, I remained in the shower, dried myself with a towel and began my experiment. I let my arms hang loose at my sides and repeated several times the sentence, "My arms and hands are heavy, warm and loose."

The results of this simple experiment astounded me. My arms and hands flushed to an almost uncomfortable degree. My hands became heavy like lead and throbbed with raw energy. What I expected was a mild hand-warming response—perhaps more pronounced than the responses I was accustomed to with my simple hand-warming exercise. What I did not expect was that my fingertips would throb and pulse so powerfully. I became excited as I recognized how valuable this phenomenon could be in dissolving visceral resistance.

I asked some of my patients to do this simple experiment without telling them about my own experience. Most of them reported exciting responses. The observations of some were identical to mine. Next, I asked a few of them to repeat the experiment and tell me if they succeeded in perceiving clear, strong pulses in their fingertips. Some replied that they already had. Others promised to repeat the experiment and let me know about the results. Most confirmed the perception of unmistakable pulses.

It is one thing for a health professional to ask patients to warm their hands in a laboratory surrounded by complex electromagnetic equipment. It is an altogether different thing for an individual to make a personal discovery of tissue energy in his or her bathroom. That's when I realized how valuable pulses could be for introducing patients to autoregulation. Still, I did not know at that time how important this phenomenon would become to my work.

PULSES LEAD TO THE HEART

It wasn't until I was lying in the sun one afternoon that the clinical relevance of pulses occurred to me. Was it possible, I wondered, to sense my heart rhythm through autoregulation? I thought of several methods, nothing worked.

Success in autoregulation requires that we abandon our usual competitive, cortical strife for control. It calls for a non-goal-oriented, if-it-happens-it-happens, limbic mode. Remember, the core concepts of autoregulation are:

1. Cancelling cortical clutter
2. Sensing tissue energy

3.   Allowing that gentle energy to guide us to a higher healing state

Autoregulation is not about clever thinking. In fact, the principal hurdle in its path is head-fixation. Chronic thinking leads to an unending recycling of past hurts and precycling of feared, future misery—the two favorites of the cortical monkey. Recycling misery feeds the reverberating cycles of old hurts, long-gone pains, and past memories of sadness.

I realized that the answer to the riddle of heart rhythm, if there was one, would come to me while in the perceptive limbic mode, not in the thinking cortical mode. And that is exactly what happened two days later, during my morning limbic ghoraa run.

Exercise speeds up the heart rate. Most people who do not exercise regularly often feel a loud thumping of the heart in the chest during sudden and unexpected bursts of physical activity. A mother dashes after her child who is running toward a speeding car. After snatching her child, she halts and suffers from heart palpitations.

After my morning limbic ghoraa run, I often do some leg-raising exercises while lying on a carpet. Sometimes this follows a brief period of jumping rope briskly. On one particular day, as I lay down on the carpet for stretching my back muscles, I could feel my heart beating fast. Rather than let the mind wander, I stayed with and became keenly aware of my heart rhythm. I decided to follow the heart rhythm rather than continue with my usual back exercises. As I expected, my heart rate gradually returned back to normal. But something was different this time. Even though my heart was beating with its normal, regular rhythm, I was still able to clearly sense the heart rhythm. The obvious question was whether it would be possible for me to bring back this awareness without first going through a period of exercise. This is where directed pulses seemed to offer an interesting and clinically useful possibility. What would happen if I first sensed pulses in my fingertips, then directed them to my heart?

The question raised an exciting prospect. To this end, I did the following simple test: I brought strong pulses to my fingertips with my standard autoreg exercises. I then tried to carry these pulses to the area of my left chest where I had felt the heart rhythm after jumping rope briskly. It worked. I was now able to sense the heart rhythm just as I had after the exercise. (See the latter part of this section for a description of pulse methods.)

The next step was simple. I tested this method with many of my patients. With few exceptions, they were able to feel the pulses in their fingertips, then direct them to the heart and perceive the heart rhythms.

TWO CHALAZIA SHRINK AND DISAPPEAR

I developed a chalazion, a type of lump, in the upper eyelid of the right eye. It was of the size of one half of a pea. A chalazion is a lump formed by an intense and indolent inflammation of specialized sweat glands in the eyelids. These glands, called meibomian glands, are modified to produce an oily secretion. In chalazia, oily secretions leak out of inflamed glands and form a central cyst. Frequently, the inflammatory process results in abscess formation. Sometimes an abscess breaks through the inner membrane of the eyelid and ruptures into the eye. This can have serious consequences. The treatment generally consists of removal of the chalazion by surgery.

Within a few days, a second chalazion appeared close to the first one. The first chalazion grew to the size of a full pea and the second to one half that size. I thought about consulting an ophthalmologist and preparing myself for surgical removal of the chalazia.

I also thought about doing an experiment with directed pulses. I considered the possibility of avoiding surgery by bringing pulses to my eyelids and flushing them with abundant blood. It seemed possible to heal the chalazia with this approach.

All healing occurs with energy. At the level of individual cells in the human body, and at the level of the minute structures within these cells, energy is generated by complex chemical reactions. Nature has designed these reactions to create high energy bonds (called ATP bonds in medical terminology) and to release energy from these bonds in times of need. A disease state represents such a time. All energy reactions require oxygen and micro-nutrients. Tissues can obtain these elements only through blood. It seemed logical, though simplistic, that chalazia could heal if only I could somehow flush the tissues of the eyelid with blood.

But the surgeon and the pathologist in me raised a warning signal. The inflammation in chalazion causes death of tissues and produces scar tissue. Over the years I have examined hundreds of chalazia under the microscope. I regard this lesion with caution in terms of its ability to destroy healthy tissues.

Could I selectively bring the pulses to one eyelid? Could I effectively sustain such pulses for a long enough period to affect the chalazia? Could mere pulses in the eyelid really clear the pool of oily secretion, arrest inflammation, and prevent scar tissue formation? Would it not be risky to adopt an untried approach to a potentially serious health problem? Even if the pulses could dissolve the chalazia, would they recur? Why not get rid of the chalazia with surgery once and for all?

These were all valid questions. Still, I decided to go ahead with the idea. After all, surgery would always be available to me.

This simple idea turned out to be not only theoretically valid but both feasible and clinically valuable. It provided me with a firsthand, personal confirmation of the practical value of directed pulses.

By this time, I had become quite proficient at bringing pulses to my fingertips then directing them to the chest area for sensing my heart rhythm. With the very first attempt, I brought strong pulses to my right eyelid, naturally and effortlessly. Sustaining the pulses in the right eyelid also turned out to be quite an easy task. I brought the pulses to the eyelid by repeating five times each of the following three sentences.

My right upper eyelid is throbbing.
My right upper eyelid is tingling.
My right upper eyelid is pulsating.

After I succeeded in getting strong pulses in the right upper eyelid, I let the pulses go on. Every now and then, when I lost the pulses in the eyelid, I brought them back again by repeating the usual autoreg method for it. I sustained these pulses for over 15 minutes. After a break of several minutes, I brought the pulses back in the right upper eyelid for a second period of about 15 minutes.

The size of a chalazion can be easily measured. One can roll a finger on top of a chalazion pressed against the eyeball and obtain a fairly close measurement of its size. I measured the size of these two chalazia before and after the two periods of pulses in the eyelid. The chalazia shrank to two-thirds of their original sizes after application of the pulses.

Hard to believe.
Harder to comprehend.
Hardest of all to accept the utter
simplicity of it.

The temptation to dissolve the two chalazia with more pulses in the eyelid was clear. Instead, I decided to prolong this experiment. I did not practice the method for the pulses in the eyelid for the next three days. During this time, the chalazia grew back to their original sizes. At this time, I resumed the pulse methods, and practiced for 4-5 times a day, for 7-10 minutes each time. The chalazia shrank down to about one-fourth their original size in four days.

I decided to continue this experiment for some more time. I stopped the pulse exercise for four days. Once again the chalazia grew back close to their original sizes. I waited three days and started the pulse exercise for the third time. It took me five days to completely clear the chalazia. More than six years have passed, and the chalazia have not recurred.

HIVES, SWOLLEN EYES, STUFFED NOSE AND AUTOREGULATION

Sometime later, I developed a severe food allergy reaction. My left arm developed hives extending from the shoulder to the elbow. My eyes became red, itchy and swollen. My nose became congested. My heart rate quickened and developed palpitations. I reached my office and pulled out adrenaline and Benadryl injections. Reassured by immediate access to these drugs, I decided instead to try the pulses. I reasoned that I could flush the affected tissues with the pulses and eliminate all the chemicals like histamine that cause hives, redness, itching and nasal congestion. Further, the flush of new blood would bring a fresh supply of the enzyme, histaminase, and other related enzymes, which the body uses to break down histamine and related chemical compounds.

I directed pulses to my left arm. The hives cleared in about seven minutes. Next, I brought the pulses to my eyes. Some minutes later I felt the itching and swelling around my eyes subside. Next, I focused on to my nose.

Research in medicine requires discipline, diligence, perseverance and luck. It is always demanding. Often, it is frustrating. Infrequently, it has its light moments. Bringing the pulses to my nose turned out to be one of those light moments. Strong pulses in my nose converted nasal congestion into a total nasal blockage. No matter how I tried to figure out a way to open my nasal passages with some autoreg method, I drew a blank. That evening I completed my office hours with a totally blocked nose, courtesy of the pulses.

Several months after this incident, I drank some fresh vegetable juice. I didn't realize it included carrots, to which I am allergic. I felt uneasy within a few moments and developed a full-blown allergic reaction with heart palpitations, tightness in the chest, swelling around the eyes and hives. This time, dissolving the allergic reaction with autoreg came readily to me.

This reaction occurred about 15 minutes before I was to attend a meeting of the Medical Executive Committee at Holy Name Hospital. Needless to say, I was on time for the meeting which lasted more than four hours. None of my colleagues suspected that 15 minutes before the meeting, I was in the middle of a severe food allergy reaction. During my days as a physician in the emergency department, I treated such reactions with oxygen, intravenous drip and injections of adrenaline and Benadryl. For patients in my age group, I sometimes hospitalized the patient for extra safety.

I did not need any further proof of the safety and efficacy of autoreg. But some questions remained:

First, would the pulses work for everyone? Second, how many other clinical disorders can be successfully addressed with directed pulses?

FIRST, DO NO HARM

I now started earnestly looking in earnest for ways to build upon these observations. Do no harm, first and foremost, is the enduring principle of good medicine. I recognized that beyond my full commitment to the principle of doing no harm were many essential ethical, moral and legal issues that had to be addressed. Informed consent, safety and efficacy, proper research protocols and controls, even the placebo effect, are among the most important issues. But, most critical of all was being truthful to myself.

ARE PULSES REAL?

Are pulses real, or an imagined response to hypnotic suggestion? Do arteries really throb with pulses, or is it an illusion created by a professional with his clever words?

Many of my patients asked this question during the initial period of autoregulation training. This question is also raised often by professionals who have not experienced such energy responses themselves. Their interest in the subject is purely intellectual and that, of course, is the problem.

During training sessions, I ask everyone in the laboratory to tell me whether or not he felt any energy response. Most individuals say yes, then go on to describe their individual responses. It is not uncommon for some people to feel no energy response during the first couple of exercises. When asked if they think pulses are a real phenomenon, they usually shrug and look askance at the others who said they felt them. In such instances, I make a mental note of that and proceed with subsequent exercises. With rare exception, those who didn't feel pulses in the first exercises do so during subsequent training. When asked the same question about whether pulses are real or not, they grin broadly and nod affirmatively.

The pulses are indeed a real phenomenon. They can be readily monitored with a device called a plethysmograph, an electronic device that measures the range of expansion of tiny blood vessels in the skin. This non-invasive device can be expediently attached to a fingertip with a Velcro band. In my autoregulation lab, I demonstrate to my patients the dynamic moving graph of their pulses on a computer screen.

THE WAY WE LOOK AT THE WORLD AROUND US DETERMINES THE STATE OF OUR BIOLOGY

During initial autoregulation training, most of my patients are amazed at the way their biologic profiles change from cortical to limbic modes with autoregulation and back to the cortical mode when they stop autoregulation. These patterns often change instantaneously as the individual moves from a meditating mode to a thinking mode.

It is my practice to guide my patients through 15-minute

periods of autoregulation, then stop to explain the various elements of their electrophysiologic profiles. Invariably, during a training session of two and a half to three hours, I am able to demonstrate rather dramatic examples of this phenomenon to my students. The way we look at life around us determines whether we keep our arteries open or closed. All we need to do in the context of autoregulation is to be aware of our tissues and not to allow our minds to punish the tissues by closing off the arteries.

FINGERTIPS TO FINGERTIPS PULSES

I focus on the fingertips during early training in autoreg for a simple reason. Fingertips contain the richest supply of sympathetic nerve fibers. It is easy to see the wisdom of Nature in this. We use our fingertips for more functions than any other body organ. It also means that the walls of arteries in our fingertips have the tightest reins on them from the vaso-motor center in the brain. It also explains why our fingers and hands are the first body organs to feel cold when we are stressed or become depressed.

There is yet another simple method that many of my patients found to be very useful during early training. This method is especially valuable for those who do succeed in getting the pulses when training with a professional but are unable to get them on their own.

In this method, I ask my patients to hold their hands together in their laps with the fingertips of one hand touching the fingertips of the other. Juxtaposition of the fingertips assists in the perception of the pulses. Again, once a person succeeds in getting the pulses, he should separate his two hands to see if he can sustain the pulses when his fingertips are not touching.

Children learn autoregulation fast. They can be quickly taught to ease up on these autonomic reins on their arteries and let the pulses flow freely.

PULSES IN THE WASH BASIN

I wrote earlier that a vast majority of patients in my autoregulation class learn the method of directed pulses during the very first training sessions. It was different when I began teaching autoregulation to my patients about 10 years ago. At that time, many patients were frustrated by their inability to perceive any energy in their tissues with autoregulation. This was quite common among very ill patients. Even when some of them felt the pulses during my autoregulation class, they were unable to perceive or sustain pulses later when they tried the method on their own. It didn't take long before their angst became my frustration. I began to think of ways that I could help such patients overcome their systemic resistance.

The answer to the riddle became obvious one day in my laboratory when a woman in her mid-eighties related her experience. She had patiently sat through the training session for more than two hours without perceiving any energy in her hands as other patients in the class related their positive experiences. After the last autoregulation exercise, suddenly her face beamed with excitement as she loudly proclaimed that finally she had felt the pulses. Then she added, "I guess it happened now because my hands have been slowly and steadily warming during the class, even though I didn't feel clear pulses."

Like a flash, her comment gave me the idea of using warm water for the initial warming of hands, before beginning autoregulation. The next question was simple and predictable: What would be the simplest and most convenient way to warm hands?

In the method of pulses in the washbasin, a person dips both hands in a washbasin full of lukewarm water for five to ten minutes. When the temperature of the hands and fingers rises to that of the warm water, the person takes his hands out of the washbasin, dries them and begins autoregulation.

I have now validated the clinical efficacy of this method with extensive experience. Most patients who report initial difficulties with autoregulation find this method very useful in breaking the initial systemic resistance.

Pulses in the washbasin may be tried in a kitchen or bathroom sink, or in a warm water bathtub.

AUTONOMIC AND SOMATIC NERVOUS SYSTEMS

The nervous system in the human body—I was taught in medical school—comprises two distinct and discrete systems: a somatic nervous system that is under our voluntary control and an autonomic nervous system that is beyond our control. When we lift a glass of water, we willfully use muscles in an arm. This is an example of the functioning of the somatic nervous system—the thinking mind directs activity in muscles. When a person's blood pressure rises due to tightness in his arteries and he tries to order his tightened arteries to loosen up, nothing happens. (If the thinking mind was capable of such a feat, none of us physicians would ever take drugs for high blood pressure.) That is an example of autonomic function—a bodily function that is outside the reach of the thinking mind.

All our prevailing medical ideas of the function of the heart rate and rhythm, arterial tone, electro-magnetic energy in skin and muscles are based on this fundamental distinction between somatic and autonomic nervous systems. And so are ideas concerning the treatment of diseases affecting these organs.

Earlier work with biofeedback research led many investigators to conclude that autonomic nervous functions were also under voluntary control. The evidence for this viewpoint was derived from changes observed during biofeedback in heart rate, blood pressure, brain wave patterns and a host of other autonomic functions. This led to the widespread—and, in my view, mistaken—belief that the mind-over-body healing works. And that the thinking mind can learn to control the function of the heart, arteries, bowel and other body organs previously thought to be outside its reach. This erroneous belief also spawned the now thriving mind-over-body industry.

The distinction between the somatic (voluntary) and autonomic (involuntary) nervous systems is the primary reason why mainstream physicians do not put much stock in the mind-over-body healing notions espoused by the New Age gurus, and so heartily accepted by the general public. On this issue I stand firmly among my colleagues in the mainstream. The thinking mind does not—it cannot—heal the injured tissues. How can it? How can the thinking mind direct the healing phenomenon in injured tissues when it does not even understand it? To date, I have never met a person who claims to understand how healing occurs. Specifically, how does an injured cell know it is injured? How does a cell know its neighbor cell has died so it must multiply to fill the void left by the dead cell? And how do multiplying cells know when there are enough of them and they can cease replicating? A cell is a cosmos. Within it lie myriads of organelles. How do the organelles on one side of the cell know those on the other side have been zapped by radiotherapy or chemotherapy? When a child is hit by a car and loses a lot of blood, the cells in his bone marrow multiply rapidly to make up for the blood loss. How do the parent cells sitting smugly in the bone marrow know their offspring cells have been lost through gaping wounds in the skin?

One can ask such questions endlessly. Pathologists like me who have studied injured cells and tissues with microscopes for decades know there are no valid answers to any of those questions. The thinking mind simply does not know the answers. And yet, the gurus of mind-over-body healing continue to incubate grand schemes for using the mind to ordain healing in injured tissues.

I do not believe the thinking mind can ever heal injured tissues. In the same vein, to date I have never seen any evidence that the thinking mind can normalize raised blood pressure or slow the heart rate. These functions of the autonomic nervous system are manifestly outside the domains of the thinking mind. I address this subject in greater detail in the companion volume, *RDA: Rats, Drugs and Assumptions.*

Artists, musicians and poets usually find the principles of

autoregulation—autonomic training with energy dynamics—simple to understand and its practice easy to follow. I suppose it is because they are comfortable with abstract notions of life and energy. This group usually progresses rapidly, and I am able to see objective, electrophysiologic evidence of this progress during the very first training session. Lawyers and accountants often have more difficulty in the initial stages. Physicians often find autoregulation tedious, as do nurses to a lesser degree.

AUTOREGULATION ISN'T MIND-OVER-BODY HEALING, IT'S THE EXACT OPPOSITE

In my view the core belief of the biofeedback community that individuals can be trained to bring involuntary autonomic nervous functions under voluntary control of the thinking mind is erroneous.

So then, how does one reconcile the commonly observed phenomenon of "mind-over-body" control of asthma, colitis and PMS with self-regulation with the clear inability of the thinking mind to understand the healing response in injured tissues, let alone direct it with volition? The answer to that question is really quite simple: In self-regulation, the mind does not do any healing. Rather, when it is excluded—cancelled out with any method—the body slips into its natural state of healing energy. Thus, healing in self-regulation isn't a mind-over-body phenomenon, it's the exact opposite.

I address this subject in more than one place in this volume because I see it as the single most important obstacle in the path of healing among my patients.

> *Healing energy events take place when we are unfocused. Good things happen when we escape the tyranny of the thinking mind.*

I measure the results of such training sessions with accurate, objective, and reproducible electro-magnetic technology. It is quite rare for me to see a patient who fails in this completely. Needless to say, some people learn much faster than others. At times, the progress of patients in the throes of intense chronic suffering is slow.

Exercises for the Pulses

The following is the text of the autoreg tape I use for my patients. You may wish to use this text to prepare a tape for your own use in your own voice. I encourage my patients to do so. I also encourage them to add to this text additional material which they may find suitable. For the beginner, I recommend my own tapes (available from the Institute, (201) 586-4111).

This text for my tapes is copyrighted material, and may not be used to prepare tapes for sale or distribution to others in other ways.

In autoregulation, words are not important; the energy responses to which they lead are. Words are used only to cancel the cortical clutter and escape into limbic openness. The gentle guiding energy knows how to direct itself to the parts of the body under duress.

The tone of the voice, the emphasis on certain words, the spacing between successive sentences, and intervals between the various steps of this autoregulation exercise enhance its clinical benefits. The reader may begin autoregulation with my tapes, suitable tapes prepared by other professionals, or make his own tapes using the text that follows. Again, the core idea of autoregulation is to enter a healing energy state. It matters little what particular words, phrases or sentences can help an individual to enter the healing energy state that I describe in this volume.

In the tape text that follows, I take the beginner through some simple but effective steps that I have found to be useful after extensive clinical experience. This tape is for initial training in autoregulation. Our objectives at this stage are to learn how to be aware of our patterns of circulation, our breathing cycles, and the electro-magnetic energy in our skin, muscles and other tissues. These basic skills are essential for success in advanced methods of attending to different parts of our biology with autoregulation. It is important for the reader to practice basic autoregulation methods before seeking higher energy states that are only possible with deep *methodless* spiritual work.

PULSES WITH AUTOREGULATION TAPE

Assume the comfortable position you were in when we did autoreg in the lab together. You are sitting comfortably, at the edge of the chair. Your back is straight, maintaining the natural forward curve. Your knees are about 12 inches apart. Your feet are flat on the floor. Your hands are resting on your thighs, your palms facing upwards. Your eyes are closed. Move your shoulders gently and let the muscles settle in so you feel your arms hanging loose and free from your shoulders. If you wish to change your position to make yourself more comfortable during autoregulation training, please feel free to do so. The position I describe is the ideal position for most people who practice autoreg.

As we begin autoreg, our cortical mind rebels. It asserts itself in many ways. It will wander off. When that happens, we will let it do so. We will not fight it. We will stay with the autoreg steps. Our cortical mind will begin to judge and censor us. We will let it do so. If it distracts us with angry thoughts, we will let it do so. If it brings us images of past hurts, we will let it do so. We will stay with the autoreg steps. If it argues with us, and tells us autoregulation will not work, we will let it do so. We will stay with the autoregulation steps.

After the initial instruction, I give my patients a tape that I specifically prepare for this purpose. (This tape is available from the Institute.) With practice, most people can learn, within days or weeks, how to do the pulses without any external help from a tape or a professional.

Patients with severe chronic ailments, as I mentioned earlier, usually require extended training with a professional.

Together we will free limbic healing energy from the captivity of the thinking cortical mind.

✳✳✳✳✳✳✳✳✳✳✳

Breathe in and feel your stomach gently roll out.
Breathe out and feel your stomach gently roll back in.
Breathe in and feel your stomach gently roll out.
Breathe out and feel your stomach gently roll back in.
Breathe in and feel your stomach gently roll out.

Breathe out and feel your stomach gently roll back in.
Breathe in and feel your stomach gently roll out.
Breathe out and feel your stomach gently roll back in.

****

My hands are heavy and warm.
My hands are heavy and warm.
My hands are heavy and warm and limp.
My hands are heavy and warm and limp.
My hands are heavy and warm and limp and loose.
My hands are heavy and warm and limp and loose.
My hands are heavy and warm and limp and loose.

****

My feet are heavy and warm.
My feet are heavy and warm.
My feet are heavy and warm and limp.
My feet are heavy and warm and limp.
My feet are heavy and warm and limp and loose.
My feet are heavy and warm and limp and loose.
My feet are heavy and warm and limp and loose.

****

My hands and feet are heavy and warm and

limp and loose.
My hands and feet are heavy and warm and
    limp and loose.
My hands and feet are heavy and warm and
    limp and loose.
My hands and feet are heavy and warm and
    limp and loose.
My hands and feet are heavy and warm and
    limp and loose.
My hands and feet are heavy and warm and
    limp and loose.
My hands and feet are heavy and warm and
    limp and loose.

****

My leg muscles are heavy and warm and limp and loose.
My leg muscles are heavy and warm and limp and loose.
My leg muscles are heavy and warm and limp and loose.
My leg muscles are heavy and warm and limp and loose.
My leg muscles are heavy and warm and limp and loose.
My leg muscles are heavy and warm and limp and loose.
My leg muscles are heavy and warm and limp and loose.

****

My thigh muscles are heavy and warm and limp and loose.
My thigh muscles are heavy and warm and limp and loose.
My thigh muscles are heavy and warm and limp and loose.
My thigh muscles are heavy and warm and limp and loose.
My thigh muscles are heavy and warm and limp and loose.

My thigh muscles are heavy and warm and limp and loose.
My thigh muscles are heavy and warm and limp and loose.

My shoulder and neck muscles are limp and loose.
My shoulder and neck muscles are limp and loose.
My shoulder and neck muscles are limp and loose.

****

I am on a beach. It is a clear day. The sky is deep blue. The breeze is soft and gentle on my face. I see the waves breaking on the white sand. I see gulls floating on the water. The breeze is soft and gentle on my face. I see the waves breaking on white sand.

I see water waves breaking on the white sand.
I see water waves breaking on the white sand.
I see water waves breaking on the white sand.
I see water waves breaking on the white sand.
I see water waves breaking on the white sand.
I see water waves breaking on the white sand.
I see water waves breaking on the white sand.
I see water waves breaking on the white sand.

****

I see seagulls floating in the air.
I see seagulls floating in the air.
I see seagulls floating in the air.

I see seagulls floating in the air.
I see seagulls floating in the air.
I see seagulls floating in the air.
I see seagulls floating in the air.
I see seagulls floating in the air.

****

I see water waves breaking on the white sand.
I see water waves breaking on the white sand.
I see water waves breaking on the white sand.
I see water waves breaking on the white sand.
I see water waves breaking on the white sand.
I see water waves breaking on the white sand.
I see water waves breaking on the white sand.
I see water waves breaking on the white sand.

****

My hands are heavy like lead, and limp and loose.
My hands are heavy like lead, and limp and loose.
My hands are heavy like lead, and limp and loose.
My hands are heavy like lead, and limp and loose.
My hands are heavy like lead, and limp and loose.
My hands are heavy like lead, and limp and loose.
My hands are heavy like lead, and limp and loose.

****

My fingertips are throbbing.
All ten of my fingertips are throbbing.
All ten of my fingertips are throbbing.
All ten of my fingertips are throbbing.

My fingertips are tingling.
All ten of my fingertips are tingling.
All ten of my fingertips are tingling.
All ten of my fingertips are tingling.

My fingertips are pulsating.
All ten of my fingertips are pulsating.
All ten of my fingertips are pulsating.
All ten of my fingertips are pulsating.

My toes are throbbing.
My toes are throbbing.
My toes are throbbing.

****

I can imagine the space in the back of my throat.
I feel the space in the back of my throat expand when I
    breathe in.
I feel the space in the back of my throat expand when I
    breathe in.
I feel the space in the back of my throat expand when I
    breathe in.

I can imagine the volume of my right hand.
I can feel my hand swell up as I breathe in.

I can feel my hand swell up as I breathe in.
I can feel my hand swell up as I breathe in.

I feel energy in my right hand.
I feel energy in my right hand.
I feel energy in my right hand.

I feel energy in both my hands.
I feel energy in both my hands.
I feel energy in both my hands.

I feel energy in my hands and feet.
I feel energy in my hands and feet.
I feel energy in my hands and feet.

I feel energy in all parts of my body.
I feel energy in all parts of my body.
I feel energy in all parts of my body.

****

I will now count to three, and this will end the autoreg
session. If you feel that your body tissues are loose and
limp and limbic, and wish to stay that way, please do so.
You may end autoreg at a later time when that feels right
to you.

Three--two--one.
You may gently open your eyes.
Gently stretch your fingers and toes.
Sit comfortably for a few moments. Then you may slowly

rise. Practice minute-reg as often as you can during the day, while doing your day's work.

An experience can only be experienced.

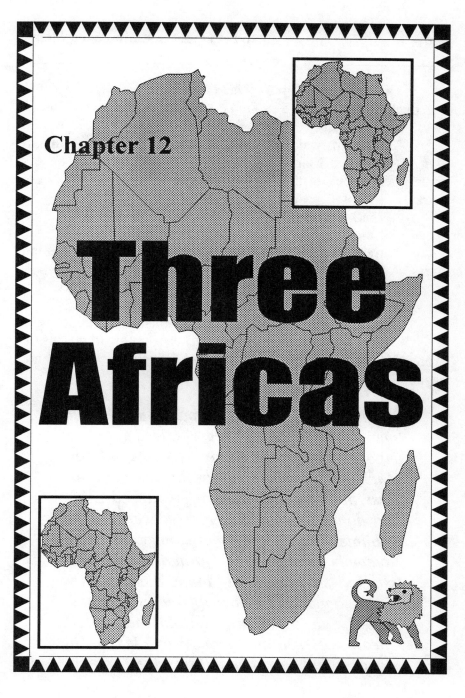

Chapter 12

Three Africas

One evening Choua joined me under a large tent that was pitched on the lodge grounds. He was carrying some books.

"I want to read you some passages from Karen Blixen's *Out of Africa* and Mary Lefkowitz's *Not Out of Africa,*" he said as he opened one of the books to where he had placed a book mark.

"What's it about?" I asked.

"Stress."

"Stress?" I said, surprised. "I didn't know Blixen was into stress. And Lefkowitz, isn't she a professor of history?"

"One is about stress in the high art of governance, and the other is about *creating* history."

"Creating history? No one *creates* history," I countered.

"You can if you happen to be a creative history professor. Listen closely. First, I'll read Blixen," he grinned and began:

> *At that time, it came to pass that the old men of the neighborhood resolved to hold a Ngoma for me. These Ngomas of the Ancients had been great functions in the past, but now they were rarely danced ...The old dancers when they arrived were a rare, sublime sight...they were naked, as if solemnly stating the formidable truth... chalked stripes running along their crooked limbs...emphasizing the stiff and brittle bones underneath the skin...The old men didn't speak, not even to one another...Just as the dancers had arranged themselves for the*

dance, an Askari from Nairobi arrived at the
house with a letter for me, that the Ngoma
must not take place...During all my life in
Africa I have not lived through another
moment of such bitterness. I had not before
known my heart to heave up in such a
storm against the things happening to me.

"Africa is a violated land," I commented, when Choua
closed the book and looked up. "And Africans are a..."
"A wounded people," he completed my sentence.
"Yes. But tell me, why did the British stop some naked,
rickety old men from their ritual dance? What could some
emaciated men with crooked limbs have done? What could the
British possibly have gained from stopping them?"
"If you want to subjugate a people completely, you must
first humiliate them completely," he replied. "You must hit them
hard where it hurts most."
"But why focus on a bunch of old dying men?" I asked,
perplexed.
"Stress was the instrument of power for the British. In
African cultures, the young look up to their elders for guidance.
If you want to demean the young, you must begin with their
elders. So the British played their stress card—and did so
ruthlessly while the young looked on. Before the British could
install their new colonial order of slavery, they first had to
uproot and torch the existing native structures."
"Man's cruelty to fellow man."
"The British took their lessons from nomad lions. When

those cats kill the patriarch lion and take over his harem, they eat the cubs of the killed patriarch in full view of the cubs' mothers. Those nomad lions know something about control and subjugation."

"All that melodrama aside, Choua, why did the British outlaw innocent tribal ritual dances?" I persisted.

"You don't understand, do you?" he grimaced. "Listen to another Blixen passage:

> *The old Kikuyu themselves stood like a herd*
> *of sheep, all their eyes under their wrinkled*
> *lids fixed upon my face...Some of them*
> *made little convulsive movements with their*
> *legs; they had come to dance, and dance*
> *they must. In the end I told them that our*
> *Ngoma was off.*

They had come to dance, and dance they must," Choua repeated the words as he looked up from the pages of the book.

"That's sad! Very sad!" I responded.

"The British weren't into making the natives sad," he said in a dark voice. "They were empire builders, and empires cannot be built on sentiment. They wanted to be supreme and have their subjects wholly subdued —and that meant complete and utter humiliation of the natives." He finished speaking, rubbed his temples with both hands, then resumed reading *Out of Africa*.

The old Kikuyu women have had a hard life, and have themselves become flint-hard under it. They were more difficult for any disease to kill off than their men. They had borne a number of children and had seen many of them die; they were afraid of nothing.

Africans were a resilient people and Blixen wasn't the only who knew it. The British also knew it."

"Do you really believe the British had a plan to outlaw African ritual dances to destroy their culture?" I asked, still doubtful.

"And to demoralize them," he continued. "The colonists wanted to prove to the natives that their great Spirits were utterly helpless against the British. To demonstrate that all their great ceremonies held to please their pagan gods could be abruptly halted by a mere piece of paper from Nairobi."

"How awful."

"Right, how awful!" His eyes narrowed. "To subdue the young volatile African blood, the colonists dealt blows where they were most vulnerable. And nowhere is an African more vulnerable than when he abides by the tribal laws set forth by his elders. The British understood that fired up by the ritual—no matter how feeble the old dancing men—the young Africans could be dangerous. The British understood that their edicts against a handful of old men baring their bones in a ritual dance were more lethal than kegs of gunpowder."

"So what happened? Did Blixen fight back?" I asked.

"How could a single Danish woman stand up to the British Raj? How could she dare defy even the local Nairobi overlords?" Choua replied.

"How sad! I'm glad all that is behind us now." Choua's words distressed me.

"Behind us?" he scowled.

"I mean those awful things don't happen anymore."

"Stress was, and continues to be, a weapon of colonialism —and colonialism thrives as well as it ever did."

"That's not quite right," I challenged. "There may be some inconsequential pockets of colonialism left in some remote areas of the globe, but its core idea is dead."

"That's not quite right," he mocked. "The core of colonialism was—and continues to be—racism. And racism is as robust now as it ever was. Only its garb has changed in some places. Listen to this passage from Martin Bernal's *Black Athena*:

> *Putting the Indo-European, Semitic and Egyptian roots together, I now believed that—with further research—one could provide plausible explanations for 80 to 90 percent of the Greek vocabulary...Astour had demonstrated that anti-Semitism provided an explanation for the denial of the role of the Phoenicians in the formation of Greece... Clearly there were very profound cultural inhibitions against associating Egypt with Greece.*

"I'm glad someone is putting African history in its right

place, and bringing some objectivity to it," I said, after he finished reading. "That should heal some wounds. It should bring back the pride of a rich heritage for culturally robbed African children."

"You're a dreamer," he mocked.

"Black children have been impoverished for decades by a distorted history that credits the Aryan race for all achievements in science, art and philosophy. It's about time someone set the record right."

"Dream on, professor," he taunted. "That's not the way things are. That's not how it works."

"What do you mean?" I asked, perplexed.

"Some history professors contemptuously pronounce that Afrocentricism is nothing but a cheap excuse to teach myth as history. To them it is sacrilegious for anyone to hold that the Greeks were not the inventors of philosophy, science, democracy and every other decent thing."

"That doesn't surprise me. After all, hasn't that been the standard version of history taught in schools and colleges for centuries?"

"It's hard to eat crow," Choua chirped, then added, "What are the history professors going to do now? Tell everyone that what they taught as facts were mere fiction? For decades they've painted a pretty picture in which every good thing was attributed to their master Aryan race—and every barbaric thing to Africans and Asians. And now someone has the audacity to challenge their most sacred beliefs—to undo their core notion of racial superiority."

"Bernal is just one historian," I countered. "His is a sole voice presenting a contrary viewpoint. That hardly establishes his position as the truth. Even if Bernal is right, his conclusions need to supported by additional research."

"For once, you're absolutely right," he laughed out loud.

"I'll now read a passage from Professor Mary Lefkowitz's *Not Out of Africa*. She does exactly what you predicted. Listen to this:

> *I shall show that the notion that Egyptian religion and philosophy had a significant influence on Greece is a cultural myth...In the fifth century B.C. Herodotus was told by Egyptian priests that the Greeks owed many aspects of their culture to the older and vastly impressive civilization of the Egyptians. I shall explain why in this matter the Greek writers are not as trustworthy as they claim to be.*

Professor Lefkowitz is evidently committed to the dogma of intellectual superiority of the master Aryan race. She is obsessed with the notion that the Greeks owed no debt to any other people. She abhors the idea that Greeks learned things about life from the Egyptians. What amuses me is not her historio*poetic* prowess, it's ..."

"What's historio*poetic*?" I interrupted him. "Did you just make that word up?"

"Historiopoetics relates to creation of history—not a bad word for making history," Choua chuckled. "Professor Lefkowitz researches and writes well, as she *creates* history," he went on. "What amuses me most is her claim that she is more trustworthy than the Greek historian, Herodotus. She wants us to believe that what she writes in the 1990s about fifth-century Egyptians is more authentic than what Herodotus observed as he traveled throughout Egypt at that very time."

"That's audacious," I said.

"Chutzpah! That's chutzpah," he groused.

"The ancient Greek historians probably did make some mistakes, just as historians do today," I defended Lefkowitz's viewpoint.

"Why does white history always err on the side of whites?" he countered. "Why don't European historians sometimes make mistakes on the Egyptian side? Why do they keep stubbornly pronouncing that the Greeks invented the human intellect?"

"That's absurd. Nobody says the Greeks invented the human thinking faculty."

"When I first saw the Parthenon," Choua continued, ignoring my comment, "I knew God had walked on the Acropolis, the 'High City' of ancient Greek kings long before Pericles' architects drew their blueprints for the great temple. Then his builders subtly curved marble to create optical illusions of a perfect temple," he continued. "The stunning result is silence in stone that makes God palpable."

"God becomes palpable, eh?" I chided.

"Yet sometime later, when I walked the long Avenue of Sphinxes, with the sculptured ram heads completed by the Great Ramses II linking the Temples of Luxor and Karnak," he went on, again ignoring my sarcasm, "I knew that God must have had a better time in Luxor and Karnak then he did at the Acropolis."

"You should know, Choua. God speaks to you," I taunted.

As much as I wanted to pull Choua's leg, I couldn't disagree with him. No one who has stood before Ramses' temple at Abu Simbal would ever contest Choua's claim. Nor can anyone who has ever seen the great Obelisk at Luxor not feel utterly humbled. At the Parthenon, I felt a sinking sense of personal inadequacy. The Parthenon cannot be comprehended. But it was different at Luxor and Karnak. There I felt God's presence. For the first time in my life, I realized what primitive man, emerging out of the great Rift Valley, must have felt when he first recognized there was something larger, much larger—something beyond the capacity of his physical senses and the reach of his imagination. Years later, we named that something spirituality.

"Tell me, Choua, why would it matter whether the ancient Egyptians bequeathed more to us or to the ancient Greeks?" I broke the silence.

"It matters only to those who are still obsessed with notions of racial superiority," he muttered without looking at me. "Evidently—or, should I say as far as I know?—the great Egyptian civilization preceded the Greek civilization by more than a millennium. The ancient Greeks themselves wrote about what the Egyptians bequeathed to them. The reverse cannot be said. Yes, the Greeks were magnificent builders, but none could hold a candle to Ramses II. His temples and palaces —whatever is left behind now—are far greater in scale and splendor than anything the Greeks could ever build."

"Is that why you see God more clearly reflected in the glistening granite of Karnak than in the radiant white marble of the Parthenon?" I teased.

"White marble looks prettier; dark granite is sturdier. But I don't exalt one type of stone over the other. It's just that the dark granite stone pulls at me more than the pale marble does."

"We're talking about the Egyptians and Greeks, how did we end up with stones?" I asked, bemused. "What's the point of all that?"

"There isn't any point," he grinned mischievously. "I'm quite content in letting the historians slug it out among themselves. I don't particularly care what they *create* and what they revise when they rewrite history. It all came from the Rift Valley of East Africa anyway. But for now it doesn't matter."

"What doesn't matter?" I asked, irked by his flight of ideas.

"It's silly to hang on to obsolete notions that pale skin covering a skull hides more intellect than a black one. The real threats facing humankind are anger and chemicals. Neither anger nor chemicals discriminate between blue eyes and black eyes—between blond hair and black hair. Earth is a shrinking planet. John Donne was right. 'Send not to know for whom the bell tolls, it tolls for thee.' We're all in it together —the mess we have made of our earth."

"Are you saying history, as a science, isn't important anymore?" I asked, incredulous.

"History was never a science," he posited. "Nor is it now. Science is pure observation. And history, by definition, cannot be pure observation. It is merely a set of conclusions drawn from piecing together ancient shards and stones. And we all know that newly discovered shards and stones continually change our notions of ancient history based on previously discovered relics, don't they?"

"So?"

"Each of us has to be rooted in our own soil."

"Right! But, isn't that soil one's heritage? One's culture and history?"

"That soil isn't history. It's the present," he replied testily.

"A person's lineage doesn't matter anymore, is that it?" I asked, bewildered.

"Past glory is a shared human heritage. It all came from Africa, as we believe now. If and when someone discovers evidence of human perception, sensitivity, creativity and tools elsewhere in the world that predates the African civilization, I'll gladly change my opinion. For now, Africa is the birthplace for all of us." A mysterious smile spread on Choua's face, then he walked away without caring to hear my response.

WHOSE KENYA IS IT ANYWAY?

On the morning of our return from Kenya, Sarah dropped Talat and me off in downtown Nairobi. She needed some time to complete her fellowship work before leaving for the U.S. She suggested we lunch at Handi, the most recommended Indian restaurant in Nairobi. We walked around, then went to the observatory at the top of Jomo Kenayatta Center —named after the Kenyan anthropologist who later served as the first president of independent Kenya—for an aerial view of the city. At about noon, we returned to the Nairobi streets, and I asked a passer-by for directions to Handi. The man, a Kenyan of Indian descent, asked us to follow him as he turned onto a side street. On the way I asked how long he had been in Kenya and what he thought was the most important change Nairobi had experienced in those years.

"I came here as a boy, almost forty years ago," he replied. "Last week, I returned from London after a short visit. I realized that Nairobi had once been as clean as London is now. It was a safe city when I first got here. You never saw any trash on sidewalks," he said sourly, then, pointing to some Africans walking toward us, he added, "Of course, *they* weren't allowed within the city limits in those days."

I decided not to ask any more questions. Talat and I walked in silence a few paces behind him. He wore a brightly colored, glistening polyester suit that reminded me of what our son, Omar, once said on his return from a trip to Costa Rica. I'd asked him to name two things that impressed him most about Costa Rica. "Rain forests and polyester poverty", he had replied. To break the monotony of following the man in silence, I tried to guess what line of work he might be engaged in. Perhaps a government employee, I thought.

After walking a few blocks, he abruptly stopped, turned to face us, looked Talat in the eye and said, "This country has gone to the dogs." Talat's face went blank. Then he gave us directions to Handi and disappeared in the traffic.

"Nothing has really changed in a hundred years," Choua murmured, as we sat for lunch in the restaurant.

"What do you mean?" I asked, though I understood what he alluded to.

"It was the same way in 1893 when Ghandi went to South Africa, wasn't it?" he frowned.

"What was the same in 1893?"

"You know what the West Indian writer, S. Naipaul, wrote about Ghandi and his feelings for Africans—or shall we say lack of them."

"What did he write?" I asked, my curiosity piqued.

"I bought this book yesterday from a street vendor," he replied, pulling a copy of *India: A Wounded Civilization* by Naipaul, out of his pocket. He opened the book to a page he had marked with a piece of paper, and read:

> *The adventure never ceased to be internal:*
> *so it comes out in the autobiography. And*
> *this explains the most remarkable omission*
> *in Gandhi's account of his twenty active*
> *years in South Africa: Africans...The*
> *Africans vanish in Gandhi's heart-*
> *searchings: they are the motive of a vow,*
> *and thereafter disappear.*

Interesting, isn't it?" he smirked.

"Men's hearts take time to change," I replied.

"Africans in Africa were an unwanted presence for Europeans. When Europeans allowed Asians into Africa to run errands for them, Africans became an unwanted presence for the immigrant Asians as well," he went on darkly.

"Things aren't that bad now, are they?" I tried to lighten up the conversation.

"Do you know what I find astonishing in the words of that Indian in the polyester suit?" he asked.

"What?" I asked, amused that the man's polyester suit had also made an impression on Choua.

"He told us he had just returned from England. Now that's quite amusing. The English look at Indians in England as an encumbrance. He must know that, and that must be demeaning for him. Yet, here in Nairobi, he considers Africans an encumbrance."

"Men have short memories," I said.

"Short memories?" he grimaced. "That Indian doesn't seem to recall what he left behind in London a day earlier."

THE FIRST AFRICA:
AN AFRICA OF HEAVENLY HEAVEN

"There are three Africas," Choua said as we wandered through Nairobi streets after lunch.

"Three Africas?" I asked, puzzled.

"First, there's the Africa of a heavenly heaven."

"Africa of a heavenly heaven?" I asked, puzzled.

"Yes, of a heavenly heaven. A pure and pristine heaven —unpolluted by power grid lines, radio frequencies and smog of toxic fumes."

"Oh, that!" I said, then asked, "What's the second Africa?"

"Why is the Serengeti openness so exhilarating?" he asked, ignoring my question. "Why are the rains more cleansing here? Purifying and enriching? And why are the rainbow's colors sharper here? Why is the sky spiritually uplifting?"

"You just told me why. It's the absence of smog."

"This Africa lures, holds and captivates," he continued. "It's a place where the sheer beauty of the savannah hurts the eye. But there is more to the Africa of heavenly heaven than that," he added whimsically, then looked up.

"What?" I asked, my curiosity kindled.

"Its spirituality! Its divinity! The Africa of heavenly heaven is different because one can feel a link with the larger *presence* here. It's stronger than anywhere else."

"Can you see God more clearly here?" I provoked.

"It is purity of existence," he replied evenly. "It is Africa's nativity. It is the way it *was*."

"Not quite," I challenged him. "As pure and noble as the Serengeti may appear, I doubt there's any part of it that hasn't been violated by man."

"The heavenly heaven belongs to humans as humans belong to it. It's where all life comes from," Choua went on.

"Do you mean the energy of sunlight which turns into the chemical bond energy of chlorophyll, which, in turn, sustains the earth's food chain?"

"Heaven was man's link with the energy of that *presence* that permeates and surrounds him always—above, below and in every other direction."

"*Was?*"

"It was an early discovery of man. Africans preserved their history largely by ritual. But the Jains in India—in the oldest known civilization—carved images on stones to express their notions of human suffering and the nature of their God-man relationships as early as five thousand years ago, possibly even earlier."

"What do those stone objects show?"

"Among the artifacts unearthed in archaeological digs of the pre-historic Indus valley civilization in western Pakistan there are figures of a nude yogin, a woman in meditation. The yogin is in the characteristic Jaina *kayotsarga* posture, which symbolizes perfect bodily abandonment. Along the nude yogin were found bull emblems and nude male Harappan torsos that are thought to point to the prevalence of worship of Rsabha, the First Lord, of Jaina tradition. Those ancient Indians had great insight."

"What insight?" I asked, a trifle put off by his shifting thoughts.

"That man cannot resolve the larger problems of the human condition by clever thinking alone," he replied solemnly. "He must surrender to the larger *presence* for guidance."

"Are we talking about Africa or India?" I asked, irritated.

"The Africans also understood the human need for spirituality—a dimension they realized extended well beyond their physical or intellectual perceptions. The Africans had their own versions of the ancient Jain doctrine, which is *ahimsa*—respect for all life. They didn't carve their notions onto stones, perhaps because they *lived* them and the tribal elders were content in passing them along to the younger generations in dance rituals, like the Ngomas that Karen Blixen wrote about in *Out of Africa.*

"Is that why you read that passage from her book?" I asked.

"The Jains understood about the purity of heart and the sanctity of all life," he went on. "Wild animals were their tutors. The Africans understood things like purity of heart and the sanctity of all life. They learned their lessons from wild animals. The ancient Jains enunciated the principle of nonviolence, and so did the Africans—a very long time before Ghandi did. Lord Bhagawan Mahavira, the historical figure of Jainism, was the twenty-fourth *Tirthankara*—a crossing-maker, one who crossed over to Enlightenment —and an elder contemporary of Buddha. The African tradition goes back even further."

"Are you saying spirituality was invented in Africa?" I mocked, exasperated by his endless wandering.

"No one 'invented' spirituality," he groused. "The human need for the spiritual is as old as humankind. The African searched for the meaning of his life, looked up and understood there was an *organizinginfluence* out there —although he could not perceive it with his physical senses. He created his ritual to forge a connection with that presence. What you dismiss as his barbaric pagan ritual was his celebration of that organizing influence."

Choua paused —the sort of pause that does not invite interruption —then he went on.

"Jainism in ancient India took root in a peaceful civilization, not in a superpower. Hence its concept of human behavior is in man's reverence for *all* life. The Jains enunciated the principle of *Ahimsa* —an injunction against all violence, intended, expressed or inflicted through thought, word or action. When you gloat about the philosophy, science and wisdom of the ancient Greeks, you should know they did not invent humanism."

"But the Greeks clearly left behind a rich legacy, didn't they?" I countered.

"While the Greek supergod, Zeus, was establishing a name for himself by chasing immortal goddesses on Mount Olympus and mortal ladies on earth —as well as earthling boys when the opportunity arose —the African was a humanist. And a very long time before that, the African had emerged from the Rift Valley, looked up and understood that he must submit to something larger than himself—something that his physical senses couldn't perceive and his intellect couldn't reach."

"The spiritual?" I guessed.

"Yes," he replied and looked up again, his eyes slowly closing.

THE SECOND AFRICA: AN AFRICA THAT BLEEDS

"The second Africa blisters and bleeds," Choua resumed as we walked down the street. Some children were leaning against a filthy wall plastered with cow dung cakes. Their rickety legs hung below the dirty rags that served as shorts. Their bloated bellies protruded above their waistlines.

"That's not a pretty sight," I remarked, quickening my pace, as if distance could dull my perception of the deprivation those hungry children faced.

"The second Africa is a violated land—a deeply wounded and scarred place. This Africa also hurts the eyes, but in different ways. One only sees the victims here, not the victimizers. It also makes the heart hurt in ways one didn't know existed. Poverty perturbs anywhere, but African poverty suffocates."

"What about the third Africa?" I wanted to change the subject.

"This second Africa is also about the essential incompleteness of the human condition," he persisted. "It is a place where a person is uncertain, uneasy, empty and hollow—without knowing why." Choua fell silent.

I saw Talat some paces ahead of me. She was looking back and wanting me to catch up. I moved briskly. "The sight of those children makes you sick, doesn't it?" she asked. Then added, "But what can be done? Maybe the tourist dollars will help. Why else would anyone come here? But that's not quite true." She corrected herself. "Africa is about something else, though I haven't quite figured it out yet."

We finally managed to hail a taxi to the airport. Nairobi, like all poor large cities of the world, is a place where visitors like to leave in a hurry. Eyes are jarred by dilapidated houses, streets strewn with decomposing garbage, rickshaws pulled by half-naked sweating coolies, and unending streaks of emaciated men and women leaning against dirty walls.

"The spiritual African is old and dying," Choua spoke as we approached the airport ramp. "The young African is hungry, ready to plunder —and kill—if necessary."

"What about the third Africa?" I repeated my earlier question.

"The third Africa." He squinted and looked away.

"Yes, tell me about the third Africa," I pleaded earnestly.

"The third Africa is there, but you have to look harder to see it."

Before I could say anything, he opened the taxi door, stepped out and disappeared in the airport terminal.

THE MASAI

Second only to the Serengeti lion, Masai warriors of East Africa have enchanted the European eyes most.

From the beginning, Masai tribes peacefully shared the Serengeti Plains with animals. The tsetse fly saw to it that the Masai cattle didn't crowd out other animal life. The tsetse fly causes fatal trypanosomiasis in cattle, but wild African animals are immune to it. This arrangement came under jeopardy when the British took a fancy to the Masai homeland and decided they needed an expanse of hunting ground—a sort of *divine Disneyland*. They forcefully expelled the Masai from many of their native lands to create huge game parks. That is one action the British took in colonial east Africa that I can't fault. Ironically, in the Masai tragedy lay the only chance mankind had to save the Serengeti Plains from itself.

Masai men are tall and lithe. From a distance, they seem to glide in the tall grass, as the ochre-red of their togas slips through the contrasting golden-brown of the grassland. Up close, you can see their silver neck amulets and the black-and-white ostrich feather headpieces that frame their thin faces and large yellowed teeth.

The Masai were idealized by the Europeans as a proud and indomitable people who remained impervious to the colonial designs that so readily subverted the Kukuyo, the Masai's shorter, chunkier neighbors to the south. European intellectuals were fascinated by what they regarded as the fierce independence of these warriors—although what great wars they fought and won isn't clear from their history. Cattle folk have not been great warriors in other parts of the world.

We were fortunate to spot several Masai warriors up close during our brief stay in Kenya. The management of Serengeti lodges, like all good hotel administrators, go to considerable lengths to provide their guests with a genuine Masai experience. At the Keekorok Lodge in the Masai Mara Game Reserve, we saw the Masai warriors dance. Wearing their traditional ochre-red togas and positioned in rows of two, they held long spears in their hands and gracefully waved their ostrich-feathered headdresses to the rhythm of the drummers. The highlight of the dance was a competition among the dancers to find who could jump the highest. For this competition, each warrior stepped into the middle while others surrounded him forming a small circle. The more the jumping warrior could be seen above the heads of others encircling his frame, the greater the applause he received from his comrades. High jumping in place is a Masai dance tradition in which young men boast about their tall frames.

The next morning in the dining hall, I spotted one of those warriors among the waiters, then another and another. I told Talat about my exciting discovery. Together we began to count the warriors until we identified all of them. Then we realized that all the other lodge guests were doing the same—and were equally amused. All the warriors doubled as waiters during the day and entertained the guests with Masai dances in the evening. We ended the next three evenings in three different lodges of the Masai Mara Game Reserve by experiencing the *genuine* Masai culture in *exactly* the same way. As I looked around, it seemed most of the lodge guests would have preferred to be at the movies.

The lodges in the Kenyan game reservations we visited were awash with purple, crimson and red bougainvillea. Orange trumpet flowers and baboons in the fever trees enhanced the spectacle. But I had no idea that the spectacles that would most enthrall tourists were the sumptuous sprawls of extravagant buffets and exotic cocktails. Apparently the lodge managers not only observed the opulence of Marriott and Hilton brunches in the States, they found ways to exceed their western counterparts. After lunch we saw grossly overfed, lethargic and bored American teenagers slump in overstuffed chairs. The teens were waiting to be transported in safari vans to where lazy cats snoozed in the sun. Men, sporting safari suits and wearing khaki hats purchased at African kiosks, stumbled and strutted among the teenagers. Women shopped in the gift shops. Still, they made the effort to be in the Serengeti, I thought. They ought to be commended for that.

MASAI WARRIORS FOR ETHNIC DIVERSITY

On a return trip from the safari, Sarah suggested that we might consider a trip to Mumbasa. I felt a childlike excitement. The name Mumbasa is etched deep in my boyhood memories. Locating the town on a coastal map, I tried hard to recall what associations with the town's name kept it from being obliterated in my memory during the years I hadn't heard the town's name mentioned again. Perhaps it was the memory of enchanting stories of Arab pirates who plundered the coastal villages, or the accounts of the ivory trade that I had heard. I didn't recall any stories of *the black* ivory trade, in which the traded commodity was African flesh. Or, perhaps it was something more mundane. The word Mumbasa might have seemed bombastic to a Pakistani boy learning English as his fourth language.

"What is Mumbasa known for?" I asked Sarah, trying to imagine what an African trading town, with a history of dominance by Arab sheiks, might look like in the late twentieth century.

"Ethnic diversity," she chuckled loudly.

"Arabs and Portuguese?" I tried to recall who the colonists were before the British.

"No, not that kind of diversity," she giggled naughtily, then looked at Talat.

"The Hindus, Sikhs and Muslims?" I asked, puzzled by her impish giggle.

"No, this is an altogether different type of diversity. This is a Mesai warrior-European woman thing," she laughed.

"Warrior-woman things? What's that?" I asked, my puzzlement growing.

"European women visit Mumbasa to rent the companionship of Mesai warriors for a week or two," she explained with a laugh, then added seriously, "but it is a place worth visiting."

We couldn't arrange plane tickets for Mumbasa. Instead, we flew to Lamu, a small, sleepy, Arab coastal town north of Mumbasa. Human excreta flowed freely through the small gutters situated in narrow alleys at the center of town. The town had an interesting garbage removal plan. Donkeys with fungus-eaten hides moved around freely, feasting on large piles of garbage at many street intersections.

On the docks at Lamu, a young Arab man waiting for a boat asked me where we had come from. I told him we had arrived from the United States. He told me he had never been to the United States but that he had vacationed extensively throughout Europe and the Middle East. Curious as to how a young Arab man from Lamu could afford extended vacations in so many countries, I asked if his family had business in those countries. He chuckled and explained that he was befriended by an older German woman who took him along during her travels to faraway countries. Then he'd returned to his hometown, not unhappily, it seemed to me. I asked why he had left the woman. "One tires of that sort of thing after a while," he explained, then added, "It wasn't difficult. She wanted a change too." Masai warriors, Italian women, Arab youngsters, older German ladies, patriarch lions with their harems, nomad lions and their conquered concubines in estrous!

"It's all the same," I thought I could hear Choua summing things up. I turned sharply to face him. He was nowhere to be seen.

In Mumbasa, European ladies rent Mesai warriors for ethnic diversity. In Nairobi, it works the other way. One evening, Sarah took Talat and me to Buffalo Bill, a part-covered, part-open night club in Nairobi. The place teemed with black ladies of the evening. They were amused by our presence among them and greeted us with polite, subdued smiles. The waiters of Buffalo Bill were impeccably professional when Sarah ordered decaffeinated coffee for the three of us. We learned that the Kenyan beauties there generously shared their HIV viral loads with their white male guests from North America, Europe and Australia. Also shared, and equally as generously, I imagined, must be herpes, hepatitis, cytomegalic and Epstein-Barr viruses. "What is good for the goose is good for the gander," Choua would have said.

FAYEMI'S AFRICA

In 1995, Professor Alfred Olusegun Fayemi published *Balancing Acts*, a picture-essay book of life in west Africa. He graciously offered a copy of his book to Talat and me as a gift. In the foreword written by Professor Molefi Kete Asante, Chairman of African-American studies at Temple University in Philadelphia, I read the following:

Finding the soul of Africa exposed in laughter, joy, pain, work, praise, and business, Fayemi has snapped the essence of the meaning of the drama and the charisma of life in West Africa. But how can one photograph charisma? There is something innocent, playful, serious, coy, and resolute about these photographs as if the photographer is telling us something about himself. This is unlike the familiar photographer who seeks to see but only sees what is given.

To Professor Asante's profuse admiration of Professor Fayemi's work, I only add this: Every black, brown and white person interested in the soul of Africa should view this collage of pictures. No one needs to do justice to Fayemi's pictures. The pictures do justice to him.

One day Choua picked up *Balancing Acts* and buried his head in its pages. I looked at it for some moments, then returned to my work. Some minutes passed before Choua broke the silence.

"When Fayemi's African beauty stands in front of her thatched hut," he spoke finally, "she does so with a purity that transcends all human perceptions."

"I know which picture you're looking at. She *is* a pretty woman," I said, then quickly added, "I don't mean the Julia

Roberts' sort of *Pretty Woman*."

"When his native woman plaits her daughter's hair," he went on, not acknowledging my stab at humor, "that's all she does—with remarkable simplicity. And when two women visit a clinic with their sick babies nestled in makeshift sheet knapsacks, their gentle smiles and shining eyes reassure total strangers."

"He has some quality pictures in that book."

"The elderly potter woman is so absorbed in her craft, it seems she isn't making the pot, the pot is making her."

"I don't know about the pot *making* her," I said, "but the two *are* one."

"His street barber wears a lily white robe as he caresses the shaved, lowered head of his customer. Both are true to life."

"Fayemi's takes some quality pictures, doesn't he?" I repeated.

"It's not about taking shots," he snapped. "It's about life. It's about human suffering, anguish and endurance. Fayemi has put into pictures what Sinclair Lewis put into words."

"What words?" I asked, irritated.

"Man will not only endure, man will prevail."

WHY AREN'T FAYEMI'S FOLKS FURIOUS?

"Africans are a wounded people. They have been exploited and violated for centuries. They have been bought and sold. Everything African has been defiled. Tell me, Choua, why don't people who populate Fayemi's pictures look sullen?"

"Because they're Africans," he shrugged.

"C'mon, that's no answer. Why aren't those folks

furious?" I pressed.

"Didn't you look at his pictures? I thought you loved his book." His forehead wrinkled.

"Yes! yes! I did. Didn't I tell you so? But that doesn't answer my question."

"I think it does." He stared at me for a while, then resumed. "Don't the innocent faces of boys wearing little turbans in their Quran class answer your question? Look again at the beaming face of the little girl in the white uniform at the head of the kindergarten class line at the Mary Immaculate School. Doesn't she tell you anything?"

"They're children. What do they about know how their ancestors were violated?" I replied.

"Exactly my point!" Choua became animated. "Don't you see the miracle of Africa in those pictures? Don't you see how alive those faces are? No doubt many of their parents live anguished lives, but you wouldn't know it by looking at those children's faces. Isn't that a miracle?"

"In that sense, it is," I confessed. "But what about Fayemi's adults who endure drought and disease? How can they look so serene?"

"In Djenne, Mali, against the backdrop of the famous mud mosque, the marketplace bustles. Yet there is no sign of fear or strife. There are no uneasy, frightened faces eager to finish their business and return to the safety of their homes. Are there?"

"No. But I'm sure many of those folks won't have enough to feed their families in the evening. Why aren't they fretful and furious?" I persevered.

"Notwithstanding the Western press, Africans aren't a furious people," he replied.

"That's not true," I snapped. "Didn't you read about the 1990 hijacking of a middle-aged missionary couple near Narok

in *Into Africa?* The natives forced the husband to watch while
they raped his wife to death. And don't you remember the news
article reporting the hijacking of a safari caravan in the
Serengeti, while we were there?"

Choua stiffened visibly, then asked "What do you see in
Fayemi's picture of the women-hawking-food scene in Mopti,
Mali?"

"Women hawking food. What else?" I replied, dropping
my voice as I realized my questions jarred him.

"What do you see on their faces?"

"They exude life. But that's precisely my question. How
can they be so poor yet look so rich? They all carry heavy clay
vessels, balanced precariously on their delicate necks and heads.
How can they look so exuberant?"

"What do you see in the rice-and-bean-selling scene?"

"The same things."

"And at the Friday prayer scene in Dakar, Senegal?"

"Men kneeling in prayers."

"And at the wedding scene in Parcelles, Senegal?"

"Women dancing. Dancers and drummers facing off."

"What do you see in their faces? What thoughts do you
think populate their heads? Do you think they're real people?"
He fired away.

"Yes, Fayemi's folks are real people. They are alive. But
that doesn't answer the questions I ask. They live hard and
diminished lives. Sometimes their sick children sleep hungry at
night. Why aren't they sullen? Why don't they sulk? Why aren't
they furious for what has been done to them?"

"Look harder," he cajoled.

"Don't be silly," I replied, hiding my bitterness. "Why
don't the Fayemi folks show depression in their eyes? Don't
they ever suffer mental illness? Why don't any of them look
bleary-eyed?"

"Because they sleep well," he laughed.

"No, seriously, Choua, aren't they ever anxious? Smitten by panic attacks? Don't their hearts ever palpitate —cause mitral valve prolapse? No one looks sullen or agitated. Why aren't they ever in the throes of sugar-insulin-adrenaline roller coasters?"

"Because Fayemi's Africans don't crave sugar." He laughed out loud.

"I can't believe all of Fayemi's folks are free of the demons that haunt my patients in the United States. Yet, that's what I want to know. Do you understand any of that?" I finished, exasperated.

Choua looked at me with solemn eyes for a long while. I stared back at him. Then slowly his face softened and a mystic smile spread on his face.

"You think African children are poor because they walk barefoot. And American children are rich because they have closets stacked with shoes. You see African children impoverished because they're run to their schools in rags and wallow in dust under the acacia trees where they sit to take lessons. And you see American children as privileged because their classrooms are air-conditioned. After the schools is over, the Africans walk back to their mud huts while the Americans are picked up by school buses. But there is more to a child's poverty or richness than shoes and school buses. You fail to see something far more important. How often does a little American girl leave for school and carry with her the neuroses of her parents? How often does a little African girl do that? How often does an American boy return to a home torn by anger and hostility? How often does an African boy do that? How often is an American child tormented by nightmares? How often is an African child troubled by ugly dreams?"

"The African belongs to his tribe. Who does the American belong to? Where does in your order of richness and privilege fit in the isolation and alienation of American children? Your eyes hurt when you see emaciated children withering away in an African famine. But you fail the see the rivers of anguish in the silent eyes of abused American children. Teenage suicide is rampant in the United States. Why don't African teenager seek refuge in death?"

Choua stopped, stared past me at the wall behind my desk for several moments, then briskly walked out.

GIMME FIVE

Matthew is a seven-year-old autistic child. He never spoke a single word until he was almost six years old. He suffers from multiple food and mold allergies. Just like most of the autistic children I have seen, in a follow-up visit a few months after starting our nutrient therapies and allergy desensitization, Matthew's mother reported some improvement in his general behavior. Then she tearfully told me that Matthew had finally started to call her mom and speak a few other words.

Encouraged by the news, I told Matthew's mother I wanted to try something different. My approach was simple: Would Matthew respond further if we found someone to coach him? The two elements of effective coaching would be frequency of contact and absence of censorship. I knew that in children with attention deficit disorder and hyperactivity a similar approach had been reported to be effective by Edward Hallowell, M.D., author of *Driven to Destruction*, and by others. I asked if she had a neighbor who might be willing to make brief one- or two-minute daily contacts with Matthew (or less frequently). The coach would simply repeat a few predetermined sentences, then finish by saying something encouraging to him. The person who agreed to such coaching would have to establish a bond with Matthew, not only for the boy's sake but also so that the coaching wouldn't be tedious. I ended by giving Matthew's mother an example of what I meant. The coach could use simple sentences such as: "Hi, Matthew. How are you today? What did you do yesterday? What are you going to do today? Matthew, I think you're a great guy."

Profound isolation and the inability to respond to common situations of life are, of course, central problems in autism. At least in theory, attempting to break the barriers of inward isolation of autistic children seemed worth a try.

As simple as this concept might seem to the reader, it was awkward to explain it Matthew's mother. She had consulted several specialists at the clinic for child developmental disorders at the university who established the diagnosis. She also saw some neurologists who agreed with the previous diagnosis and told her to accept it. I wondered how she might react to my suggestion of coaching by a nonprofessional. Even if she was amenable, I recognized the difficulty of finding someone suitable and willing to make such a commitment. She listened to me, first with growing curiosity and then with blank eyes. I began to see the futility of my approach. She nodded, but it was just a show of politeness, I was sure. I moved on to some items about his nutritional plan.

Suddenly, her eyes brightened. She smiled and blurted,

"Oh, my God, so that was it?"
"What?" I asked, puzzled.
"Gimme five! *That's* how it worked," she went on excitedly.
"That's how what worked?" I asked.
"Gimme five," she laughed.
"What's that all about?" I asked.
"Oh, Dr. Ali, you would love it. I'm sure of that." She stopped laughing and told me the following:

Once she saw a janitor —a black American —pass by at school and Matthew's eyes lit up. It seemed strange to her, but she thought nothing of it. Of course, until then she had never seen Matthew acknowledge anyone, let alone greet them with bright eyes. A few days later, the same thing happened. She became curious and asked Matthew's teacher about it. The teacher laughed and said that she had also noticed it. Matthew's mom then decided to talk to the janitor. He was baffled by her inquiry, then explained that all he ever did was to ask Matthew to give him five when he saw him in the morning. At first, Matthew accosted him with the usual autistic indifference. But the janitor persisted with that simple sentence every time he saw Matthew. One day, Matthew surprised the janitor by stealing a quick glance at him before walking past him. The janitor persisted. Weeks passed, then one day Matthew stopped for a moment, looked up at the janitor and blinked his eyes. The janitor was encouraged. Finally it happened. One day when the janitor approached Matthew, the boy slowly raised his hand and gently touched the man's fingers. A current seemed to have passed from hand to hand. From then on, Matthew always stopped and put his hand in the janitor's when the latter asked for it.

| **CWC: COACHING WITHOUT CENSORSHIP** |

I thought about how much we physicians learn from our patients. I wondered if there were a professor of psychiatry anywhere who could have explained the essence of coaching without censorship more eloquently than that janitor. Was there a psychologist around who could have touched Matthew the way that man with wash rags and dirty pails of water did?

I asked Matthew's mother how it was between Matthew and the janitor now. She told me the janitor had left the school. We spoke some more about the possibility of employing this strategy. Tentatively, I asked if she would discuss the matter with her husband, and if he was agreeable, to look for someone suitable for coaching without censorship. Would their mailman be open to such a suggestion? I wondered. Probably not. He would most likely dismiss such a suggestion as a prank. I finally made the suggestion that she look for some suitable person to resume where the janitor left off. She smiled back but said nothing.

Many psychiatrists and psychologists painstakingly classify children's learning disorders into rigid, neat categories of hyperactivity syndrome, attention deficit disorder (ADD), pseudo-ADD and autism. I see no clear distinctions between these overlapping clinical syndromes. As far I can see, such children are born with some genetic handicaps. Some malaligned genes render them vulnerable. Their nerve cell mismatches cause neuronal misfiring—vagaries of neurotransmitters that confound the disadvantaged brain cells. Equally important are nutritional, environmental and stress-related oxidative coals that fan the flames of malfunctioning genes. Unfortunately, most psychologists and psychiatrists are not trained to diagnose and manage those triggers; hence, their unyielding boundaries between hyperactivity and learning disabilities; between learning disabilities and ADD; between ADD and pseudo-ADD; and between all of the preceding and autism. As Choua puts it ungenerously, these specialists are gleefully unburdened by any knowledge of human biology, metabolism, nutrition and environment.

Then I wondered if that janitor ever realized the precious gift he gave Matthew —then, me. How could he? He was a mere janitor.

Who among the several professionals hired by Matthew's school would have the clarity of vision, or courage of conviction, to credit a janitor where the professional and all his peers had failed so miserably?

Maybe that was what Choua wanted to tell me about Fayemi's African children, but didn't. There must be autistic children among them —although perhaps not as many as we have in the United States. The neuronal mismatches that set some children up for autistic suffering are much more likely to become unmasked by devastating sugar-insulin-adrenaline overloads and incremental chemical triggers in American children. How do African tribesmen manage autism in their children? I wondered.

Perhaps Choua is right. Perhaps Fayemi's Africans are

blessed with that janitor's gift of communication. Perhaps their tribal elders have a sense of such things. Perhaps they can sense the anguish of little children incarcerated in their silos of silence—unable to engage in even the most primitive dialogue with other living beings. Perhaps in Africa everyone is like that janitor.

****

Multiple caregiving and fostering are two common distinctive African forms of nurturing. In multiple caregiving, a unique African tradition, the mother passes her baby around to other caregivers, usually close or distant relatives...This system of nurturing ensures that the infant interacts regularly with several different individuals.

Fayemi
Balancing Acts

Africans also have an innate sense of nature and human ecorelationships. Of course, they don't have to contend with man-made chemical avalanches. "Fayemi's Africans are in a better position to cope with ADD, hyperactivity and autism than either your clinical ecologists or psychiatrists," I could almost hear Choua proclaim.

AN INDIAN'S SILENCE

The next patient I saw after Matthew that day was a psychology professor. He had noticed Matthew and his dad in the waiting room while Matthew's mom spoke with me. After taking a chair in my office, the psychology professor spoke.

"That boy is autistic, isn't he?"

"Yes. Did he ask you to give him five?" I asked.

"No," the professor replied, a trifle confused, then laughed and continued, "but he knew what I was doing without once looking at me."

"What were you doing?"

"Observing him."

"Why?"

"To communicate with him."

"Did you succeed?"

"Yes."

"How do you know?" I pressed.

"I just *know*," he shrugged, then grinned and continued. "I guess I know the same way that one of my Native-American Indian friends knows. Sometimes, when I visit him at his reservation near Lake Ontario, I tell him things. He doesn't respond, and I wonder if he hears me. Days later I find out he not only heard me, he also understood what I wanted to say but couldn't find suitable words. Native-Americans communicate well in silence, though that's now a dying art. That autistic boy also communicated with me, without once directly looking at me."

Then I told him the story Matthew's mom had just told me.

"The young men and women in my psychology class are interested in spirituality, not psychology," he said. "I would love to teach them spirituality, but the curriculum committee at the college would be on my back."
"Why?" I asked.
"They're adamant about my sticking to classical psychology."
"What's that?" I prodded.
"You know *that*, don't you?" he laughed. "Our beloved obsessive-compulsive model."

We then moved on to discussing aspects of the EDTA chelation therapy that he was undergoing for cardiovascular problems. Choua sat silently throughout my visits with Matthew's mother and the psychology professor. After the professor left, he spoke,

"Do you know why the curriculum committee at his college strictly prohibits discussion of spirituality in his class?"
"How can anyone discuss spirituality in a psychology class?" I asked.
"That's not what I asked," he groused. "I asked you why do they prohibit it."
"I don't know. Why don't you tell me?" I said, hiding my irritation.
"Spirituality makes psychology irrelevant, that's why," Choua winked and walked out.

PERCEPTIONS OF A CHILD
WITH DOWN'S SYNDROME

Many years ago I worked as an emergency room physician at Irvington General Hospital in Irvington, New Jersey. As I now write about Matthew, the janitor and the psychology professor, I am reminded of the story of a child with Down's Syndrome whom I saw in the emergency department. The child was about eight or nine years old, and was brought to the hospital after falling and injuring his head in a playing field. It was an unusually hectic day. There were several victims of traffic accidents who required immediate care. All the stretchers in the emergency department were occupied. I decided to see the child while he sat on a stool by my desk.

Children with Down's Syndrome are friendly, loving and lovable. He grinned broadly as I examined his scalp wound and shone a light in his eyes to evaluate the state of his pupillary reflexes. Saliva drooled from one corner of his mouth to which he was mercifully oblivious. I decided to sew his wounds while he sat on the stool by my desk, then send him to the radiology department for skull X-rays. It was a deviation from the normal procedure. I did so in view of the limited space available and my sense that if I didn't do it then, the poor child may have to wait for some hours. That meant he had to stay on that stool until a nurse could lay a suture set on my desk.

I returned to completing the clinical charts of other trauma patients and felt his gaze on my face. I looked up and smiled. He was ecstatic. Then a strange thing happened. His eyes moved to one corner of the emergency room where a nurse frantically tried to pull muddy shoes off the feet of a traffic accident victim. The little boy watched her intently. At one point, the nurse turned to say something to me. The boy caught her eye and flashed a broad smile. The hassled nurse frowned, though, I'm sure, not at the boy. He froze for several moments, then slowly lowered his eyes—as if caught in a shameful act of invasion. I felt amused but decided not to say anything to the boy or to the nurse. Several minutes passed while I waited for my suture set and a nurse to assist me. Ever so slyly, the boy raised his head and looked at me. I had no doubt that his sad and silent eyes were asking me for permission to smile. I patted his cheeks with both hands. The boy sighed with relief. Minutes later, he began to explore the rest of the emergency room and his eyes drifted then to the opposite corner of the emergency room where another nurse was replacing sheets on a stretcher for another patient. As his eyes found hers, she sent him a warm, pleasant smile. The boy responded with visible enthusiasm, then he looked back for my approval. I touched his shoulder, again with both hands.

The boy had to stay in the emergency room for a few hours. There were delays at every step. There was considerable delay in the X-ray department. Then the lab took its time. During this time I observed something that I will forever treasure: the sensitivity and perception of a little boy with Down's syndrome. All during that time, every time the first nurse—the one who had inadvertently frowned when he first glanced at her—passed by him, he stiffened. And every time the second nurse—the one who had responded warmly and kindly to his exploring eye—passed by, he grinned and nodded.

Textbooks describe children with Down's syndrome as perceptually impaired. Some perceptual impairment!

THE TYRANNY OF TIGHT BIRTH CANALS

"Fayemi's Africans have no need for primal screams," Choua's words brought me back.

"Why not?" I asked.

"They have no festering wounds inflicted during birth by their mothers' spastic birth canals."

"You don't believe that, do you?"

"It's not a question of whether I believe it or not. It's those primal scream gurus who convince their patients that their psychiatric problems are rooted in birth traumas."

"How?"

"If you ask them, they'll tell you manic-depressive patients owe their anguish to maternity nurses who held the baby back during labor until the doctor could arrive to deliver the baby and bill the patient for his services."

"That's a new one for me," I laughed out loud. "It's all preposterous."

"The primal scream folks will tell you that the same thing happens when delivery is blocked by a uterine fibroid and a Caesarian section becomes necessary. What such births do is stamp in cyclic personalities. Later in life, when the going gets tough, the cyclical prototype kicks in, causing compulsive shopping sprees and irrepressible check-writing. A little more anguish and these cyclical impulses turn into obsessive-compulsive demons that wreak havoc on those persons. People despair and become obsessed with all kinds of morbid thoughts."

"So mothers alone are to be blamed for psychiatric disorders. Dads go scott-free. Is that it?" I asked, amused by the thought.

"Dads also contribute," he replied somberly.

"Do the primal scream specialists find such problems predominantly in women the way Freud did?"

"Oh no! They also describe case histories of hunky football players who lived in terror because they're afraid that deep down they might be homosexual."

"How do those players know that?"

"They get 'funny' feelings when they tackle other players."

"Wow! That's something." I couldn't hide my surprise. "Tell me, what did they find was wrong with those football players?"

"Some of them required constant treatment for a full year before their therapists convinced them that the root of their problems was the deprivation of their father's love."

"What proof do those primal scream specialists have that psychiatric disease is caused by cruel birth canals and nonloving dads?"

"Primal scream specialists are unburdened by any need for proof," Choua chirped. "They simply know what they know. They're Freud's disciples. And Freud never believed he required evidence to support his theories of mental illness either. Now, if you don't understand something that simple, that's your problem."

"Tell me, Choua, do Africans also suffer from the tyranny of constricted birth canals and loveless fathers?" I asked.

"Nope!" he replied curtly.

"Why not?"

"They do not suffer from such vaginal tyranny and

paternal deprivation because no African therapists have convinced them of it," he chuckled.

"So you don't believe in birth canal traumas?"

"Those traumas aren't afflicted by spastic uteri and constricted vaginas; they're caused by constricted thought canals, mostly in their therapists' minds," he replied scornfully.

"What did those poor therapists do to you to make you so angry?" I chided.

"Fayemi's Africans are not afflicted by any unremitting anguish for self-realization," he continued, ignoring my question.

"Why?"

"Because they do not need to be *realized*. They *are* real."

"How so?" I persisted.

"They are realized every moment by a heavenly heaven above them and a sacred earth below them. Luckily, they're spared the great insight of mind-over-body gurus," he said, brimming with sarcasm.

"What else do Fayemi's Africans not need?" I provoked.

"Fayemi's Africans do not yearn for actualization."

"Why is that?"

"*Actual* people do not need to be *actualized*," he grinned, then added. "They are actualized by every breath of life."

"And they are *individuals* so they don't need to be *individuated*, right?" I baited.

"Right! Right! You get the message now," Choua chirped.

"Okay, if Fayemi's Africans don't much care for European notions of psychological enlightenment, what do they think about spirituality?"

"They know what it *is* to be spiritual, but they don't much care whether they can define to your satisfaction what the spiritual might or might not be." A mysterious smile spread over Choua's face as he turned his face toward distant hills.

"How about divinity?" I pressed.

"Fayemi's Africans do not seek divinity either. They don't need to. Their elders have taught them that the Divine lives within them. They *are* divine. That's all there is to it."

"That's not much help, Choua," I complained. "At every step, you say they know it, yet they don't care to talk about what they know."

"It was the same way with ancient Chinese, wasn't it?" he continued cryptically.

"What was the same? Now I'm utterly lost," I replied, exasperated.

"Fayemi's Africans know something about the teachings of the Chinese sage, Lao-tzu, the master of the law of reversed perceptions," he grinned.

"What's the law of reversed perceptions?" I asked, more baffled.

"That true security is in knowing that there can be no security," he bared his teeth mischievously. "And that real certitude is in understanding that there can be no certainty. Insecurity is the child of desire to be secure, as uncertainty is that of hunger to be certain."

"Wow! Those Africans know all that," I teased. "I didn't know Lao-tzu ever taught in Africa. Did he?"

"Lao-tzu only saw what was there to be seen—and so do Fayemi's Africans," he replied and looked away.

"They know so much about insecurity and uncertainty, Choua. Tell me who do they think is spiritual?" I returned to my original question.

"They know who is a spiritual Hindu," he replied without looking at me.

"Who?" I asked, my curiosity piqued.

"Fayemi's Africans know what it is to be a spiritual Jew," he went on, ignoring my tone of surprise.

"Who is a spiritual Hindu? Who is a spiritual Jew? What are you rambling about?"

"A spiritual Hindu is one who can help a wayward Muslim return to the truth of Islam."

"What was that?" I asked, suddenly hit by his idea. "Say that again, Choua."

"Who is a spiritual Jew?" he continued, ignoring my question. "A spiritual Jew is one who can help a Christian disillusioned with Christianity to rediscover the truth of Christianity."

Choua gazed at me in silence as I tried to decipher the meanings of his glib words. Then he laughed, winked and walked out. What would a primal screamer say to that? I wondered. How would he relate to the silence of the Native-American? Or to Choua's notions of spirituality? How would Alfred Adler, the Austrian psychiatrist who founded the school of "individual psychology", have laughed at Choua's simplistic notions? How would Carl Gustav Jung, the master of the art of individuation, have told Choua off? Freud was the great guru of things penile and vaginal. How would he have scoffed at Choua's simplemindedness?

HOW COULD I BE ALL STUPID IF GOD IS WITHIN ME?

The day after I spoke to Matthew's mother, I had a follow-up visit from a woman in her seventies. The woman had initially consulted me for swelling in her legs, varicose veins, arthritis and concentration difficulties. She brought her copy of

RDA: Rats, Drugs and Assumptions and asked me to autograph
it. I complied with her request and thanked her for asking me
to do so. Curious about how she'd gotten through the book with
her considerable concentration difficulties, I asked her how
much she'd actually read.

"Up to the bookmark," she beamed, showing me the
bookmark at about the middle of the book. Then, turning
suddenly sullen, she added, "But I don't understand it."

"You will when your concentration improves," I tried to
reassure her.

"It's not that. I don't understand because I'm stupid," she
spoke, a hurt expression spreading over her face.

"That's not true," I countered.

"Oh yes, it is!" she tried to smile. "That's what everyone
tells me. I know I'm stupid."

"There is a part that is stupid in each of us," I persisted.
"But, there is also a part that is wise in each of us. I do things
that are stupid, then I regret that I did them."

"Don't say that, Dr. Ali, you write all those books and
you help all those sick people," she countered eagerly, then her
voice fell, "I've been told I'm stupid."

"So have I," I tried to humor her. "There's a part in each
of us that is demonic. Then there's a part that is divine."

She stared at me with blank eyes, as if trying to figure
out whether I was being cruel or compassionate. I returned her
stare in silence. She regarded me for several long moments. I
wondered what conclusion she would finally arrive at: Did I
mean what I said, or did I make fun of what she was convinced
was a sluggish mind? Finally, she broke into a broad grin, shook
her head approvingly and spoke.

"Dr. Ali, I'm a Christian. I know God lives within me. You have to be right. How could I be all stupid if God is within me?"

There are no stupid people in Fayemi's Africa. Nor do I remember any in Kirto, my ancestral village in Pakistan. Yes, there are people who see, hear, smell or imagine things differently in Kirto and in Africa. Kirto folks, as well as tribal Africans, have ancient traditions of regarding such people differently, but they know they are not stupid. They know being different is not being stupid. I once knew someone like that elderly woman in Kirto. He roamed the village alleys, sometimes talking to himself, sometimes to goats and sheep. We knew he was different but not stupid. Sometimes he said things that seemed incongruous, yet they hung in the air for hours afterwards. What he uttered seemed to hang forever after he uttered them. Days and weeks—and sometimes months—later we understood what he meant. What did he see when he spoke those words? We wondered. What did he hear? Or smell? We realized God bestows gifts on people in ways that aren't always clear to us.

After finishing my visit with the woman with concentration difficulties, I saw her older sister who suffered from crippling arthritis. She told me about her dreams that predicted events that later came to pass in stunning detail. Whose voice did she hear? Who told her about the shape of things to come?

Who knows who is stupid? I wondered.

One day, several weeks after our return from Kenya, I remembered my conversation with Choua about the three

Africas. His first Africa was the Africa of heavenly heaven, and the second the Africa that bleeds. But what was his third Africa? I tried hard to recall but drew a blank. When I ran into Choua next, I asked him about it.

"The third Africa, eh?" he chuckled.

"Yes, the third Africa. I remember the first two Africas, but I can't remember the third."

"You missed the whole thing, did you?" he searched my eyes.

"What thing?" I was baffled.

"Didn't you tell me you read *Balancing Acts* cover to cover?" he asked impishly.

"Yes. But so..."

"So that's your answer," he replied cryptically.

"What?" my confusion grew. Then, tentatively, I asked, "Is the third Africa Fayemi's Africa?"

Choua smiled but said nothing.

****

I've had the great honor to be associated with Professor Alfred Olusegun Fayemi for over 20 years. We practiced pathology and did research at Holy Name Hospital, Teaneck, New Jersey from 1974 to 1982, and together published over 75 scientific papers. We also wrote eleven books for pathologists preparing for speciality board examination. At present, he is Chief of Pathology at St. Mary's Hospital, Hoboken, New Jersey, and a senior consulting physician at the Institute of Preventive Medicine, Denville, New Jersey.

Chapter 13

Saying No to Chemotherapy

Treatment decisions facing patients with cancer were once simple and easy to make.

Surgery, radiation and chemotherapy were considered *scientifically proven,* effective therapies. The physician's word was gospel, and there was no room for doubt. Decisions about cancer therapies were easy precisely because there was no choice—and no stress.

However, there was no choice in cancer treatment because patients were uninformed. In the past, patients often went for a second opinion about chemotherapy. That second opinion was, of course, never different from the first one. This confirmation was reassuring to the patient and made his decision easier to accept. The consulting doctor who rendered the second opinion always agreed with the referring physician. (As conventional wisdom goes, you don't bite the hand that feeds you. Giving a different second opinion would jeopardize chances of receiving future consults.)

Consensus medicine is comfortable for physicians, and it also brings comfort to the patient.

A second opinion in mainstream medicine is **one** *opinion for which the patient pays twice.*

> The Cortical Monkey and Healing

Now all that is changing rapidly. Many cancer patients are

well-informed. They read about alternative therapies that are being used in foreign countries and in the United States. They are aware that there is a mushrooming *underground* of unapproved therapies. Physicians vigorously caution their patients against the dangers of unapproved therapies, but patients are increasingly rejecting that party line. Almost everyone knows of patients who were told surgery had removed the whole tumor or chemotherapy had burned down all of the cancer, yet the cancer returned and killed the patient. They also know of patient who clearly died of "approved" chemotherapy drugs rather than of their cancer. Many people also know of people who opted for "unapproved" nondrug cancer therapies, and who lived without cancer for decades.

Few things are as stressful as the decision to choose the right operation and whether or not to accept chemotherapy. Cancer drugs are invariably very toxic and seriously damage the immune system. Most people know someone who had chemotherapy and have seen the havoc it wreaks.

Although many oncologists believe the toxic effects of chemotherapy are reversible, I have yet to hear a patient say he was the same person before taking chemotherapy as he became after it. This phenomenon is common knowledge among well-informed people. And yet, oncologists continually tell patients are continually that by not taking chemotherapy they are destined for certain death, as if certain death is something patients taking chemotherapy can escape.

GRANDPA GUIDES FROM HIS GRAVE

Patty, a woman in her early forties, came to my office one day. She looked anxious and distraught to a degree I had never seen before. When I had cared for her two little boys for multiple food and mold allergies, she always looked serene. I knew something extraordinary had happened. When I asked what the problem was, she smiled bravely and said,

"I have a difficult problem this time. It is breast cancer, and I'm facing some difficult decisions. I have two little boys whom you know. I have a loving husband. I have to survive this cancer."

Patty had her breast cancer diagnosed by a biopsy. She asked me whether she should follow the biopsy with a lumpectomy and node sampling or mastectomy. I told her both were reasonable options, and asked what her personal preference might be. She said she would rather choose a mastectomy. I supported her decision, and advised her to take an intravenous nutrient infusion before and after the surgery to promote healing and minimize the possibility of infection. I further asked her to return for a consultation and management plan after surgery.

Three weeks later, Patty returned for advice. Fortunately, her axillary nodes were found to be free of cancer. Predictably she had been advised to undergo chemotherapy by an oncologist. She told me she was very troubled by the prospect of serious immune injury caused by chemotherapy drugs and asked whether that was the right course of action for her. I told her she was not facing an immediate decision and that she could think about it. Furthermore, I advised her to seek a second opinion from another oncologist. She said she already had done so, and the second oncologist concurred with the first. She now wanted an opinion on non-chemotherapy options.

Patty was uncomfortable with some of the answers she had received from her oncologists. Specifically, she had asked about the possibility of chemotherapy causing a second cancer and had been told that such a risk didn't exist. She had considerable difficulty accepting that statement. She asked me if I agreed with the statement. I told her that such a risk was very difficult to assess because there are simply too many variables. I thought about a recent report in the *New England Journal of Medicine* that reported somewhat higher risks of cancer developing in the opposite breast of women taking chemotherapy than in the control group who did not. Then my mind wandered to a conversation Choua and I had about the report some days earlier.

A SACRED DECEPTION

One day I reviewed the slides of biopsies and surgical cases for the monthly breast-cancer conference at the hospital. My administrative assistant told me she would distribute copies of a current article on the value of chemotherapy in treating breast cancer. She also said the article had appeared in the April 6, 1995, issue of the *New England Journal of Medicine* and had been widely reported in newspapers, radio and TV. She then suggested that I might want to glance at the article before the meeting. I gave the article a cursory look and showed it to Choua.

"Interesting!" Choua spoke as we walked backed to my office after the conference.

"What's interesting?" I asked.

"The folks at the National Institutes of Health traveled all the way to Italy to prove that chemotherapy effectively treats breast cancer."

"Why?"

"I suppose because it's easier for oncologists to sell the program to Italian women than to American women."

"That's ludicrous," I rebuked him.

"Then why pay Italian doctors American dollars to test chemotherapy drugs?" he pouted.

"I'm sure they didn't give Italian doctors American money to do that research study. Doctors don't get money when they conduct research studies."

"They don't?" he frowned.

"You've a warped mind," I scolded him. "What difference does it make whether the study was conducted in Italy or in Kenya?"

"I guess you're right," Choua smiled impishly. "It makes no difference what country the study was done in as long as the folks at the National Institutes of Health have the ability to draw wrong conclusions."

"Oh shush, Choua. You are annoying," I said, irritated. Then I asked, "What did the study say anyway?"

"The report declared emphatically that chemotherapy works in treating breast cancer," he replied.

"That's not unexpected. So?"

"After pronouncing chemotherapy effective on the front page, the report later gives detailed statistics."

"Which support the front page conclusions, right?" I asked.

"Wrong," Choua chirped.

"Wrong? How can that be? Didn't you just say the front page concluded that chemotherapy works?"

"Yes, it did," he winked.

"So, what's the catch?" I asked, perplexed.

"That's the fascinating part. The report showed that 20 years after giving chemotherapy for node-positive breast cancer, eleven percent of women given chemotherapy were alive without disease, while ten percent of those in the control group who were spared toxic drugs did as well."

"Are you saying chemotherapy improved the disease-free survival only by one percent?" I challenged him. "I don't believe those numbers. Are you sure you are citing the data correctly?"

"Take a look yourself," Choua thrust the article at my face.

"I can't right now. I have to sign out some biopsies," I replied, pushing the article away from my face. "Why don't you tell me more about it?"

"That one percent advantage in the chemotherapy group was outnumbered by new cancers that appeared in the opposite breast of those in the chemotherapy group," he smirked.

"That's understandable. What are the data?"

"2.2% women in the control group developed a second cancer while 3.4% did so in the chemotherapy group. That's a difference of 1.2%—a trifle more than the 1% difference between the disease-free survival rates in the two groups. Now, if they would publish their data again in ten years, they will surely find..."

"That overall disease-free survival would be actually higher in the control group," I completed his sentence.

"Yeah," he jeered.

"What else does the article say?" 1 asked.

"Actually, it isn't what they say, but what they omit, that's interesting," he winked again.

"What's that?" I asked, puzzled.

"They diligently hid the data pertaining to cancers found in other body organs in the women of the two groups. Surely, chemotherapy would have caused cancers in other body organs as well."

"Oncologists insist that doesn't happen," I provoked him.

"Of course!" he thumped the table contemptuously, causing vibrations in the video screen attached to my microscope.

"Calm down, Choua," I admonished him. "I am trying to look at slides, and you are shaking my microscope."

"I'm sorry," he relented. "How can those oncologists say, with straight faces, that chemotherapy does not cause more cancers in other body organs when they know it does so in the breast?"

"That's a surprise. Why wouldn't they report additional cancers in other body organs?"

"Is that really a surprise?" he pouted. "Either they didn't bother to keep a tally of other cancers, or they deliberately withheld the data. Now that shouldn't surprise you, should it?"

"You see things with your cyclopean eyes," I teased. "What else?"

"They deftly avoided the subject of the toxic effects of chemotherapy on various body organs as well. Clever rascals, those researchers."

"That's not being true to research."

"Truth in research, eh!" Choua mocked.

"Don't you think researchers are obligated to include adverse data when they report favorable data?"

"Are you really that naive?" he scowled. "Since when have men of money in medicine worried about truth in reporting? You should know better. You wrote the *Rats* book."

"Okay! Okay!" I yielded. "But didn't you tell me that the efficacy of chemotherapy in that report was widely reported in the media? How did that happen?"

"Miracles of medical statistics, my friend," he scoffed.

"How did they do that?"

"Simple," he laughed. "They reported data for the earlier years of the study that favored the chemotherapy group."

"So, chemotherapy was beneficial. The *Journal* was right after all."

"Right, but with an incomplete story."

"What is the complete story?"

"They prudently kept quiet about the higher risk of additional cancers, and didn't raise ugly questions about why chemotherapy was not a poison for the group of Italian women when it's a poison for everyone else. That's a sacred deception, isn't it?"

Choua walked over to the window before I could respond. He looked out and was soon lost in deep thought. I knew nothing volatile would be forthcoming for a while and returned to my slides.

****

When my wandering mind returned, Patty, my patient with breast cancer was staring at me.

"You were thinking about something, weren't you?" she asked.

"No. Yes." I was flustered that she caught me in my reverie.

"About what?"

"About the benefits of chemotherapy."

"About the difference between the touted and actual benefits of chemotherapy. Wasn't that it?" she smiled disarmingly.

"Yes," I admitted.

"Tell me, would you take chemotherapy if you were in my position?"

"I don't know," I smiled back. "I don't know how I would face such a decision. It isn't easy."

"So, you would?" she asked, her eyes intensely fixed on mine.

"I didn't say that," I hastened to add. "In fact, I probably wouldn't. But such decisions are never easy. I don't know what I would do if I had to advise my wife about it. The long-term results of chemotherapy are dismally poor. Some studies do show some short-term benefits, but what makes the decision more difficult is that chemotherapy results are compared to control subjects who do not receive nondrug therapies."

"But you would put yourself on a comprehensive non-chemotherapy protocol, wouldn't you?"

"I definitely would."

"Why?"

"For obvious reasons—herbs for their known anticancer effects, nutrients for their immune enhancement, slow and sustained exercise for fitness, and meditation and spiritual work for escaping the cruelty of cancer statistics."

"And, knowing what you know about the ways chemotherapy destroys the immune system, would you still take chemotherapy?" she pressed.

"I probably wouldn't."

"I really don't think you would take chemotherapy for my kind of breast cancer," Patty smiled knowingly.

"Probably not," I repeated.

"So, what next?"

"Has anyone died in recent years that you loved deeply?" I asked.

"Yes, my grandfather," she beamed. "I was very close to Grandpa. I guess I still am."

"Good!" I replied. "Here is what I suggest. Visit his grave three times during the next several days. Maybe there you will find an answer you are comfortable with."

"How do you know that?" she asked, bewildered.

"I don't know that. I just think it might work," I replied.

"Well, I've already done that once."

"Do that some more," I advised.

"I think I know what Grandpa will tell me," she smiled and left.

I took up the chart of the next patient, looked at the progress sheet to read the notes I made during the preceding visit. Within moments, the staff ushered in my next patient. The office hours ran late that evening, as they usually do. It was past eleven p.m. when I prepared to leave the office.

"Why didn't you tell her about the full risk of chemotherapy?" Choua asked curtly, standing at the office door.

"Because it is not clear to me how to balance that risk against the risk of saying no to chemotherapy. That's why," I replied.

"Not clear to *you* or not known?" he scowled.

"Okay, not known to *me*," I replied with irritation.

"Have you never seen a case of a cancer caused by chemotherapy?" he persisted.

"How does anyone know whether a second cancer was caused by chemotherapy or just developed coincidentally?" I asked, feeling a bit angry.

"There are statistics on that," Choua was unrelenting.

"Statistics!" I mocked. "Since when are you impressed by medical statistics? Aren't you always knocking medical data?"

"What about that Kaposi sarcoma that you diagnosed in a patient receiving chemotherapy for malignant lymphoma?"

"What about that?"

"Multiple nodules of Kaposi sarcoma developed within months of starting chemotherapy for lymphoma, but then the tumor nodules spontaneously regressed months after chemotherapy was discontinued."

"I remember that." I recalled the case clearly. "But you can't cite such anecdotal case reports when someone asks your opinion about the treatment of his cancer, can you?"

"Do you what know an oncologist said at the tumor board meeting?"

"What was that?"

"He said I know chemotherapy doesn't work for anaplastic cancer of the lung, but I still believe in it for its possible anecdotal value."

"Anecdotal value?" I looked askance. "Hard to believe an oncologist would say something like that."

"Especially because that's exactly the argument they use to dismiss the holistic physicians' reports of positive results with nondrug therapies," Choua chimed.

"Still, that sort of information is not adequate in discouraging anyone from taking chemotherapy," I explained my position.

"You will change your position," Choua stated emphatically.

"I wish I had a better handle on the benefits of anticancer herbal therapies, organic coffee enemas, bio-oxidative therapies, charge neutralization techniques, light therapies and other therapies. I wish some group of knowledgeable, diligent physicians would undertake a careful study of integrated nonchemotherapy therapies to come up with a clear sense of what can be achieved in this area. Wouldn't that be wonderful?"

"Yes, it would be wonderful," Choua agreed, gazed at me intently for a long while, then asked, "Why don't you?"

Before I could say anything, he stomped out of my office.

****

It has been over a year since Patty saw me for advice about chemotherapy. She seems remarkably at peace with her decision to say no to chemotherapy. She has traveled and attended some workshops about nonchemotherapy options for cancer. She is taking the anticancer herbs, nutrients and coffee enemas that we prescribed. The last time I performed a microscopic oxidative stress test (MOST Test), her blood cells and plasma proteins showed minimal evidence of oxidative injury (as is shown by other people in good health without cancer). All her other blood tests are also negative.

The day she came to tell me of her decision to turn down chemotherapy, I was impressed by the serenity on her face. It wasn't that she didn't understand the gravity of her decision. Rather, her serenity existed because she arrived at her decision from a higher visceral-intuitive level—in the presence of her grandfather. The old man helped his granddaughter from his grave.

her grandfather. The old man helped his granddaughter from his grave.

****

Life is not a "brief candle." It is a splendid torch that I want to make burn as brightly as possible before handing it on to future generations.

George Bernard Shaw

Chapter 14

Is There Another Door?

We Americans are a technically oriented people. We assume that we can resolve any problem as long as we can muster the right technique. Such thinking serves us well in surgery, trauma and the management of acute medical conditions. But when it comes to stress, anxiety, sleep disorders, disease prevention and other chronic disorders, such an approach brings poor results.

Yoga is currently experiencing a resurgence in the United States. And for good reason: Its value in self-regulation, disease prevention and reversal of many chronic health disorders is well-established. The central purpose in all yogic practices is the search for spirituality. The ancients were very clear about this purpose. The word yoga means linkage with God. (One meaning of the Holy Language word Mitzvah is also linkage). Yet today we seem to think that yoga simply involves contortions of the human frame and that success can be achieved only when one looks like a pretzel. I commonly see the same mind-set applied to self-regulation among my patients.

Sometime ago, a schoolteacher consulted me for chronic sinusitis, headache, fatigue and depression. Initially, he learned autoregulation well and regularly followed my nutrient prescriptions and allergy treatment. Consequently, his fatigue and depression lifted, and he obtained much relief from headaches. After the first two follow-up visits, however, I didn't see him for several months. Then he returned and told me of his recurring symptoms. I found out—as I had expected—that he discontinued the practice of autoregulation and took his nutrient protocols irregularly.

Such cases don't surprise me. Many patients go through cycles of compliance with our management plans, experiencing symptom relief followed by noncompliance and symptom relapse until our preventive measures become a part of their daily routine. So, I advised him to begin my therapies again and to practice autoregulation consistently. After obtaining positive clinical results a second time, he disappeared yet again.

One day the schoolteacher returned, looking more tired, distraught and depressed than ever before. He told me that nutrient therapies were insufficient in reducing his stress, which had mounted at school and at home. I listened patiently to his complaints and prepared to emphasize the need for consistent autoregulation. But before I could say anything, he smiled laconically and, touching his forehead with his index finger, said, "Dr. Ali, it gets stuck here. Is there another door?"

A DOOR FOR LETTING ONE OUT

What gets stuck where? I recognized that *what* for him is the limbic openness and *where* is the skin of his forehead—or, perhaps the frontal bone of his skull. *Is there another door?* I wondered.

The cortical monkey doesn't let up. It forever recycles past misery, and when that isn't enough, it engages in its other favorite activity: pre-cycling feared, future misery. These unrelenting demands of the thinking mind continually beat up on tired tissues. And the monkey throws hurdles in the path to limbic openness in ingenious ways. I realized that my schoolteacher envisioned his forehead as the door through which he could enter a limbic state. Yet the skin represented a closed door to him. How ironic! The limbic state is about openness—about an escape from the dark cortical tunnels of the thinking mind. The limbic state is a spiritual dimension. He seemed to think spirituality resides in the skull.

It fascinates me how we think of mechanical barriers even when we talk about spirituality. Is it because being centered is hammered into us all our lives? We are taught that being well-centered is being wholesome. Enlightened psychologists tell us to look inward for our core being. Even the New Age gurus preach to their faithful about looking inward for the *center*. Is our core really in our skull? Is the center situated in the pineal body, as melatonin enthusiasts seem to believe? Or, does our center reside in some other sacred part of our body?

Is it possible that humans have no center other than that of the *larger presence* that surrounds each of us? Perhaps that *presence* has no center either? *Is it simply a vast openness*, devoid of all human notions of "centeredness?"

I define limbic openness as freedom from the limits of the physical body as well as the confines of the thinking mind. *Limbic openness is as much outside us as it is within us.* It isn't something that we let into our body—through the skin of the forehead or any other part of the body. It is a continuum that permeates and surrounds us. The limbic state is not about being centered—as we often envision. Rather, it is about being "uncentered."

Where does our preoccupation with "centeredness" come from anyway? Is centeredness a legacy of a primitive epoch when a man's cave might have appeared to him as the center of his universe? Is it a notion of a period when men might have guarded the turf of their tribes as the center of the land—as lions do the territories of their prides today? Or, is it our heritage from the Ptolemaic period when Egyptian pharaohs proclaimed they were the emperors of Earth—which was the center of the cosmos—and that the sun circled around it. Copernicus laid that idea to rest long ago. But we seem to cling to notions of centeredness forever.

There is indeed another door, I wanted to tell the school teacher. But the door isn't for letting things enter the center of our being—it is for letting us out to the limbic openness that has no center.

BUILDING ON SOMETHING "DIFFERENT"

Jack, a West Coast chemical engineer, was once a "universal reactor." He told me he had become sensitive to almost all foods, pollens, molds and chemicals. Stresses of such sensitivities led to the development of incapacitating Sjogren's syndrome—an autoimmune disorder in which the eyes and mouth become painfully dry because the natural secretion glands in these organs have been destroyed. At one point, Jack had to stop working. For several months he lived like a hermit in the mountains of the western United States.

Through patience and perseverance, Jack saved his life. Reading about the nature of his illness and taking many natural restorative therapies, he became adept at rotating and diversifying his foods and at avoiding exposure to chemicals.

Jack called me to ask if autoregulation might alleviate some of his residual symptoms. I said it probably would, and a few weeks later he flew to the East Coast for training in autoregulation. After some introductory comments, I wired Jack to the electrophysiologic equipment I use and began to explain the basic principles and practice of self-regulation. After listening to me intently, he said,

> *"All my life I have lived in what you call the cortical mode. I know my mind is always cluttered, but I just can't shut it off. I know my disease cannot be treated with drugs. I react to all of them. I am very careful in choosing my foods. I'm meticulous in avoiding chemicals. I have saved my life with these precautions. But I know I am not a well person. In all my readings and travels, it never occurred to me that the answer to my disease could be in my own breathing and my own pulses."*

Jack was evidently fascinated with the autoregulation approach. As we proceeded with actual training, however, he was unable to bring the pulses to his fingertips or to any other part of his body. The video screen showed no appreciable changes in his profiles of the heart, arteries, skin and muscle energy patterns. After several attempts, I asked,

"Did you feel anything?"
"Oh yes!" he replied.
"What?" I asked, encouraged.
"I don't know."
"Something different?" I pressed.

"Yes!" he smiled, "But I don't know what it might be."

"Pleasant or unpleasant?" I asked.

"It wasn't unpleasant. I suppose it might have been pleasant," he answered tentatively.

"Well, then we will stay with this something different and pleasant," I replied.

It is important for the beginner to build on whatever works for him. If it is only something "different and pleasant," it must be accepted as such. This something "different and pleasant"—or different and unpleasant—holds the key to success in autoregulation. It is the first element of self-discovery in the exploration of one's biology and the awareness of one's tissue energy. Success in the more advanced and effective methods, such as directed pulses, limbic breathing, body scanning and tissue energy sensing, usually follows without significant difficulty.

SOMETIMES ARTERIES TAKE THEIR TIME

In chronically ill patients arteries sometimes take a while to respond to autoregulation. One needs to be patient at these times, as there isn't much anyone can do to force arteries to respond quickly.

One patient with extreme cold sensitivity showed a starting fingertip skin temperature of 79 degrees. Her temperature failed to show any response during autoregulation training. After about fifteen minutes, I decided to move to the next patient. As I removed the electrodes from her skin, I explained that her profile on the video screen demonstrated an absence of response, and I tried to reassure her. But she was so disillusioned by the failure of her arteries to respond that I reattached the electrode sensors to her skin, and we began autoregulation again. This time her tissues responded as if floodgates had opened. Her skin temperature shot up in a matter of minutes. Evidently, the stress of being on the machine further tightened her arteries during the first attempt. But this time her temperature rose from 79 to 91 degrees right before our eyes. The flush of heat to her hands brought tears of joy to her eyes.

Why didn't her arteries open during the first session? Why did they do so the second time around? The patient was *trying* to make things happen. She was using some mind-over-body technique. Why did her arteries finally open and flood the starved tissues of her hand with blood? Most likely, she was uncertain about what I would do next. When her thinking mind let up for a few moments, the muscles in her arteries also let up, letting blood rush to her skin and raising her skin temperature.

I learned an important lesson: One must be prepared for delays in tissue energy response. Notwithstanding the prevailing notion of mind-over-body healing, tissues are not subservient to the dictates of the thinking mind. Injured tissues do not seem to care much for the mind's exhortations. Tightened arteries do not open to accommodate the demands of the thinking mind so that a headache is relieved. Tightened bronchial tubes do not heed the pleas of the thinking mind as it tries to bring the asthma attack under control. A rebellious bowel in spasm is equally immune to appeals for mercy by the thinking mind. Extensive clinical experience has convinced me this is so.

Indeed, it is when we escape from the cortical clutter that

energy responses begin to take form. Such observations continue to reinforce my view that the common notion of mind-over-body healing is a fallacy.

HANDS THAT DISSOLVE

At the end of autoregulation classes, I usually ask my patients to describe any perceptions of energy they might have felt during the training period. Most people describe their perceptions as heaviness, warmth, a sense of magnetism, tingling, throbbing or pulsating. Some patients slide deep into a limbic mode and, when asked to reconstruct events in that state, use interesting expressions. During the last several years, many people have described it, saying:

"My hands were floating."

****

"For a while, I couldn't feel my hands."

"I had a sense that my hands were not attached to me anymore."

****

"Thin air! That's what I thought my hands were."

****

"I had a very strange experience," a man said one day.
"Pleasant or unpleasant?" I asked.
"Pleasant, but strange." He smiled.
"What did you feel?" I asked.
"My hands dissolved—they literally dissolved."

EYES THAT WILL NOT PULSATE

Eyes often bear the brunt of the trickery of the cortical monkey. Such was the case for a 43-year-old woman who consulted me for severe anxiety, daily headaches and depression.

She was unable to hold her management position at her company. A particularly distressing symptom, she told me, was a continuing difficulty with her eyes. She described the problem as a persistent stress that often progressed to unrelenting tightness and searing pain. Initially, I expected the problem might be rather easy to correct with pulses directed to the eyelids. Until then, most of my patients had not experienced significant difficulty in directing pulses from their hands to their eyelids. Indeed, pulses in eyelids had been a major breakthrough when I addressed the problem of my own eyelid chalazia with autoregulation.

The woman showed considerable visceral resistance to autoregulation. This resistance did not exist because the concept of self-regulation was foreign to her. Rather, the severe anxiety and depression made it difficult for her to feel energy in her tissues. After much effort, she learned several autoregulation methods, such as pulses and limbic breathing. Every time she had an office visit with me, she spoke about her unrelenting eye symptoms. And every time, I emphasized the need for autoregulation with a special emphasis directed to pulses in the eyelids. She would listen to me patiently, then shake her head and say, "If only you knew how hard I try."

Some years later, the woman became an expert at limbic breathing and other methods of tissue sensing that I taught her. She could usually control her headaches and pull herself out of depression. She returned to work, running a large office and managing personnel problems. Yet, no matter how hard we tried to direct pulses to her eyelids, we failed. Exasperated after prolonged unsuccessful attempts, one day she sadly remarked, "I don't think my eyes will ever pulsate. I think this agony will exist forever."

Perhaps someday she and I will unravel the mystery behind that inability.

PULSES: ANY TIME, ANYWHERE, UNDER ANY CIRCUMSTANCES

Initially, during autoregulation training, I focus on methods of pulses, limbic breathing and tissue energy sensing. My basic purpose in training is to teach patients how to do autoregulation any time, anywhere and under any circumstances. Only when sick people reach that stage can autoregulation become a viable alternative to drugs (along with optimal nutritional and environmental therapies).

Meditation can help maintain good health. In my experience, however, such meditation, in and of itself, is insufficient for the reversal of chronic disease. Any method of self-regulation done for 10 to 15 minutes a day is not enough.

As I mentioned earlier in this chapter, some people seem to slide naturally and effortlessly into these methods. Others require considerable practice. Those in the throes of long-term chronic and indolent disease may find it very difficult, indeed impossible at times, to learn these methods. Persistence is the only way for such individuals. And persistence, I might add, is hardest for those debilitated by prolonged suffering.

A person needs to learn the basic autoregulation steps before learning to experience directed pulses. Guidance from an experienced professional is often necessary for most people and, for the chronically ill, it is essential.

Below are some simple, practical approaches a person can practice to become skillful at autoregulation. In time, this activity becomes a part of one's day, without constant reminders from anyone else and without the frustration that many patients suffer in self-regulatory work.

PULSES IN THE KITCHEN

During my early work with pulses, I often thought of ways to help many of my female patients who were experiencing highly stressful periods. One day while I was washing dishes in the kitchen, the warm sink water brought pulses to my hands even though I wasn't thinking about it. It then occurred to me that this might be a good time to direct pulses to my legs. My legs complied rather easily.

I find warm water on my hands while washing dishes very comforting. Perhaps this is so because I don't clean dishes often. I know that most women who wash dishes daily find this chore uninviting, and it frequently leads to family arguments. Here is my suggestion to women—and men—who regularly wash dishes: Be aware of your legs and feet when the warm sink water warms your hands. With time, awareness of the tissues in your feet and legs will bring perceptions of energy to those tissues. It's far easier to feel the energy of leg tissues when your hands are in warm water than when they are cold. If necessary, repeat this phrase several times, "My feet are heavy and warm. My legs are heavy and warm."

If you practice this exercise for any period of time, the likelihood is that you can turn an unwelcome chore into a period of profound visceral-intuitive calm and energetic renewal. And, perhaps in time it will help you discover that spiritual language of silence which transcends all need for expression. Perhaps one day you will discover the limitless limbic openness in which no beings can be alone, isolated or without linkage to the larger *presence* that surrounds each of us.

ENERGY AWARENESS IN THE LIVING ROOM

A person can take the same approach while relaxing in his living room. While listening to radio or watching TV—radio is a far better choice than TV—one can become aware of one's hands, fingers, feet or legs. Again, if necessary, repeat several times, "My hands are heavy and warm. My feet are heavy and warm. My legs are heavy and warm." These autogenic suggestions become unnecessary with practice, as tissues then begin to respond on short notice.

Who knows when the gentle guiding energy of the leg tissues might overtake a person? Who knows where it might lead?

ENERGY OF TRIVIA

Another simple approach to learning autoregulation is to become aware of trivial items in one's field of vision. For example, trivial items might include a dried leaf seen through a window, a bird on a ledge, a wild flower in the yard, a patch of melting snow, a clay item on a fireplace (that one purchased many years ago but never bothered to look at), or even a crumpled piece of paper that a child might have carelessly thrown on the floor before running off to school.

In essence, this is giving the cortical monkey a taste of his own medicine. Although the cortical monkey loves to recycle past misery or pre-cycle feared, future misery, this monkey has no capacity for looking at a patch of snow, a bird on the ledge or a clay item on the fireplace. Once the monkey's unrelenting clutter is swept away by the presence of trivia, spontaneous energy responses follow.

Trivia, in such circumstances, become objects of enlightenment. Sometimes I see people travel long distances in search of enlightenment. Little do we recognize that the presence of a clay item on a fireplace can lead one to as powerful a spiritual experience as a Himalayan vista.

SCANNING THE BODY

Sensing tissue energy is an essential element in all types of self-regulation with energy. Autoregulation is no exception. Just as a person can sense warmth in the hands or pulses in the fingertips with simple self-suggestive sentences, it is possible to sense the energy of other tissues with a similar approach. Sensing is then followed by "staying with the energy" in the tissues or body organ.

Talat uses the expression "scan the body, then respond to what needs responding." It is a succinct description of a method that she has used extensively for herself and for many of my patients that she attends to. She recommends the following simple steps:

1. Scan the whole body for uneasiness, discomfort or pain—slowly moving from hands, arms, shoulders, neck, head, face, torso and legs.

2. Isolate tissues under duress. Keep your awareness fixed on those tissues.

3. Sense the energy or absence of it in the tissues that are the focus of your awareness.

4. Breathe into—or into and through—the tissues under duress. A simple method for this is to repeat any of the following sentences several times until one begins to sense an energy response in that particular tissue:

    4.1 I breathe in and my right hand swells with energy.
    4.2 I breathe in and feel both my hands swell with energy.
    4.3 I breathe in and feel my eyes swell with energy.
    4.4 I breathe in and my right thigh swells with energy.
    4.5 I breathe in and feel my back muscles swell with energy.
    4.6 I breathe in and feel my abdomen swell with energy.

I suggest the reader learn the basic autoregulation method I describe earlier in the chapter, Directed Pulses, before trying any of the above simple suggestions.

Some readers may raise an obvious question here: Aren't these examples of mind-over-body healing? On a superficial level, they are. But as I discuss in many parts of this volume, these practices are, in reality, examples of giving the cortical monkey a taste of his own medicine. By breathing into or through a tissue under duress, what we really achieve is stillness in the mind. We exclude the mind from our state. Or, to be more precise, we use breathing methods to break the chains of the cortical clutter. Once we perceive the tissue energy, we are guided by the gentle limbic healing energy.

THE LIMBIC HEALING POWER OF WATER

Water fascinates people—perhaps because life began in water, and living beings that preceded us crawled out of water to inhabit land.

Water has enormous limbic healing power. I don't think it is purely serendipitous that most of the great shrines were built close to water. Historians often hold that great cities grew by large bodies of water because of their obvious value in transportation. But it seems likely that the nuclei of the world's great cities took form by the water first to fulfill a human spiritual need, then mushroomed into great commercial centers.

Man has had a lasting romance with bodies of water,

whether it be the fountain Zum Zum of prophet Ibrahim in Mecca or Thoreau's Walden Pond. All bodies of water—great rivers, mountain streams, lakes, bayous, fjords and open seas—have inspired man and brought him spiritual insights and growth.

People generally need no coaxing to seek respite from life's troubles by going near water. The cortical monkey, given half a chance, will keep a person away from the limbic healing power of the water, just as it does so in other places. We face the same problem near water as we do away from it: how to cancel the cortical clutter and still the mind.

To allow water to perform its healing miracle, a person needs to let his eyes fall on water—a still water surface, running water, water in mist form, or water in waves or rapids—and to keep the eyes there. *That's it*. The water *knows* how to take over. Of course, that's not likely to happen if someone is chattering at us all the time, so silence is necessary, *then the language of silence takes over.*

When the cortical monkey refuses to let go, the best way to keep out of its path is to breathe limbically.

THE LIMBIC HEALING POWER OF A CANDLE

Fire, the ancients knew, has a healing power.

Humankind has engaged in fire rituals since ritual came into existence. The ancients considered fire as one of the five basic elements essential for the human condition. Fire was—and continues to be—a major part of many religious ceremonies. At least one religion considers fire as the principle divine symbol.

Boy scouts and girl scouts learn to sleep by warm fires during their field trips. At some intuitive-visceral level, those young people understand fire is much more than just a source of warmth. Men and women discover the joys of slumber by the fireside. Again, they know there is more to fire than just its hypnotic effect. The flames and warmth of fire create the physical state that facilitates healing processes.

Candles are used to celebrate companionship and kinship and to illuminate dining tables for family togetherness. In these ways we savor the joys of flames without any critical appreciation of the comforting qualities of fire.

The flickers of a candle flame, I found out many years ago, can be wonderful companions in a person's journey to the land of silence. They numb the cortical monkey.

As a practical suggestion for enhancing the value of candles in meditation and spiritual work, I recommend that my patients simply sit quietly by a candle and let the flickers of the flame numb the monkey. Simply be with the flickering of a flame or the silence of a stone. *There is nothing metaphysical there.* It is simply being with a flame or a stone—nothing more, nothing less. If the monkey makes you fidget, so be it. Please know he can't do that forever.

Again, if the monkey persists in its relentless chatter, a useful, practical step is to breathe limbically. Between the flicker of the candle and slow breathing, one should be able to banish the beast.

PULSES COME NATURALLY TO CHILDREN

Children learn autoregulation very quickly. I cannot recall an incident when a child did not perceive pulses on the first training session. Adults carry a heavy load of disbelief, and disbelief is hard to unload. But children are different.

Children don't have preconceived notions of what a chronic headache is. They do not know yet what the irritable bowel syndrome is. To them a headache is just that—a headache. It isn't yet a *diagnosis* of chronic headache. If they learn that a certain way of breathing or pulses can clear their headache, they simply try it, and if that works, they use it. To a child, a tummy ache is just that—a pain in the tummy. It is not yet a diagnosis of irritable bowel syndrome. If he is taught limbic breathing and finds it works for his tummy ache, he will simply do it.

Regrettably, our schools are teeming with medical experts eager to label simple problems of sugar-insulin-adrenaline roller coasters and food sensitivities with elegant, creative and *scientific* diagnoses. There are, in fact, new breeds of pediatric psychologists and gastroenterologists who diligently "educate" their little patients about the subtleties and intricacies of medical diagnoses. Sadly, and all too often, I see children who are well-schooled in the names of their chronic head, bowel and attention disorders.

One day a woman asked me to see her nine-year-old son who had been recently *diagnosed* as having irritable bowel syndrome. She was adamant about the diagnosis because it had been determined by a world-class pediatric gastroenterologist who had completed a colonoscopy on the child. When I asked if the specialist had performed any food and mold allergy tests, she replied, "No. The doctor does not believe in food allergies. He thinks it is a hoax perpetrated by quacks." The boy—as is often the case in such children—had received many courses of antibiotics. As I began to explain my view of the bowel as a delicate ecosystem that is easily battered by antibiotics, she shifted restlessly in her seat. Then she looked askance, as if I had just confirmed her gastroenterologist's perception of nutritionist-physicians as quacks.

HEADS THAT ACHE, BOWELS THAT BLOAT

"Drug medicine in the United States is committed to keeping the ill incarcerated in an illness mode. Do you remember you wrote those words in *Canary?*" Choua asked.

"I remember," I replied.

"Drug medicine in the United States is totally focused on what's wrong with the patient," he went on. "When patients consult their physicians, the question is always the same: *What do I have?* Of course, you physicians are only too happy to comply and supply the answer in ingenious ways."

"You have a different proposal, do you?"

"Often, there is much irony as well as humor in your answers, though you seldom recognize it." He ignored my question. "I will cite two examples."

"Go on."

"Patients with chronic headaches suffer for years from headache attacks. And for years, they receive advice from TV commercials instructing them to take this or that over-the-counter painkiller. When the sufferer can no longer cope with his chronic headaches, he turns to his primary care physician who orders a host of laboratory tests. When the results come back negative, the physician writes a prescription for some painkiller, hoping the patient hasn't already tried the drug he prescribes. Right?"

"So?"

"When the pill doesn't work, the physician refers the headache sufferer to a neurologist who conducts a thorough clinical evaluation and a complete work-up. He performs brain wave graphs and a spinal tap for the study of the fluid that bathes the brain. Next, he orders X-rays and MRI scans of the head and neck. Several weeks—and a few thousand dollars later—the patient returns to the neurologist for a final verdict. The neurologist now looks straight into the eyes of the patient and pronounces, with great clinical authority, that the diagnosis for the patient's malady is *chronic headache.* He then proceeds to prescribe exactly the same over-the-counter painkillers the patient was taking before seeing his primary care physician. Do you see the comedy?"

"It's tough when all tests are negative, yet the patient continues to suffer," I replied.

"Don't you see the absurdity?" he frowned.

"Go on, Choua, tell me about the other example," I goaded him.

"A similar comedy takes place when a patient suffering from chronic irritation in the bowel approaches his primary care physician. For several years, the patient has suffered from abdominal bloating, flatulence, cramps, excessive mucus in the stool, and episodes of diarrhea and constipation. Much like the headache sufferer, for years he has taken over-the-counter drugs to relieve his abdominal symptoms to no avail. Finally, he consults his physician who orders a battery of tests and prescribes an antispasm drug, which he hopes the patient has not heard of before."

"It's hard this day and age for a physician to prescribe something the patient hasn't heard of," I commented.

"I know," he grinned. "The drug companies are out to educate the masses with their clever drug ads, sometimes even before their salesmen hit the doctor's office. It is difficult for you physicians to maintain an aura of clinical authority unless you can throw around the names of drugs and procedures that your patients have not heard previously."

"That doesn't happen frequently either."

"I know that too. Now, when the results of the laboratory tests return inconclusive, the primary care physician refers the patient to a gastroenterologist who orders his share of laboratory tests, X-rays, and CAT scans of the abdomen. In the end, the gastroenterologist performs an endoscopic examination of the inner stomach and colon. When this testing is complete, the gastroenterologist summons the patient for the verdict. He reviews all the test results, and delivers authoritatively his clinical opinion: *You have irritable bowel syndrome*. Neither the physician nor the patient sees the absurdity in all that."

"What else can a gastroenterologist say?" I asked.

"The gastroenterologist's prescription is usually no different from what the patient was taking in the first place," he continued, ignoring my question. "Yet, sometimes the doctor is fortunate to have had a drug salesman bring a brand-new *cure* for irritable bowel syndrome only days earlier. The patient leaves satisfied and hopeful that the new drug will work. Again, no one sees the absurdity."

"What causes a headache when the MRI scan tests negative for a brain cancer?" I provoked him.

"And what irritates the bowel when the bowel X-rays are

negative for tumors, and the bowel biopsies show no specific inflammation?" he went on. "These awkward questions are never raised in drug medicine. Neurologists generally don't think of mold allergy, and gastroenterologists rarely understand how food incompatibilities and yeast overgrowth irritate the bowel. If the patient does raise such ugly questions, the medical specialist glibly dismisses the question with an authoritative directive: 'Cause of this is unknown.' Unknown to whom?"

"In mainstream thinking the cause of inflammatory bowel disease remains unknown."

"And unknowable," Choua mocked.

"Well, I don't know ..."

"You physicians are so infatuated with *scientific* medicine that the absurdity of its diagnostic labels escapes you completely. You move from what the patient *has* to what he needs: *the drug of choice.*"

"So what's the solution?" I asked.

"Solution!" he frowned, stared at me for some minutes, then briskly walked out.

TRUE AUTOREGULATION IS METHODLESS

Autoregulation in its purest form—guided by tissue energy responses, as I define it—is a methodless state. In such an energy state, there is no right method nor wrong technique. All notions of right or wrong are based on human perceptions, and perceptions are, of course, the first casualties of the limbic energy state. This simple concept is difficult for many patients to grasp.

When I do autoregulation myself, I do not chant words. I

do not use tapes. I use no directed pulses. I make no conscious attempt to breathe limbically. I do not use any methods of tissue sensing—or scanning the body tissues, as Talat puts it. All these methods are valuable for the beginner but unnecessary for experienced meditators. None of that seems necessary to me. I simply become aware of my tissue energy, then I am there—floating effortlessly in a deep, sustaining limbic silence. With long years of experience, I have reached a stage in which my tissues begin autoregulation when they need it, spontaneously and effortlessly. On rare occasions, when I sense rising tension in my tissues and my immediate circumstances do not allow me to break away, I take a few limbic breaths and I'm a free person again. (I describe limbic breathing in the companion volume, *Lata and Limbic Breathing*.)

This easy facility for entering the limbic mode—an effortless, guiding, healing, energy state—is a continuing gift of God to me. When God chooses to take this gift away from me, I hope He will leave me with enough fortitude to be grateful for the time I had the facility. I am fully aware that easy access to the limbic mode doesn't come easily to everyone. One does not go about appropriating to oneself such divine gifts. *This is a point of crucial importance.* I go to lengths to explain this to my patients. Fortunately, there are significant benefits to self-regulation, even during early periods of training when a full limbic escape is problematic.

IS THERE ANOTHER DOOR?

The search for a correct meditation technique—another door, as my schoolteacher patient put it—continues to be a problem for the Western mind. In what Western philosophers often term "rationalistic orientation," Descartes pronounced that the mind can achieve *certain* knowledge *only* by discerning clear, distinct and self-evident truths. Those truths to him concerned the observable concept of matter, force and inevitably a mechanical concept of the universe, as he set out to liberate science from theological dogma and animistic superstition. Descartes's disciples, in their zeal, mapped out a new universe—one totally devoid of human purpose, intelligence and meaning. Only that which could be directly—and narrowly—observed was acceptable to them. Of course, spirituality was rigorously excluded from their rationalistic and mechanical concepts of the universe.

But what is *certain* knowledge? Can the knowledge of love, kindness, beauty, music and art be considered certain? If not, where do we place such knowledge in the clear, distinct, self-evident—and cold and impersonal—Cartesian universe? What does one think of the essential humanity of humans? Of their spiritual essence? Of their yearning for linkage with the larger *presence?*

THE MYSTIC AND THE SCIENTIST

In *Rats, Drugs and Assumptions* I say that science has not failed medicine; rather, medicine has failed science. In its purest form, science is observation. That is just as relevant to the larger issues of human needs and the human condition. There is nothing unscientific about human experience in the realms of higher states of consciousness, meaning of life and death and spirituality. While they may not fit into the clear, distinct and self-evident world of Descartes, their legitimacy cannot be questioned.

In this century alone, how many structures of force and matter, forming the basis of the Cartesian theory, were dismantled because science moved from one set of observations to another? Science is self-correcting. It follows nature, which has its own schedule for revealing knowledge—its own order of enlightenment. What amazes me most about science is how faithfully it continues to be in line with the insights of the ancients and how scientists keep trampling the footprints of the mystics.

The wisdom of the empiricist precedes the scientist wherever he goes.

SANCTITY OF THE MOMENT

The past lives in the present. This is the core belief of

many therapists and their subjects in the world of psychotherapy. It seems that the main lesson a therapist insists on teaching his client is that the suffering of the present can be alleviated only through visiting past miseries.

But the lesson that my patients have taught me is that the past robs the present. When allowed to do so, past suffering creates a phantom suffering for the present. It also pollutes the future. The cortical monkey, as I wrote earlier, is obsessed with recycling past misery. When that doesn't suffice, it loves to pre-cycle feared, future misery.

What is suffering but perceptions? All perceptions can be dissolved by changing the level of consciousness. So all suffering can be mitigated. To do so, one has first to learn how to banish the cortical monkey. This is one of the oldest lessons mankind has learned. (The lesson is about 9,000 years old, according to some Jain relics unearthed in recent decades in Mohangu Daru, Pakistan.)

When in the throes of unremitting suffering, a person has a choice. He can search for the meaning of present suffering in past misery. Or, he can simply be in the present and obliterate his pain by entering higher states of consciousness. Which path should one take? He can seek meaning in the clever reconstruction of his past life with a therapist. Or, he can follow the spiritual path of the ancients and learn the language of silence. I know silence can be suffocating, but that is only the case for those who have not mastered the art of silence. True silence never suffocates. This is an important point.

The path of the mystic—which is the road to spirituality—admits no subservience to the past. The mystic has no use for dredging past dirt or for the packaged wisdom a therapist turns that dirt into. The mystic wants to be open to the moment—its reality, its truth, its beauty and, of course, its *sanctity*. Each moment to him is a reflection of that *larger being* that permeates *his* being at all times. He seeks linkage with the *larger presence* that surrounds him at all times.

A therapist loves clocks. Often, he keeps two clocks. One clock is shared with the client. This clock makes it easier to mark time for both. Another clock faces only the therapist so he can unobtrusively make sure that the client's chatter doesn't go beyond the allotted time.

Mystics abhor clocks.

A therapist thrives on the nuances of his client's words. For him no words are too simple to take for what they say. No gestures are without deeper significance. Words are not his craft, yet words are the only crutches he can stand on. Without those crutches, the therapist is off balance—and lost. When a client repeats his story endlessly, the therapist is forever ready to give a different meaning to each rendering of the same story. He doesn't protest repetition. Why should he? More repetition means less new material with which to contend. He remains impassive and impervious to his client's wailing. His professional standards call for no emotional responses. The client can spill his guts out, but the therapist remains unruffled. His eyes never blink, never blanch, never widen, or narrow. The client's words reach him and are absorbed in the thick air of his consultation room.

Words irk the mystic, and repetition stifles him. He knows only too well the infatuation of the cortical monkey for recycling past misery and pre-cycling feared, future misery. He has learned that the spiritual is not beholden to past sadness or to imagined future shocks.

The therapist thrives on repeat business. I quote below a passage from a book in which someone recounts her therapy years:

> *Therapy had become part of my landscape. I saw Dr. Parks two days in a row, had a day off, came once more, then marked the time through the weekend until my next session.*

> *You're going to therapy three times a week?" a friend asked. "I can understand going once or twice a week, but three times! Don't you worry about running out of things to say?...You can't pretend that you don't remember what you were talking about the last time you were there.*

The mystic's landscape is different. He beholds the Eastern sky at sunrise and the western sky at sunset. He doesn't need to pretend anything. He never sees the same horizon again. He doesn't worry about what he talked about the last time. His language of silence has no repetition. He is aware of the hollow words of the cortical monkey.

The therapist fishes deep in the dark recesses of his client's mind. Sometimes he confuses his client's dark recesses with his own. Who suffers? Who observes? It isn't always clear.

The writer continued:

> *Dr. Park's office was a point of warmth whose power source, I sometimes felt, was me—my limitless, bottomless, effortless, feverish churning.*

The mystic knows that a psychiatrist's couch can never be a power source. Indeed, it is unlikely that anyone can ever find a limbic escape—and serenity—on a couch recycling past misery. Neither are limbic escapes possible only during retreats in the Poconos or Appalachian Mountains. Meditation by a garbage dump in Newark can be just as enlightening as a view from Mount Washington. A tree seen through one's own office window can be more calming than all the elegant insights of a Park Avenue specialist, perhaps more so because the specialist most likely will be busy feeding the cortical monkey a rich meal of what the monkey loves most, analysis and reanalysis.

Does that mean everyone in therapy should get out of it? Not at all. My purpose in juxtaposing the therapist's goal with the mystic's "goallessness" is to make an essential point: *Healing is not an intellectual function.* When an orthopedic surgeon puts two broken ends of a bone together and immobilizes the fracture in a cast, he is *not* healing the fractured bone. He only seeks to create a condition in which healing—a natural spontaneous process—can proceed unimpaired. A good therapist seeks to do the same.

An orthopedist's patient and a therapist's client must

recognize the essential nature of the healing process. A person who moves from one therapy session per week to two, and then to three, and continues for years and years is sadly mistaken about the nature of the healing process.

RICH IN SLAVERY,
POOR IN FREEDOM

Hope is essential for healing. Therapy is clinically beneficial in serious chronic illness if it holds out hope for the patient. (This is just as true when hope is held out by a family member, a friend or a clergy.) By creating hope—and sustaining it through difficult initial periods—good therapists can facilitate the recovery process.

How does a therapist create hope from the unending rehashing of old pains? How can he sustain hope by visiting and revisiting past hurts?

The world of therapy has long held that past suffering is like a deep tissue abscess. Until the deep-seated exudate of the psyche is let out, healing cannot begin. My patients have taught me a different lesson. *Suffering cannot be alleviated by mere probing.* Indeed, it feeds the insatiable appetite of the monkey for recycling misery. It is as if every week, the package of pains is opened, rearranged and repackaged, then neatly placed back to be opened the following week—or the following day as in the case I cited above.

Long-term therapy, which relentlessly delves into the same

issues month after month, year after year, is a form of slavery. The therapist unwittingly incarcerates his client deeper and deeper into a pathologic dependence. I consider it entrapment, albeit perpetrated in good faith. Sometimes the entrapment is regarded as an enhancing experience. Can slavery be enriching?

The mystic shirks relationships that lead to dependence.

Received wisdom rarely reveals truth in healing. Walking out of a therapy session feeling better is not the same thing as the true enlightenment that periods of deep, healing silence bring. Good therapy is self-limiting. Enlightenment is not pathologic dependence that grows with time, year after year, paid for at hourly rates.

As a practical matter, serious life-threatening psychosis, anxiety, panic reactions and depression do not respond to therapy anyway. The patients in such states require potent psychotropic drugs to pull them out of their neurotransmitter vagaries.

The best results I have seen in such serious conditions are obtained with the judicious use of drugs, an ample supply of oral and injectable nutrients, such as: magnesium, calcium, potassium, taurine, vitamin B_{12} and other members of B complex; avoidance of sugar-insulin-adrenaline roller coasters; normalization of hormonal dysregulations; restoration of damaged bowel, blood and liver ecosystems; slow, sustained exercise; and effective methods of self-regulation and spiritual work.

GRATITUDE AND THE SPIRITUAL

Mysticism cannot be manufactured on short order.

The limbic language of silence is a gift from the Divine. It may be easy to achieve for some, yet difficult for others. Training in forms of self-regulation, such as autoregulation described earlier in this volume, is necessary for learning deep meditation. But all that does is take a person to the periphery of the spiritual realm. No human effort can guarantee success in entering that domain. Standing at the periphery, each of us must accept his essential humanity. There are no doors to be found and entered—no conduits to be negotiated.

This is a point of considerable importance for persons facing highly stressful situations. Such people should be grateful when they make any progress in learning the limbic language of silence. And they should be profoundly grateful when they are granted ready access to a limbic energy state. Also, they must accept when progress in this path is not forthcoming. *That acceptance is the hardest thing to achieve in energy and spiritual work.*

Gratitude, not happiness, is the operative notion in the spiritual search.

TYRANNY OF LIMITS

Someone said limits are not bad, they simplify life.

Two questions arise in my mind when I hear such ideas: First, what are those limits? And second, who sets them up?

When a surgeon takes a biopsy of a breast tumor for a frozen section study and waits for me to determine whether the tumor is benign or malignant, he sets a limit on me. He must have the report within fifteen minutes so the patient isn't kept under anesthesia any longer than necessary. I understand that. In the laboratory we set limits, within which our quality-control data remain, before we report blood glucose levels or other test results.

It is a tragic error when such notions are carried to the domains of the spiritual. The spiritual realm recognizes no limits—it has no boundaries. Hence, no doors.

The problem with limits is in defining what they are and who sets them. As I write this, I hear a TV evangelist tell his congregation about what the Spirit told him during a foreign crusade. He wanted to do what the Spirit told him to do, yet he wondered whether it was really the Spirit that spoke to him or Satan. Back to square one! Who decides what spiritual limits are? And who sets them?

There are similar problems with the limits set by the

therapist. Therapists may protest that they never set limits. *But they do.* Analysis is all about limits. Without concepts of limits, there can be no notions of deviations. And, of course, analysis is about deviations—about departures from what the therapist considers normal. And what is normal for one therapist, as we all know, is abnormal for another. Who do we believe?

The mystic has no use for limits. How can he? He doesn't even see them.

SILENCE OF A STONE

A stone can be as eloquent as poetry. Sharing the silence of a stone can be a deeply spiritual experience. All one needs to do to listen to the eloquence of a stone is to look at it—and do so without any purpose, goal or preconceived notion.

Here is what I tell my patients about meditation with a stone: Find a stone in your backyard. Sit next to it and let your eyes stay on it. *That's it.* You will have your thoughts. There is no need to fight them. Simply do not try to make things happen, nor try to understand if anything unusual is experienced. Sit silently by the same stone, keeping your eyes on it the whole time a few times a day, for a few minutes at a time or longer if you wish.

The cortical monkey will, no doubt, have a lot to say about the silence of a stone. It will ridicule the stone, and, when that doesn't suffice, it will ridicule you. Simply keep your eyes on the stone. The monkey might next call the whole exercise absurd. Yes, the stone is silent. So the monkey might provoke you, saying: The dumb stone has no voice. It cannot utter a word. What do you expect from it anyway? Isn't it a stone? Simply keep your eyes on the stone. The monkey will probably bring up the matter of wasting time, or berate you for reverting back to primitive stone worship. Stone worship, it might argue, was discarded centuries ago when man became enlightened. Why bring it back?

The monkey might persist: What's the relevance of a stone?

The cortical monkey is forever into *relevance,* isn't he? That reminds me of a young girl who complained bitterly to her girlfriend about her boyfriend. Her friend listened patiently, then said,

"He doesn't misbehave. He doesn't lie to you. He doesn't cheat on you. He is always there for you. How many girls do you know who have such boyfriends?"

"That's not the point," the first girl replied.

"Then, what's the point?" the friend asked, perplexed.

"You don't understand my problem. He is decent and all, but he never does anything. All he ever talks about is the *relevance* of things."

The monkey might ask: How long are you going to stay with that stupid stone? His persistence might create anxiety for you. It might even trigger a tightness here or a muscle spasm there. None of this should surprise you. The cortical monkey cannot cope with silence. Silence suffocates him. The monkey thrives on argument and repetition. Simply being in the presence of a stone is a punishment it cannot bear. When nothing else works, the monkey might get plain angry and strike back, creating yet more troubling thoughts and more ugly scenarios.

How can the silence of a stone be a spiritual experience? The monkey might challenge you next. Here is a little trick for the monkey, to give him a taste of his own medicine. Each being is an energy being. And so is a stone—albeit a denser form of energy than beings that breathe, move and eventually waste away. Energy has a language of its own—a language that transcends the ordinary notions we excel in articulating. A stone also has a language—the language of silence. Stones have always communicated with people at much deeper levels. Consider the holiest of all objects in the Islamic world: *Hajjar-e-Asswad*, the Black Stone of *Khana Quabba* in Mecca, or the Wailing Wall in Jerusalem.

A stone communicates differently—energetically, at higher intuitive-visceral levels, far beyond the reach of the cortical monkey.

Each energy being is linked to every other being. It follows that your energy is linked to the energy of stone. And, yes, so is the stone's energy linked to the energy of that larger *presence* that surrounds each of us at all times. Hence, even in a purely physical sense, a stone can provide a linkage with the larger *presence* for those who may have trouble experiencing that *presence* directly. How does one know when that *presence* will grace him through the linkage of that stone? One doesn't. And that's the point of taking oneself to the presence of a silent stone.

From extensive clinical experience, I know that beginners are served well by two approaches: the silence of a stone in the backyard in summer and the light of a candle in the kitchen or living room in winter. These two methods require nothing more than patience and persistence. No special equipment is needed. No elaborate preparations are necessary. They *always work,* though the results can be maddeningly slow in some cases. The cortical monkey has no antidote for them.

MINDFUL MEDITATION

A type of meditation coming into vogue is "mindful" meditation. Some stress managers are enthralled by it. They boast of its superior clinical efficacy. To support their claims, they cite elegant, controlled studies on the value of mindful meditation conducted at famous universities.

What is mindful meditation? If the term is true to itself, it must mean the mind must be kept full during meditation, or is at least is at center stage. The experts of mindful meditation, whom I have consulted about the nature of their craft, are usually unclear about the role of the mind in their work. They talk about things I cannot fathom, and I wonder if they themselves understand what they say.

I'm afraid I don't understand what *mindful* meditation is. What my patients teach me daily is this: *The mind is the culprit.* This has also been my own experience. And this was clearly the experience of the ancient masters of meditation. The whole purpose of meditation is to escape the tyranny of the mind. Why bring the mind back into meditation?

We simply think too much. The mind creates anxiety,

fear, malaise and ennui. Chronic thinking paralyzes. Turning and twisting thoughts over and over in the mind distorts them. The cortical monkey loves to recycle misery. When that isn't enough, it pre-cycles feared, future misery. This *is* the battle of our time. John Lennon said, "Life is what passes us by when we plan our future."

The mind is well-versed in the risks we face in our daily lives. Within us lurk the unseen chemical villains—splitting and shearing DNA in cells and driving mutated molecules into malignant behavior. Aluminum, mercury and other toxic metals sit in our brain cells, insidiously eroding them from within. Years later, we develop Alzheimer's disease and other types of senile dementia. Our air is polluted. Our water is contaminated. Our food is laced with killer molecules. Our minds are abraded by such knowledge every day. Shouldn't we be uncluttered for a little while during periods of silence and meditation?

The mind copes daily with the possibility of random crime and targeted terrorism—not only in streets where we fear strangers, but also at workplaces where those we know are often more threatening. Shouldn't there be periods of escape from that fear?

When the fear of the known does not suffice, the mind engages in fear of the unknown. Shouldn't we be fearless at least during meditation?

So why bring the mind into meditation? Could it be that the masters of mindful meditation know something about marketing that we don't? They go to such lengths to differentiate their meditative technique because they know effective product differentiation is essential for successful marketing.

BEAUTY AND THE LANGUAGE OF SILENCE

Sometime ago, during a cruise on the Norwegian fjords, I was much distracted by people around me. As I usually find in traveling abroad, we Americans were the loudest among a very large, multinational group on the ship. At every turn of the fjord there were boisterous cries of appreciation for the beauty of the waterfall and the mountains. Indeed, the scenery was overwhelmingly beautiful. The water pummeling down the mountainsides was ravishing.

The loud noise of tourists was not limited to admiration of the scene. A large flock of seagulls hovered close to the deck, literally begging the visitors for alms. Some travelers obliged and threw snacks at the birds who swooned gracefully to catch the food in midair. Then followed a rush to the snack bar, and pretty soon a huge number of adults and children excitedly shared stale snacks with the seagulls. This time, the Japanese made the most noise. For a short while, the feeding game amused me, but then the shouting grew irksome.

I wondered how different my experience might be if I were to look at the mountains, waterfalls and water but say or hear not one word about their beauty for the remaining hours of the day. To do that, I had to blot out the surrounding clutter. I looked at Talat and found her staring blankly at the fjords. I told her about my idea and asked if she cared to join me in limbic silence. She nodded in agreement. We moved to a less crowded part of the deck and began limbic breathing. We discovered something valuable: One can talk about beauty with cortical clutter or know it with the limbic language of silence. A place is far more enchanting when the mind is silent.

SILENCE: A MENTOR OR TORMENTOR

For some people, silence is a marvelous mentor. For others, silence is also a great tormentor.

I frequently refer to the clinical benefits of the language of silence in my writings. I continue to be amazed at the healing capacity of silence as well as at the disease-causing potential from the noise of a cluttered mind. People who learn the language of silence heal well. Those who do not often continue to suffer.

Below, I include the text of an exercise I conduct with my patients during autoregulation classes. I call it Chambers of Silence. The purpose of this exercise is to introduce them to the subject of the language of silence. I highly recommend it to the reader. It is a simple exercise that any reader can do on his own using this text. He or she may make a tape with this text for personal use.

(This material is copyrighted and may not be used to make tapes for sale or for any other use. This text is also available on a tape with my voice and may be obtained from the Institute of Preventive Medicine at 201-586-4111.

Chambers of Silence

I am walking down a narrow cobblestone alley. There are small stone and brick houses on each side of the alley. The houses have large wooden doors with black wrought-iron bolts. I look up. The sky is deep blue, though the sun is hidden behind the houses. The alley ends at a stone archway through which I can see a cobblestone courtyard flooded with sunlight. There is a fountain in the middle of the courtyard. I walk slowly and approach the archway. Now I see the water of the fountain glistening in the bright sunshine. I look down to see the mosaic of stones that make up the street, then up to see the dark blue sky again. When I reach the stone archway, I pass underneath it. Standing in the courtyard now, I look to the right and see a row of small chambers with small wooden doors. I look to the left and see another row of small chambers with small wooden doors. I stand there in the courtyard, looking at the fountain and the drops of water shining splendidly as rays of sun touch them.

I know the chambers on the two sides are windowless and empty. There are no rugs in them. I am aware that I can enter any of them and stay as long as I wish. I must begin, however, with the first chamber on the right side. If I wish to move on, I must leave the first chamber, slowly walk across the courtyard to the first chamber on the left side and enter it. Again, I have the choice of staying in the second chamber or moving on. To do so, I again have to slowly cross the courtyard and enter the second chamber in the row on the right side of the courtyard. This is the way I have to move if I wish to change chambers. At any step, I can simply stop and stay by the fountain, or do anything else.

Now, I begin my slow walk to the first chamber. I open the wooden door gently. It is a small, windowless chamber. There is neither furniture nor a rug. I close the door behind me, walk to the middle of the chamber and stand there. I know my choices. I can simply stand or sit there for as long as I wish or until I finish this period of meditation. Or, I can leave this chamber, slowly walk across the courtyard, and enter the first chamber on the left side. Again, I know that chamber is also windowless, without a rug or furniture.

Now, I stand in the center of the first chamber. It is cool, dark and peaceful here. Here I stand.

I have led hundreds of patients in the Chambers of Silence exercise. Almost at all times, I myself stay in the first chambers throughout the period of meditation. I have experienced many fascinating limbic experiences during these periods. Usually, the cool, dark chamber gets flooded with lights of many colors within several minutes of my entering the first chamber. Sometimes windows appear in the walls, and through them I can see waves of blue ocean and hear the sounds of waves breaking on white sand. At other times, limbic images follow each other in quick successions—forming composite pictures of places I have visited and others that are totally unknown. Then, there are energy responses in various parts of my body. These experiences are never undesirable or bitter. I feel no inclination to leave the chamber and seek other experiences in other chambers.

Many of my patients also stay in the first chamber, describing images and energy responses similar to mine. In other patients, I have recognized several interesting patterns of limbic, energy and cortical responses. Some patients become fearful of the darkness and find the small chamber suffocating. They quickly leave the chamber and sit by the fountain until I finish the period of meditation. Others describe irksome or distressing sensations or images that drive them out of the chamber. Many patients restlessly wander from chamber to chamber seeking relief from their suffering.

I have observed a clear correlation between the discomfort in the chambers of silence and a state of inner tumult—a condition of adrenergic molecular hypervigilance that literally causes a molecular burn-out of human energy, detoxification and neuroreceptor enzymes.

Those under emotional and physical stress often find the experience in the chamber of silence jolting, whereas experienced meditators find the silence in the chamber liberating and enriching. The important point is this: All images and energy responses in the chambers of silence are true-to-life. There are no right or wrong things to do in this type of meditation. A person needs to allow herself or himself to be gently guided by limbic energy. Of course, this type of meditation clearly tells people how much distance they need to cover before adrenergic hypervigilence subsides and the natural energy patterns in the human body are liberated from the tyranny of the thinking mind.

BEWARE OF THE CORTICAL MONKEY IN SUPPORT GROUPS

An effective support group can be enormously valuable for

persons in the throes of a debilitating chronic illness. I know of no remedy that has helped people afflicted with alcoholism more than Alcoholics Anonymous. Similarly, I have personal knowledge of other support groups, such as Recovery, that do splendid work in creating a healing environment. This is all the more remarkable because such support groups succeed in areas where Star Wars medicine fails miserably. Similarly, I have seen good results in patients who join bereavement groups and other support groups.

The key element for success in a support group is not the knowledge of the group leader, nor is it his facility with clever words. Neither is it his ability to make people laugh—or cry. (An inappropriate laugh can be fuel poured on the fires of suffering.) Furthermore, it matters little whether or not the group leader has a wildly successful personal story to tell. The group's knowledge of the resources required to cope with the specific health disorders is clearly very useful to the newcomer. In my view, however, this is not the main reason for a person to seek a support group.

On the other hand, I have also seen situations where the activities of the support group exacerbate the stress of the person seeking relief. Regrettably, such instances are becoming more frequent. An increasing number of patients with debilitating chronic fatigue, fibromyalgia, cancer, paralyzing multiple sclerosis and other disorders tell me about their disappointment with the support groups they attended.

A young man suffers from fibromyalgia—a condition of chronic fatigue associated with muscle pain and tender points in muscles in various parts of the body. There are no drugs that can cure fibromyalgia, however in my experience it is a reversible condition—though in some cases it may require many months of comprehensive nondrug restorative therapies. That young man told me that the people in a fibromyalgia support group he attended tried hard to convince him that there was no hope of recovery for him. They advised him to simply accept the fact that he has to live a severely limited life from then on. They also advised him not to waste any money on any treatment. When he protested that he wasn't ready for such a dire forecast, they adamantly stressed that fibromyalgia is irreversible, claiming that all nondrug therapies, which are touted to reverse the disorder, are pure fraud perpetrated by greedy doctors. Not unexpectedly, he returned home deeply disappointed.

(I might add here that in most cases of fibromyalgia, long-term nutritional support with intramuscular injections of nutrients is required. Furthermore, minerals such as magnesium, calcium, potassium and molybdenum, and vitamins such as B_{12} and pantothenic acid is essential. Of course, we administer these therapies along with our integrated holistic programs for restoring the battered bowel, blood, liver and other ecosystems of the body.)

"I'm a young man," he continued. "I have young children. I can't give up. I have been so successful in my work on the stock market floor. The pain in my muscles is debilitating, yet I press on. I need someone to tell me this thing is reversible. I simply can't give up. I need help. Can you do that, Dr. Ali?" he pleaded.

"Yes, you'll get better," I replied.

"When?" he asked eagerly.

"Unfortunately, it takes time. The progress can be maddeningly slow," I cautioned.

"But, you do think I can get better."

"Yes."

"That's all I need to know. I can fight as long as I have to. And, I'm not going back to that depressing support group where everyone is so negative."

(At the time of this writing this young man is feeling, in his own words, "much better".

A MOTHER DENIES THE POSSIBILITY OF HER DAUGHTER'S RECOVERY

A growing number of support-group leaders form strong opinions about the irreversibility of their particular health disorders. The group leaders frequently express their personal prejudices as established scientific knowledge. Tragically, they sometimes do so even when scientific facts are evidently to the contrary. In *The Dog, Directed Pulses and Energy Healing,* I write about several of my patients who were infected with HIV viruses 12 to 15 years ago and who still live and hold jobs. They had the courage to say "No!" to AIDS drugs and took the holistic and spiritual approach to that problem. I remember how during the early 1980s, infection with HIV viruses was predicted to be uniformly fatal.

The problems created by fatalistic leaders of support groups were brought home to me during a recent TV debate in which I participated. My opponent was president of the local Chronic Fatigue Immunodeficiency Disorder (CFID). It was my first encounter with someone who was absolutely convinced that chronic fatigue syndrome is utterly irreversible.

In writing *The Canary and Chronic Fatigue,* I knew I would offend many people. The *Canary* is a powerful advocate of chronic fatigue sufferers—human canaries, as I call them. Many mainstream physicians still deny the problem exists at all, proffering the old all-in-the-head story. The few physicians who admit that debilitating fatigue may be a real phenomenon find they are helpless since there are no drugs that can provide long-term relief. Long-term drug use invariably compounds the problem.

Most insurance companies take their cues from practitioners of drug medicine and usually do not reimburse human canaries for natural, nondrug therapies that *do* reverse the disorder. Even the judges in disability cases usually side with the insurance companies and mainstream physicians who deny that chronic fatigue is a real problem.

(The recent emphasis on giving fatigue sufferers large doses of cortisone, beta blockers and drugs that affect the cholinergic part of the autonomic nervous system is a tragic error. It is bound to fail over the long haul, and it will further damage the patients' battered antioxidant, enzyme and immune systems. This is a safe prediction because steroids work by suppressing the immune defenses and the other two drugs also work by blocking or impairing essential healing mechanisms.)

Consequently, I knew *Canary* would leave me open to criticism, but I never dreamed the first public attack on my position that chronic fatigue is reversible would come from the mother of a young woman disabled by it.

Several minutes before we went on the air, I was introduced to the CFID chapter president. I had been told by the producer of the TV show that her daughter had been disabled by chronic fatigue several years earlier. While shaking her hand, I said,

"I hear your daughter has a fatigue problem."

"She doesn't have a fatigue problem," she shot back, withdrawing her hand abruptly. "She suffers from chronic immunodeficiency syndrome."

"I meant that," I added hastily, stepping back a little.

"No, it's not the same thing," she growled. "She does not have a fatigue problem. She suffers from CFID syndrome."

"I hope she feels better." I tried to disentangle myself from a conversation that seemed to degenerate into an argument by the minute.

"No, she won't," she snapped. My explanation seemed to make her angrier. "I know there will be no answer for CFID in my lifetime."

"I wouldn't lose hope," I said and removed some papers from my briefcase just to end the conversation.

"You are dreaming." Her anger was unmitigated.

She left the room for some time, then returned, eyeing me suspiciously. I buried my face in my papers.

"I don't think you understand CFID," she resumed testily. "The people you claim you can help do not suffer from CFID."

"My associates and I see many very sick people who are totally disabled by persistent chronic fatigue. Most of them get better, though sometimes it takes several months," I explained.

"No one with CFID gets better," she nearly screamed.

I went back to my papers.

On air, the TV host began by asking me what I thought caused chronic debilitating fatigue and to describe the programs for fatigue reversal. I briefly outlined my basic theory that chronic debilitating fatigue is caused by oxidative damage to enzymes of digestive-absorptive, detoxification, neurotransmitter and energy systems of the body. Next, I mentioned our nondrug nutrient and herbal therapies, and our program for autoregulation. The president of the local CFID chapter repeatedly interrupted, despite pleas from the host not to do so. When she was asked to comment, she repeated her viewpoint that CFID is irreversible, and reiterated her belief that a treatment for her disabled daughter would not be found during her (the president's) life.

When the host opened the telephone lines, the first caller told us on the air that my therapies nearly killed her. I asked if she would identify which therapy she was referring to. She then changed her line, saying it would have killed her had she tried it. She couldn't provide specific information about the therapy to which she referred. The next two callers assaulted *Canary*, again without citing specifics.

After finishing our TV appearance, the CFID chapter president and I walked to our cars in the parking lot of the TV station. I said goodbye to her and inadvertently repeated my wishes for her daughter's recovery. I realized my error, but it was a moment too late.

"There will be no cure for CFID in my life," she erupted again, then continued in controlled anger. "I know my daughter won't get better in my life. I'm sure of that. You were a dead man before you came here. I had called Drs. ABC and XYZ (two CFID experts who, like her, firmly believe in the irreversibility of CFID). They told me you don't understand CFID."

"I still hope your daughter feels better," I repeated. (This time, I must admit, I did so deliberately to provoke her for my amusement.)

"You were dead before you came," she crowed contemptuously.

(I later received a call from the television show's producer expressing his regret about the hostility of the callers whom he recognized as plants by the president of the local CFID chapter.)

Although I held my ground during her assaults before and during the TV show, I found the woman's comments in the parking lot unsettling. During the drive back, I couldn't help but wonder why a mother would respond so violently to the mention of possible recovery. It was the one time I wished I had taken more psychology courses in college. Perhaps then I could divine what distressed that mother about the possibility of her daughter's recovery. Perhaps I could understand about the inner workings of a mother so wrought by her daughter's illness that the possibility of healing irked her so. As hard as I tried, I drew a blank.

Some hours later on the highway, a possible answer arose in my mind. I suddenly recalled the case history of a woman I had seen some years earlier.

A beautiful young woman consulted me for a severe case of eczema on her hands, arms and face. After a diagnostic work-up, she received allergy and nutrient therapies from our Institute. She was always accompanied by her mother during her office visits. Initially, her eczema improved visibly, then relapsed. (This is not unusual when patients do not follow their food plan and consume allergic foods.) Over the months I noticed something that I hadn't encountered earlier. Whenever I asked how she was doing, her answer was positive when her mother wasn't in the room but negative when her mother was within hearing distance. Curious about that, I asked some nurses if they had also noticed the change in the woman's responses when her mother was close by. They laughed and told me that they found the circumstance just as amusing. I next asked if the nurses had an explanation for this unusual situation. Again, they laughed.

One said, "She is so beautiful, yet has no boyfriend. Maybe the mom fears that if her eczema clears up she might find a boyfriend and leave her. You know she has no other children and apparently has no other interests in life."

Could it be that the daughter of that CFID chapter president is a victim of similar hidden fears of her mother? I wondered.

BE A PART OF SOMEONE'S HEALING

In cases where intense suffering persists despite a good program of nondrug therapies, and when progress in meditation is blocked by unremitting suffering, I turn to my court of last appeal: I make vigorous efforts to get the patient seriously involved in someone else's healing.

The reader might ask, if that really works, why not simply start there and skip the nutritional, environmental and other therapies? The answer is that most patients when we first see them are not prepared for such spiritual dimensions in their recovery process. Also, we obtain far better clinical results when all nondrug supportive therapies are used. As for the healing effects of being part of someone else's healing, the literature of the world is replete with stories where such involvement alone led to the healing of chronic health disorders.

There is no healer other than the *larger presence* that permeates each of us at all times. So what do I mean when I suggest that a patient become a serious part of someone else's healing? How does one person heal by simply observing another's healing? This question would have been impossible for me to answer during the more than 25 years when I was involved in drug medicine. At that time, I would have dismissed the notion as an apocryphal old-wives' tale. But, since I began to see biologic phenomena as energy relationships many years ago, I have little difficulty seeing the underlying energy dynamics. The healing response not only creates powerful healing dynamics for that person, it does so for those who observe healing intimately as well. I believe this is the main reason that physicians and nurses with an intense passion for their work can care for severely ill patients for long hours and decades yet remain healthy themselves. Without that healing response, physicians and nurses would expect to have short life spans—if for no other reason than because they are exposed to infectious agents much more frequently than others.

(I have known several physicians who were active—and some still are—in their professional work until their nineties. All of them were—and are—passionate about their work in healing. I have never thought about it before, but as I write now, I try to think of a physician who is professionally active in his nineties and who isn't passionate about healing. I can't think of a single such physician, or a single such nurse.)

How else does being a part of another's healing help one heal? *In giving we receive.* All great cultures of the world have recognized that. When a sick person goes out of his way to care for another, in the giving he unwittingly receives. Again, it is an aspect of the healing energy dynamic. People who might dismiss this phenomenon as a mere play on words will never experience this essential aspect of healing. I'm sure physicians who have watched people live who shouldn't have according to medical texts—and those who died but shouldn't have—will attest to the simple truth of my words.

It is one of the profound medical ironies of our time that older physicians who understand such dimensions of healing rarely talk or write about them. They are often intimidated by the medical statistics rattled off by young academic doctors. The older physicians then shy away from asserting their most treasured clinical observations of the healing phenomenon. Cold, mechanical Star Wars medical technology prevails. Subtle but essential aspects of healing are ignored—casualties of our infatuation with synthetic chemicals and surgical scalpels.

There are many ways a person can be a part of someone else's healing. Perhaps the simplest of all is finding an ill, elderly individual in one's neighborhood and visiting that person with a flower or a sandwich. Simply *be* with that person for as long *you* wish. There is no need for an agenda.

If that person likes being read to, the problem is solved in an elegant way. Literature contains many gems about the healing of the sick. Any public library will furnish a person with an unending supply of such reading materials. Again, the trick is to not let the cortical monkey trip you. Stay with simple stories of healing and prayer.

Shun the New Age gurus who exhort you to intellectualize about the reasons why you become sick. I know of a woman who developed a cancer in her ovary. She was vehemently told to peer back into her past, draw pictures of images she sees there and chant until she can figure out why she developed her cancer in the first place. She was deeply offended by that advice. She asked me what I thought of that approach. I told her that I didn't think the DNA molecules in her ovary much cared for such exhortations of the cortical monkey. It is true that unrelenting stress lowers resistance—impairs the repair of oxidatively-injured DNA in cells by DNA repair enzymes, in my language. But I had seen no evidence yet that mental games of drawing pictures by the cortical monkey has any healing benefits.

Indeed, I think such healing schemes are nothing more than cruel intellectual pranks of the cortical monkey. *Healing is not an intellectual function.* I repeat this sentence often in my books because this is one of the most important insights into healing that my patients have given me.

BEFRIENDING SOMEONE WITH A SIMILAR PROBLEM

Befriend someone with a similar problem. Compassion comforts. And it works both ways—for those who give as well as for those who receive. It is not difficult to do because most communities in the United States now have support groups for major types of chronic disorders. Again, be wary of cortical monkeys at support groups. You look for spirituality, not clever medical tricks for goading the recalcitrant healing responses in the body. You are much better off leaving that to your physician—as long as he is not too infatuated with synthetic drugs.

Befriend an animal. Animals communicate limbically, not cortically. Animals are not into clever healing schemes of the human mind. They facilitate healing responses by simply being. And that is the essence of the healing response.

A FATHER'S CRUELTY

Cruelty takes many shapes, and few are as hurtful as a father's cruelty.

Amy, a woman in her forties, consulted me for severe stress, anxiety attacks, heart palpitations and chest discomfort. Like other patients, she made good progress with our holistic approach to her problems. One day she arrived looking very distraught. Her eyes were red from crying. Her husband sat by her pensively. I reviewed her clinical chart, then looked at her.

"I was very close to my mother," she spoke softly, trying desperately to hide her sadness. "She fell ill some months ago, then died rather unexpectedly. I was devastated. During the last few months of her life, I visited her almost daily, cooking meals for her and my dad. Dad has always been difficult, and Mom's illness seemed to affect him in a strange way. He became increasingly hostile toward me. Just before Mom died, my brother visited us after some years. He was accompanied by his girlfriend. My father made it a point to be very friendly to my brother's girlfriend in my presence. That annoyed me but I kept quiet. When my mother died, as if I wasn't shattered enough, he started talking about giving the house to his son and his girlfriend, and moving in to live with them. Then my brother and his girlfriend left."

"Did that ease things a little?" I asked.

"No," she blurted, then spoke softly, "I know my mom would have wanted me to cook for my dad. So I did that every day. But there was no change in my father's hostility. He insults my cooking. And that's not where he stops. The other day..." she stopped in midsentence and sobbed.

I looked at her husband. He nodded sympathetically.

"The other day," she resumed after some moments, "he said, 'Why don't you fire that doctor of yours and find a good one who can get rid of some of your ugly fat.' He said that while I was cutting down a small tree in his yard, which he asked me to take down."

Cruelty has many shapes. I continue to be amazed at how inventive some people are in finding new ways to be cruel.

"Is there ever a pleasant visit with Dad?" I asked.

"No," she replied, trying to smile bravely.

"Why do you go there every day?"

"I think my mom would want me to make sure that he has something to eat. He can't cook, you know."

"Couldn't you order food in for him on some days?" I suggested, recognizing that she could afford that.

"Oh, he looks so old, weak and pathetic. He can't do anything. I *have* to do his laundry," she replied firmly.

"Not going there on some days might ease your pain a

bit. "

"Yes, it might, but my mom..."

"Maybe some days you can cook and some days you can order in," I continued.

"That would be a big help," the husband spoke hopefully.

"Why don't you consider that?" I asked her.

"My mom..." she left her sentence unfinished and broke down again.

"When your panic attacks and heart palpitations stop, try thinking again about what your mom would have wanted you to do. In the meantime, do only what you can and want to do. Go spend some time by your mom's grave. Simply be with her. And try not to figure out why your dad does what he does. Escape the tyranny of the thinking mind."

"The cortical monkey?" she asked, then laughed.

"Yeah, the cortical monkey. Go to your mom's grave and lose him. Hasn't he tortured you enough?" I laughed and so did her husband.

"And you think that would do it?" she expressed doubt.

"I don't know if it will or not. But you'll find out if you go there. Would silence by your mom bother you?"

"Are you kidding?" she cheered up. "I love that."

"You've thought enough. And that hasn't worked," I added. "These are not the kind of problems that one can clever-think his way through. You now need a no-thinking approach. There has to be some time for silence by your mom's grave. And do get some calcium, magnesium and B_{12} shots. Those nutrients help in stressful times. They will help settle the aching heart."

Silence has an enormous healing capacity. She looked much calmer a week later.

SCULPTOR IN THE SKY

The sky tugs at me more in many ways—more than any mountain or ocean ever did. It is, of course, present everywhere for anyone to seek solace from. All one needs to do is to look up. I highly recommend the sky to people interested in self-regulation, meditation and spiritual work. Below, I have reproduced a few pages of text from *The Ghoraa and Limbic Exercise.*

There is a sculptor in the sky with a gift for every moment. Look up with the language of silence, receive the gift and treasure it.

Life on planet Earth is sustained by a spinning ball of fire—the sun. The sun gives us light and energy. Light and energy bring forth life.

Living things need light to sustain them. Some rare species of fish that live in total darkness in caverns deep in large caves are an exception.

Tiny buds raise their little heads from beneath piles of dirt seeking the light and warmth of the sun. Sunflowers follow the motion of the sun. Little saplings covered by thick brush of the forest floor lean and bend and twist to peek at the sun. The young leaves at the treetops surge high to claim the early rays of the morning sun. Butterflies come to life with the rising sun and so do woodpeckers. Roosters have different kinds of light sensors. They know when the sun will rise before it actually rises.

The sky reveals. It enlightens. It offers communion. It nourishes. It sustains. It does so at every single moment. Early man knew it. The Egyptians and Sumerians knew it. The men of the Age of Reason knew it. And those who flew up to touch the moon knew it.

On Sunday afternoons I drive West to Blairstown for evening office hours. I drive with my cortical monkey part of the journey, but during most of my trip I am with the sculpture in the sky. The Western sun paints the sky in a hundred different colors and in a thousand different shades. The dimly lit clouds have a way of reaching the deepest recesses of human perceptions — and the human soul.

Early man from the Rift Valley in Central Africa—the Serengeti Plain of Choua's lions—looked up to the sun when he was overwhelmed with grief. He did the same when he was happy and wanted to celebrate. When things happened that he didn't understand, he looked up again for answers. There he found his *spirits, his gods.* His children, the early Egyptians had many gods, but the god they revered most was the sun god, Amun-Ra. They sought sustenance and looked for protection from the elements, from this god. The sun was a mere creation of our lord God, the men of religion derided the ancients. The sun cannot create anything, they exclaimed with scorn. It only does what the Lord, Our God, wants it to do. Still the men of religion conducted their sacred rituals by the sun. They taught their folks to begin their fasts before sunrise and break them by taking cues from the sun. The men of religion often had trouble with what was visible in the sky — perhaps because it distracted them in their pursuit of their gods who lived above it.

There is a gold-colored relief in the tomb of King Ikhnaton, who is best known for his outspoken challenge to Egyptian polytheism. He declared that the only god was Aton. The gold relief shows the king, his wife, Nefertiti, and their two daughters. One of the princesses sounds a sistrum. The king and queen make offerings of flowers to the sun, which hangs above as a sun-disk with the traditional uraeus. It is a precious work of art, stunning in detail and overwhelming in sheer beauty. There is something touching in this relief. A careful look reveals the sun rays turning into little arms as they reach down to make contact with the royal family: God himself reaches down to His people.

The ancient Egyptians had many gods. They had Isiris, Isis and Horus—the father, mother and the son gods. There was Thoth (a cousin of my cortical monkey and my favorite) —the baboon-headed god who invented hieroglyphics—and Anubis, the jackal-headed god who protected the dead from the evil spirits. They had loin-headed gods, cow-headed and snake-headed gods. Egyptians loved to restructure their gods. But there was no god like their sun god, Amun-Ra. At night he traveled below the belly of earth Egypt and emerged from the East in the morning with life, light and love.

From where did the Egyptians inherit their preoccupation with the sun? Perhaps it emerged from their need for linkage with what must have seemed to them as the center of things in the sky. And what about their ritual of looking up to the sun for their supreme god? I suppose they learned that from their ancestors from the Rift Valley of Central Africa. Early man in Africa searched for linkage with something larger than himself. He found that linkage in the sky and sun. He bequeathed those insights to his descendants, the Egyptians. Man's link with the sun and the eastern sky goes back a long way.

Every Sunday, I drive West to my Blairstown office. And every Sunday, I see the sky painted crimson, red, pink, purple, silver and gray. The sky changes by the moment. I see sun rays turn into little arms that extend down to the creation below, God reaching down to His people. Unkind images of yesterday melt away as do the feared miseries of tomorrow. What permeates the world above and around Interstate 80 is the sunlight, sunlight filtering through the skies in an ever-changing mosaic of light, life and love.

HEART OF THE FIGHTER

One afternoon Talat and I went for a walk in New York's Central Park. We sat on the stairs of Bethesda Terrace by the fountain at 72nd Street and watched as Aki Sato, a talented Japanese choreographer and dancer, performed her "dance symphony." Her companion distributed a leaflet indicating that in her dance "space," Aki defines space by the stretching and luxurious splaying of her lithe body on the brick terrace. In "Prayer," insupportable burdens are lifted by a body that flies up freely—hoisted by the very weight and number of those burdens. Aki is an enchanting dancer.

On the back of the leaflet was some ancient Japanese writing. Below, I have reproduced portions of that text.

> *What kind of world could there be on the other side of the mountain?...Perhaps up on the mountain, it looks like people are fighting far below...If we don't knock on the door of the heart of one of the fighters, we won't know what they are fighting for...*

> *What could be on the other side of the door? Could someone be standing on the other side of the door, just like we are: wanting to open the door, just like we are? The moment we open the door and step forward, perhaps we'll be able to meet someone.*

Who is on the other side of the door? Who is that someone being written about? A family member? A long forgotten friend? An animal? *A stone?*

*If we don't knock on the door of the heart of one of the fighters...*Is it all about fighting? About knowing what the fighter is fighting for? About making peace with the fighter? Or, about opening the door to his heart?

Perhaps it's not about doors at all. Perhaps the imagined

doors are in walls that truly do not exist—walls that we create, and boundaries that we draw out of nowhere. A door has no presence except when there is a wall. It's the wall that gives an existence to a door. Perhaps the ancient writer who penned those lines was not into doors. He wrote about the doors only because he wanted to write about walls. Doors are not important, walls are. Perhaps that writing was about the larger *presence* that surrounds each of us at all times. That *presence* has no walls, nor can there be any doors to it.

I read the leaflet, then gave it to Talat. Her face broke into a smile when she read about the doors. I'd finished this chapter earlier that morning and had read some paragraphs to Talat before we left for Central Park. She smiled and returned the leaflet.

توں کتھے کتھے لبیں اونوں لو لیا

توں جتے جتے جاویں او لو لیا

In vain, you search for Him everywhere.
Wherever you go, He is there.

Chapter 15

The Seven for Stress

In this chapter I suggest seven ways to cope with stress, prevent disease and promote health. The following definition of what health is and isn't provides a practical framework for the suggestions I make.

WHAT IS HEALTH?

How is health defined in drug medicine? It isn't. The subject of what health is—and what it isn't—is scrupulously avoided in our medical schools, hospitals and physicians' offices. We dismiss any reference to it by mumbling something unintelligible about the physical, mental and emotional aspects of health.

But what are the physical attributes of health? How do we define mental health? What is emotional wholeness? I have attended thousands of medical lectures since entering King Edward Medical College in 1958, yet I can't recall ever hearing a serious attempt to answer these questions. Why?

I myself never reflected on these questions throughout the more than 25 years that I worked as a disease doctor of drug medicine. It was only when my interest shifted from disease to health that the issue caught my attention. So, what is health?

Health is rising in the morning with a sense of the spiritual—without any need to analyze what the spiritual might be. In health, spirituality—trust in the larger *presence*—displaces the practice of psychology in one's work.

Health, at a deeper level, is resonance with the larger *presence* that permeates and surrounds each of us at all times.

Health is waking up in the morning with a deep sense of gratitude —gratitude not for any particular accomplishment, *but for simply being*. Recently I made some comments about this aspect of health during a lecture at the American Academy of Otolaryngic Allergy. In the audience was a Greek surgeon who later expressed his frustration at my comments, "This is utterly new to my Greek way of thinking." Well, if the concept of gratitude for simply *being* is foreign to us, we need to learn about it.

Health is waking up with a sense of energy, going through a day's work with that same sense of energy and returning to bed at night with it.

Health is having as much energy before meals as after them.

Health is the ability to treasure personal time in silence —alone or with family and friends. Relentless thinking—head fixation, as it may be called—is a major stressor, and eventually causes dis-ease and disease.

Health comprises living with dynamic and vigorous bowel ecosystems—having two or three effortless and odorless bowel movements a day without mucus and cramps.

Health comprises dynamic and well-preserved blood, liver and other body ecosystems.

Health is having intact and functioning cell membranes

that mark the boundaries between life within the cell and that
which exists outside it. The cell membrane separates the
internal order of a cell from external disorder. It is a living,
breathing, spongy and porous sheet that regulates the two-way
energetic-molecular (EM) traffic between cells and the soup of
life that bathes them.

Returning to the first element of resonance with the
larger *presence*, health is the sum total of all atomic, cellular and
molecular resonances that exist within the human frame. I do
not consider this an abstract and metaphysical notion. Common
sense holds that a part cannot exist without some relationship
with the whole. Since each of us is an energy being that is part
of the larger world, all of us have a definite relationship with all
the energies around us that exist on the planet Earth —and those
beyond. It is an elementary fact of physics that all bodies in an
energy field resonate with that field. An amoeba resonates just
as each cell in the human body does. Such atomic and cellular
resonances, in my view, represent the essence of health of a
being.

I will illustrate this concept with a simple example. The
surface of a healthy cell resonates with a weak negative surface
charge of about -3 microvolts. A cancer cell, by contrast, is
highly charged and resonates with a much higher charge that
may reach a value of -200 to -250 microvolts. In a type of
treatment I call tumor potential restoration (TPR), I apply a
positive electrode to the surface of a malignant tumor and
regularly observe the charge to change within seconds —as
electrons fly towards the surface of the tumor and then to the
electrode with the speed near that of light. Similar energy
dynamics, reflecting changes in molecular and cellular
resonances, take place in all heathy cells during metabolism and

in abnormal cells in other disease states, though we cannot observe them with available technology. I am confident that future advances in physical energy technologies will allow us to observe and document other examples of molecular and cellular resonances.

But, what is the source of such resonance? We may call it solar radiation, stellar radiation, cosmic or geomagnetic waves, or by any other name. I concede that the core energy aspects of that *presence* are—and I believe, will always remain—unknowable. All the technology of humankind has not—and I believe, will never fully—explain the essence of those energies. No doubt we will learn more about aspects of that *presence* as our technology advances. But my strong sense is that no matter how much our science advances, we will never know the essentially unknowable aspects of that *presence*. Thus, I come full circle back to where I started —that we humans must accept the spiritual as beyond the reach of our physical senses and intellectual capacity.

The element about the health of cell and plasma membranes in my definition of health may seem tedious to some readers. In the following passage, which is an excerpt from the companion volume, *RDA: Rats, Drugs and Assumptions,* I present a conceptual framework for what I call EM medicine.

The essence of EM medicine is to seek a genuine understanding of the energetic-molecular dynamics of cells before the cells are injured, and not on our notions of cellular injury as seen through a microscope after the injury has occurred. All nondrug, restorative therapies that I use to reverse chronic disease, and describe in this series of books, are based on EM dynamics of health. This model of clinical medicine promotes health with natural therapies that revive injured bowel, blood and cellular ecosystems.

It is not uncommon for me to hear mainstream doctors criticize holistic physicians for their "unscientific" methods. They consider all drug therapies scientific and scornfully dismiss all nondrug, empirical therapies as forms of quackery. The truth is that empiricism in medicine is a valid science. Empirical medicine relies on sound clinical observations —and observation, of course, is the purest of all sciences. Thus, it is far more scientific to base one's restorative therapies on a genuine understanding of bowel, blood and cellular ecosystems than to simply suppress symptoms of diseases with drugs. Sick humans are not mere bits of bowel to be examined with a microscope, nor are they slices of diseased skin to be covered with steroid creams. It is far more scientific to consider a sick person as a whole organism in stress and holistically address all the issues of his illness rather than test for one or two hormone levels in the blood and prescribe replacement hormonal therapy.

Drug medicine essentially is a medicine that blocks human energy, detoxification and digestive-absorptive enzyme systems. Drugs, as useful as they might be in the management of acute illnesses, block normal healing processes —and, hence, do not constitute a true solution to problems caused by damaged body ecosystems. Furthermore, drugs, as we all recognize, eventually lose their effectiveness as human metabolic enzymes devise new ways to bypass their blockade.

WHAT HEALTH IS NOT

Health is not the mere absence of disease. Health has nothing to do with the whimsical notions of RDAs (Recommended Daily Allowances) to prevent a handful of nutrient-deficiency syndromes, nor is it the "balanced diets" prescribed by doctors who practice drug medicine and consider nutritional medicine quackery.

Health is not the euphoria of eating, nor is it the denial of dieting. Health is not preoccupation with recycling past miseries, nor is it pre-cycling feared, future misery. Health is not living with regrets, nor is it an obsession with control in life.

So why do mainstream physicians shun the subject of health? The answer is really quite simple: *None of the essential aspects of health defined in this chapter can be addressed with drugs.* There are no drugs that make us spiritual or bring us gratitude and freedom from anger. There are no drugs that teach us the limbic language of silence or extinguish the oxidative fires of stress. Drugs cannot revive injured energy enzymes, nor can they repair damaged detoxification enzymes. There are no synthetic chemicals that can upregulate energy and fat-burning enzymes. Drugs cannot restore a damaged bowel ecosystem nor can they strengthen a weakened blood ecosystem. Drugs cannot normalize disrupted EM dynamics of the cell and plasma membranes.

Injured tissues heal with nutrients, not with drugs. Indeed, the tools of modern medicine—drugs and surgical scalpels—are singularly ineffective in coping with the stressors of life today and in promoting health.

The First Path:
Spirituality Through Silence

The true answer to the problem of stress is spirituality—not psychology. Stress is an integral part of the essential injury-healing-injury cycle of life. Both injury and healing are spontaneous phenomena. Healing is not an intellectual function, because the mind cannot order healing in injured tissues. The thinking mind—the cortical monkey in autoregulation language—endlessly recycles past misery. And when that is not enough, the mind precycles the fear of future misery. The cortical monkey thrives on doubt. It embellishes fear. Relentless recycling of past pain or feared, future suffering can drive body tissues into rebellions, but it cannot coax rebellious tissues to function in healthy ways.

Psychology is no substitute for spirituality. The ancient notion of the mind-body-spirit trio is this: Whatever can be experienced with the physical senses or perceived by the mind cannot be spiritual. For the spiritual to be discrete from the body and the mind, it must be beyond the reach of either. One cannot reach the spiritual by seeing, smelling or hearing—or by superior thinking. Indeed, if that were true, there would be no need for the trio. The popular press is infatuated with the mind-body connection! Has it lost sight, then, of the third element?

How does one go about searching for the spiritual? One doesn't.

The spiritual involves surrendering in silence to the larger *presence* that surrounds and permeates each of us. Why is silence essential? Because sights, smells and other sensory perceptions are aspects of the physical body—and language is the mind's turf. Clever thinking, alas, is just that: thinking. And thinking, as I write above, is not spiritual. Consequently, a thinking mind cannot be banished with clever words.

In the chapter, Is There Another Door, I suggest some simple ways to escape the tyranny of the thinking mind—the relentless clutter of the cortical monkey. What that monkey cannot cope with is the silent energy of the spiritual. Specifically, I make two suggestions that I have found to be clinically useful: meditation with the silence of a candle flame in winter and with the silence of a stone during summer. For further details about these two methods, I refer the reader to the chapter, Is There Another Door? In essence, with these simple approaches to meditative silence, one lets either the flame of a candle or the mellow color of a stone to lead him to perceive one's essential link with the larger *presence*. These simple approaches are usually far more rewarding—and revealing—than an elaborate ritual. The *Holy Quran* puts it thusly:

Paradise is nearer to you than the thongs of your sandal.

I have seen few exceptions to the clinical value of silence: for example, the early phases of severe anxiety states, frequent panic attacks and depression. Metabolic roller coasters in anxiety and panic disorders may make silence unbearable during meditation. In that case the practice of saying the rosary and mantras, chanting or listening to spiritual music often helps to reduce the inner turmoil that can make silence suffocating.

Depression is a serious disorder of neuronal and neurotransmitter function, which is frequently made worse by metabolic roller coasters. In many cases meditative silence initially exaggerates these malfunctions. Here again, healing sounds can be of great value during the initial stages. After they are stabilized, I strongly urge my patients with anxiety-panic disorders and depression to learn the profoundly healing practice of silence. Indeed, in my clinical experience positive long-term results for such disorders cannot be obtained without persistent and prolonged spiritual work.

The Second Path:
Spirituality Through Service

Some of my patients have taught me an important
lesson: Reaching out to others can be a powerful healing
influence for the sufferer himself. Again, in the chapter entitled,
Is There Another Door, I suggest several ways to do so, such as
helping an elderly person with ordinary chores, befriending a
sick child or being kind to an animal. This path to healing is
especially therapeutic for those who are very sick and have been
so for long periods of time.

> *The reward for reaching out to someone in
> need is not what one receives for it but what
> one* becomes *by it.*

The essence of reaching out to someone in this context
is simply a matter of being with the sick or needy. Certainly,
what doesn't work is telling a seriously ill or a severely
depressed person to cheer up.

Sometimes I hear visitors at hospital wards ask questions
that reveal a morbid curiosity about the patient's prognosis.
Family members of cancer patients often tell me about the
number of months or years the ill person is expected to live. Of
course, they have obtained such information from the patient's
doctor. It amazes me that there are physicians who are so

insensitive—and ignorant—as to make predictions about who will live and for how long. As for the family members and friends, their morbid curiosity about the precise dating of death seldom remains shielded from the sick.

There is a profound irony in this. What comforts the sick and suffering most are compassion and empathy, and there is no better way to express that than with silent presence. A visitor's curiosity about the nature of the sickness may be offensive to the sick. What the ill person needs most is to be with someone who can comfort him by his presence, and who is available to be spoken to, if and when the sick person wishes to do so.

****

A true gift of service is the gift of presence, and the essence of that presence is listening to what goes unspoken.

The Third Path:
Gratitude, Not Happiness

Happiness is an illusion. That is one reason why no two people ever agree on what constitutes happiness. No matter how one chooses to define happiness, it is an empty notion—now you have it, now you don't. Few things make people more unhappy than the search for happiness.

The best reason for practicing gratitude that I know is that it makes getting out of the bed in the morning less demanding. For others, it makes the morning hours a profoundly spiritual time.

Practicing gratitude does not require elaborate rituals or travel to exotic places. It can be practiced anywhere, at any time. It requires neither outside support nor special inner capacity. I have seen patients live with profound gratitude even as they suffer a progressive paralysis of body muscles caused by multiple sclerosis or amyotrophic lateral sclerosis. I know many young people who are incarcerated at home with disabling chronic fatigue, yet they are grateful for simply being alive. I also know chronically ill and angry patients for whom the word gratitude is a cruel joke. They rage, without quite understanding why they are consumed by overwhelming resentment. For the former group, gratitude is a river that flows endlessly, neither revealing its true origin nor its destiny. For the latter, gratitude is an impenetrable wall.

How does one practice gratitude? How does one learn to know, trust and surrender to the larger *presence* that surrounds and permeates each of us at all times—the divinity within each human being? There are, of course, no simple prescriptions. First and foremost, one must learn to live with the essential insecurity of life. What is freedom? To the extent that human beings can be free, it is the freedom from the need to be free that sets us free. To the extent that we can feel secure, it is the recognition that there can be no complete security in life. Thus, freedom and security are the gifts we receive when we learn to trust that larger *presence.*

How does one become aware of that *presence*? Natural beauty requires no endorsement from mere mortals. Yet when we see a sun lowering behind crimson clouds, we speak of the magnificence of that scene. Then we try to *do justice* to that scene. But does that magnificence really need our endorsement? Does the *presence* in that magnificence really need us to do justice to it? We look at the snow-capped peaks of a tall mountain and excitedly talk about its stunning grandeur. We strive to do justice to it. But does the *presence* in that mountain really need our justice? We witness the innocent beauty of a wildflower, marvel at it, then seek words to do justice to it. Does the *presence* in that wildflower require any justification from us to be? How did we get so messed up? How did we get so infatuated with ourselves? And with the notion that sunsets, mountains and wildflowers need our approval for their existence?

How does one become aware of that *presence*? I return
to the question. We cannot do so by doing justice to that
presence. Rather, we need to let that *presence* do justice to us,
approve and endorse our existence. It takes a certain innocence
free from the cortical clutter to know that *presence* in that
sunset, that mountain peak and that windflower. That is the
simple way.

The energy of that *presence* surrounds and permeates us,
just as geomagnetic fields do. We can discern the magnetic
fields only when we open ourselves to them with appropriate
sensors. It is a crude analogy, but to be aware of that *presence*
we also need to open ourselves. Then we don't need stunning
sunsets or lofty mountain peaks to become aware of that
presence. We can do so just as well by looking at dust particles
shining in the shaft of light entering a room through a window,
or through the dim flame of a candle reflected in a rusty door
knob. *That awareness is the gratitude that sets us free*. So it
follows that we can receive all the freedom and security we
need through the light reflected from a door knob—or, when
walking on a sidewalk, by the light absorbed in a shriveled dry
leaf that the wind might blow toward us.

Gratitude may be practiced anywhere, anytime, through
any trivial object—for there is divinity in all trivia just as there is
divinity is each of us.

****

*We can know only as much divinity as exists
within us.*

The Fourth Path:
Control of Metabolic Roller Coasters

Many people live on metabolic roller coasters. Some are on sugar-insulin roller coasters, while others suffer adrenaline-cholinergic roller coasters. Biology, I write earlier, is a kaleidoscopic mosaic. Sugar-insulin-adrenaline roller coasters trigger neurotransmitter roller coasters, resulting in anxiety, headaches, lightheadedness, heart palpitations and panic attacks. Many patients describe electric shocks in their muscles and skulls. Many women live with PMS, wild mood swings and hot flashes caused by estrogen-progesterone-adrenaline roller coasters. Yet others are tormented by neurotransmitter roller coasters. In my clinical work, I consider the elimination of such roller coasters a primary goal.

CONTROL OF SUGAR-INSULIN-ADRENALINE ROLLER COASTERS IN THE MORNING

Sugar dysfunction is the primary threat to human health today. I devote the chapter, Lions, Hypoglycemia and Insulin Roller Coasters, to an in-depth discussion of this subject. The best way to preserve the integrity of carbohydrate metabolism is to protect it from large and sudden sugar overloads. For this purpose, I recommend the following for breakfast: Take one and one-half heaping tablespoons of a suitable soy, milk, egg or rice protein formula with abundant amounts of fluids, such as organic vegetable juices, in the mornings. If deemed desirable, the taste of this formula may be changed by adding small amounts of fruit juice or club soda. I discuss this subject at length in my series of videos outlining programs for weight control, management of hypoglycemia and nutrition for a healthy life span. (These videos are available from Life Span Videos at 201-586-9191.)

I drink 16 or more ounces of water with nutrient supplements the first thing each morning. For my own breakfast, I put one and one-half heaping tablespoons of soy or rice protein powder in 8 ounces of organic vegetable juice, then add another 8 ounces of water. Such fluid intake assures me a state of overhydration and obviates any need for coffee or tea. Readers may wish to add a piece of fruit to their protein drink for additional support or add small amounts of fruit juices or natural carbonated waters to change the taste of the protein drink. I include additional information about the composition of protein protocols later in this chapter.

CONTROL OF SUGAR-INSULIN-ADRENALINE ROLLER COASTERS IN THE EVENINGS

I protect the carbohydrate metabolism of my patients during afternoon and evening hours with prescriptions for supplemental cold-pressed essential oils to be taken *cold*. Specifically, I prescribe two or three tablespoons of one of the oils included in my list of recommended oils an hour or so before dinner. The oil may be taken with steamed vegetables (cooled to avoid oxidation of essential oils), salads, goat or sheep cheese, a small amount of grapefruit juice, or simply taken alone.

ESSENTIAL OILS ARE NOT FATTENING

Essential, unoxidized oils speed up fat metabolism. This is a widely misunderstood aspect of human metabolism. Essential oils provide a steady-state source of energy, and prevent sugar-insulin-adrenaline roller coasters. Other clinical benefits of essential oils include their value in the prevention and management of the following disorders:

1. Coronary artery heart disease and other vascular disorders.
2. Various types of arthritis including rheumatoid arthritis, lyme arthritis, psoriatic arthritis.
3. Skin disorders such as dryness, eczema, atopic dermatitis and psoriasis.
4. Dry eyes syndrome and other types of chronic eye irritations.
5. Asthma and other chronic lung disorders.
6. Immune disorders.
7. PMS and other hormonal disorders.

Why should essential oils be beneficial in such diverse clinical disorders? What is the common denominator? The simple answer is that all cell membranes need essential oils for their structural and functional integrity. And the health of any cell, tissue or organ cannot be preserved without healthy cell membranes —hence, the clinical efficacy of essential oils in diverse clinical disorders. I discuss this important issue at length in the companion volume, *RDA: Rats, Drugs and Assumptions.*

LIST OF RECOMMENDED COLD-PRESSED OILS	
Extra virgin olive oil	Flaxseed oil
Sesame oil	Grapeseed oil
Avocado oil	Pumpkin oil
Safflower oil	Canola oil
Garlic oil	Cod liver oil*

* Cod liver oil is very rich in vitamin A, and I recommend that it be taken in a small dose of 1 teaspoonful once a week. An exception to that general recommendation is the control of acute viral infections when cod liver oil may be taken in larger amounts and for longer periods of time such as 5 to 7 days.

RECOMMENDATIONS FOR OIL ROTATION

I recommend to my patients that they obtain any two oils from the above list and take them on alternate days. After finishing the first two oils, they purchase the next two oils from the list and so on. Such a rotation plan assures an excellent mix of oils and one need not worry about the adequacy of supply of omega-3, omega-6 and omega-9 groups of fatty acids.

I prefer the essential oil supplementation program outlined above to the traditional way of prescribing one or more oils in capsules for three main reasons:

1. Supplemental oils taken cold with steamed (and cooled) vegetables and salads can make a delicious meal.

2. Three tablespoons of such oils equal 20 or more of the generally available oil capsules, and ingestion of such a large number of oils is cumbersome.

3. The cost of such oil supplementation is usually less than equivalent amounts of other choices, such as evening primrose oil, borage oil and black current oil.

CONTROL OF HORMONE ROLLER COASTERS

For eliminating hormonal roller coasters, I find a combination of folic acid (5 to 15 mg), DHEA (25 to 100 mg) and a progesterone skin cream derived from wild yams effective for most of my patients. Some other natural therapies that I use in rotation include dong quai, black and blue cohosh, licorice, false unicorn root, fennel and sarsparrilla. I include additional comments about this important subject later in this chapter.

Ample but judicious prescriptions for minerals and vitamin supplements are also needed for controlling metabolic roller coasters. These micronutrients are essential for promoting a steady-state metabolism of proteins and fats, and for preventing sugar roller coasters. Again, I state my recommendations for nutritional and herbal support for chronic stress later in this chapter.

The Fifth Path:
Preserving the Integrity of the Bowel, Blood and Other Body Ecosystems

Human antioxidant and immune defenses are plants rooted in the soil of the bowel contents. The bowel ecosystem is as diverse and delicate as any other in nature. It interfaces with the outside world on one side and with the blood ecosystem on the other. The blood ecology, in turn, integrates with liver, kidney and brain ecosystems. Human health, in essence, is a dynamic ecologic equilibrium among the various body organ ecosystems.

Few things are as distressing as seeing little children who live on antibiotics. In so doing, food and mold allergies that set them up for recurrent infections go unrecognized. Their delicate bowel ecosystems are battered repeatedly with broad-spectrum antibiotics that violate their antioxidant defenses. When their oxidative metabolism causes behavior and learning difficulties, school psychologists promptly label them with hyperactivity and attention deficit disorders, or refer them to their pediatricians who readily oblige the psychologists with Ritalin prescriptions.

Many women suffering from severely battered vaginal and urinary ecosystems are prescribed one course of antibiotics after another. The symptoms caused by such ecologic disruptions are vigorously suppressed with yet additional doctors. Not infrequently, they are completely unaware of the true nature of their suffering. I discuss these subjects at length in the companion volume, *RDA: Rats, Drugs and Assumptions.* Attempts to resolve issues of stress with therapies based on the prevailing—and simplistic—fight-or-flight notion of stress are bound to fail, and they do.

Similarly, there are important ecologic considerations affecting home and work environments. I refer readers interested in this subject to the companion volume, *The Canary and Chronic Fatigue.*

Since health is ecologic equilibrium, it can only be preserved with ecologic thinking. Until mainstream physicians learn to think ecologically, people who suffer chronic stress have no choice but to learn about ecologic balances in the body and how to preserve them.

The Sixth Path:
Rejection of Diagnostic Labels that Tell Us Nothing About the Nature of Suffering, but Hide Much.

Every day in my clinical practice I see patients who are tortured by meaningless diagnostic labels. Their physicians use those labels to justify the use of symptom-suppressing drugs. Those diagnostic labels reveal nothing about the true cause of their suffering. Yet the patients remain trapped in stress-causing disease modes of thinking.

I see chronic fatigue sufferers tormented with yet another diagnostic label of neurally-mediated hypotension (NMH). They are prescribed steroids and drugs that affect the heart activity without any regard to the stressors that overdrive the heart. Their allergic triggers go unrecognized and unmanaged. They live on sugar-insulin-adrenaline roller coasters, but such metabolic stressors are never addressed. Their battered bowel ecosystems are further battered with antibiotics —the simmering oxidative coals in their blood continue to damage cell membranes of blood corpuscles and cook enzymes, hormones and proteins just as the white of an egg is cooked when it is boiled. The NMH gurus never bother to ask the simple question: What injures the autonomic receptors of people who suffer from NMH? They contemptuously dismiss the possibility of such injury by environmental pollutants. Or by unmitigated oxidative stress of unrelenting adrenergic overdrive. It is sad because a physician could recognize the underlying cause with a mere drop of patient's blood and some skill with a microscope.

Disruptions of urinary ecosystems occur as consequences of battered bowel ecosystems—except in uncommon cases of structural obstructive lesions of the bladder and related organs. I see little girls who suffer from repeated urinary infections and young women who are given the label of interstitial cystitis for similar problems. They are given repeated courses of antibiotics that further damage their delicate ecosystems. When that doesn't work—and why would it?—they undergo urethral dilatations in operating rooms. Their pediatricians and urologists completely ignore all issues of antibiotic abuse, food and mold allergy, overgrowth of yeast and disease-causing bacteria in the bowel, and parasitic infestations.

Hyperactivity and attention deficit disorders are almost always associated with food allergy, mold sensitivity and digestive-absorptive dysfunctions of the bowel. Such individuals crave sugar and suffer wide mood swings caused by sugar-insulin-adrenaline roller coasters. School psychologists are only too eager to provide suitable diagnostic labels and the pediatricians are prompt in dispensing Ritalin, Cylert and dexidrine. Neither the psychologists nor pediatrician seem to have any sense of the nutritional deficits that feed those disorders, nor of the relevant allergic triggers.

I see patients who are troubled by a cardiologist's diagnosis of mitral valve prolapse, while the real problem is a heart overdriven by sugar-insulin-adrenaline roller coasters. In the chapter, Lions, Hypoglycemia and Insulin Roller Coasters, I describe the true nature of mitral valve prolapse in patients without structural damage to the valve. Training in effective methods of self-regulation is too cumbersome for cardiologists. Why waste time teaching anyone breathing methods to relieve the symptoms when beta blockers can be doled out so conveniently?

Coronary heart disease is caused by oxidative injury to intima (cells lining the arteries) and connective tissue (collagen and other substances that hold intima cells together as mortar holds bricks). Cholesterol is an innocent bystander molecule in the saga of coronary disease. No one has ever described any mechanisms by which cholesterol —a weak antioxidant —can inflict oxidative injury to vessel walls. But cholesterol cats—the money men of cholesterol industry—are not troubled by such questions. They know there is much money to be made by selling cholesterol-lowering drugs. Predictably such drugs do not work. But, that doesn't matter either. Cholesterol cats have enough money to hire drug doctors and fly them everywhere singing the cholesterol songs of their drug masters. How many people suffer heart disease while worrying about their cholesterol numbers? Cholesterol cats are not interested in that question either.

I see patients who have been prescribed antianxiety drugs for stress without any attempt to understand the underlying cause. I see patients given drugs for gastritis and irritable bowel syndrome without any consideration to the issues of disrupted gastric and bowel ecology. The list of such symptom-suppressing labels is a long one.

I see people for whom the diagnostic labels are more tormenting than their violated bowel and gastric ecosystems. The same happens for sufferers of sinusitis, chronic headaches, PMS, chronic fatigue and many other ailments.

I provide detailed explanations of the energetic-molecular events that create specific stress patterns in various chapters of this volume. I suggest the reader consider a second reading of selected chapters to feel comfortable with the scientific underpinnings of the health-disease (dis-ease) continuum that I address in this book. For this purpose, I recommend the following chapters: 1) Stress and the Fourth-of-July Chemistry; 2) Lions, Hypoglycemia and Insulin Roller Coasters; 3) Adrenergic Hypervigilance, Mitral Valve Prolapse, Dysautonomia and Chronic Fatigue Syndrome; and 4) Anxiety, Lactic Acid and Limbic Lions. I refer the professional reader to my book *Nutritional Medicine: Part I—Intravenous and Intramuscular Therapies.*

The Seventh Path:
Optimal Hydration, and Nutrient and Herbal Support of Body Ecosystems.

When injured tissues heal, they heal with nutrients not with drugs. This is self-evident and holds true for all the ecologic disruptions I refer to in this volume.

I introduce the subjects of optimal hydration and supplemental nutrient and herbal support at the end of this chapter for a specific reason. For many people, popping vitamin and herbal pills seem to be an easy remedy for stress. But it doesn't work that way.

Buckets of water are not sufficient for saving a house on fire. Similarly, a tablet or two of multivitamins and herbal pills cannot extinguish the leaping oxidative flames of a Fourth-of-July chemistry. What is needed is a deep visceral-intuitive stillness that lifts one to higher spiritual states.

With that cautionary note, I include below brief comments about the optimal state of hydration and lists of vitamins, minerals, essential amino and fatty acids and herbs that I have found to be of special value in the management of chronic stress and anxiety. Again, I prescribe nutrients to prevent metabolic roller coasters that feed other stress responses. I provide detailed information about the mechanisms of action of most of these agents in the companion volumes, *The Butterfly and Life Span Nutrition* and *The Canary and Chronic Fatigue.* I refer the professional reader to *Nutritional Medicine Part I: Intramuscular and Intravenous Therapies.*

STATE OF OPTIMAL HYDRATION

My patients who lead stressful lives frequently complain that they need to drink large quantities of fluids to take their prescribed nutrients and herbs. I tell them that is good news. If nutrient protocols force them to increase their water intake, so much the better!

Water is an essential macronutrient. Water is nature's best diuretic. It is the most efficient detoxifying agent in the human metabolism. Water is the simplest solution to acidotic overload in conditions of stress. Water can significantly reduce the stress of allergic and sensitivity reactions. Water is the cheapest diluent for environmental pollutants. Need we search for more reasons to benefit from an ample intake of water—the miracle substance of all life?

The simplest and most effective practical measure for reducing the excessive acidotic—and oxidative—stress on biology in chronic stress is to dilute and eliminate the acidotic—and oxidative—molecules with increased fluid intake. Parenthetically, one of the fundamental changes of the general aging process is cellular aging. Aged cells are shrunken and dehydrated. Chronic stress is clearly a state of accelerated molecular and cellular aging. A state of overhydration is not only desirable, but necessary. One-third of kidney disease in the United States is considered to be iatrogenic —caused by prescription drugs. Three major culprits are nonsteroidal anti-inflammatory painkillers, antibiotics such as aminoglycosides and contrast media used for scans and x-rays. The simplest safeguard against such kidney damage when taking drugs is optimal hydration.

I recommend a six-ounce glass of suitable fluid every three hours. Frequent urination is a very small price to pay for upregulated energy enzymes. I refer the reader interested in further information about this critical subject to the companion volume *The Butterfly and Life Span Nutrition.*

MELATONIN FOR SLEEP

Melatonin is an excellent choice in promoting natural, deep sleep for people with sleep disorders. It is a natural hormone produced in the pineal gland during the night hours and normally assures restful sleep during the dark hours. I usually prescribe a small initial dose of 1.5 milligram to be taken at bedtime. Such a dose may be repeated during the early hours of the morning if found necessary. If a small dose is not effective, I recommend larger doses of 3 to 10 milligrams.

Notwithstanding the furor over melatonin use created by the media, with extensive experience, I have not found any adverse effects of melatonin when used in the above-mentioned doses. Furthermore, in recommended doses, there is no serious potential for increasing autoimmune injury as is believed by some. Melatonin plays a role in the regulation of thyroid function. It provides a counterbalance to the estrogen overload which most American women are subjected to with prescriptions for synthetic hormones and xenoestrogens (environmental pollutants with estrogen-like effects). I discuss this important subject at length in the companion volume, *RDA: Rats, Drugs and Assumptions*.

NUTRIENT AND HERBAL SUPPORT FOR STRESS

Below, I include lists many of the vitamins, minerals and herbal protocols which I have found to be useful for restoring the abnormal chemistry of stress in my clinical practice. I do so to provide the reader with some general information about my clinical approach to stress, and not to recommend any specific therapies for any specific health disorders. Books such as this are no substitutes for experienced professionals.

CAUTION
I do not recommend that any reader should attempt to manage his specific health disorder with any of the protocols outlined in this volume. For that purpose, I strongly urge the reader to obtain advice from an experienced clinician.

IMPORTANT NUTRIENTS AND HERBS FOR STRESS		
VITAMINS	**MINERALS**	**HERBS**
B_5 (pyridoxine)	Calcium	Anise
B_6 (pantetheine)	Chromium	Chamomile, Catnip
B_{12} (cobalamine)	Magnesium	Ginkgo biloba
C (Ascorbic acid)	Molybdenum	Passion flower
Choline, Inositol and methionine	Potassium	Skullcap St. John's Wort
Niacin	Selenium	Valerian
Taurine & Others	Zinc	Wild yam

Vitamin B complex, vitamin C and lipotropic factors (choline, inositol and methionine) play many essential roles in the chemistry of stress responses. I discuss these beneficial roles fully in the companion volume, *The Butterfly and Life Span Nutrition*. I describe the desirable effects of magnesium, potassium and taurine later in this chapter. Here I make some brief comments about personal experience with the herbs I choose to include in the table.

First and foremost, it is important to use herbs in moderate doses and in rotation. *All herbs become drugs if used in large doses and for long periods of time.* Indeed, historically most drugs were isolated from herbs and plant sources.

Valerian root in doses of 400 to 1,000 milligrams taken at bedtime enhanced the quality of sleep for most of my patients. For patients with severe stress, anxiety and depression, I prescribe 400 to 500 milligrams two or three times during the day. If necessary, I add melatonin in doses of 1.5 to 10 milligrams to promote restorative sleep. (Also see the note about melatonin below.)

Chamomile taken as tea or in capsule form is helpful in chronic stress and anxiety states. It may be safely added to prescriptions for valerian. I usually prescribe two cups of tea or a capsule containing 250 to 400 milligrams once or twice daily.

St. John's wort and Ginkgo biloba in doses of 250 to 500 milligrams, two or three times a day, are valuable additions to my total program for the management of unrelenting chronic stress and depression.

Passion flower, catnip and skullcap are mild herbs that have been extensively used for managing irritability, anxiety and stress. I sometimes prescribe these herbs in combination and rotation with others included in the above table.

Anise (licorice) is useful for adrenal support. However, this herb should be used only under close supervision of an experienced clinician, especially when used by people with a history of high blood pressure.

Hormonal imbalances almost always occur in chronic stress. Estrogenic overload, in my view, is one of the primary health hazards facing American women. I recommend 10 to 15 milligrams of folic acid to prevent troublesome hot flushes and other estrogen-related symptoms. A natural progesterone preparation, such as one derived from Mexican wild yam is valuable for providing a counterbalance to estrogenic overload. I usually recommend the application of one-third to one-fourth teaspoon of natural progesterone cream to the skin of the upper chest or face at bed time for a period of two weeks before the menstrual period. For postmenopausal women, I recommend the use progesterone cream during the last two weeks of the month.

COMPOSITION OF NUTRIENT PROTOCOLS

The following are the compositions (per tablet or capsule) and dose schedules of nutrient protocols that I prescribe in my practice for chronic stress. I provide this information as general information for the reader, not as specific prescriptions for treating specific health disorders.

VITAMIN C PROTOCOL	
Vitamin C (niascorbate)	750 mg
Vitamin C (calcium ascorbate)	250 mg
Bioflavonoids (citrus)	50 mg
TPM PROTOCOL	
Magnesium (carbonate, sulfate)	150 mg
Potassium (citrate)	50 mg
Taurine	250 mg
TAURINE PROTOCOL	
Taurine	500 mg

I usually prescribe a daily dose of 3 or 4 tablets of Vitamin C protocol as a part of my general program of nutrient supplements for healthy individuals as well as for my patients with chronic stress. My recommendations for patients with chronic stress for daily doses of TPM and Taurine Protocols are two tablets of each protocol.

TPM protocol is one of my key nutrient protocols for stalling oxidative cell membrane injury in chronic stress states. Oxidant injury pokes holes in the cell membrane —and for that matter, in the plasma membranes of cellular organelles —and causes "leaky cell membrane syndrome." (I coin this term to humor my colleagues who thrive on inventing diagnostic labels.)

The SAD (standard American diet) is in a sad state indeed. It makes us potassium-poor, magnesium-deficient and taurine-depleted. Thus, I've found my TPM Protocol to be valuable in clinical practice. This formulation is also effective for regulating bowel transit time and managing cases of chronic constipation.

Taurine —an antioxidant, and my favorite for reasons given below—is present in all cells and has been ascribed many protective roles in the brain, heart and kidney cells. On one of my office walls I have hung a large, complex chart that shows innumerable metabolic pathways and interrelationships among various amino acids with unidirectional, bidirectional and multidirectional arrows. Some time ago, my eyes wandered over that chart before settling on taurine. I noticed something that I never had before: The taurine box showed arrows coming in from different directions —cysteine, cysteic acid and hypotaurine —but no arrow going out. Why would that be? I wondered. Why would nature design pathways like that if not to ensure that other amino acids were to be used to produce taurine, but taurine was to be reserved for some higher function?

ANTIOXIDANT PROTOCOL	
Vitamin A (acetate)	2,500 IU
Beta carotene	2,500 IU
Vitamin C (calcium salt)	200 mg
Vitamin E	100 IU
Bioflavonoids (citrus)	100 mg
Choline bitartrate	40 mg
Zinc (gluconate)	5 mg
Selenium (sodium)	50 mcg
Taurine	100 mg
L-Methionine	40 mg
L-Cysteine hydrochloride	270 mg
L-Glutathione (reduced)	25 mg
N-Acetyl-L-Cysteine	25 mg

I generally recommend one or two tablets daily of the above antioxidant protocol initially. After a satisfactory clinical response, I generally reduce the dose to one tablet daily.

ANTISTRESS PROTOCOL	
Vitamin B_1	30 mg
Vitamin B_2	30 mg
Niacin	150 mg
Pantothenic acid	30 mg
Pyridoxine	220 mg
Folic acid	400 mcg
Vitamin B_{12}	200 mcg
Vitamin C	100 mg
Vitamin E	100 IU
Biotin	100 mcg
Choline	50 mg
Inositol	50 mg
Magnesium (oxide)	25 mg
Zinc (chelate)	4 mg
Manganese	10 mg
Potassium (citrate)	2 mg
L-Phenylalanine	100 mg
L-Tyrosine	75 mg

I usually recommend two tablets of the above antistress

formulations for my patients with chronic stress. If I find it necessary to consider additional nutrient support to alleviate anxiety, stress, sleep difficulty and panic attacks, I usually add one of the herbs mentioned earlier in this section.

MINERAL PROTOCOL	
Magnesium	175 mg
Potassium	35 mg
Zinc	7.5 mg
Manganese	5 mg
Calcium	75 mg
Copper	0.75 mg
Iodine	50 mcg
Chromium	100 mcg
Boron	1 mg
Molybdenum	50 mcg
Selenium	3 mcg
Vanadium	50 mcg
Phosphorus	70 mg
Vitamin D_3	75 IU

I usually recommend three tablets of the above mineral formulation to be taken with the evening meal.

PANTOTHENIC PROTOCOL	
Pantothenic acid	165 mg
Pantetheine	100 mg
Folic acid	50 mcg
PABA	5 mg
Potassium (citrate)	2 mg
L-Arginine	25 mg
L-Histidine	25 mg
L-Ornithine	5 mg
Aloe	5 mg
Licorice root (GLGE)*	50 mg
Spirulina	20 mg
* Deglycerrizinated	

     I usually prescribe two tablets of this formulation for all of my patients. Like the TPM protocol, this is also one of my staple nutrient protocols. There are three main reasons: 1) Pantothenic acid and pantetheine play critical roles in energy enzyme pathways and are necessary for production of acetyl Co-A, which is an important molecule in the release of chemical bond energy of foods during metabolism; 2) these two micronutrients are essential for many detoxification pathways; and 3) these vitamins, along with vitamin B_{12}, are among the principal growth factors for the health-promoting bowel flora. The bowel, of course, is where all immune battles are fought—and won or lost—in the body.

CAL-MAG PROTOCOL	
Calcium (carbonate, citrate)	240 mg
Magnesium (carbonate, sulfate)	240 mg
Vitamin D_3	50 IU

I prescribe one or two tablets of this protocol for most of my patients. The case for supplemental calcium for the prevention of osteoporosis has been grossly overstated by the dairy industry. As I indicate earlier, my patients benefit much more from larger amounts of supplemental magnesium than calcium, and so I often prescribe magnesium and calcium in rations of 2:1 or 3:1. Indeed, I have seen reversal of osteoporosis with an increase in bone density obtained with magnesium and calcium supplementation in such ratios given along with wild yam progesterone.

On the other hand, I do not agree with nutritionists who hold that calcium should not be given along with magnesium because these two minerals compete with each other in some cell membrane functions. While it is true that magnesium is nature's calcium channel blocker, it is important to recognize that when two elements function closely with each other in human metabolism, the clinical results are superior when both are administered together, albeit one in much larger amounts than the other. The same holds for zinc and copper and some other micronutrients. For instance, the most common abnormality I see in mineral analysis in my practice is a deficiency of copper associated with an excess of zinc—no doubt due to the common practice of taking supplemental zinc and ignoring copper.

PROTEIN & PEPTIDE PROTOCOLS

Peptides are hydrolyzed or partially digested proteins. I use three protein and peptide formulations in my clinical practice and prescribe one or more of the same for all of my patients. I recommend that they take one and one-half heaping tablespoons of one of the three protocols with organic vegetable juices or other suitable nonsugar liquid in the morning for breakfast. As I indicate earlier in this chapter, this practice is extremely effective for eliminating troublesome sugar-insulin-adrenaline roller coasters as well as in providing all essential amino acids for the production of enzymes, hormones and structural proteins in the body. All three protocols contain about 90% of their calories in amino acids.

Except in cases of food allergy, I recommend that they rotate these protein formulations as follows:

Protein & Peptide I	Once weekly
Protein & Peptide II	Twice weekly
Protein & Peptide III	Three times weekly

     The rationale for my recommendation is as follows: Protocol I is derived from milk and egg protein and hence is most desirable from the standpoint of its amino acids diversity. However, the high frequency of food allergy in my practice makes this formulation less desirable. Protocol III is derived from rice proteins and is the least desirable from the standpoint of amino acid diversity. However, it is best tolerated by allergic individuals. Protocol II, derived from soybean, falls in between the other two, both for diversity of its amino acid content and allergenicity. Following are compositions of my three protein and peptide formulations per heaping tablespoon.

PROTEIN AND PEPTIDE PROTOCOL I	
Protein & Peptides, egg & milk	19.5 gm
Carbohydrates	2.0 gm
Fats	0.2 gm
Calories	84
PROTEIN AND PEPTIDE PROTOCOL II	
Protein & Petides, soybean	17.4 gm
Carbohydrates	less than 2 gm
Fats	less than 0.2 gm
calories	53

PROTEIN & PEPTIDE PROTOCOL III	
Protein & Peptide, rice	19 gms
Carbohydrates	2.5 gms
Fats	0.3 gms
Calories	90

Other suitable sources of proteins for such protocols include rice and spirulina. I discuss my reasons for prescribing protein protocols with breakfast earlier in this chapter.

ENHANCEMENT OF LIVER DETOXIFICATION DEFENSES

The liver is *the* detoxification organ of the human body. Not surprisingly, this organ has fascinated men and women in the healing professions since antiquity. Presently, the role of the liver in health preservation holds fascination for many in natural medicine. The main reason for this fascination is that clinical disease is increasingly caused by a growing pollutant body burden. However, my research and clinical work in battered bowel ecosystems has led me to conclude that the liver cannot function, well except when it is shielded by the gut. Hence, the gut ecosystem—in my view—is the true interface between man and his environment and must be recognized as the principal detoxification organ. Notwithstanding, I recognize that chronic stress sufferers require extra support for their liver antioxidant and detoxification enzyme systems. For this purpose, I liberally use several herbs and some nutrients combined in the following three Liver Ecology Protocols.

LIVER ECOLOGY PROTOCOL 1	
Dandelion root	100 mg
Beet root	50 mg
Black radish	50 mg
Goldenseal	50 mg
Catnip	50 mg
Methionine	400 mg
Choline	200 mg
Inositol	20 mg
LIVER ECOLOGY PROTOCOL II	
Turmeric	100 mg
Milk thistle	100 mg
Red clover	100 mg
Ginger root	100 mg
Goldenseal	100 mg
Jerusalem artichoke	100 mg
Fennel seed	100 mg

In my clinical practice, I liberally prescribe the above two protocols in combination and rotation to provide support for the liver in chronic stress states. However, detailed discussion of how to use these protocols is outside the scope of this book. I do not recommend that the reader take any of these protocols without the supervision of an experienced natural health practitioner. As presented here, I include the composition of my two liver ecology protocols for the general information of the reader.

HORMONAL DYSREGULATIONS

The thyroid, pancreas and adrenal glands are a troubled trio in chronic stress states. Regardless of the initial events that set the stage for chronic stress, the accelerated oxidative molecular injury to human enzyme pathways seen in chronic stress will *always* lead to oxidative damage to enzymes and receptors that preserve the functional integrity of these three body organs.

I reproduce some modified text from the companion volume, *The Canary and Chronic Fatigue,* to briefly address these issues. Optimal management of these hormonal dysregulations, as well as those of the estrogen-progesterone-testosterone axis, requires supervision by an experienced clinician. Thus, the following comments are only intended to provide the reader with some general information.

THE TROUBLED TRIO

Accelerated oxidative injury in chronic stress almost always leads to thyroid dysfunction, cold sensitivity and low body temperature.

Accelerated oxidative injury in chronic stress almost always leads to pancreatic dysfunction and sugar-insulin-adrenaline roller coasters.

Accelerated oxidative injury in chronic stress almost always leads to adrenal dysfunction and progressive stress.

The thyroid gland is the primary gland that regulates the body temperature —and through it the metabolic functions of *all* energy and detoxification enzyme systems of the body. Thus, undue sensitivity to cold temperatures and lack of energy are two of the major clinical symptoms of chronic fatiguers.

The pancreas regulates the blood sugar level. Beyond that, through its insulin secretion, it profoundly affects a host of other molecular dynamics and cardiovascular functions. Injury to the pancreas causes the sugar roller coasters that are well known to chronic fatiguers. Sugar roller coasters induce insulin roller coasters that, in turn, bring on adrenaline roller coasters. Adrenaline roller coasters, of course, cause the symptoms that are commonly associated with hypoglycemic symptoms such as sudden mood swings, weakness, sweating, nausea, palpitations and lightheadedness. Almost all chronic fatiguers suffer from such symptoms at one time or the other.

TIRED AND EXHAUSTED ADRENAL GLANDS

When death follows prolonged, chronic disease, the adrenal glands often show enlargement at autopsy, a process called adrenal cortical hypertrophy. In chronic, unrelenting disorders, the adrenal glands become exhausted and appear shrunken.

It is my practice to assess adrenal stress in my patients with a 24-hour urinary steroid profile that includes the following metabolic end products of adrenal hormones as well as some closely related sex hormones:

SOME IMPORTANT ADRENAL HORMONES

DHEA	Tetrahydrocortisol
Pregnanediol	Tetrahydrocortisone
Preganetriol	11-Ketoandrosterone
Etiocholanolone	11-Hydroxyandrosterone
Androsterone	11-hydroxyetiocholanolone

In the early stages of stress, some of the hormones

included in the above table, or their endproducts, are excreted in urine in larger amounts. For example, I often see higher levels of endproducts of cortisone and cortisol in patients with early stages of chronic fatigue. This indicates an adrenal overdrive state. In later stages, some of these products are increased while others are reduced, reflecting a state of early adrenal failure. In yet later stages, I see reduced urinary excretion of many products without any associated increases in others. Finally, in very advanced stages, there is marked reduction in excretion of most products while the levels of others such as DHEA and etiocholanolone approach zero, indicating adrenal exhaustion.

The adrenal glands play many roles in chronic stress states including the following:

1.   'Fight or flight' hormones —adrenaline and its cousin molecules, catecholamines —that help us gear our energetic-molecular defenses for coping with life-threatening events.

2.   Cortisone and its cousin molecules that energize the receptors —including those for adrenaline —for various body functions.

3.   Aldosterone hormone that regulates kidney function and consequently the water and salt balance of the body.

4.   DHEA (the "mother" hormone that prevents accelerated aging), androgen (male) and estrogen (female) hormones that provide a counterbalance to such hormones produced in other organs of the body.

The adrenal gland is regulated in large part by ACTH (adrenocorticotrophic) hormone produced by the pituitary gland, which in turn is regulated by the hypothalamus. It was entirely predictable that the adrenal-pituitary-hypothalamus axis would draw much attention from stress researchers. Below, I summarise some important research findings in chronic stress states:

1. High blood cortisone levels in the early and low levels in later stages of chronic stress.

2. High blood levels of ACTH—not unexpected, because the pituitary senses the low adrenal activity and tries to drive it harder.

3. Low prevalence of dexamethasone nonsuppression.

4. Increased sensitivity (and reduced maximal response) of the adrenal gland to ACTH and reduced maximal response of the adrenal glands.

5. Reduced ability of CRF (corticotrophin releasing factor) to stimulate ACTH release.

(J Clin Endocrinol Metab 73:1224; 1991)

TEMPERATURE DYSREGULATION IN STRESS

Chronic stress sufferers often have a significant problem

with cold hands and feet by the time they consult me. Eventually all people suffering from unremitting stress develop temperature dysregulation and low body temperature —and with that lose the efficiency of their enzymes, much like a defect in the furnace reduces the efficiency of a home heating system. There are five core points in this discussion:

First,

adrenaline and related stress hormones are potent vasoconstrictors. When present in excess, those hormones cause spasm of the muscle in arterial walls, narrow the lumens of vessels, impede the flow of blood in tissues and cause the tissue temperature to fall. Every week, I spend about three hours in my autoregulation laboratory teaching my patients how to flush their cold hands and feet with warm blood by allowing their arteries to open up by shutting out the thinking mind. I do not recall a single laboratory session in which one or more patients did not see their skin temperature shoot up from below 80 degrees to 90 degrees or over. Clearly, this is an autonomic function. (The term autoregulation actually derives from my early work in this area, when I used to call it autonomic regulation. My patients shortened it to autoregulation, then to autoreg.) Equally clearly, such a rise in skin temperature cannot be attributed to thyroid manipulation because no thyroid hormone is used in such work. Furthermore, temperature regulation through thyroid hormone therapy takes several days or weeks, whereas I observe changes in the skin temperature in minutes.

Second,

accelerated oxidative injury in chronic stress damages the membranes of red blood cells and makes them sticky, resulting in cellular sludging. I commonly observe large clumps of red blood cells when I examine a drop of blood from patients suffering from chronic stress with a high-resolution microscope with phase-contrast and dark-field optics. Normally, tiny blood capillaries in tissues open wide enough to let only one or two red blood cells flow through them side by side. Large clumps of blood cells cannot flow freely through capillaries, and literally choke off tiny capillaries.

Oxidative injury also causes blood platelets to form clumps that impede blood circulation and increase blood coagulability. The same holds true for the white blood cells, though to a lesser degree.

Fourth,

accelerated oxidative injury damages the receptor sites of the autonomic nervous system, and so causes autonomic dysregulations. This adds to the vasoconstriction caused by excess adrenaline and further lowers the tissue temperature.

Fifth,

accelerated oxidative injury in chronic stress eventually leads to hypothyroidism. I am certain that the mechanism of such injury is accelerated oxidative injury to the enzymes which are necessary for production of metabolically active thyroid hormones from their inactive precursor. Furthermore, I confidently predict that this will be proven with future research.

Underactivity of the thyroid gland slows down the entire metabolism and results in a fall in the body temperature. Even a small drop in body temperature, such as three-quarters to one degree, can significantly impair enzyme efficiency, sometimes causing as much as a 50% drop. *Lowering the body temperature by one-half to one degree has the same effect on human metabolism as lowering the thermal efficiency of a home heating system—the fuel burns inefficiently. The firm proof for this phenomenon is the common observation that people living highly stressful lives feel much better and more energetic on days when their temperature is normal and do poorly on days when their temperature is low.* This question, within the context of human total body metabolism, has not been well investigated. I am confident that when it is, it will reveal a large drop in metabolic enzyme efficiency—a major physiologic handicap for those with low body temperature.

Many environmental pollutant molecules such as dioxins show close structural similarity to thyroid hormones and fool thyroid receptors on cell membranes. Thyroid dysfunction so caused further slows down metabolism. This mechanism, though not directly related to the stress chemistry, adds to the degree of thyroid gland injury.

TEMPERATURE UP-REGULATION WITH T₃ AND T₄ THERAPIES

This subject is generally considered very complex. It need not be. Below, I describe how thyroid dysfunction occurs in chronic stress states. Seven mistakes are commonly made in this area:

First,

the impact of persistently low body temperature on energy and detoxification enzymes is not recognized, either by the patient or the physician. The fundamental difference between living beings and nonliving things, as I wrote earlier in this volume, is that living beings are enzymes beings, and all enzymes are temperature-dependent.

Second,

the enzymes that convert inactive and weakly active thyroid hormone precursors to active hormones are damaged by oxidative injury. I am certain of this, though this has not yet been proven with actual studies. This oxidative injury leads to diminished production of active T_3 hormone and persistently low body temperature. The proof of this is in the common observation that body temperature cannot be normalized in many patients even with large doses of natural thyroid extract or synthetic T_4 preparations, such as synthyroid. Yet, the temperature rises within days when optimal doses of T_3 are used. Furthermore, oxidative injury damages the thyroid hormone receptors. I address this subject later in this section.

Third,

in the prevailing dogma of endocrinology, thyroid function is frequently assumed to be normal if the commonly performed T_4, T_3 uptake, quantitative T_3 and TSH tests show negative results. Rather large drops in the blood hormone levels are ignored simply because the test value falls within the "normal" range. The frequency with which otherwise knowledgeable physicians make this mistake amazes me. For example, the normal range for T_4 in most laboratories is 4.5 to 12 mcg/ml. However, a fatigue sufferer with a normal hormone level of 12 mcg/ml might drop it by 50% down to 6 mcg/ml. According to the prevailing dogma, this would be considered a negative result, while in reality it represents a significant degree of hypothyroidism (underactive thyroid gland).

Fourth,

hypothyroidism is assumed to exist when the body temperature is below normal, and no attempts are made to investigate dysfunction of the autonomic nervous system. Predictably, when low body temperature is due to autonomic dysfunction, thyroid replacement fails to restore the body temperature to the normal range.

Fifth,

the dose of thyroid hormone is continually increased even when such therapy neither affords clinical benefits nor raises the body temperature. I have seen cases where the dose of T_4 or T_3 was pushed to a very high value with resulting rapid heart rate, palpitations, and in some cases, cardiac arrhythmia.

Sixth,

insufficient attention is paid to the impaired function of the adrenal gland and other hormonal dysfunctions that frequently coexist with underactive thyroid status. The oxidative injury that slows down enzymes involved with thyroid hormone synthesis can also be fully expected to slow down the enzymes that are essential for production of adrenal hormone. This indeed does happen. The blood levels of DHEA, an adrenal hormone, are almost always low, often markedly, in patients with persistent chronic fatigue.

Seventh,

little, if any, attempts are made in clinical endocrinology to consider the nutritional basis of hormonal dysregulations. This is remarkable because even a cursory look at the biochemistry charts outlining enzyme pathways shows how multiple nutrients are essential for each enzymatic step in hormone synthesis.

I carefully study temperature dysregulation in all patients with chronic illness using appropriate blood tests and asking the patient to take oral as well as axillary (underarm) temperature readings immediately after waking up and before getting out of bed. The oral and axillary temperature readings are again taken three and six hours after the morning reading. In addition, I ask the patient to record his/her pulse in the morning. These steps are repeated on three consecutive days.

The oral temperature should range from 98.2 to 98.6 degrees. Axillary temperature should range from 97.5 to 98 degrees.

In my clinical practice, if the body temperature is more than a half degree lower on average, I address all the issues listed above. For thyroid hypofunction, I usually prescribe a small dose of one grain of natural thyroid extract (Armour brand). Four weeks later, I do a clinical evaluation and repeat body temperature readings — oral, axillary or both, depending on the pattern of temperatures observed during the initial readings. If the small dose of thyroid extract fails to raise the body temperature to the desired level, I increase the dose by small increments such as one-half to one grain at a time. *It is essential to monitor the pulse rate during all types of thyroid therapy.* I clearly instruct the patient not to increase the thyroid dose if the pulse rate begins to rise by more than 10 beats per minute above the initial reading or when the pulse rate climbs above 90 per minute.

T₃ TEMPERATURE UP-REGULATION

At times, thyroid extract therapy fails to give any clinical benefits and low body temperature persists. After careful re-evaluation, if I still think the thyroid gland is not functioning properly, I move on to the use of small doses (7.5 to 30 mcg daily in two divided doses) of slow-acting T_3 preparations, and increase the dose in small increments of 7.5 mcg (as suggested by my friend, Dennis Wilson, M.D.), carefully watching the pulse rate and body temperature and looking for clinical signs of improvement.

In my office, I use temperature and pulse sheets for recording daily temperatures, pulse rates and symptom scores. I designed these worksheets specifically to assist and guide the patient in following my instructions. I cannot overemphasize the *absolute* need for careful monitoring of both body temperature and pulse rate so that an overcorrection of the thyroid gland does not lead to hyperthyroidism and excessive stress on the heart.

DHEA, PROGESTERONE AND RELATED HORMONAL DYSREGULATIONS

Accelerated oxidant injury in chronic stress states also causes dysfunctions in other hormonal systems in the body. I see clinical evidence of this in almost all patients with severe chronic fatigue. Although laboratory evidence of dysfunction is easily established for some hormone systems, such as DHEA for the adrenal glands—it is not so apparent for other hormone systems, such as female and male hormones. The main reason for that is that we have a strong overload of synthetic hormones caused by: 1) hormone prescriptions by doctors; 2) prescriptions of other drugs such as beta blockers that mimic hormonal effects; 3) the addition of hormones to animals feeds; and 4) pesticides and related compounds that compete with hormones for their receptor sites. I discuss this subject at length in *RDA: Rats, Drugs and Assumptions.*

DHEA

DHEA, dehydroepiandrosterone, is a primary adrenal hormone which serves as one of the body's major anti-aging hormones. In contrast to steroids that depress our antioxidant and immune defense systems, DHEA supports such defenses. (I will let you in on a secret: Holistic physicians prescribe DHEA liberally for their family members, and most of them take it themselves for enhancement of their general antioxidant and immune defenses.) I consider this an excellent agent for restoring the damaged antioxidant and immune defenses of chronic stress sufferers. Indeed, it is a very rare patient who does not report beneficial results within weeks or months of taking it.

I frequently use DHEA in a daily dose of 50 mg for the first three months and then reduce the dose to 50 mg on alternate days. In most cases, such therapy may be discontinued within several months when normal enzyme functions—and energy levels—are restored.

1. DHEA has many established beneficial effects on the immune system.

2. Stress states are associated with suppression of several immune functions; DHEA prevents that.

3. Blood DHEA levels are usually reduced in chronic fatigue sufferers, and replacement therapy with DHEA improves the overall energy level and reduces many associated symptoms.

4. DHEA opposes the physiological effects of cortisone in several animal models.

5. DHEA levels drop in serious infections, including AIDS, indicating progression of disease, and the levels rise during recovery.

6. DHEA protects immune cells against acute lethal viral infections (including viral encephalitis).

7. DHEA regulates many immune cell functions and the production of hormone-like mediators called lymphokines. It helps generate many desirable molecules (such as IL-2) and prevents the excessive production of some undesirable ones, such as interleukin 4 and 5 and gamma interferon that can impair our immune defenses. A role of DHEA in the cause of systemic lupus—an autoimmune disorder—has been suggested.

FEMALE HORMONAL DYSREGULATIONS

Biology adapts to the environment slowly—in fact it can take millennia for the body to adapt to adverse changes in the environment. On the other hand, oxidant injury can damage genes quickly—perhaps in some hours.

Menstruation is nature's design to ensure the continuity of the human race. To this purpose, the endometrium —the inner lining of the uterus —prepares itself for conception every month. That is the natural order of things, and was established to preserve Homo sapiens in an era when the principal threat to the survival of humankind was extinction by a shrinking population. Predators and accidents were the principal threats. Human genes needed to be preserved, and the simplest and most efficient mechanism for that was more babies.

Times have changed —and so have the demands for survival. Now the twin principal threats to humankind are progressive environmental oxidant stress and overpopulation, each feeding upon the other. Families today cannot afford pregnancy at the rate planned in nature. Natural monthly demands of the endometrium for pregnancy cannot be met, and hence are foiled every month.

How does the endometrium prepare itself every month for its evolutionary role? By putting out bursts of estrogen. How does the body cope with such bursts of estrogen in the natural order of things (when pregnancy does occur)? By providing a counterbalance with bursts of progesterone from the corpus luteum of the ovary as the fertilized egg settles into the pregnant endometrium. What happens when the endometrium prepares but the fertilized ovum does not make the scene?

Disillusioned —and frustrated —the endometrium strikes back. This is the natural order of things. And this is where female hormonal problems begin. Surprisingly, unbridled estrogen is the villain for women today—not estrogen deficiency. Estrogen, like magnesium, acts as a calcium channel blocker as well as a dilator of blood vessels. Thus, insufficient estrogen supply leads to dysregulation of several cardiovascular responses. In a sense, the hot flashes of menopause are the confused responses of an estrogen-deficient body—estrogen withdrawal symptoms are akin to the misery of a cocaine addict when his fix is not forthcoming.

BALANCING ESTROGENS AND PROGESTERONES

Accelerated oxidative injury in chronic stress can damage enzymes involved in the synthesis of estrogen and progesterone as well as their corresponding receptor molecules. This indeed does happen. It is very common for women with severe stress to suffer from menstrual irregularities, severe PMS symptoms, and, in persistent cases, absence of menstruation. *The return to normal menstruation is utterly predictable when chronic stress is managed well and enzyme functions are restored.*

In my clinical practice, I generally address female hormonal dysregulations with a broad holistic approach that includes one or more of the following measures:

1. Folic acid in daily doses of 10 to 30 mg, especially for menopausal flushes.
2. A natural progesterone preparation (cream or oil derived from Mexican wild yam) used during the last two weeks of the cycle—or the last two weeks of the month for menopausal women. I recommend one-third or less of a teaspoon of the cream to be applied to the skin of upper chest, neck or face at bed time.
3. Modest doses of DHEA (25 to 100 milligrams are helpful in intractable cases.
4. Herbs with hormonal activity such as dong quai and black cohosh.

Should synthetic estrogen be used to prevent osteoporosis? Only as a last resort. Osteoporosis is caused by oxidant injury to hormone receptors and enzymes involved with the laying down of new bone. I discuss this subject at length in *What Do Woodpeckers Know About Osteoporosis?* The best prevention of osteoporosis is a reduction in total oxidative stress—with optimal choices in the kitchen and self-regulation—and direct vertical stress on the axial skeleton with rebounding exercises such as jumping rope or using a trampoline. I recommend *The Ghoraa and Limbic Exercise* for a discussion of exercise for osteoporosis.

For prevention and reversal of osteoporosis, I liberally use a natural progesterone product as described above. When clinical situations compels me to consider the use of estrogen, I prefer to use estrogen formulations that contain higher amounts of estriol (the "good" estrogen) derived from natural sources such as soybean. It is a rare woman who does not respond to integrated, holistic nondrug therapies to such a degree that the use of synthetic estrogens become necessary.

In closing this section, I wish to emphasize that the best strategies for control of chronic stress are optimal choices in the kitchen, oral nutrient and herbal therapies, immunotherapy for IgE-mediated allergy when such allergy exists, intramuscular and intravenous nutrient infusions for managing acute conditions such as common infections, self-regulation, and slow, sustained, nongoal-oriented (limbic) exercise. Furthermore, that hormonal therapies for chronic stress states should not be undertaken without the supervision of a knowledgeable physician.

LIMBIC EXERCISE FOR STRESS

Limbic exercise is meditation in motion. I use this term for slow, sustained, noncompetitive and nongoal-oriented exercise. Such exercise done *every* day is an integral part of my recommendation for stress control and disease prevention. The core philosophy of such exercise is to integrate physical exercise with deep meditative and spiritual work. Is meditation in motion possible for everyone? Extensive clinical experience has convinced me that it is not only possible, it is essential for a long-term strategy of good health for the entire life span. (See *The Ghoraa and Limbic Exercise* for more on this subject.)

Silence can bring suffering or serenity depending on what secrets we keep—and from whom.

Chapter 16

The River Does Justice to Me

One never sees the same river again, so goes an ancient saying. Those words often come to me when I look out our apartment window and see the Hudson River. The river is gray, often carries jetsam and there is always some garbage at the bank. My mind's eye sees the industrial effluence hidden below the water's waves.

Looking to the north, I see several boats at the marina on 79th Street. Often there is a tugboat or two floating on the river. Looking south, I usually see large cruise ships docked at the piers. Those huge boats must add their share of exhaust pollutants to the river. Across the river, I see the New Jersey bluffs, and beyond that, the ugly masses of concrete that form New Jersey's high-rise apartments.

I stare at the river impassively for a few moments, imagining what the river might have been like a hundred years ago and what it might become when our children's children are grown. As with other ecosystems of planet Earth, the river ecology is diverse and dynamic—but it is also *delicate*. We often see the first two attributes of a river's ecology, but we rarely have a real appreciation for its delicacy. I read that the Hudson River is becoming cleaner because of recent laws that strictly regulate the dumping of industrial waste. But I fail to discern any visible signs.

One late afternoon, Talat and I returned to our apartment after a walk in Central Park. Choua sat by a table near the window overlooking the river. The sun sank low behind the New Jersey condominiums, its rays luminous behind thin crimson clouds. As I approached the window, Choua stood up and walked away, leaving two sheets of paper on the table. I picked them up and read.

Sometimes my eyes stay with the river.
Then the river changes.
It comes alive.
The sun reflects on it.
The water glistens.
The wind turns luminous on its waves.
The river widens.
The river lengthens.
It flows.
It grows.
Colors appear that were not there.
Colors come closer.
Colors recede.
Trees line up on the Manhattan bank of the river,
        then   form mosaics.
Bluffs grow taller on the Jersey bank, then thin out.
The waves turn, twist, merge into each other.
The sun draws ripples of spreading gold on the river.
The Hudson changes by the moment,
        just as the ancients knew every river does.
My perceptions change, then dissolve.
Then the river takes over.
Then I know I'm only there.
Then I have no thoughts.
I have no perceptions.
There are no walls, no doors.
There is limbic openness.
I am.
The river *is*.
I do not do justice to the river.
The river does justice to me.

I finished reading the first sheet, then picked up the

second and read.

> *I don't search for God. How can I search for Him when He is always within me?*

Chapter 17

Why and How Do Not Matter

Bob, a brilliant engineer in his mid-forties, suffered from ALS, which is Lou Gehrig's disease. He sent me a letter some months ago. I scanned his letter as I do other letters, standing by my desk. It is hard for me to read every word of what people send me by mail. So I read hurriedly, passing over the kind remarks and greetings that many patients and readers send.

I quickly passed over the beginning sentences of Bob's letter. Halfway through the letter, I realized what Bob had written in the opening sentence. I read again the opening sentence of the letter, felt a sharp chill in my spine and stopped abruptly. No one had ever written such a thing to me. I sat down on my chair and started to read it slowly, word by word. Then I read the letter a second time and knew that I was going to forever treasure that letter above all other letters I had received, or would. I wondered how I was going to respond to a letter like that.

The next day I called Bob and thanked him for the letter. He accepted my gratitude shyly—and awkwardly. Then I asked for his permission to read it to my staff and some other patients. He graciously obliged. I have read his letter on several occasions in my meditation workshops. Every time I read it, it touches me and I see how deeply it moves the listeners.

Bob's letter has been a gift that keeps giving. I will always treasure it. Below, with his permission and a deep sense of gratitude to him for having written that letter to me, I reproduce the full text of Bob's letter:

9/28/95

Dear Dr. Ali,

I may be doing the last of my handwriting so I decided to write and not type. I have experienced exciting changes over the past couple months. Although I am a little concerned about losing my right arm (my left has been gone for two years) and some/most of my independence, I feel like the good things far outweigh the bad. I have discovered spiritualityfor the first time in my life. I was always running—I was ambitious and aggressive as many others are in business USA. I always thought God was man-made in order to squelch our fear of death. But now I know something is inside me—I found that non-thinking/all-knowing place—maybe its heaven? I believe the power to cure is there. I don't know if I can tap into it—but if not, I still have found my soul. No matter what, the rest of my life is changed. I only regret not discovering this place sooner. I feel full of light and I no longer (most of the time) judge people as much. There are people that hurt me, but it just seems to me that they are not in touch with their souls. They really are good in spirit, they are just out of touch. I know I can't change them and wouldn't try. I have enough to handle right now. I only wish my wife & kids could know the "steel" I feel so they will feel good about life and accept changes in me. You talked about cancer the other night—this seems a bit different to me. I have never had cancer, but I think it would be easier at first but more difficult as time goes on. I was told at diagnosis, unconditionally, that I will die of ALS by about five neurologists. At first I had no hope. I could and did finally accept this for me—we all must die anyway. But I fought and fought for understanding because (I think now) of my children. They are 2, 4 and 6 years old. My work is not finished and this is the only remaining frustration I have. Also, I feel terrible about the tremendous burden on my wife, Denise. I have watched you now for several months and I have learned so much. I know you do not have much time for individual patients. I see how hard and long you work and I know you do not do it for ambition, ego or money. *You really care and try to reach as many patients as possible. I believe this. Also, most important, you gave me hope. There is no greater gift than hope. Ironically, now I no longer need the hope so much. And I no longer need the understanding. Why or how do not matter-when the bigger picture starts to form. One more thing (now that I have complimented you)-someone in your office missed a $250 service charge on me for vitamin shots. [I figured if I wrote a long and very dull letter with many thoughts poorly organized you might not get to this part and I would keep my money & be morally justified (ha). But if you are still reading than I may be a better, more interesting writer than I thought.] Early on- when we first met-you told me to write to you on occasion about what I am feeling. Well you asked me for it. Take care-you & your family.*

Sincerely,
Bob Z.

"I may be doing the last of my handwriting so I decided to write and not type." I had felt a chill when I read Bob's letter

for the first time. And I feel a chill again now that I write about it. A patient chooses to send his last handwritten words to his physician! What greater honor can any physician ever hope for?

Bob knew he may not be able to write again as the paralysis of his hand became complete, and he chose to honor me with his last hand-written words! His physician of all the people! Where does one draw the grace to do such a thing? Has any physician ever received a note from his patient more overwhelming than that? I wondered as I felt a crushing weight of gratitude.

"I was told at diagnosis, unconditionally, that I will die of ALS by five neurologists. " I feel a lump in my throat as Bob's words reverberate in my mind. *"But I fought and fought for understanding because (I think now) of my children—they are 2, 4 and 6-year old. "* I tried to understand too—make sense of what could not be made sense of. How does one understand what Bob was going through? How did any of Gehrig's fans understand what he must have gone through? An image of Gary Cooper at Yankee Stadium rose in my mind. He played Gehrig in a movie (I think it was *Pride of the Yankees*) and made a moving speech—Gehrig's farewell to his fans. He must have made many of them weep—just as Cooper did in the movie.

"Also, most important you gave me hope. There is no greater gift than hope. Ironically, I no longer need hope so much. " Bob's words returned with a rush of sadness and confusion. *"And I no longer need understanding. Why and how do not matter —when the bigger picture begins to form. "* The big picture! A prayer rose to my lips: Allah, when it is time for you to take back from me all your graces, please leave me with just one last gift: the grace to accept your will the way Bob has accepted it.

Glossary

Adaptation response (general):
A set of biochemical changes that is believed to prepare an organism to cope with the stress of a demand for change.

Adrenal glands:
A pair of glands weighing about one-half ounce and situated above the kidneys. These glands produce adrenaline and steroid hormones. It is commonly —and, in my view, inaccurately —believed to be the primary body organ involved in the stress response.

Adrenaline rushes:
Blasts of adrenaline produced in sudden shock states that quicken the heart rate, tighten the muscles and cause anxiety.

Adrenaline:
A hormone produced by the adrenal glands plays many roles in human biology, and is believed to cause the stress response.

Adrenaline roller coasters:
Repeated adrenaline rushes that follow each other, creating sharp peaks and deep troughs of adrenaline levels in the blood and tissues.

Adrenergic hypervigilence:
A state of overproduction of adrenaline hormone and related hormones that keeps various energy pathways revved and causes molecular burn-out.

Aging-oxidant molecules:
A family of oxidant molecules that cause death and decay in cells and tissues. See oxidation.

All-in-the-head syndrome:
A derisive term used by many doctors to dismiss patients with chronic complaints as malingerers —such symptoms are believed to be false and imaginary. See shirker's syndrome.

Amino acids:
Building blocks for proteins, amino acids are simple nitrogen-containing molecules.

Amitriptyline:
A tricyclic antidepressant drug. Brand name: Elavil.

Antihistamines:
A class of drugs that controls the symptoms of allergic reactions by blocking the action of histamine, a substance that is released from mast cells and, in turn, causes the release of many inflammation

mediators.

Antioxidants:

Molecules that prevent oxidation (loss of electrons) of other substances. Antioxidants of interest in human metabolism include vitamins such as vitamins A, C and E as well as minerals such as selenium.

Antioxidant defenses:

Host defenses against oxidative molecular injury. See oxidation.

Anxiety state:

An abnormal state of undue anxiety about real or imagined adverse events. In severe forms, anxiety causes loss of appetite, difficulty with sleep, jitters, indigestion, heart palpitations and missed heart beats.

Arrhythmia:

Irregular heartbeat. Sometimes the individual can sense the irregular rhythm of the heart as skipped beats.

Arteriosclerosis:

Commonly called hardening of the arteries, arteriosclerosis is a disease process characterized by plaque formation on the inside walls of arteries. It leads to heart attacks, strokes and leg cramps while walking due to insufficient blood supply.

Ativan:

A commonly prescribed antianxiety drug. Generic name: lorazepam.

Attention deficit disorder:

A disorder of children as well as adults characterized by inattentiveness, impulsivity and inability to perform ordinary chores at home and at work. See hyperactivity syndrome.

Autism:

A disorder characterized by severe inability of the subject to react to ordinary stimulations and to communicate with family members and friends. The resulting isolation, unless averted, causes serious developmental problems.

Autoimmune disorders:

An individual's immunity turned against himself. A class of disorders in which an injured immune system produces antibodies directed against the body's own molecules, cells and organs. These autoantibodies may cause widespread tissue damage. See lupus, multiple sclerosis and hyperthyroidism.

Autonomic nervous system:
> A part of the nervous system that is believed to be outside voluntary control, for example, nerve cells and nerve fibers that regulate normal heart rhythm and rate.

Autoregulation:
> A process by which a person enters a healing energy state.

Biology:
> A branch of science that deals with the structures and functions of living beings.

Blood ecosystem:
> A diverse, dynamic and delicate biochemical ecosystem of blood components circulating in blood vessels that actively interfaces with the bowel, liver, brain and other ecosystems. This concept contrasts with the traditional view that sterile blood circulates in a closed system of arteries and veins. The circulating blood is an open ecosystem in the sense that there is an ongoing free entry into it of bacteria, viruses and parasites from the bowel and other ecosystems of the body.

Bowel ecosystem:
> A delicate, diverse and dynamic ecosystem composed of chemical (food elements and digestive-absorptive enzymes) and biologic elements (bacteria, viruses and parasites).

Bulbectomy:
> An operation in which the olfactory bulb essential for the sense of smell is removed.

Cellular ecosystems:
> The internal environment of cells and intracellular organelles that sense—and respond to—changes in the tissue fluid that bathes cells.

Chelation:
> A process by which metals are eliminated from the body by binding them to substances with a special affinity for such metals. When used to reverse coronary artery disease, chelation employs EDTA as the chelating agent for calcium deposits in the plaque lining the arteries.

Cholesterol:
> A waxy, fatty substance in the blood that is incorrectly considered to be the cause of heart disease, stroke and instances of common heart attacks.

Cholinergic:

A part of the autonomic nervous system that provides a counterbalance to adrenergic nerve receptors and messenger molecules such as adrenaline. See adrenaline.

Chronic fatigue syndrome:

A chronic state of undue tiredness that lasts for more than six months and results in more than a fifty percent reduction in physical activity. It is associated with immune dysfunctions; dysfunctions of the thyroid, adrenal and pancreas glands; and disorders of mood, memory and mentation.

Coronary arteries:

Arteries that supply blood to the heart muscle.

Cortical:

In autoregulation terminology, cortical indicates a thinking state in which the mind counts, calculates, computes, competes, censors and cautions. The cortical mind creates images of suffering and disease. It is a competitive mode in which one yearns for control, further compounding the problem. In contrast, limbic in autoregulation terminology cares and comforts. It creates images of relief and health, and so mitigates suffering. In the limbic mode, human energy pathways are in a steady state and facilitate the healing response.

Cylert:

A drug used for attention deficit and related learning disorders.

Cytomegalovirus:

A common virus that causes fever and may involve any body organ, especially when the immune system of the individual is compromised by antibiotic abuse, chemotherapy, radiotherapy and environmental toxins.

Decerebrate:

An animal in which a part or whole of the brain has been removed.

Dexedrine:

A drug (dextroamphetamine sulfate) that stimulates the nervous system and is often used for attention deficit disorder and related conditions.

DHEA:

Dehydroepiandrosterone, a "mother" hormone produced in the adrenal gland that orchestrates the production of estrogens,

progesterones and testosterone in the body. It is also considered to
be an anti-aging hormone.

Diagnostic labels:
The diagnostic terms that are employed in drug medicine to justify
the use of symptom-suppressing drugs but reveal nothing about the
cause of the illness. For instance, irritable bowel syndrome, chronic
headache and restless leg syndrome.

Directed Pulses:
A term used in autoregulation to indicate enhancement and
perception of ordinary arterial pulses in different parts of the body.

Distress:
A state of harmful stress, contrasted to eustress, which is believed
to be a helpful state of stress.

Diuretics:
A class of drugs used to treat excessive accumulation of fluids in
tissues. These drugs promote loss of fluids from the kidneys.

Dysautonomia:
A disorder of autonomic nervous system that often causes
disturbances in heart rate, blood pressure, sweating and control of
urination.

Dysfunction:
Malfunction in the cells and tissues.

Dysregulation:
Abnormalities in the regulation of various molecular functions in
the body. For instance, excess of synthetic chemicals with estrogen-
like activities interfere with normal hormonal functions in women
and cause such disorders as endometriosis.

EDTA:
Ethylenediaminetetraacetic acid, a substance used in chelation
therapy to eliminate toxic heavy metals in cases of metal poisoning
and to reverse coronary heart disease.

Elavil:
A brand name for a tricyclic antidepressant drug called
amitriptyline. Other brand-name drugs that contain amitriptyline
include Endep, Etrafon, Limbitrol and Triavil.

EM medicine (energetic-molecular medicine):
A type of medical practice in which therapies are based on
energetic-molecular events that occur *before* cells and tissues are

damaged and disease develops, rather than on how tissues look under a microscope *after* they have been damaged.

EM traffic:

Energetic-molecular events that take place at the cell and plasma membranes in health and disease, and represent the essential energy dynamics of living beings.

Endothelins:

Substances produced in the blood vessel wall and other parts of the body that serve a large number of functions, such as the control of blood flow within arteries and the regulation of many hormonal functions.

Enzyme:

Catalysts that facilitate biochemical reactions in the body. Enzymes are delicate proteins that are highly vulnerable to oxidant stress.

Epstein-Barr virus (EBV):

A common virus that causes infectious mononucleosis (kissing disease), and was at one time thought to be the cause of chronic fatigue syndrome.

Estrogens:

A class of female hormones essential for normal fetal development, and for maintenance of menstruation and other female reproductive functions. Opposed by progesterones.

ETS:

See endothelins.

Eustress:

Eustress is considered a type of stress with healthful effects.

Fatigue:

Undue tiredness. Also see chronic fatigue syndrome.

Fourth-of-July chemistry:

A state of chemistry in which electrons are fired excessively and randomly in various tissues, causing widespread damage to cellular enzymes, membrane receptors, membrane channels, enzymes, hormones and neurotransmitters.

Glucose:

A simple six-carbon sugar molecule that is utilized in the tissues for energy production. In the brain, glucose is almost exclusively utilized for all neurologic functions.

Glucose roller coasters:
A term I use for rapid changes in the blood sugar level creating high peaks and deep valleys. Synonymous with rapid hyperglycemic-hypoglycemic shifts.

Growth hormone:
A pituitary hormone that promotes growth during childhood and prevents premature aging.

HDL cholesterol:
High-density lipoprotein, the "good" cholesterol that is supposed to prevent coronary heart disease. The higher the blood level, the lower the presumed risk of heart disease. I say presumed because this is an overly simplistic view.)

Herpesvirus:
A family of viruses that causes common fever blisters in the mouth as well as genital lesions.

High-energy molecule:
A molecule that contains chemical energy bonds that may be broken to release the energy contained in them. For example, glycogen is a high-energy molecule that contains many energy bonds. When it is broken down into smaller sugar molecules, energy is released for muscular activities or other energy functions in the body.

HIV:
HIV (human immunodeficiency virus) causes AIDS (acquired immunodeficiency syndrome).

HMO:
Health maintenance organizations, in essence, are insurance companies that specialize in reducing costs by controlling the spending of doctors.

Hyperactivity syndrome:
A syndrome usually diagnosed in children whereby a child is restless, impulsive and unable to perform common chores at home or at school.

Hyperadrenergic state:
A state in which excessive release of adrenaline and related stress molecules causes restlessness, anxiety, insomnia, heart palpitations and stress.

Hypochondria:
Neurotic conviction of the existence of an imaginary illness. Derived from hypochondrium —a region of abdomen located below the cartilage of the breast bone —thought to be the seat of melancholy in premodern times.

Hyperglycemia:
Opposite of hypoglycemia. A state of raised blood sugar level. Persistent hyperglycemia is the essential feature of diabetes.

Hyperthyroidism:
An autoimmune disorder characterized by overactivity of the thyroid gland that causes undue sensitivity to high temperatures, speeded-up metabolism, sweating, weight loss and heart palpitations. See autoimmune disorders.

Hypoglycemia:
Opposite of hyperglycemia. A state of low blood sugar —usually lower than 50 mg/Dl —associated with symptoms of weakness, jitters, anxiety, heart palpitations, nausea and sweating.

Hypothyroidism:
Opposite of hyperthyroidism. An autoimmune disorder characterized by underactivity of the thyroid gland that causes undue sensitivity to cold temperatures, fatigue, dry skin, weight gain, hair loss and sluggish metabolism.

Hysteria:
A type of neurosis characterized by vulnerability to suggestion, amnesia, emotional instability and related mental disturbances.

Infarction:
Death of tissue due to the sudden interruption of its blood supply. Example: myocardial infarction causes heart attack.

Insulin:
A *storage* hormone produced in the pancreas gland that regulates blood sugar levels by promoting storage of glucose in tissues as fat. It also facilitates the entry and utilization of sugar in cells.

Insulin roller coasters:
Sharp peaks in blood insulin levels followed by precipitous drops, which represent the dysregulation of insulin production in the pancreas gland.

Ischemia:
> A condition of diminished blood supply to tissues. Examples: ischemia of the heart muscle, which may cause heart attacks, and of the brain, which may lead to stroke.

Jung, Carl Gustave:
> Eminent swiss psychiatrist, an early friend of Freud, who later forcefully disagreed with many aspects of Freudian psychology.

Kukuyu:
> The largest native tribe of Africans in Kenya.

Language of silence:
> In autoregulation terminology, it is an intuitive-visceral stillness that enlightens without any analytical activity: equivalent to a profound meditative state in other disciplines of meditation.

LDL cholesterol:
> Low-density lipoprotein that is often considered "bad" cholesterol. A raised blood level of LDL is considered a risk factor for heart disease.

Life span:
> The length of one's whole life. For humankind, it has been estimated to be between 100 and 110 years.

Life span enzymes:
> Enzymes that promote health and allow a living being to achieve his or her expected life span. Also see enzyme.

Limbic:
> Limbic indicates a calm, comforting, noncompetitive healing energy state. The autoregulation term refers to a nonthinking, noncompetitive, nongoal-oriented, steady healing energy state. The limbic state "cares and comforts," and "creates" images of health and healing that mitigate suffering. The cortical state, by contrast, indicates a thinking state in which the mind counts, calculates, computes, competes, censors and cautions. It creates images of suffering and disease. It is a competitive mode in which one yearns for control, further compounding the problem.

Limbic breathing:
> In autoregulation terminology, a type of breathing that profoundly affects the energy state of an individual. Limbic breathing is an enhanced energy state in which the breathing-out phase of respiration is prolonged in a slow, sustained fashion following a

brief effortless breathing-in period. Very effective for reducing stress, slowing quickened heart rates, normalizing high blood pressure, and managing other chronic disorders.

Limbic exercise:

A type of nongoal oriented, noncompetitive exercise in which slow, sustained physical exercise is combined with meditation.

Limbic language of silence:

In autoregulation terminology, this expression refers to reaching higher energy states with periods of silence and meditation.

Low-energy molecule:

A molecule with few energy bonds or electrons available for transfer to other molecules. See high-energy molecule for further explanation.

Lupus:

An autoimmune disorder in which a confused immune system turns on the body's own tissues and produces destructive antibodies that damage various body organs. Full medical name: systemic lupus erythematosus.

Mantra:

A word or a short phrase that is repeated often in one's mind to induce a contemplative state. In Hinduism, mantras are used in prayers and incantations, and are believed to be sacred words that embody the divinity invoked.

MAO:

Monoamine oxidase (MAO) inhibitors are a class of antidepressant drugs.

Masai:

A tribe of native Africans in Kenya and Tanzania romanticized by Europeans as fiercely independent.

Melatonin:

A hormone produced in the pineal gland that promotes natural sleep during night hours. It also helps people and animals adjust to various seasons.

Metabolism:

The complex of biochemical and physical processes involved in the maintenance of life. Metabolism comprises reactions necessary for breakdown of food substances for release of chemical bond energy (catabolism) as well as those for synthesis of structural and functional molecules for cellular and tissue build-up (anabolism).

Metabolic Roller coasters:

This term is used in this volume for abrupt changes in the blood and tissue levels of sugar, insulin, adrenaline, cholinergic hormones and neurotransmitters. Sharp rises and sudden drops in the levels of such molecules cause a host of symptoms such as anxiety, the jitters, nausea, weakness, sweating and heart palpitations.

Mind-body-spirit:

A spurious concept of using the thinking mind to force healing on injured tissues.

Mitral valve prolapse:

A condition in which a chronically overdriven heart muscle stresses the mitral valve. The mitral valve leaflets bulge (prolapse), become floppy, and fail to prevent the backflow of blood from the left lower chamber of the heart to the left upper chamber. Except when it is associated with a mitral valve damaged by rheumatic fever or other conditions, it is *not* a specific heart defect. The proper holistic approach is to address all the elements that overdrive the heart of each individual patient.

Molecules:

A group of atoms with defined atomic arrangement within its structure.

Multiple sclerosis:

An autoimmune disorder that damages the insulation material in nerve fibers called myelin sheaths.

Murmur:

An abnormal heart sound produced by turbulence in the flow of blood within the heart. It may be caused when the heart is overdriven, when one of the heart valves does not open fully (stenosis), or when it does not close fully (regurgitation).

Myocardial infarction:

Death of the heart muscle; heart attack, in common terminology.

N^2D^2 medicine:

A type of medicine in which a practitioner's work begins with a search for the name of a disease and ends with the selection of a name of a drug. In N^2D^2 medicine, no consideration is given to ecologic and nutritional factors in the cause of disease. This type of medicine is expressed as follows:

$$N^2D^2 \text{ medicine} =$$
Name of a disease   X   Name of a drug

In N^2D^2 medicine, a doctor begins care of a patient with a disease name and ends with a drug name.

Natural selection:

According to Darwin's theory, natural selection is a phenomenon that results in the survival of the fittest individuals and species. Seen in light of modern genetics, natural selection refers to gene mutations that favor survival of the species and so preserve and prolong the survival of the new (genetically altered) species. Mutations that adversely affect the survival result in extinction (being selected out) of that species.

Neuron:

A nerve cell present in the brain and nerve ganglia of many body organs.

Neurotransmitters:

Molecules that facilitate communications between nerve cells.

Nitric oxide:

1) A simple but essential molecule composed of one atom each of nitrogen and oxygen. In human tissues, it regulates the caliber of small blood vessels and so regulates blood pressure within normal limits. It also functions as a hormone in many different organs of the body.

2) A colorless gas composed of one molecule of oxygen and one of nitrogen. It is an important messenger molecule that is produced in the cells lining the blood vessels, brain, immune cells and many other places. Among its many metabolic roles is regulation of blood circulation.

Obsessive-compulsive disorder:

A type of neurosis in which the sufferer feels compelled to think or do nonsensical things. If such a compulsion is resisted, the individual becomes dysfunctional.

Organ ecosystems:

An ecologic community of biochemical and biologic elements together with its physical environment situated within a specific body organ. For instance, liver ecosystem, brain ecosystem etc.

Ovary:

An organ in the female pelvis that produces ova (eggs) for conception and various female hormones.

Oxidation:

Loss of electrons (tiny packets of energy) from an atom or a molecule. In common language, it may be seen as decay of high-energy molecules into low-energy molecules. Oxidation in nature is a spontaneous process—it requires no outside programming. Examples of oxidation in nature include spoiled fruit, rotten fish, rancid butter, decomposed grass, and denatured energy enzymes that cause chronic fatigue.

Oxidative fires:

A term I use for accelerated oxidative molecular injury that literally cooks enzymes, hormones and other essential molecules in the blood and tissues.

Oxidative injury:

Injury to molecules and tissues in which the mechanism of the injury involves the oxidation or decay of high-energy molecules into low-energy molecules.

OSHA:

Occupational Safety and Health Administration.

Palpitations:

A rapid heart rate that causes an uncomfortable perception of heartbeats in the chest.

Pancreas:

A gland situated behind the stomach in the upper abdomen that produces insulin, glucagon and other hormones for regulation of carbohydrate metabolism.

Panic attacks:

Attacks of extreme anxiety caused by fear of things that do not happen; for example, a sudden sense of doom and fear of heart attack when such an attack has been ruled out repeatedly.

Pantothenic acid:

Vitamin B_5

Pyridoxin:

Vitamin B_6

Pathology:

The study of disease processes and their clinical and laboratory manifestations.

Paxil:

An antidepressant drug.

Phobia:

An irrational, often morbid, fear of things that do not take place.

Physiology:

The branch of biology concerning the function of organisms.

Pineal gland:

A gland located near the base of the brain that produces a hormone called melatonin to induce sleep.

Plaque:

An area of swelling involving the inner lining of an artery caused by tissue injury and accumulation of oxidized and denatured fats, with or without surface ulceration or blood clot formation.

Platelets:

Irregularly shaped particles in circulating blood that contain essential blood clotting factors.

PMS:

Premenstrual syndrome of irritability, cramps, headache, mood swings and water retention that often precedes the menstrual flow. PMS is caused by hormonal imbalance.

PPO:

Preferred provider organization. An organization of health care providers established for the purpose of standardizing provider fees.

Precycling feared future misery:

In autoregulation terminology, it is a neurotic compulsion to indulge in disturbing thoughts about the future.

Prilosec:

An antiulcer drug that works by inhibiting the proton pump involved in the production stomach acid. Generic name: omeprazole.

Progesterone cream:

A progesterone cream derived from wild yam.

Progesterones:

A class of female hormones that provide a counterbalance to

another class of female hormones called estrogens.

Prozac:

An antidepressant drug.

Psychoneuroimmunology:

A branch of medical science that deals with links among aspects of the psyche, the brain and the immune system.

Psychosomatic:

A disease process that is assumed to be caused by disorders of the mind.

Quran:

The holy book of Islam. It is the sacred text of revelations made by Allah to Prophet Muhammad. The holy book is often referred to as Koran by nonmuslims.

RDA:

An abbreviation for the recommended daily allowance, RDA refers to amounts of nutrients considered sufficient to prevent a handful of nutrient deficiency diseases. RDA is the prevailing —and a pernicious —notion that holds that nutrients play no roles in the healing phenomena in injured tissues, and thus are of no value in the clinical management of ecologic, immune and nutritional disorders.

Reactive hypoglycemia:

Abnormally low level of blood sugar thought to be caused by anxiety and emotional disorders. True hypoglycemia, by contrast, is considered to be caused by a dysfunction of the pancreatic release of insulin. This distinction in my view is artificial and clinically irrelevant.

Reduction:

In scientific chemistry terminology, the term reduction refers to the gain of electrons by molecules —the opposite of oxidation. When oxidation and reduction occur together, it is called a redox reaction.

Relaxation response:

A set of exercises designed to reduce stress and a set of biochemical changes associated with relaxation described by Harvard professor, Herbert Benson, M.D.

Ritalin:

A drug that stimulates the nervous system and is used for patients with attention deficit disorder.

Selye, Hans:
> A noted stress expert credited with popularizing the fight-or-flight stress response.

Serengeti:
> A large wildlife preserve in Kenya and Tanzania in East Africa.

Shirker's syndrome:
> A derogatory term used to describe patients who complain of undue tiredness, and who are erroneously labeled by their physicians as malingerers.

Silence of stone:
> In autoregulation terminology, it is a method of achieving an intuitive-visceral stillness by simply looking at a stone. No attempt is made to banish one's thoughts during this practice.

Somatic nervous system:
> A part of the nervous system that is under voluntary control. Examples: use of legs for walking and of hands for holding.

Somatization:
> Development of bodily dysfunction in response to emotional triggers.

Somatopsychic:
> An adjective for organic medical conditions that secondarily affect the mind.

Spirituality:
> Dimensions of human existence that cannot be perceived by physical senses and are beyond the reach of human intellect. I consider spirituality to be the linkage with that larger presence that surrounds and permeates each of us at all times. In my view, it has nothing to do with clever thinking and is quite distinct from intellectual achievement.

Spontaneity of healing:
> A natural healing phenomenon that occurs without external aid. In essence, all healing is spontaneous.

Spontaneity of living:
> A philosophy of life that fosters heeding natural impulses of essential human goodness. In autoregulation terminology, it is living a life uncensored by the cortical monkey.

Spontaneity of oxidation:
> A natural phenomenon in which high-energy molecules

spontaneously undergo decay and are turned into low-energy molecules.

Stress:

Usually defined as a fight-or-flight response to demand for change. The term was coined by Walter Cannon and popularized by Hans Selye. In this book, stress is regarded as the essential process of decay and dying in living beings —the injury-healing-injury cycle of life.

Stress test (of the heart):

A test for adequacy of the blood supply to the heart muscle. In this test, the heart is first stressed by exercise (treadmill or exercise cycle) and then its performance is evaluated with a cardiogram or a thallium scan.

Syndrome of just being sick:

A term first coined and later abandoned by the noted stress expert, Hans Selye.

Taurine:

A derivative of the amino acid cysteine, 2-aminoethane sulfonic. It is an important cell membrane stabilizer which is found in all cells. For this reason it is liberally used in clinical nutritional medicine. Taurine was so named because it was first isolated from ox bile (*taurus* in Latin means bull.)

T_3:

A hormone produced by the thyroid gland to regulate metabolism and body temperature. It is formed by the breakdown of its parent hormone called T_4.

T_4:

A hormone produced by the thyroid gland to regulate metabolism and body temperature.

Thallium scans of the heart:

A type of heart scan that shows patterns of circulation in the heart muscle and is used for diagnosing coronary artery disease.

Thyroid gland:

A gland situated in the front of the neck that produces hormones to regulate metabolism. Underactivity of the gland is called hypothyroidism; overactivity is called hyperthyroidism.

Tourette's syndrome:

A syndrome characterized by involuntary muscular twitches, ticks, learning disabilities and uncontrollable use of foul language.

Triglycerides:

A type of fatty substance in the body which, when present in excessive amounts, is considered to be a risk factor for common heart attacks and strokes. In my view, this risk is grossly exaggerated by physicians who prefer to prescribe drugs rather than take a natural approach to prevention of heart disease.

Valium:

An antianxiety drug. Generic name: diazepam.

Vasodilatation:

Opening up of blood vessels—a process of relaxation of the muscle in the walls of arteries that results in improved blood circulation and oxygenation of tissues.

Vasospasm:

Spasm of the blood vessels.

Viruses:

A family of microbes that cannot be seen with ordinary microscopes and generally can thrive only within the host's cells. Examples: HIV, EBV, CMV and herpesviruses.

Zoloft:

An antidepressant chemically unrelated to tricyclic and tetracyclic antidepressants. Generic name: sertraline hydrochloride.

Index

Original and innovative....

Original and Innovative Solutions to the problem of dieting and the ill-health associated with it.

The Oxidative theory on the cause of aging and disease and its acceleration in the dieting process.

The No-Diet Diet Book

The Butterfly and Life Span Nutrition
Majid Ali,M.D.

ISBN 1-879131-01-3

A celebration of motion...

How does an African tribal messenger run on his wilderness trail? What state of energy is he in? How does an American executive run on his sidewalk? What does his cluttered head demand from his tired and hurt tissues? How do hurt tissues rebel? Can physical exercise provide a deeply personal, treasured retreat from the relentless chatter of the thinking mind?

The Ghoraa and Limbic Exercise

Majid Ali, M.D.

One of America's foremost spokespersons for preventive medicine and author of the *Life Span Library:*
• *The Butterfly and Life Span Nutrition*
• *The Cortical Monkey and Healing*
• *The Canary and Chronic Fatigue*

With chapters on sugar-burning and fat-burning exercises, up-regulation of fat-burning enzymes, stretching, limbic pacing, exercise for heart disease, chronic fatigue, osteoporosis, arthritis, bowel disease and other disorders.

A book of exercise for those who have been left behind by the fads of the fitness industry.

A wonderful book about the joys of fitness without the burden of goals.

An exercise book like no other
Celebrating all motion as exercise

The Ghoraa and Limbic Exercise
Majid Ali,M.D.

ISBN 1-879131-02-1

Chronic fatigue is reversible!

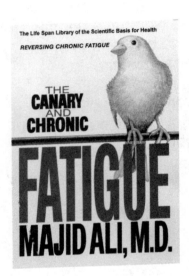

The definitive book on chronic fatigue.

Providing not only the clinical outlines for non-drug reversal of chronic fatigue, but also the rational and scientific basis of hope and optimism that is so sorely lacking in 'human canaries'.

Reversing chronic fatigue <u>without</u> drugs and <u>with</u> hope and non-drug therapies

The Canary and Chronic Fatigue

Majid Ali,M.D.
ISBN 1-879131-02-1

**A book about a changing medicine
for a changing time.**

A book about:
A changing medicine for a
changing time.

Freedom from disease
and dependency on drugs.

Self-regulation for
respiratory, cardiac
and chronic disorders.

Disease reversal without drugs

The Cortical Monkey
and Healing
Majid Ali,M.D.

ISBN 1-879131-00-5

**Muscles, tissues, and cells do not lie...
The cortical mind can...**

*...A novel energy-over-mind
approach to healing*

The Dog, Directed Pulses, and Energy Healing
Coming to bookstores soon

Science has not failed medicine...
Medicine has failed science...

The Life Span Library of the Scientific Basis of Health

A book about one physician's search for
the cause of disease and truth in medicine

RDA
RATS, DRUGS
and ASSUMPTIONS

From the author of
The Canary and Chronic Fatigue

MAJID ALI, M.D.

*A book about one physician's search for the
cause of disease and truth in medicine*

RDA: Rats, Drugs, and Assumptions
ISBN 1-879131-07-2 670 pages

For the Professional or advanced reader

The Life Span Library of the Scientific Basis of Health

The Principles and Practice of Nutritional Medicine

Part 1: Intramuscular and Intravenous Therapy

Majid Ali, M.D.

The Principles and Practice of Nutritional Medicine
Part 1: Intramuscular and Intravenous Therapy
ISBN 1-879131-13-7